Robert Louis
STEVENSON
A Life Study

Robert Louis Stevenson,
engraving after a photo taken in Australia in 1893

Robert Louis STEVENSON
A Life Study

Jenni Calder

A strange trade this voyaging, so vague, so bound-down, so helpless.

Robert Louis Stevenson,
letter to Sidney Colvin

New York   Toronto
OXFORD UNIVERSITY PRESS
1980

First published in the United States of America 1980
by Oxford University Press, Inc.

First published in Great Britain 1980
by Hamish Hamilton under the title *RLS: A Life Study*

The publishers acknowledge the financial assistance of the
Scottish Arts Council in the production of this volume.

Library of Congress Cataloging in Publication Data

Calder, Jenni
Robert Louis Stevenson: a life study.
1. Stevenson, Robert Louis, 1850-1894—Biography.
2. Authors, English—19th century—Biography.
PR5493.C25   1980   828'.809   [B]   80-15715
ISBN 0-19-520210-4

Printed in the United States of America

in memory of my mother
and for Alan and Liz

CONTENTS

	Preface	xiii
1	The Hills and the Firth	1
2	The Shadow of the Child	26
3	A Heart of Fire	53
4	This Damned Life	78
5	The Mountains of the Moon	101
6	In Extremis	123
7	Too Little in Life	150
8	Hadden Doon by the Bubblyjock	177
9	A Weevil in a Biscuit	200
10	Times are Changed since the Lothian Road	225
11	Burgundy or Daybreak	245
12	Far Better Fun than People Dream	264
13	Hard Work and Short Commons	289
14	No Rest but the Grave	313
	List of Robert Louis Stevenson's Works	333
	Select Bibliography	334
	Notes	339
	Index	351

ILLUSTRATIONS

Robert Louis Stevenson in 1893 (*Mansell Collection*)   *frontispiece*

17 Heriot Row (*Radio Times Hulton Picture Library*)   11

Old Town of Edinburgh, seen from the New (*Mary Evans Picture Library*)   16

Swanston Cottage (*Radio Times Hulton*)   22

8 Howard Place (*Radio Times Hulton*)   29

Page from *A Child's Garden of Verses* 1896 (*Courtesy of the Trustees of the British Museum*)   31

Alison Cunningham (*Radio Times Hulton*)   35

Louis with his mother (*Radio Times Hulton*)   39

Louis and his father (*Radio Times Hulton*)   45

RLS at about twenty-six (*Mansell*)   59

Sidney Colvin (*Mansell*)   67

Edmund Gosse (*Mansell*)   90

Siron's Inn, Barbizon (*Lady Stair's House, Edinburgh*)   97

Fanny Osbourne (*The Beinecke Rare Book and Manuscript Library, Yale University*)   106

Group in the garden of Chevillon's Inn, Grez (taken from W. H. Low's *A Chronicle of Friendship*, Hodder & Stoughton, 1908)   109

Frontispiece of the first edition of *Travels with a Donkey* (*British Museum*)   121

_____ (*Lady Stair's House*)   135

_____ Joe Strong of *The Silverado*
_____ Stevenson's *Works*, 1894–8, British   145

_____ ds (*Radio Times Hulton*)   16_

_____ re Island (*Lady Stair's House*)

_____ ll)

x *Illustrations*

Chalet La Solitude, Hyères (*Radio Times Hulton*)   187

RLS, painting by Sir William Blake Richmond, 1887
   (*National Portrait Gallery*)   197

Henry James (*Mansell*)   208

Lloyd, Fanny and Louis at Saranac Lake (*Lady Stair's
   House*)   232

W. E. Henley (*Mansell*)   238

Medallion in bas-relief by Augustus St Gaudens (*Mansell*)   243

Fanny Stevenson (*Radio Times Hulton*)   259

Lloyd, Fanny, Louis, King Kalakaua and Margaret
   Stevenson in the cabin of the *Casco* (*Lady Stair's House*)   268

Aboard the *Equator* (*Radio Times Hulton*)   276

Vailima, Samoa (*Mansell*)   292

Louis and Belle in the library at Vailima (*Radio Times
   Hulton*)   301

Group on the verandah at Vailima (*Radio Times Hulton*)   307

One of the last photographs of RLS (*Mansell*)   330

PREFACE

I have called this book a life study, not a biography, because it has not been my intention to set down all the known facts of a very fully documented life. I have attempted to explore and explain a man and writer rather than to produce a final round-up of evidence. The experience has been at every stage challenging and exciting.

The task would have been impossible without the work of two scholars who have pioneered a reassessment of Stevenson. *Voyage to Windward* by J. C. Furnas and *Robert Louis Stevenson* by David Daiches remain unchallenged landmarks in Stevenson studies. My gratitude to Joe and Helen Furnas, for their enthusiastic help, their hospitality and their friendship, is immeasurable. My gratitude to David Daiches, my father, is for much more than the interest and encouragement he has given me during my work on this book. I owe thanks, too, to the Scottish Arts Council, for a generous grant that enabled me to make an essential trip to the United States, to Professor Alistair Fowler, to Miss Marjorie Wynne and the staff of the Beinecke Library, Yale University, for their courteous and friendly help, and, once more, to the staff of the National Library of Scotland, my second home while working on Stevenson. I am grateful to Colonel and Mrs Clifton-Brown for showing me Cockfield Rectory, and to Mrs Kathleen Macfie and Mrs Jane Thomson for showing me 17 Heriot Row and Swanston Cottage respectively, and to Mr John Delahant for especially opening up for me the Stevenson house and museum at Saranac Lake. Many friends and colleagues and members of my family have helped the progress of this book in ways of which they are perhaps unaware: my thanks to all of them.

My debt to Angus is beyond words.

Phi

Robert Louis
STEVENSON
A Life Study

Chapter 1

THE HILLS AND THE FIRTH

. . . as long as we have the hills and the Firth we have a famous
heritage to leave our children

Edinburgh: Picturesque Notes

On the eighth of April, 1871, Robert Louis Stevenson and his
father walked from the New Town of Edinburgh to the little
village of Cramond, a few miles distant on the shore of the Firth
of Forth. At that time the handsome mid-Victorian
developments to the north of the Water of Leith, which edged
the New Town, merged into pleasant farmland and woods;
beyond the green, the blue of the Firth, beyond that, on a clear
day, the hills of Fife. Glimpses of water and hills continually
surprise one in the heart of Edinburgh's grey stone. For
Stevenson they were a temptation and a reassurance. He never
liked to be far from water and hills.

On that spring day Stevenson was in his twenty-first year. He
was thin, narrow-chested, his face long and mobile. He had
much to say to his father on that walk. When he talked his
gestures were fluid; not much like a Scot, in fact, many people
said. His hair was long, his dress eccentric. He was rarely at a
loss for words, but it wasn't always easy to talk to his father. As
the two of them followed a route they knew well, Louis Stevenson
– Louis was the name he used – spoke about how he felt himself
unable to take up the profession on which his father's heart was
set. Thomas Stevenson was a lighthouse and harbour engineer,
and his work had everything to do with the Scottish coasts. His
own father had built in the Firth they walked beside the great
Bell Rock lighthouse, and had then recorded the heroic saga of
the building. And it was a profession of heroic proportions.

Towards the end of his life Stevenson was to reflect wistfully
on whether he could not have been an engineer and created
David Balfour too. Now, in his twenty-first year, he wanted more
than anything to try his hand as a writer, and this was what he

told his father. It was a heavy blow for the older man. A few days earlier his son had delivered a paper to the Royal Society of Arts, 'On a New Form of Intermittent Light for Lighthouses', which had been much praised and awarded a silver medal. Louis perhaps wanted it to be clear that it was not lack of ability that prompted his retreat from the profession, but he chose a moment to break the news when his father was full of pride and confidence in his son. Louis was his only child. The Stevensons were a family of engineers. There had been three generations of them, and Thomas Stevenson's two brothers also followed the profession. Through it the family had achieved distinction and status. They had left their permanent marks on the Scottish coastline and the Scottish islands in defiance of wind and weather. Thomas Stevenson had prepared his son to take up this heritage.

Yet perhaps he did have doubts. There were those who had been aware of Louis's lack of real interest in engineering.[1] Thomas may have tried to reassure himself on that difficulty, but it was impossible to close his eyes to his son's ill health. The supervision of harbour works and lighthouse building was a rough business. Louis's frail body could not have held out long against the savage onslaughts of sea and wind. Even the streets of Edinburgh were often too much for him, and were to become increasingly so. Knowing this, and loving his son deeply and possessively, it was probably easier for him to accept Louis's rejection.

Accept it he did. 'Tom wonderfully resigned', his wife registers in her diary entry for that date.[2] A compromise was reached. Louis was to safeguard his future by studying for the Bar. The legal profession was eminently respectable and had contributed much to Edinburgh's wealth and status. It was a way of life accepted and approved by the circle in which the Stevenson parents moved; the sons of numerous New Town families were studying law. If he passed his Bar examinations Louis would have professional qualifications on which he could fall back if the risky enterprise of establishing himself as an author was not a success. Also, and importantly, Thomas Stevenson was a man of substance. In condoning his son's ambitions he was in effect preparing himself to become, if necessary, his financial prop, which was indeed what happened, as Louis himself was often wryly to acknowledge. Without the family of engineers it is unlikely that there would have been a *Treasure Island*, or a *Kidnapped*, and Jekyll and Hyde would not have established their vivid presence in the English language.

Father and son made their way amicably home to Heriot Row, perhaps the New Town's most spacious and dignified street. In some ways it was a miracle that Louis had survived until his twenty-first year. He had so often been ill as a child, delirious with high fevers, in bed for weeks on end. His mother's diary records his illnesses, and with almost equal regularity the deaths of young cousins and the children of friends. Diphtheria and scarlet fever were two of the common killers. Mrs Stevenson frequently attended the funerals, and every small coffin she laid eyes on must have reminded her of the frailty of her own only child.

Now he was a young man of charm and wit who often troubled his parents for quite other reasons. In the autumn of 1867 he had become a student at Edinburgh University, but he followed none of the courses he registered for with any real attention. Formal learning did not interest him; it was not only that he had little enthusiasm for the engineering classes he was expected to attend. He had never excelled during his rather sporadic school career, and he was not to do so at the University, at least not in the accepted fashion. He was a frequent truant from classes, and preferred to spend his time walking, talking and drinking – or rather, spending a lot of time in bars making a little money go a long way. When he did attend lectures he usually sat reading or writing at the back of the room. Extant lecture notes are liberally decorated with drawings and snatches of verse.

But his natural charm, and more cultivated winning pose, made it easy for some more conventional beings to forgive his bohemian lapses, and he was thoroughly good company. If he made no attempt to distinguish himself academically, if he despised such aspirations as he resisted the values that his father's generation represented, he became distinguished in other ways. He was recognized on the streets, though not always by name, known in the dives he frequented as 'velvet coat', because he wore one, notorious for his practical jokes, valued for his conversation, regarded askance by many for his gestures against the bourgeois, self-esteeming, prudish society of professional, middle-class Edinburgh. He cultivated the society of underdogs and prostitutes, the denizens of the decaying, overcrowded Old Town, abandoned by the upper classes when the carefully planned New Town beckoned them down to elegant terraced houses, wide, well-ordered streets, railed gardens and more discreet sanitary arrangements.

The University itself was only just beyond the tiered High Street closes which contained endless fascination for Stevenson. In one of those closes, a century or so earlier, Deacon Brodie, a richly symbolic figure for Stevenson, respectable cabinet-maker by day, burglar by night, had carried on his trade. In another the notorious Burke and Hare, grave-robbers and murderers and ironically two of Edinburgh's best remembered sons, had, less than half a century before, planned their exploits. The dual nature of Deacon Brodie and the twist of irony that connected Burke and Hare with Edinburgh's world-wide reputation in medicine (for they provided the bodies, the raw material of medical experiment), represented for Stevenson an essential truth about the city.

It was a truth that was exposed at every turn. The hotching, sordid life of the Old Town's lands (tenement buildings) and closes sprawled on the doorstep of the University. Towering over the New Town on the south, flanking it to the east, and a short walk from its smart West End were the rendezvous of criminals and prostitutes, seedy howffs, shebeens like the one Stevenson himself describes in 'The Misadventures of John Nicholson', areas of an underground life that the decent preferred to forget. And at any moment, turning the corner from a dense slum or breasting a cobbled slope one might catch sight of green hills or the glint of water.

A century earlier Edinburgh had been only the Old Town, crowded tenements piled along a rocky spine that sloped from the castle down to the less aggressive Palace of Holyrood. The castle must have always looked as if it had grown out of the rock. Behind Holyrood was the King's Park, where Prince Charles Edward had mustered his Jacobite army before marching south, and behind that the leonine volcanic humps of Arthur's Seat. From the castle ramparts the full richness of hills, Salisbury Crags, Arthur's Seat, the Pentlands, the Braids, the Moorfoots, the Lammermuirs, the Ochils across the Firth, and perhaps a glimpse of the summit of Ben Ledi, north of Callender, all reminders for Stevenson of Jacobites and Covenanters and Border raids, of rebellion and fanaticism, of a savage past from which he was never able to escape.

On that crowded ridge aristocrats and lawyers, traders and thieves, doctors and washerwomen had lived on top of one another. They had shared the tenements, though not at the same level: the poorest at the top, up five or six or even ten stairs, a long way to carry water from the few sources of street supply, the wealthiest in the middle, at a distance from the effluvia of the streets. But they had passed each other on the stair, drunk in the same taverns, literally rubbed shoulders. Space, for living and working, had been at a premium. In the flats of even the nobility the children had often slept on beds that were laid out on the living-room floor at night. Often the only room for both business and pleasure had been in the tavern.

The abandonment of the Old Town by the well-to-do had left it an increasingly overcrowded and unkempt morass. But it was a morass that almost seemed to mock the elegance below.

> From their smoky beehives, ten stories high, the unwashed look down upon the open squares and gardens of the wealthy; and gay people sunning themselves along Princes Street, with its miles of commercial palaces all beflagged upon some great occasion, see, across a gardened valley set with statues, where the washings of the Old Town flutter in the breeze at its high windows.[3]

Stevenson wrote this when he was well established in his writing career. It was what he grew up with. His understanding of the full complexity of this clash of contrasts came gradually, but even as a very young child he was aware of their existence. The castle's 'brute mass' that was 'rooted in a garden',[4] Georgian elegance eroded at the edges, such images were deeply imprinted on the child's mind.

When Stevenson was growing up the New Town was no longer fresh and exciting territory, with memories of green fields and wild life lingering behind the facades and the measured curves and angles. It had become stolidly established. Begun towards the end of the eighteenth century it suggests an effort, perhaps unconscious, to compensate for the cramped conditions on the castle ridge. Space is still the essence of the New Town. The ceilings are high, the streets are wide, the squares and circles are generous, parks and gardens everywhere interrupt the ranks of grey terraces. Heriot Row, where from the age of six Louis grew up, faces railed gardens of grass and shrubs and trees, and behind the terrace the slope falls away to allow a scarcely interrupted view northwards. As a young man he was there intermittently until his father's death in 1887. When respectable Edinburgh moved down from the castle rock it gained space and less polluted air and cleaner streets, but to match the superiority of its new surroundings it took upon itself also formality, constraint, the outward signs of propriety, and the casual, unpretentious ways of the Old Town were carefully forgotten. When Louis made his way back up the Mound to the High Street, or to Lothian Road that stretched southwards away from the island of respectability, or to Leith Walk that bordered it on the east, he was searching for the things the New Town had lost, for community with the unpretentious, for a more naked grasp on life, for a more honest attitude to human fallibility.

But Edinburgh had perhaps always been a city with a split personality. Many of the grimmer aspects of Scotland's past seem to concentrate in the lowering castle, which is at the same time the city's most spectacular feature. New Town enlightenment highlighted Old Town barbarity, as middle-class propriety effectively emphasised lower-class squalor. The tension between the agonised Calvinist outlook of a man like Thomas Stevenson, in whose conscience guilt was like a running sore, and the attitudes of those who tried to preserve the vestiges of Edinburgh's intellectual and artistic heyday was palpable. From the middle of the eighteenth century to the beginning of the nineteenth Edinburgh had blossomed. It had been a European capital in every sense. Many of Europe's boldest thinkers, writers and livers had been Edinburgh men, or Scots drawn to Edinburgh. The architectural glories of the New Town, the challenging ideas of Adam Smith and David Hume, the rich triumphs of Sir Walter Scott, had been matched by the less spectacular achievements of a confident professional class, lawyers, doctors, engineers, flourishing merchants, and a relaxed and generative social life in which conversation and the appreciation of good claret were highly valued.

Robert Louis Stevenson was born too late for this. Scott was dead eighteen years before his birth. He suffered, like all his generation, from a twin inheritance that he could not do much with: the rich and challenging ideas and expression of the Enlightenment, and the often hard-won, strongly established financial stability of the respectable middle class. Often, and paradoxically, the one seemed to symbolise the other. The order and harmony of Georgian Edinburgh represented for Stevenson a complacent and self-approving class; Scott was innocuous reading for all ages and both sexes. Edinburgh had become a European backwater. Stevenson would linger on his walks between Old and New Town and lean over the parapet on the North Bridge to watch the trains steam out of Waverley station. 'Happy the passengers who shake off the dust of Edinburgh and have heard for the last time the cry of the east wind among her chimney pots,' he wrote.[5]

The illustrious pre-Victorian generation had passed away. Ambitious Scots now looked across the Border for the centre of intellectual and artistic life. Stevenson was born into the atmosphere of mid-Victorian achievement, represented for him intimately and conclusively by his own father. But a sensitive, questing mind detected beneath the achievement the frailty and the hypocrisy, and an experimentally inclined young man soon discovered that respectable Edinburgh, douce, but with the devil hovering at the shoulder, had another aspect. The drinking habits, for instance, of the legal profession, were notoriously excessive. Stevenson's best and closest friend, Charles Baxter, was a lawyer who first cheerfully, then tragically demonstrated this. His habits of good-natured inebriation slid into alcoholism. The extent of prostitution was no less than in other money-making cities of comparable size. (Thomas Stevenson helped to run a rescue operation for fallen women.) There were poverty and beggary and crime which high principles and regular church-going could not cope with.

Louis Stevenson rarely had enough money in his pocket to escape from the bourgeoisie through drink. His father kept him on an allowance of £1 a month, feeling that all his needs could be supplied at home – he was not an ungenerous man, but wanted some control over his son. For the same reason Louis could not often buy either solace or adventure from women. But it cost nothing to observe, or to absorb, an atmosphere. For one reason or another experience, for most of Stevenson's life, was often a matter of observation and absorption. In Edinburgh as a young man the society of those beyond the reach of the law and the concern of the establishment was his chosen alternative to middle-class manners and morals. He said little to his parents about how he spent his time, but often found them, still waiting, when he returned in the small hours along gas-lit Heriot Row, after an evening in a brothel off Leith Walk, perhaps, or in the howff of the sour-natured Brash in Lothian Road, a favourite haunt when he was in Baxter's company.

The urge to write came early. It went hand in hand with an addiction to stories and dramatising, which emerged in earliest childhood. As a schoolboy he was producing magazines almost single-handed, as a teen-ager he was experimenting with novels. By the time he was a student he had taken a grip on his inclinations. 'It was not so much that I wished to be an author,' he wrote later, '. . . as that I had vowed that I would learn to write.'[6] Observation was part of the learning. He would sit in the gloom and tobacco smoke of a low-ceilinged howff with his pencil busy in his notebook. He would drink beer and pretend it was burgundy. Writing, perhaps, was a way of reducing the distance between what he could see and what he could know. It was a way of coming to terms with experience and lack of experience alike. And there was no other way. The potential of words is unique, unlike anything else. Very early in his life Stevenson recognised the value of language, and his incessant practice with the tools of his trade, his attitude to writing as a skill which had work and effort could transform into an art, indicate his deep respect for what words could achieve. It is doubtful whether he himself gained the summit of achieve-ment as a writer, or even realised his own potential, but he understood the possibilities. That understanding of what words can do with and for the imagination and experience informed every stage of his personal and professional life.

Edinburgh certainly fed his imagination. Louis's childhood had been circumscribed by illness and long periods of little association, at home or at school, with other children. An energetic, over-energetic at times, imagination compensated for activities that seemed beyond his reach. As a student he saw no cause to rein in this enticing gift, and as a denizen of Edinburgh, a city where still the past is never allowed to lie down and die, where in his everyday comings and goings he could not avoid the continual stimulus of the sombre outline on the ridge, castle, cathedral, kirks and uneven lands, or the sound of bugles and drums drifting down in the evening, and the mingling with lines from those authors who had already captured something of the city.

Robert Fergusson especially ran through his head, celebrating in wry and vivid poetry the robust life of the city, the dirt, the smells, the drunkenness, the riotous inclinations of Auld Reekie's citizens, with the 'black banditti', the City Guard, ineffectually policing. Fergusson had been born exactly a century before Stevenson and lived only twenty-four years. There were times when Stevenson was convinced his own life would be equally brief. He felt a powerful affinity with the poet, whose productive writing life was only about three years. Here was a man who lived without restraint and who wrote about the real life of the city, about ordinary people, servant girls gossiping on the tenement stairs, dandies getting splashed in the filthy streets, drunks staggering home at night, 'Some to their wife, and some their wench', and how the young Stevenson, nursing a bitter hatred of hypocrisy, must have relished these lines:

> On Sunday here, an alter'd scene
> O' men and manners meets our ein:
> Ane wad maist trow some people chose
> To change their faces wi' their clo'es,
> And fain wad gar ilk neighbour think
> They thirst for goodness, as for drink:
> But there's an unco dearth o' grace,
> That has nae mansion but the face,
> and never can obtain a part
> In benmost corner of the heart.
> Why should religion make us sad,
> If good frae virtue's to be had?

Na, rather gleefu' turn your face;
Forsake hypocrisy, grimace;
And never have it understood
You fleg mankind frae being good.[7]

When Stevenson later wrote about the negative morality of
Christianity, about how Calvinism seemed calculated to 'fleg
[frighten] mankind frae being good', he surely had these lines in
mind. And another writer inevitably inserted his presence into
Stevenson's experience of Edinburgh, Walter Scott, who
contained the Old Town so richly in *The Heart of Midlothian*, and
expressed it so heroically in verse, like this:

Dundee he is mounted, he rides up the street,
The bells are rung backward, the drums they are beat;
But the Provost, douce man, said, 'Just e'en let him be,
The Gude Town is weel quit of that Deil of Dundee.'

As he rode down the sanctified bends of the Bow,
Ilk carline was flyting and shaking her pow;
But the young plants of grace they look'd couthie and slee,
Thinking, luck to thy bonnet, thou Bonny Dundee!

With sour-featured Whigs the Grassmarket was cramm'd,
As if half the West had set tryst to be hanged;
There was spite in each look, there was fear in each ee,
As they watch'd for the bonnets of Bonny Dundee.

Come fill up my cup, come fill up my can,
Come saddle your horses, and call up your men;
Come open the West Port, and let me gang free,
And it's room for the bonnets of Bonny Dundee![8]

For Stevenson, instinct and imagination called forth the echo of
bugles and hoofbeats on the cobbles. He could not take off on a
horse through the now defunct West Port. The trains that
steamed southwards out of Waverley, named for Scott's first
novel, were his equivalent.

It was rich material for Stevenson, and the longing to escape
that possessed him sometimes heightened it. Edinburgh both
stimulated and restricted. 'There are hills beyond Pentland and
lands beyond Forth', Scott's 'Bonny Dundee' goes on to say.
Stevenson's imagination enriched his life, and it constantly

17 Heriot Row

tempted him, to explore as well as to write. Initially as a writer he tried too hard to discipline his mind's eye, and produced careful, clever but constrained pieces. He was to write at his best when his imagination was controlled and intensely focused, but not restricted or formalised into pleasing phrases.

It was not easy for Louis to explain to his father how he felt about writing, but it was perhaps easier to do it on a walk, in the open air, out of the city. They had had disagreements before, and the worst place for an argument was probably the drawing-room of 17 Heriot Row. Both parents must have been worried at the curious behaviour and bohemian tendencies of their son. He dressed oddly, walked the streets in black shirt and neckerchief under his velvet jacket, talked strangely, even when making an effort to be decorous, was smitten at turns by excessive laughter and excessive gloom. His narrow, elongated fram long thin fingers, gleaming eyes, accentuated the oddness of his dress. His parents could not have known the whole truth of how Louis spent his time, but there were rumours, and he hated feeling that he had to tell them lies. For of course they did ask where he had been and what he had been doing. Thomas Stevenson was certainly uneasy. Louis's friends appeared to be the respectable sons of respectable New Town families. Charles Baxter's father was a lawyer, Walter Ferrier was a professor's son, and another Walter the son of James Young Simpson, famed discoverer of chloroform: a generation of sons of middle-class achievement. But the opinions that Louis expressed were disturbingly iconoclastic. He had read some dangerous authors, Charles Darwin and Herbert Spencer, and racy French novelists. He would not fit into the narrow lanes of progress within which Thomas Stevenson worked and assessed the possibilities of life. Louis had no wish to upset or antagonise his parents, but the effort to be both honest and tactful was often too much for him. If he succeeded on this occasion, and the lack of stormy repercussion suggests that he did, admirably, two years later he was to initiate a period of acute distress for both himself and his family by confessing to an even more radical disagreement. But meanwhile he had won the legitimisation of what had been for a long time his most serious occupation. He stuck to his side of the bargain, and pursued his studies in law and passed, when the time came, the Bar examinations, but privately he was determined to go all out to become a writer. For the first time it began to look like a real possibility.

He had already produced a quantity of work – novels, dramatic verse – destroyed much, tried over and over again for certain effects, experimented with different styles. He sat scribbling at the back of lectures, or in the gloom of Rutherford's, a howff in Drummond Street, handy to the college and frequented by students, or in his room at the top of 17 Heriot Row looking out over the grass and the pond and the trees of Queen Street Gardens, and thinking perhaps of Ruskin's scathing opinion of Edinburgh, delivered during a visit a few years after Stevenson was born.

Walk around your Edinburgh buildings, and look at the eight of your eye, what will you get from them? Nothing but square-cut stone; square-cut stone – a wilderness of square-cut stone for ever and for ever; so that your houses look like prisons, and truly are so; for the worst feature of Greek architecture is, indeed, not its costliness, but its tyranny. These square stones are not prisons of the body, but graves of the soul.[9]

Stevenson experienced the tyranny of the neo-classical terraces, but understood it more deeply and historically, even at the age of twenty, than Ruskin, himself of Edinburgh origins, did. If he pulled restlessly away from New Town propriety he did not cease to feel the intimate relationship with the past, and the truth that the New Town was in its way as expressive as the Old.

What Edinburgh had been was almost within living memory. In 1831 Edinburgh author and lawyer Henry Mackenzie, remembered best for his novel *The Man of Feeling* (1771), had died in Heriot Row. A generation before that Heriot Row had still been Woods Farm, where Mackenzie himself had shot snipe. Queen Street Gardens had once been a natural wilderness that lay between the first and second stages of New Town building. Now it was tamed and regularised. The mid-Victorian generation, those who had reached success and prosperity in the middle of the century, relished the taming of both natural and urban wildernesses. If Ruskin diagnosed the result as a soul-destroying architectural wasteland, Stevenson was able to understand it as a reflection of the deeply engrained duality of Scottish culture and self-awareness. Edinburgh's expansion, which continued rapidly, ate up the green and swallowed villages whole, like Victorian expansion everywhere, but the lines of communication with the past seemed infinitely elastic. From Telford's magnificent Dean Bridge, opened in the year of the Reform Bill, Louis could look down on the rural though industrial Dean Village and the mills and tanneries along the Water of Leith, cast a glance back to the castle on its rock, look over to the breathtaking ranks of Georgian housing above the water, or walk northwards to Cramond or South Queensferry, quickly leaving behind the double lines of solid new Victorian buildings. Whatever he did he could not cease to be aware of his hatred for the tyranny and his relish for the creative stimulus of his circumstances.

Inevitably he was going to need to escape, from the New Town's 'draughty parallelograms',[10] as he described the grid of streets, from the Old Town's brooding, but it was to be another year before he was able to get away, without his parents, for any length of time, and much longer before he would be able to cease to think of 17 Heriot Row as his home. To that home he had always eventually to return, wherever his wanderings around Edinburgh took him. But he was determined to make himself as free from restraint as possible. He was not going to be circumscribed by routine or regular hours. He was ready to seize on any opportunity for diversion that arose. If he ran into a friend he was delighted at any excuse to whisk him away into Rutherford's for several hours of beer and talk, as J. M. Barrie described almost fifty years later. Barrie literally bumped into Stevenson as they were both crossing Princes Street.

> Glancing up I saw a velvet coat, a lean figure with long hair (going black) and stooping shoulders, the face young and rather pinched but extraordinarily mobile, the manner doggedly debonair. He apologised charmingly for what was probably my fault . . . then, taking me by the arm . . . he led me away from the Humanities [the class to which Barrie had been making his way] to something that he assured me was more humane, a howff called Rutherford's where we sat and talked by the solid hour.[11]

The incident ended with Louis pursuing Barrie through the streets, shouting 'stop thief' and describing him to passers-by as 'a man with a wooden leg and a face like a ham' – this was long before Stevenson's characterisation of Long John Silver, though Barrie may be guilty of some transposition here.

Barrie had never met Stevenson before and was not to do so again, although they corresponded in later life. This flair for serendipity, this ability to improvise out of a chance meeting a whole day of talk and pleasure and high jinks (and he was twenty-six when this occurred) characterised Stevenson as a young man in Edinburgh. It was this more than anything that distinguished him from fellow bohemians and rebels. There were others who renounced God and middle-class morality, but few who possessed this rare talent for conjuring sheer good fun out of thin air.

There were those who were spellbound. But if the talent charmed some it troubled many. Many of Edinburgh's citizens recoiled in dismay from this unorthodox, unpredictable figure, who might for instance, as he once did, leap up from the dinner table and insist on taking over the butler's role, to the embarrassment of his hosts and the disgust of the butler. Those he charmed, he charmed for life. With one or two notable exceptions Stevenson's friends remained devoted to him and all he represented for them until his death, and devoted to his memory thereafter.

Stevenson's bohemianism was to some extent shared by a part of the student fraternity in Edinburgh. The velvet jacket he wore was the uniform of the artistically inclined, and his style was certainly influenced by his intimate friendship with his cousin Bob, who was an art student and familiar with the modes of French bohemianism. But in his first year or two at the University, Louis had few friends. There were many who considered him not only odd and outlandish, but offensive. The dominant note of the University tended to be rather grim, certainly a great deal more serious than Louis was. Here is a description of the 1880s some years after Stevenson's day, but there had been little change:

The lofty, grey walls of the University – dingy and dead like as they appear to the common passer-by, sombre and venerable as they seem to the student – look out upon the very centre of the city throng. Its austere presence sheds a lustre of academic calmness upon the busy streets around, and over the whole area of the Old Town, whose numerous libraries and book-stalls derive their existence from the intellectual activity within its walls. Generally speaking, its influence on the surrounding life is depressing. When the classes are in full operation, the procession of students that pass along the bridge, is mournful, if not funereal in effect. The young men themselves look as if they were suffering intensely, but were resolved to support their anguish with silent resignation.[12]

A university education was a very serious business for many of the students, who often resented the squandering of both time and money. There were those for whom the university provided an opportunity of self-improvement for which their parents had

Old Town of Edinburgh – seen from the New

saved and sacrificed. Barrie was one of them. In Scotland university education had traditionally been open to the sons of families that in England would never have dreamt of the possibility. For that reason learning was regarded with the greatest respect and seriousness. Stevenson's irresponsible, cavalier attitude, his scoffing at precisely the authorities and institutions that offered opportunities for achievement to the poor but decent, was not popular. *He* was all right, with his well-off father and his comfortable home. He did not have to work his way up.

So often those who saw Louis from a distance were not impressed. At that time Louis Stevenson was the queerest looking object you could conceive. To begin with he was badly put together, a slithering, loose flail of a fellow, all joints, elbows, and exposed spindle-shanks, his trousers being generally a foot too short in the leg. He was so like a scarecrow that one almost expected him to creak in the wind. And what struck us all was that he seemed to take a pride in aggravating the oddities of nature. When the weather happened to be fine – and I don't remember seeing him when it wasn't – he came in a battered straw hat that his grandfather must have worn and laid aside because it was out-of-date. Under that antiquated headgear his long, lank hair fell straggling to his shoulders, giving him the look of a quack or gipsy. He wore duck trousers and a black shirt, with loose collar and a tie that might be a strip torn from a cast-away carpet. His jacket was of black velvet, and it was noticeable that it never seemed good or new. We remarked among ourselves that there must be a family trunk full of old clothes which he was wearing out.[13]

Louis was laughed at by some. He was thought of as an eccentric, a picturesque eccentric perhaps, but not to be taken seriously – or if so, to be seen as an affront to the values of the decent citizenry.

As a small boy Louis had sometimes been teased and mocked by other children on the streets. This must have helped to breed in him a studied defiance. As a child he was often lonely. His growing up and his early adult years were often lonely too, yet he refused to adopt the conformity that would have smoothed the way for him. All those who remember him in Edinburgh comment on his unconventional dress and his independent manner. Some frankly admit that they considered him a flamboyant poseur of the worst kind. There were houses at which he was not welcome. But whatever the attitudes towards him, amused, irritated or resentful, he made an impression on Edinburgh life through his refusal to become part of its established conventions. Although there were others who rebelled, his own rebellion seemed to have a unique flavour. If there was something of affectation in his wild garb and his cheerful irreverence these things did represent for him a serious and uncompromising attitude to life. Those close to him loved him for his gaiety, his sparkling conversation, his fluid, non-Anglo-Saxon gestures, but perhaps most of all they loved him for his irresistible sincerity. The young Louis, a lone figure striding lankily about Edinburgh, his worn coat blowing in the fierce east wind, was as sincere in his rebellion as he was in anything else of seriousness that he did. And although it is easy to be misled by his pleas for gaiety, he took life very seriously indeed.

He was not entirely alone, although so much of his exploration of Edinburgh life was a solitary affair. There were those who loved his company and recognized his talents. In February 1869, in his second year at the University, he was elected a member of the Speculative Society, an exclusive club of thirty elected members who discussed and debated and were regarded as an élite. Its comfortable premises afforded an island of self-rule amidst the University. Within its walls, but not elsewhere, undergraduates could smoke, and could freely criticise and condemn. For Louis, although it took him a while to get his bearings amongst this exclusive, rather upper-class, intellectually sophisticated group of young men, the Spec., as it was called, provided a territory of real pleasure and interest. It was there that Louis began to make close friends, there that he found contemporaries who, though mostly less extravagant in their gestures, shared some of his anti-establishment tendencies. In debate Louis was witty and challenging, though not so good at putting together a closely-argued case. But more than the debates he enjoyed the more casual arguments, his chance of developing his ideas in front of a captive but genuinely interested audience, and the dinners and the wine and the relaxation. It was an excellent climate for ripening friendship.

He invited his friends home to Heriot Row. His parents were happy to arrange dinner parties for him. Louis and his father would compete with each other for dominance of the dinner table conversation. And he went to his friends' homes. Walter Ferrier and Walter Simpson both lived within a few minutes walk of Heriot Row, Ferrier down the hill in Dean Terrace, Simpson across the gardens in Queen Street then later in nearby St Colme Street. Ferrier was already well established in the drinking habits that would kill him in 1883. His mother would bitterly reprove Louis for encouraging him. Certainly he did his share of heavy drinking, usually when his own father or his friends' fathers provided the wine. Simpson, reticent in manner and intellect, had a laconic sense of humour that Louis loved. Louis and his friends, Charles Baxter too, explored drink and sex together. Their correspondence gives us an occasional glimpse of the underbelly of Edinburgh respectability, and a suggestion that their conversation wasn't always of an elevated nature. In 1877 Simpson was recording this little episode for his friend's delectation:

I was walking along the street the other night, passed two
gents one telling a story evidently & just heard (without
appreciating for a moment) these words 'so says she ye're no
gawn to mak a foreign post office of my c - - t'.[14]

After his father's death in 1870 Simpson shared a flat with his
brother and sister. The independence of this household, freed
from the presence of an older generation, appealed to Louis.

But the ideal companion for his more boyish escapades was
Charles Baxter. J. C. Furnas, in his vital, ground-breaking
biography, describes the two of them.

> Professors lecturing chill classes were annoyed when Louis,
> slight and insolently supercilious, and Baxter, bulky and
> insolently solemn, would enter, listen for a few minutes,
> exchange glances of pitying contempt – and then casually
> leave.[15]

The two derived vast amusement from practical jokes and
hilarious schemes designed to baffle and confuse respectable
Edinburgh. They sent carefully wrapped parcels of nothing to
eminent citizens, and invented fictitious persons for whom they
would anxiously enquire. It was a way of expressing their
rebellion, but it was also a way of entering into a kind of comic
opera world, for which, Stevenson felt, Princes Street and the
Gardens beneath the castle were eminently designed.[16] They
roamed around the city together and engaged unsuspecting
passers-by in improbable conversations. At the great age of
twenty-five (when he and Baxter had far from exhausted their
prankish escapades) Louis could look back fondly at a period
that already seemed irrecoverable, and talk about, in a letter to
Baxter, 'the past where we have been drunk and sober, and sat
outside of grocers' shops on fine dark nights, and wrangled in
the Speculative, and heard mysterious whistling in Waterloo
Place, and met missionaries from Aberdeen . . .'[17] An old tune
that he was to play again and again in his letters to Baxter.

It was not only young companions who were important to
Louis. He needed, and was to value all his life, the company and
the encouragement of an older, non-parental generation. In
1868 Professor Fleeming Jenkin and his wife came to Edinburgh
and settled in Fettes Row, a short walk down Dundas Street from

Heriot Row. Jenkin was Edinburgh's first professor of Engineering, and Louis was expected to attend his classes. The fact that there *were* classes in Engineering reflects the great difference between the traditional Scottish and English universities at that time. Thomas Stevenson of course knew Professor Jenkin. When Mrs Jenkin called on Mrs Stevenson at Heriot Row soon after they had come to Edinburgh, she heard Louis speak a few words out of the dark in his soft, attractive voice, and went home to tell her husband that she had met a Scottish Heine. There was some quality in him that arrested her. He was an irregular attender at Jenkin's lectures but became a zealous one at the Jenkins' home, where Mrs Jenkin, an actress of some talent, organised an annual amateur dramatic event.

Louis regularly took part in these productions, of Racine, Greek tragedy, Shakespeare, though never in a particularly distinguished part, and enjoyed it thoroughly: 'we were always sure at least of a long and exciting holiday in mirthful company', he wrote in his tribute to Fleeming Jenkin.[18] But he enjoyed not only the company, and the weeks of rehearsal and legitimate indulgence of high spirits, the taste (even when playing Racine) of the comic opera world, but the personality of Jenkin himself. He was a man whom Louis admired as an inspiring example of adventurous good. Jenkin was not at all the decorous, well-bred son of professional Edinburgh, but a man of immensely varied background and experience, whose spontaneous unconventionality often amounted to rudeness. At the same time he was 'every inch a gentleman', truly gentle, and a gentleman with a heroic personality.

> Far on in middle age, when men begin to lie down with the bestial goddesses, Comfort and Respectability, the strings of his nature still sounded as high a note as a young man's. He loved the harsh voice of duty like a call to battle. He loved courage, enterprise, brave natures, a brave world, an ugly virtue; everything that lifts us above the table where we eat or the bed we sleep upon.[19]

In Louis's appreciation of Jenkin's personality we find a key to his own. The example of the Jenkins' was an important one for Louis. He responded strongly to the man's 'brave nature' and the woman's artistic flair and real interest in him. Not only did they provide lively, congenial and interesting company, and occasions where Louis could dress up and overact and indulge some of his wilder fancies; they were a harmoniously united couple, living within the purlieus of Georgian tyranny, yet leading energetic and creative lives, spirits undampened by Calvinism or by bourgeois respectability.

Stevenson's iconoclasm did not lead him to attack marriage. He recognised and valued the loving closeness of his own parents, and years later would comment on it rather wistfully. 'The children of lovers are orphans' he wrote, thinking of the way a child can feel excluded from the parents' concern with each other.[20] In his parents' closeness lay his own loneliness, not just solitude, though there was often that too, but a profound sense of being excluded from the throbbing heart of life. It may have been this as much as his fear of passing on his physical disability that made him reluctant to have children, yet made him love them so. And it must have affected his attitude towards marriage too. An affair with a woman would have to be something special. A marriage that was characterised and limited by conventional trappings would mean little to him. He attacked a hypocritical morality, sterile conventions, lifeless religion, but he never seems to have radically questioned marriage as an institution, although by the 1870s others were doing so. It seems clear that, in his twenties, he thought in terms of sharing his life with a woman, and that his hopes for passion and romance did not discredit marriage. But it was equally clear that Louis Stevenson was highly unlikely to marry within narrow New Town society.

In the summer of 1867, before Louis embarked on his university career, Thomas Stevenson took the lease of Swanston Cottage, a modest country residence on the northern slope of the Pentland Hills. From a distance the grey-green Pentlands have a misleadingly gentle appearance. At close quarters one sees and feels their starkness. There are few trees. Their slopes seem to have been stripped and scrubbed bare by the wind. Louis often stayed at Swanston, to read and write, and to walk the hills, which he soon came to know as well as he knew the city. Before the cottage rose the modest but steep slopes of Caerketton and Allermuir, behind them the battlefield of Rullion Green, where the little Covenanting army from

Galloway was ruthlessly defeated by General Tam Dalyell in 1666, to be followed by an even more ruthless aftermath of persecution. Louis was fascinated by the Covenanters, more so than by the more romantic and colourful Jacobites, although the latter were such attractive material for literature. He brooded over Rullion Green, over the conscience and courage of the defeated, over that strain of savage fanaticism in the Scottish experience which was so disturbing, yet admirable. But the Pentlands offered more peaceful reflection too. Louis walked sometimes to the old chapel at Glencorse, a spot he would remember emotionally many years later and thousands of miles away. He would take his book to some sheltered spot and read, or watch the Swanston shepherd working his flock, or dream.

Swanston Cottage, by A. W. Henley, 1875

He was not so far away from Edinburgh that he could not walk into town when he felt inclined and spend a convivial evening. A return from such an evening with his cousin Bob he described in his diary. It was the early summer of 1872.

Splendid moonlight night. Bob walked out to Fairmilehead
with me. We were in a state of mind that only comes too
seldom in a lifetime. We danced and sang the whole way up
the long hill, without sensible fatigue. I think there was no
actual conversation – at least none has remained in my
memory: I recollect nothing but 'profuse bursts of
unpremeditated song'.[21]

Bob, artist and later art critic R. A. M. Stevenson, was the perfect
comrade. He was older than Louis, the son of Thomas's
brother Alan, who died youngish after a period of mental
instability. Bob arrived in Edinburgh in 1870 after graduating
from Cambridge. They had played together as children,
evolving highly inventive games, full of elaborate ramifications.
Bob had all the curious features of Louis's personality, only
more so. He was exuberant, eccentric, his conversation like
quicksilver, and sure to encourage any latent qualities of this
kind Louis might have. They were an irresistible double act. If
Louis had doubts at any time about his independent nature,
about his defiant refusal to succumb to the conventional, about
the attitude of most of respectable Edinburgh, Bob gave him
courage to persevere. For though Louis's prospects were
unsettled, Bob's were more so, yet Bob had no intention of
compromise. He wanted to paint, an even riskier occupation
than writing. When the two were together it was Bob who took
the lead, who made the more emphatic impression, Bob who,
for instance, first caught the eye of the woman Louis was to
marry. He was for Louis, in the 1870s, an instructor, a support,
and an inspiration as well as a wonderful sharer in joky
escapades and ebullient nonsense. Louis and Bob outdid the
practical jokes of Louis and Charles Baxter. Bob could
experiment more freely in lifestyle, in sexual relations, in
iconoclasm. Baxter, whatever his zest, had to bear in mind his
legal career, and soon his wife.

   With Bob, Louis could, from time to time at least, transcend
reality. In 1871 Thomas Stevenson had not yet detected what he
would two years later see, almost hysterically, as Bob's ruinously
wicked influence. He could not have been unaware that his son
was failing to distinguish himself academically, in spite of the
Royal Society silver medal. But he had not been alerted to the

worst of his excesses. There was nothing wrong with boyish high
spirits. There seemed to be nothing wrong with his friends. The
disappointment over his renunciation of engineering was sharp,
but he was able to come to terms with it. He loved his son
deeply. It was his tragedy that he found it so difficult to express
this love, that the pain of guilt interfered with so many of his best
feelings. But Louis understood this.

1871 was a good year for Louis. He was no longer an awkward
newcomer in university life, but had gained confidence without
compromise, and had gained friends. Towards the end of that
year, while comfortably ensconced one day in the hall of the
Spec., 'turkey-carpeted, hung with pictures, looking, when
lighted up at night with fire and candle, like some goodly
dining-room',[22] he was approached by three redoubtable and
well-established students and asked to join them in a venture to
launch a new magazine.

> We four were to be the conjunct editors and, what was the
> main point of the concern, to print our own works; while, by
> every rule of arithmetic – that flatterer of credulity – the
> adventure must succeed and bring great profit. Well, well: it
> was a bright vision. I went home that morning walking upon
> air. To have been chosen by these three distinguished students
> was to me the most unspeakable advance; it was my first
> draught of consideration; it reconciled me to myself and to
> my fellow-men . . .[23]

The magazine was a failure, but it was Louis's first taste of the
fray of the writer's world. It brought him his close friendship
with Walter Ferrier, one of the editors, and sharpened his relish
for the scene he hoped to enter.

His friends, his family and his writing were the things he took
seriously. He was to find, throughout his life, that he could not
always be faithful to all three. There were times when one had to
be sacrificed. His loyalty to individuals and his scrupulous
desire not to be hurtful were the strong moral core of his life.
His loyalty to his craft lay in the fact that he regarded it as just
that, not as a spontaneous expression of genius, or as a happy
facility with words, but as a craft to be practised and improved
and made to work.

All through my boyhood and youth, I was known and pointed out for the pattern of an idler; and yet I was always busy on my own private end, which was to learn to write. I always kept two books in my pocket, one to read, one to write in. As I walked, my mind was busy fitting what I saw with appropriate words; when I sat by the roadside, I would either read, or a pencil and a penny version-book would be in my hand, to note down the features of the scene or commemorate some halting stanzas. Thus I lived with words. And what I thus wrote was for no ulterior use, it was written consciously for practice.[24]

Some of his early works are only too clearly a product of this. But this was what both the rebellion and the seriousness were all about. He wanted to find out about life, the true values of life, and he wanted to find the right words to communicate this. In a letter of 1871 written to a cousin he said,

It is a pet idea of mine that one gets more real truth out of one avowed partisan than out of a dozen of your sham impartialists – wolves in sheep's clothing – simpering honestly as they suppress documents. After all, what one wants to know is not what people did, but why they did it – or rather, why they *thought* they did it; and to learn that, you should go to the men themselves. Their very falsehood is often more than another man's truth.[25]

The young Louis Stevenson was trying to strip the sheep's clothing from the backs of the wolves. He tried argument, he tried mockery, he tried jokes and nonsense, but he knew that the tool with which he most needed to acquire skill was the written word.

Chapter 2

THE SHADOW OF THE CHILD

The shadow of the baluster, the shadow of the lamp,
The shadow of the child that goes to bed –
All the wicked shadows coming, tramp, tramp, tramp,
With the black night overhead.

'North-west Passage', *A Child's Garden of Verses*

Thomas Stevenson married Margaret Isabella Balfour in 1848. Each came from a family of thirteen children, though eight of Thomas's siblings died in infancy. When they married Margaret was a pretty, spirited but not robust daughter of the manse, and Thomas was thirty, an already established professional man who took his occupation and his religion very seriously. Margaret had grown up in the manse at Colinton, a village upriver from Edinburgh, on the Water of Leith. It was just beyond the extending grasp of the city. Her husband had been reared on the east side, in Baxter's Place, alongside Leith Walk and under Calton Hill. Chained in the back yard for a while was a golden eagle, that Robert Stevenson had brought back from one of his trips to the islands: it 'pined and screamed itself to death'.[1] Robert Stevenson was stern with himself and stern with his children. During his frequent trips away he wrote letters to his three sons, instructive letters. 'Now the way to get money is, become clever men and men of education by being good scholars.'[2] Thomas certainly took such advice to heart. The story of Robert Stevenson and his son Thomas is an exemplative story of initiative, energy and self-discipline, a story that the industrial Revolution made possible, and Scottish alertness and high motivation brought to particularly striking success. But it is also a story of repression and uncertainty. It had not been easy for Thomas to make up his mind to become an engineer. He was an imaginative young man with uncertain romantic inclinations. His father was furious when he discovered pages of fiction written by Thomas.

Louis always hoped to find Highland ancestry for the Stevensons; an unnecessary flourish. They had been involved in much of Scotland's real achievement in the eighteenth and nineteenth centuries, trading in the West Indies as well as designing and constructing lighthouses and harbours all round the British Isles. Louis recognised this, as his recounting of the Bell Rock story, with its elemental contests and victory over the neap tides, shows. Stevenson was a kent name in Scotland, for good reason. Thomas himself invented and designed new forms of lights, for which he would not take out patents, as he did not wish to restrict the possible benefits of his knowledge and skill.

The Balfour family was adventurous in rather a different way. They had been a substantial landed family, the Balfours of Pilrig, between old Edinburgh and Leith. They had had their intimate connections with dramatic moments of Scottish history, something which was always a source of fascination to Louis. A Balfour antecedent had fought at Bothwell Brig in 1679, the celebrated defeat of the Covenanting rebellion against Charles II. Another had been ruined by the Darien disaster, the ill-thought-out attempt to establish Scottish trade in Central America in 1700. Louis could not resist the dark magic of events like these, particularly the former. He brooded on the murder of Archbishop Sharp by cloaked horsemen on a wild moor, the event which precipitated the last phase of the Covenanters' struggle. His first serious attempts at writing, discarded and destroyed, were on such subjects.

Louis's mother grew up in Colinton manse in the midst of high-spirited brothers, sisters and cousins. Several of them went to India, as the children of abundant Victorian middle-class families tended to do. Margaret's doctor brother John, home on leave in 1849 from India, the country from which British trade had brought the dread disease of cholera in the 1830s, devoted himself to fighting cholera outbreaks in and around Edinburgh. In 1866, the year of the last big cholera outbreak in Britain, he came home for good and at once threw himself into fighting the disease in Leven, Fife, where cholera had killed the previous doctor. Lewis Balfour, Margaret's father, had been minister at Colinton since 1823, but the young Louis, named after him, Robert Louis Balfour Stevenson, only knew him as an old man. His other grandfather, Robert Stevenson, for whom he was also

named, died shortly before he was born. The two families
represented solid Scottish achievement at its best. Religion,
technology, medicine; if at the end of the eighteenth century
Edinburgh was seen as a cultural and philosophical centre of
Europe, by the middle of the nineteenth it was these things that
made its reputation, and these along with soldiers that Scotland
exported so liberally to every corner of the Empire.

Thomas Stevenson, though Victorian prudence might have
suggested otherwise, fell in love. A casual meeting with
Margaret Balfour in a train led to a polite pursuit of her. He was
severe in his religious belief; a daughter of the manse seemed
appropriate. But he was also a charming talker, and had a sense
of fun and a sense of humour. Margaret Balfour could match
him in that. He was also perhaps unconsciously looking for an
antidote to the darker side of his nature, his tendency to brood
with profound pessimism over sin, his own and mankind's, and
to take the world's guilt upon his shoulders. 'A profound
underlying pessimism appears . . . to be the last word of the
Stevensons . . . their sense of the tragedy of life is acute and
unbroken', his son was to write.[3] Margaret was inclined to look
on the bright side of everything, and to avoid where possible
confrontation with the more painful realities.

The newly-married Stevensons moved into 8 Howard Place, a
rather squat and sombre Georgian terrace just north of
Canonmills on the Water of Leith. It was there that Louis was
born on 13 November 1850. The house was small, without the
more usual Georgian graciousness, and rather too near the river
for health – effluent from mills and tanneries, as well as sewage,
was poured into it. In 1853 a move was made, only across the
road, but to higher ground, on the corner of Inverleith Terrace.
There was a splendid view from the back windows, across the
squares and circles of the New Town to the castle and Arthur's
Seat, and at the front there was the rich green of the Botanic
Gardens. The house was more handsome but there was no
improvement. It was damp and exposed. Clothes mildewed in
the presses. So after four years another move was made, which
reflected Stevenson prosperity, to 17 Heriot Row, a south-facing
terrace in the heart of the New Town.

But by this time little Louis, known to his father as 'Smout', a
word that means salmon fry, was a confirmed invalid. Illness

8 Howard Place, the birthplace of RLS, drawn by A. W. Henley

was frequent from the age of two. Coughs and chills became feverish, and tended to develop into severe bronchial infections. He was also prone to gastric infections, and went through what his first biographer called 'all the ordinary maladies of childhood' one after another.[4] There were nine concentrated years of fevers and feverish imaginings, of sleepless nights, of entertainment by his own thoughts and by the stories told to him by his nurse and by his father, of games limited by confinement to bed, of interrupted schooling, of parental worry. His mother, too, was often unwell for weeks at a time. Louis may well have inherited the tendency to bronchial trouble from his mother, who shared it with her own father. Both lived into an active old age. But Louis's father too seems to have exhibited a similar disability, though it does not appear until he is older. There is mention in Mrs Stevenson's diary of both Thomas and herself suffering from slight haemorrhage of the lungs.

Wherever it came from, illness, usually centred on the respiratory system, was the dominant feature of Louis's early

childhood. For long stretches of time he occupied a strange
limbo, the half-real world of his bedroom, from which he would
look out with wide feverish eyes to the world beyond. His poems
for children, written long after, are full of the sense of looking
out to territories that are beyond the child's reach: only
imagination will take him there:

> I should like to rise and go
> Where the golden apples grow . . .[5]

They are full of the night too, darkness, night thoughts and
night spectres, the thrill and the terror of being alone in the dark
with one's own visions. Going to bed features again and again in
The Child's Garden of Verses.

> All by myself I have to go,
> With none to tell me what to do –
> All alone beside the streams
> And up the mountain-sides of dreams.[6]

It is a lonely adventure, full of strange encounters and
'frightening sights', but an adventure all the same, and the
daylight world dispels the magic as well as the alarm.

> Try as I like to find the way,
> I never can get back by day,
> Nor can remember plain and clear
> The curious music that I hear.[7]

Wistful longing, fear, loneliness, a sense of exclusion, are all to
be found in Stevenson's poems for children, which are so often
regarded as delightfully innocent prattle. He does not plumb
the depths of his terror – we find that elsewhere in prose – but
the disturbance is there. The child in his poems has often only a
tentative grasp on safety, and is often 'The Child Alone' – the
title of a series of poems. Much of the longing, the loneliness
and the fear is contained in 'North-west Passage', the title itself
suggestive of the effort to transform these into an adventure of
discovery.

> When the bright lamp is carried in,
> The sunless hours again begin;
> O'er all without, in field and lane,
> The haunted night returns again.

Now we behold the embers flee
About the firelit hearth; and see
Our faces painted as we pass,
Like pictures, on the window-glass.

Must we to bed indeed? Well then,
Let us arise and go like men,
And face with an undaunted tread
The long black passage up to bed.

Farewell, O brother, sister, sire!
O pleasant party round the fire!
The songs you sing, the tales you tell,
Till far to-morrow, fare ye well![8]

Page from an 1896 edition of A Child's Garden of Verses

Make-believe is double-edged. The 'breath of the Bogie' and the tramp of the shadows accompany the child up the stairs. The double-edge of make-believe was something the young Louis came to know well.

The Stevensons had no more children. Louis was the recipient of all the intensity of their love and care, although his father was away a great deal, and his mother was so often ill. He was the

sole recipient too of the hopes and fears of his nurse throughout
his childhood, Alison Cunningham, 'Cummy' as Louis called
her. Cummy came to the Stevensons when Louis was eighteen
months old. She was a product of strict Calvinism, born and
bred across the water in Fife, and her dark convictions were
profoundly influential on the little boy. She condemned
dramatically the works of the devil, amongst which were
included the theatre and the novel, and fed Louis on a literary
diet of the Bible and the more vivid and bloody stories of
religious dedication and martyrdom. Covenanting literature
was quite extensive, in pamphlets and books. Louis's first
acquaintance with the testimonies in *A Cloud of Witnesses* and
Patrick Walker's *Six Saints of the Covenant*, to mention two of the
best known, was early. Memories of the Disruption of 1843, the
walk-out from the General Assembly that brought the creation
of the Free Church, were still vivid. It brought in its wake an
acute religious sensibility – 'it revived the thoughts and
sentiments of the Covenanting times', one nineteenth-century
historian commented.[9] Thomas Stevenson had been in his early
twenties at the time of the Disruption. Its effect was similar,
perhaps, to the political awakening that the events of Suez
caused to the young generation of that later time.

From Cummy, reinforced by his father, Louis developed a
precocious grasp of sin. As a three-year-old, Smout played at
ministers and delivered sermons from the backs of chairs. His
mother recorded in her diary, 'Smout's favourite occupation is
making a church; he makes a pulpit with a chair and a stool;
reads sitting, and then stands up and sings by turns.'[10] This
indicated not so much a child of natural piety, as a child whose
imagination responded keenly to the vivid colours and dramatic
happenings of the Bible, colour and drama heightened by the
enthusiasm of his nurse. He quickly learned the stories from the
Old Testament, could repeat the story of Samson word for word
after hearing it once. 'It's you who gave me a passion for the
drama, Cummy,' he told the protesting Alison Cunningham
years later.[11] The emotional conviction with which she had read
the Bible and religious literature had been telling.

All this inspired his games, but it was puzzling too. '*Why* has
God got a Hell?' he asked at the age of three.[12] 'I have drawed a
man's *body*, shall I do his *soul* now?' he enquired of his mother,

at the same age.[13] His world view was already distinct. Just after his sixth birthday he began to dictate to his mother – he could not yet write – a history of Moses, in an effort to win a prize offered by an uncle. But the territory of his imagination was not for long confined to the Bible. He discovered other sources of stimulus, in the stories his father made up and told to him from the bedroom door during long wakeful nights (but why did not Thomas sit with his child, and hold him, as he lay feverish and wakeful?), and from play with his cousins at Colinton during periods of good health, and from his valued toy soldiers and brooding over the reconstruction of battles, and from Skelt's model theatre and the whole new worlds of characters and actions that he could buy and cut out and colour and manipulate.

But sin remained a chief preoccupation of the child.

> Do I not know, how, nightly, on my bed
> The palpable close darkness shutting round me,
> How my small heart went forth to evil things,
> How all the possibilities of sin
> That were yet present to my innocence
> Bound me too narrowly,
> And how my spirit beat
> The cage of its compulsive purity;
> How – my eyes fixed,
> My shot lip tremulous between my fingers
> I fashioned for myself new modes of crime,
> Created for myself with pain and labour
> The evil that the cobwebs of society,
> The comely secrecies of education,
> Had made an itching mystery to meward.[14]

This was written by the young man looking back, another indication that the grimmer obsessions lingered in the adult mind along with the happier facets of childhood. Stevenson never lost his preoccupation with evil, particularly with the duality of human nature, sin and respectability existing side by side, something he was to explore over and over again. Here is the child not seeing evil but inventing it. His earliest view of the world was one in which both sin and suffering were very present. Out of the safety and warmth, out of the love and care, came these two vivid facts, the one experienced directly in his illnesses, the other issuing forth as a conviction out of the mouths of those he loved.

Cummy's participation was, perhaps, drastic. She was a young woman when she first came to the Stevensons, bonny, and she turned down at least one suitor in order to stay with them. For Smout she was 'the angel of my infant life'; his deep love and gratitude towards her never faded.[15] She gave up her life to him, possibly kept him alive. She was his closest companion in his early years, his teacher, his nurse. Having reached almost independent adulthood he was able to write to her,

> . . . if you should happen to think that you might have had a child of your own, and that it was hard you should have spent so many years taking care of some one else's prodigal, just think this – you have been for a great deal in my life; you have made much that there is in me, just as surely as if you had conceived me; and there are sons who are more ungrateful to their own mothers than I am to you.[16]

Cummy tried, with devotion and selflessness, to mitigate the recurring illnesses and soothe the imagination she did so much to stimulate. She also tried to inject into the child an understanding of the nature of sin. Louis's sufferings were not only the result of illness, but the product of night terrors, exacerbated, doubtless, by fever, but originating almost certainly in his own mind. Cummy was a mixed blessing. Her robust and devoted care was crucial to the delicate child, and she supplied a need that his own mother was not strong enough to provide, but she also constantly stirred up that young mind that had too much time to think and imagine and invent.

> I would not only lie awake to weep for Jesus, which I have done many a time, but I would fear to trust myself to slumber lest I was not accepted and should slip, ere I awoke, into eternal ruin. I remember repeatedly . . . waking from a dream of Hell, clinging to the horizontal bar of the bed, with my knees and chin together, my soul shaken, my body convulsed with agony.[17]

The memory is painfully vivid, and redolent of that vision of guilt-ridden childhood that is so strong a feature of Victorian writing, in Dickens, in George Eliot, in Samuel Butler, in Kingsley.

Stevenson was aware of the equivocal nature of Cummy's influence, though this did not affect the generosity with which he spoke of her. She would sit up all night with him, read to him and sing to him, and enter wholeheartedly into such activities as he was able to pursue. There is something almost conspiratorial in the impression we get of child and nurse sharing in pleasures that both suspected might not in fact be allowed, such as setting forth together to buy *Cassell's Family Paper* in order to get the next instalment of the serial the two had been reading the week before. Her vigilance over Smout's health was unceasing.

I remember with particular distinctness, how she would lift me out of bed, and take me, rolled in blankets, to the window, whence I might look forth into the blue night starred with

Alison Cunningham

street-lamps, and see where the gas still burned behind the windows of other sick-rooms. These were feverish, melancholy times; I cannot remember to have raised my head or seen the moon or any of the heavenly bodies; my eyes were turned downward to the broad lamplit streets and to where the trees of the garden rustled together all night in undecipherable blackness; yet the sight of the outer world refreshed and cheered me; and the whole sorrow and burden of the night was at an end with the arrival of the first of that long string of country carts that, in the dark hours of the morning, with the neighing of horses, the cracking of whips, the shouts of drivers and a hundred other wholesome noises, creaked, rolled, and pounded past my window.[18]

The night for Stevenson was always to be sinister. In his books duels are fought, ugly transformations are accomplished, plots are laid, graves are robbed in the night. Darkness and evil are entwined.

Smout had his own way of fending off the terrors. He would tell himself stories, fantasise richly and adventurously, take himself on fabulous journeys and fight epic battles. The clues are there in *A Child's Garden*. 'Armies and emperors and kings'[19] provided the stuff of his fantasies, and here was territory that his father shared. There was nothing he enjoyed more than a good yarn, and he would spin them happily for Smout's delectation. In the autumn of 1856 Louis's ten-year-old cousin Bob came to stay. He was to spend the winter while attending the Academy, the school down the hill on Henderson Row that Walter Scott had had a hand in creating. Here at last was someone nearer his own size to share in his adventures. The two of them turned everyday occurrences into endless games. They invented imaginary kingdoms, called Nosingtonia and Encyclopaedia, and explored them and fought over them. They dressed up and painted and experimented with Skelt.

Skelt materialised on Smout's sixth birthday in the form of a model theatre he received as a present. In his essay 'A Penny Plain and Twopence Coloured' Stevenson celebrates the part that Skelt played in his childhood. He would go to a stationer's shop in Leith Walk, within a child's walking distance, which displayed a Skelt theatre in the window, each time with a different scene and set of characters, and there would make his choice, never easy, amongst the heaps of dramas about adventurers and robbers and heroic contests. 'What am I? what are life, art, letters, the world, but what my Skelt has made them? He stamped himself upon my immaturity. The world was plain before I knew him, a poor penny world; but soon it was all coloured with romance.'[20] Not strictly true: his world had scarcely been a plain one. But Skelt's characters crowded his mind still further, already peopled with Covenanting martyrs, biblical heroes, and the characters that his father invented to distract him from his fever-wrought fears. Bob helped to fill them out and bring them to life, and their hold on Louis was lasting.

> Indeed, out of this cut-and-dry, dull, swaggering, obtrusive and infantile art, I seemed to have learned the very spirit of my life's enjoyment; met there the shadows of the characters I was to read about and love in a late future . . . acquired a gallery of scenes and characters with which, in the silent theatre of the brain, I might enact all novels and romances; and took from these rude cuts an enduring and transforming pleasure.[21]

Many children exist in a border territory between fantasy and reality. Stevenson was exceptional in relishing his fantasy to such an extent that he made every effort to preserve it for the whole of his life. As a child, fantasy helped him to cope with, to find happiness in, a lonely existence dominated by ill health. As a grown man it was still a prime source of pleasure, not so much as a means of escaping reality, which he knew well enough could not be done, but as a way of making life more colourful and more interesting. In writing romances and making a claim for their importance Stevenson was insisting on the legitimacy of the imagination. There were many who were ready to succumb to such insistence.

Louis had opportunities for enacting make-believe in a more substantial way when he went to stay at his grandfather's manse at Colinton. Colinton brought him companionship: there were almost always cousins staying there. It brought a garden sloping down to the river, a churchyard, an almost rural environment. The possibilities for play were extensive.

It was a place in that time like no other: the garden cut into
provinces by a great hedge of beech, and overlooked by the
church and the terrace of the churchyard, where the
tombstones were thick, and after nightfall 'spunkies' might be
seen to dance at least by children; flower-pots lying warm in
sunshine; laurels and the great yew making elsewhere a
pleasing horror of shade; the smell of water rising from all
round, with an added tang of paper-mills; the sound of water
everywhere, and the sound of mills – the wheel and the dam
singing their alternate strain; the birds on every bush and
from every corner of the overhanging woods pealing out their
notes until the air throbbed with them; and in the midst of
this, the manse.[22]

To little Lou, as he was called when he outgrew Smout, the
house seemed a spacious mansion, and it was filled with trophies
from the east, 'the bones of antelope, the wings of albatross',
'junks and bangles, beads and screens', which gave it an exotic
flavour.[23] In the garden Lou could with ease take on the
personality of a hunter, a soldier or a Red Indian, and inspire
his cousins to similar ploys. If further diversion was required
they could conjure 'spunkies' out of the graves: the proximity of
the churchyard was a rich source of self-induced terror.
Colinton is 'the child's garden'; the trees and the birdsong, the
river and the humming mill; the companions, though there are
not many in the poems, are the cousins.

The Reverend Lewis Balfour's wife died six years before Louis
was born. The household was run with love and efficiency by his
daughter Jane, 'Auntie', 'chief of our aunts'[24] who was a
rigorous and energetic lady, but prone to spoiling her young
nephew. She would buy him tin soldiers, and his grandfather
took a rather solemn interest in his reconstructions of battles on
the dining-room table. War games became a passion he never
lost, to such an extent that there were those who said that Louis's
real ambitions were military, not literary, and was only
prevented from becoming a soldier by his ill-health. But the best
thing about Colinton was almost certainly the numerous
household. There were quantities of cousins, some briefly
visiting from India, others from closer at hand. (Some were sent
home from India for their education only to die.) Louis found

companionship, and we see him at Colinton as something more like an ordinary, high-spirited little boy, rather than as the frail, cherished, precocious only child enclosed with three adults in a narrow Georgian terrace house, in a world of coughs and fevers and wakefulness in the dark night.

Louis with his mother,
Margaret Stevenson

There were other periods too of what it is difficult not to think of as liberation. In 1857 Louis was on holiday with his parents in the Lake District, but they also spent summer holidays on the East Lothian coast and near Peebles, in the lovely country of the Tweed valley. In 1860 Lewis Balfour died, and there were no more visits to Colinton. The East Lothian and Berwickshire coast was becoming a fashionable resort area now that the railway made it so easily accessible. There were several holidays spent at North Berwick, a small seaside town about thirty miles from Edinburgh. Hotels were sprouting there, but the Stevensons rented a house. The sea, the sand and the rocks were a great joy to Louis, but so, again, were the companions he

found there, and the freedom he had in the time he spent with
them. 'Crusoeing' was the word he used to describe his favourite
seaside activities – 'a word that covers all extempore eating in
the open air: digging perhaps a house under the margin of
the links, kindling a fire of the sea-ware, and cooking apples
there . . .'[25] He remembered with special pleasure meeting his
friends after dark with bull's-eye lanterns.

> Four or five would sometimes climb into the belly of a ten-
> man lugger, with nothing but the thwarts above them . . . or
> choose out some hollow of the links where the wind might
> whistle overhead. There the coats would be unbuttoned and
> the bull's-eyes discovered; and in the chequering glimmer,
> under the huge windy hall of the night, and cheered by a rich
> steam of toasting tinware, these fortunate young gentlemen
> would crouch together in the cold sand of the links or on the
> scaly bilges of the fishing-boat, and delight themselves with
> inappropriate talk.[26]

North Berwick had much to offer. Louis wasn't able to join in
the rougher or more active games of the other boys, but on the
beach this mattered less than it did at school, where it was
definitely odd not to play football. There were the sand, and the
links, and the dark square of the Bass Rock on which Stevenson
was to imprison David Balfour years later, and the splendid ruin
of Tantallon Castle. One of Louis's companions of the time
remembered 'secret meetings at what, for us, was the dead of
night, in a small cave or fissure in the rocks at Point Garry'.[27]
    His friends remembered him as chief inspirer of their games.
'He always led the band, was always the master-spirit and
inspiring force. A kind of magnetism seemed to emanate from
him, some of his great, though then undeveloped personality.'[28]
They played at pirates and smugglers and hunted for buried
treasure. They raced model yachts and fished in the rock pools
and played at being marooned, eating raw shrimps to add
authenticity to the game. At Colinton during a similar game
Louis and a cousin had eaten buttercups and made themselves
rather ill. But he was remembered also as a strange boy, 'the thin
elfin lad with the brilliant eyes', a boy who was different.[29]
Though we can see the North Berwick holidays as rehearsals for
Treasure Island, for Louis their chief importance was as an outlet

for an overburdened imagination. It is interesting that his young adventure heroes, Jim Hawkins and David Balfour, and Dick in *The Black Arrow*, are, deliberately, rather ordinary lads, as if inside the thin, glittering-eyed invalid there was a straightforward football-playing schoolboy longing to get out.

There was another territory of escape, though a more restrained one. Thomas often took his ailing wife to Bridge of Allan, which had become a small health resort. Louis grew fond of the area, on the fringe of the Highlands, with Stirling Castle and more historic battlefields, Bannockburn and Sheriffmuir, not far away. He enjoyed his walks along Allan Water, and as an adult returned quite frequently to Bridge of Allan or nearby Dunblane, to rest and get away from Edinburgh. But it was a douce and middle-class little town, as it still is, full of quiet hotels and very respectable lodgings. It was nice enough, but there was not much excitement there, not many outlets for self-expression.

Finding expression was of the greatest importance. He found it through play, especially with other children. He found it through the taking on of other characters: his playing at ministers and reciting of poetry – his Skelt and his dressing up were all a part of that, as were of course the Jenkins' dramatics and ultimately his writing. He was always quick to see the dramatic possibilities in any situation and to convert the tedious exigencies of reality into something more palatable. On one occasion when, equipped as a soldier, his mother insisted he should wear a shawl, he made the most of it by suggesting he could be on a night march. Writing was only one of a number of his means of self-expression and not, as a small child, a major one. Before he was literate he would intone what he called 'Songstries', lengthy, semi-metrical psalm-like improvisations of dramatic themes often to do with sin and the devil. Drawing was a favourite occupation, 'but it was from a purely imitative and literary impulse', he says,[30] in other words another attempt to body forth his fancies.

He was seven before he learned to read, and so until that age was totally reliant on the stories that were told and read to him, and the stories he invented himself. He had not wanted to learn to read before then, which suggests, although he himself puts it down to idleness, that he was resisting the possibility that the story-telling might come to an end. Schooling was a problem. He was not strong enough to survive happily in the robust atmosphere of school, nor did he care enough about his lessons to feel inclined to compensate for his physical weakness through cleverness. His father, too, had a healthy suspicion of conventional learning and seems to have considered, unorthodoxly, that stories and play were just as important. He himself achieved his own successes as much through instinct and experience as through calculation. Louis's first school was down the hill at Canonmills. Rosaline Masson, daughter of David Masson, Professor of Rhetoric when Louis was a student, records that he was teased there and had a difficult time. Shortly after, when he was five years old, he went to Mr Henderson's school in India Street, just around the corner from Heriot Row. He was only there for two hours each morning, but that again didn't last long, and sickness kept him home until in 1859 he started again at the same school. Rosaline Masson writes of the neighbours seeing 'young Mrs Stevenson running the little fellow up and down sunny Heriot Row after breakfast to warm him before his school hours'.[31]

The periods of illness followed one after the other. In September 1858, for instance, a long illness began; for five weeks he was unable to sit up in bed. He couldn't sleep and had little appetite. A year later he had chicken pox, and then for most of the following winter and spring, he was ill again. In 1861 he was in bed for six weeks with whooping cough . . . and so it went on. His parents' anxiety probably did not help, and the fact that it was assumed he would be ill must have interfered with his chances of settling down at school. It was decided that he should attend the Academy, a relatively new and well-considered school, though without the more historic prestige of the Royal High School, where Thomas had gone, and which Louis would have liked to have attended. He went down the hill each morning to the long, low classical frontage in Henderson Row with the vast and (certainly nowadays) forbidding expanse of playground before it. He made friends there, but the whole atmosphere of school was alien to him. He stood out as a curious figure, though there was some kudos in being an Academy boy, and he could rattle his clacken, a wooden stick, along the railings with the other Academy boys.

He was eleven when he started at the Academy. In 1862 and 1863 there were lengthy trips abroad, partly in search of health, but on his parents' behalf this time. Thomas was ill, 'threatened with spitting blood', his wife recorded.[32] It looked as though his strenuous life, strenuous in conscience as well as in action, was taking its toll. And Margaret wasn't well either, although exactly what it was they were suffering from is not clear. They went to London and the south of England, then in the summer to Germany, Louis's first trip abroad. But Louis visited Salisbury, Stonehenge and the Isle of Wight without recording any impressions, and was equally silent about Homberg. In January 1863 a lengthier trip was embarked on which took the Stevensons first to Nice, then a month in Menton, with which Louis was to become much more familiar later, then on through Italy, Austria and Germany. Cummy went with them, and was scandalised by Continental Sabbath habits. Papist revelries were too much for her. She wrote in the diary she kept for her sister,

> The people here have been going on at a fearful rate to-day, men and boys dressed in all conceivable costumes, having false faces on and playing some kind of music. How sweet it was to leave this foolery and great rabble of people, and go into the House of Jesus! It seems some festival is going on just now before Lent. It is awful to see the dozens of priests going about, and allowing such wickedness to go unchecked, but I suppose the priests will sanction the festival. They are dark mysterious-looking men, going about with their long gowns and cocked hats, professing to be the true servants of God; verily they have their reward.[33]

It sounds the kind of scene Louis would have relished, but he was only twelve, and probably his response was tinged with guilt also. He came, after all, from a city where papists had often been bracketed with thieves and harlots. Cummy's outrage would certainly have rubbed off on him to some extent, and though his parents followed a deliberate policy of exposing themselves to other forms of worship than their own, Cummy clearly resented such contamination.

A clue to what the experience was like is given in a

reminiscence of a cousin who was with them for some of the
time. Lou was obviously a mature twelve-year-old.

> In some ways he was more like a boy of sixteen. My uncle had
> a great belief . . . in the educational value of travel, and to this
> end and for the benefit of Louis he devoted his whole energies
> to the five months abroad. In the hotel at Nice he began to
> take Louis into the smoking-room with him; there my uncle
> was always surrounded by a group of eager and aroused
> listeners – English, American, and Russian – and every
> subject, political, artistic, and theological, was discussed and
> argued. Uncle Tom's genial manner found friends wherever
> he went, and the same sort of thing went on during the whole
> journey. Then in regard to what we saw, his keen admiration
> of art and architecture seemed to be shared by Louis; they
> would go into raptures over a cathedral, or an old archway, or
> a picture.[34]

The lengthy companionship with his father and the introduction into the adult world were important. The next stage was
to have these without mother and nurse hovering in the wings.
That was to come soon.

He did not go back to the Academy. There followed a spell at
an English boarding school, Spring Grove in Isleworth, where
two of his cousins were. He was so unhappy there he felt
compelled to tell his father he wanted to leave. His letters from
school show a sense of fun, but with a pathetic strain too – he
wasn't all that grown-up. It was a great relief when Thomas
arrived to take him off to Menton, where his mother was again
escaping the harsh northern winter. Finally, in 1864, he started
at Mr Thompson's small and flexibly organised school in
Frederick Street, a short walk from home, and remained there
until he went to university. But Louis never distinguished
himself at school (although there were those later who claimed
they recognised his genius). His health was rather more stable,
but he clearly resisted any kind of institutional ambience. He
did not care for formal learning, and never would: he had better
things to do. He invented, edited, and virtually wrote single-
handed several schoolboys' magazines. By the time he had
settled at Mr Thompson's the scribbling had well and truly
begun.

Louis and his father,
Thomas Stevenson

So Louis spent little time at any institution that might have suppressed his individuality. He must have felt less of an oddity at Thompson's, where there were only twenty pupils, than in the more conformist atmosphere of the Academy or an English public school, and we can guess that he gained in confidence – for it required confidence to be the determined non-conformist that emerged in 1867 when he left school. His parents do not seem to have attempted to shape him, but to have assumed that he would accept their own deeply engrained moral and religious principles. The overriding problem of his health, their own health problems, and their deep concern for each other may have led them to neglect the challenging personality that was growing up beside them. Margaret Stevenson's total, almost childlike love for her husband is apparent amongst the ordinary concerns of her diary. She counts the days of his absences and the days to be lived through before his returns. Her loyalty was always unquestioningly to Tom, and when the inevitable frictions developed between father and son, this was a hard lesson, as it always is, for the son to learn. 'My mother is my father's wife': the only child, conscious of his oddity, with few

friends, had to come to terms with the fact that for two of the
three people he most loved he rated second best.[35] Only Cummy
was all his, and a growing lad could scarcely admit that.

By this time Louis was exploring Edinburgh more freely and
independently than he had been able to do hand in hand with
Cummy and well wrapped up against the biting wind. They had
taken their walks to Warriston cemetery, to the Leith Walk
stationer, along the Water of Leith, and around the fascinating
area where the north-east corner of the New Town shaded into
vestiges of rural communities. One of the best things about the
New Town, Stevenson felt, was that there still lingered 'this
haunting flavour of the country'.[36] It was not just that a gap in
the sedate terraces would suddenly reveal a vista of hills and
water, but that the building itself had not entirely obliterated a
rural awareness. And there were other fascinations. A
contemporary of Louis wrote of the mills and granaries at
Canonmills,

> . . . with their store of grain which we tried to reach into; the
> mill lade; the Old Coach Inn further up the road; the
> tannery; the market-garden, where we used to spend our
> halfpence on fruits in their season; the Coachmen's green at
> Bellevue, where a travelling menagerie with Tom Thumb and
> Mrs Thumb was on view for a time; the Zoological Gardens in
> East Claremont Street, where we saw the monkeys, the strange
> birds, the bears down in a pit, and got peacocks' feathers to
> our delight; while the corn was growing in the fields nearby,
> and Blondin walked on the tight-rope high up in the air down
> at Inverleith Row, and the miller's horses toiled zig-zag ways
> up the hill with their loads of flour on sled-carts for the city,
> and Jooky Reid at Bellevue chased us boys, would-be
> plunderers, away from his garden.[37]

There was plenty for Lou and Cummy to see, although the
scenes were soon to pass away, and Cummy seems to have been
as enthusiastic a walker and observer as Louis. But there was
even more to be found out when Lou set forth without the
reassurance of Cummy's hand.

Stevenson has little to say of himself as a young teen-ager. He
seems to grow at once from sickly child to prankish young man.
He has little to say about his trips abroad, little to say about

school. It may have been because neither travel nor school produced the intensified imaginative experience of the younger child. He had outgrown his earliest susceptibilities, and there may have seemed less for his imagination to build on. There were the North Berwick interludes, and those near Peebles, where Louis fought a duel with another Academy boy with real pistols and real powder (but no bullets) and redcurrant jelly to add to the effect. There he and Bob and his sister Katherine rode ponies which Lou named Heaven, Hell and Purgatory – he was on the latter. But there were probably periods when the boy felt starved of creative exploration.

One trip that clearly remedied that was his first alone with his father. In the autumn of 1863, back from the Continent, Thomas took him on a tour of the Fife lighthouses. This in itself was an event to be treasured, for it was 'without the help of petticoats'.[38] They were on their own. He was no longer a small boy in the charge of his nurse, but a boy of nearly thirteen, who would, it was understood, one day be an engineer as enterprising as his father. However, his memory is not of an enthusiasm for lighthouses and harbours, but of the particular thrill of driving over Magus Moor, the scene of Archbishop Sharp's murder.

> I still see Magus Moor two hundred years ago; a desert place, quite unenclosed; in the midst, the primate's carriage fleeing at the gallop; the assassins loose-reined in pursuit, Burley Balfour, pistol in hand, among the first. No scene in history has ever written itself so deeply on my mind; not because Balfour, that questionable zealot, was an ancestral cousin of my own; not because of the pleadings of the victim and his daughter; not even because of the live bum-bee that flew out of Sharpe's 'bacco-box, thus clearly indicating his complicity with Satan; nor merely because, as it was after all a crime of a fine religious flavour, it figured in Sunday books. . . . The figure that always fixed my attention is that of Hackston of Rathillet, sitting in the saddle with his cloak about his mouth, and through all that long, bungling, vociferous hurly-burly, revolving privately a case of conscience. He would take no hand in the deed, because he had a private spite against the victim, and 'that action' must be sullied with no suggestion of

a worldly motive; on the other hand, 'that action' in itself was
highly justified, he had cast in his lot with 'the actors', and
he must stay there, inactive but publicly sharing the
responsibility.[39]

This passage, one of the many one could choose to illustrate
crucial facets of Stevenson's relationship with the past that
shaped him, contains a most revealing clue to his attitudes. It is
the combination of violent action and the 'case of conscience'.
Frequently he harks back to this figure and this scene: murder
on a dark moor, religious fanaticism and the individual
conscience. That it should have dominated his first visit to the
locations of his father's work is significant. The pull of not so
much history as of tangible images of the past and the exciting
possibilities of historical narrative was so much greater than his
interest in the achievements of his father and grandfather.
Although he would as a grown man retell in detail, with a full
sense of the adventure and risk involved, the story of the
construction of the Bell Rock lighthouse, the dark memory of
murder and the cloaked figure of Hackston filled his mind on
this first visit to Fife.

Hackston appealed not just because he was one of history's
mysterious horsemen, but because of the twin forces of violence
and conscience that were contained in him. He was a tantalising
embodiment of what would become Stevenson's vision of the
duality of human nature, or rather a demonstration of the hold
that duality could have over Stevenson himself. The not yet
thirteen-year-old boy conjures the figure out of the sinister
moor. The awareness of duality had been developing in the
small child, the growth of a highly-strung and sensitive
conscience depending on an apprehension of evil. As an adult
Stevenson was able to write of his father, an intimate part of this,
and describe his vulnerability to guilt. 'His sense of his own
unworthiness I have called morbid; morbid, too, were his sense
of the fleetingness of life and his concern for death. He had
never accepted the conditions of man's life or his own character;
and his inmost thoughts were ever tinged with the Celtic
melancholy.'[40] Louis as a young man was quite determined to
accept the fact of death and the conditions of his own life.

'Courage and gaiety and the quiet mind', he wrote towards the end of his life, were the essential ingredients of a worthwhile attitude to life.[41] His father had courage, gaiety on occasions, but peace of mind it seems rarely. Louis's sensitive understanding of his father, which he seems to have arrived at very young and which underwent some severe tests, surely helped him to cope with his own emotional and psychological divisions. If he was able to free himself from a narrow definition of morality, his conscience remained delicately responsive to the last.

He tried to write a novel about Hackston, as he did about the Pentland Rising and Rullion Green, and other dramatic historic events. But they were all discarded. In his adolescent years he was taking writing seriously, although we can probably accept his word that his attempts were heavy-handed. By this time also the need to spend at least part of the winter in some southerly quarter had established itself, for his mother's health as well as his own. At the end of 1863 after his brief unhappy spell at Spring Grove he spent five months at Menton. It is hard to imagine how Louis spent his time if it were not with writing and perhaps drawing. In the spring of 1864 and again in 1865 he and his mother were in Torquay, where he had private tutors to keep him at his studies. Although he was now less subject to the fevers and coughs which had been a way of life in his early childhood he did not look robust. School companions remember that he did not look well and was often absent. At the age of fourteen he already had that characteristic and alarming look of emaciation.

In body he was assuredly badly set up. His limbs were long, lean and spidery, and his chest flat, so as almost to suggest some malnutrition, such sharp corners did his joints make under his clothes. But in his face this was belied. His brow was oval and full, over soft brown eyes that seemed already to have drunk the sunlight under southern vines. The whole face had a tendency to an oval Madonna-like type. But about the mouth and in the mirthful mocking light of the eyes there lingered ever a ready Autolycus roguery that rather suggested sly Hermes masquerading as a mortal. The eyes were always genial, however gaily the lights danced in them, but about the

mouth there was something a little tricksy and mocking, as if
of a spirit that already peeped behind the scenes of life's
pageant and more than guessed its unrealities.[42]

The inspiring leader of games, who had to make up through
inventiveness what he lacked in action, had become a more
sophisticated creature, turning to words now, both written and
spoken, to compensate for his ability to be strenuously active.
Almost everyone who describes Stevenson comments on the
vivacity and wit of his conversation and the eloquence of his
gestures. Partly the traits were inherited from his father, also a
winning conversationalist who charmed people wherever he
went, but it is clear that Louis deliberately cultivated this ability
and made the most of it. The bright eyes and mocking half-
smile, self-mocking as often as not, added an element of Puckish
intelligence to his – already emerging at fourteen – sophisticated
bohemian manner.

His reading of course had broadened considerably since the
days of Cummy's stories, but he still read assiduously about the
Covenanters. It is fascinating that the grim Covenanters and
bloody stories of fanaticism appealed to him more strongly
than the romantic possibilities of Bonnie Prince Charlie, and
inevitable that, sooner or later, he would make some attempt to
communicate something of that unrelenting aspect of the Scots
character in his fiction. It is there in part in some short stories
and in *The Master of Ballantrae*, but it was not until his forty-
fourth year and his last and unfinished novel *Weir of Hermiston*,
that he came fully to grips with it. He was also reading novels,
Scott and Thackeray, and he loved Dumas. As a student he read
and chose to imitate eighteenth-century essayists. He read
French with ease, and that was his route to some much loved
and much disputed-over literature. He discovered American
authors, Thoreau, Hawthorne, Whitman, and found them
exciting. The French and American influences on his work were
to be significant. He read with an eager appetite, but not only to
savour literature: he read in a search for patterns and examples
that his own writing could learn from. He had worked out for
himself that this was the way he would become a writer.

The summer after Louis's first year as a student at Edinburgh
University, a difficult year with Louis keeping up a bold front in

the face of hostility and lack of interest, he spent some time at Anstruther in Fife on his own, studying the harbour works. It did not come easily, and he wrote rather ruefully of his difficulties in letters to his father.

> When I am drawing I find out something I have not measured, or, having measured, have not noted, or, having noted, cannot find; so I have to trudge to the pier again ere I can go further with my noble design.[43]

To his mother he wrote more truculently,

> I am utterly sick of this grey, grim, sea-beaten hole. I have a little cold in my head, which makes my eyes sore; and you can't tell how utterly sick I am, and how anxious to get back among trees and flowers and something less meaningless than this bleak fertility.[44]

He found the days wearisome, but spent the evenings shut up in his little room in his Anstruther lodgings writing, and relished the fact that he was on his own and working away at what he considered really important.

Later that same summer he went with his father on a tour of Scottish lighthouses, which was part of his father's duties as Commissioner of Northern Lights. This he found much more rewarding. It involved travel, mainly by boat, often in bad weather, and he responded enthusiastically to the physical demands this made on him. He got drenched and wind-lashed as they made their way as far north as Wick. Thomas had built the Wick harbour, and was devastated when the sea battered it beyond repair. Wick was bleak too, seared by the wind, pounded by rain and the sea, but it was more challenging than the Fife coast.

There were more trips for Louis, in the summers of 1869 and 1870, north into the Pentland Firth, the notoriously wild stretch of sea between Caithness and the Orkney islands, and threading the Hebrides off the west coast. Louis enjoyed this journeying, and enjoyed the thought that Scott had made a similar trip under the guidance of his grandfather Robert, and had written *The Pirate* as a result. There were adventures, and the inevitable risks of wind and weather. He tried deep-sea diving. And there was some congenial companionship. He became friendly with

Sam Bough, the artist, and met, memorably though briefly and without knowing his name, Edmund Gosse, who was to become later a firm friend. During the 1870 trip he spent three weeks on the Isle of Erraid, where his father was supervising the construction of the lighthouse on Dhu Hearteach. He had plenty of time to absorb the atmosphere, grim sometimes but compelling, of the string of islands off the Argyle coast. He made his return to Erraid in *Kidnapped*, when he stranded David Balfour there and exposed his lack of practical understanding: David thinks himself marooned and desperately scavenges for shellfish, only to discover when he has almost given up hope that when the tide is out he can walk across to Mull, a populated island. Stevenson's story 'The Merry Men', is set on the same island.

The pleasure Louis got from these trips, and the riches he gleaned from them, failed to convince him that engineering was his calling. Perhaps his father had the chance to observe that Louis's responses were less to the challenge of harbour works than to the impressiveness of landscape and seascape and weather and the discovery of remote areas of Scotland. Whatever Louis failed to learn in the one profession the experiences provided sustaining nourishment for another. The impressions he came home with, physical and emotional, were to serve him well.

Chapter 3

A HEART OF FIRE

A heart of fire,
In the full flush of young desire
'Epistle to Charles Baxter'

For something like six years life did not change significantly for
Louis Stevenson, and that is a long time in a young man's life.
From his seventeenth to his twenty-third year the way he spent
his time remained much the same. The nature of his studies
changed, from engineering to law, but his attitude to them
scarcely at all. He roamed Edinburgh and the Pentlands,
frequented the same taverns, enjoyed the same companionship,
explored further the potential of bohemianism, for most of that
time. His genius for serendipity developed, his friendships grew
firmer, his anti-establishment ideas bolder. And all the time, as
one savours Stevenson's activities during this period, there is an
exaggerated sense of life sparkling rather frustratedly as he
copes with ill health, disappointment and the feeling of
imprisonment. From Germany, which he visited with Walter
Simpson in August 1872, he wrote to his mother:

An opera is far more *real* than real life to me. It seems as if
stage illusion, and particularly this hardest to swallow and
most conventional illusion of them all – an opera – would
never stale upon me. I wish that life was an opera. I should
like to *live* in one; but I don't know in what quarter of the
globe I shall find society so constituted. Besides, it would
soon pall: imagine asking for three Kreuzer cigars in
recitative, or giving the washerwoman the inventory of your
dirty clothes in a sustained and flourishing aria.[1]

A joke perhaps, but he *could* imagine it, and clearly liked the
idea.

Fleeting glimpses of people, moments, incidents fed his
appetite for heightened reality. The street woman to whom he

could not bring himself to give money directly stabbed his heart and vision with sudden intensity. He dropped coins on the pavement for her, because he could not bear her to see him witness her humiliation. The little boy he discovered lost and alone totally captivated him, and he wandered the streets for hours carrying the boy in his arms until home and parents were found. Such episodes reflected not only his very real and sensitive kindness, but his eye for sparks of drama in life's drabness. It was as if he were making every effort to fashion his own opera out of life, not in order to run away from reality, but to transform it.

When he fell in love he was bound to do so dramatically. The hints that there may have been love affairs during this period, that there was one particular passion which J. A. Steuart in his dubious biography describes in some detail with a young prostitute from the Highlands called Kate Drummond, can be discounted. It is hard to believe that Stevenson's spontaneous self-dramatisation would not have provided us with better authenticated evidence. An affair of any real depth or significance was unlikely to have escaped his own pen and the notice of his friends. As a young man Louis seemed to find it very hard to keep his feelings to himself.

He certainly had affectionate as well as sexual relations with Edinburgh prostitutes, and appreciated the kindness and the frankness of some of the women he encountered. There was for Louis in the directness and lack of hypocrisy in this world he moved in a dignity that middle-class Edinburgh lacked. Although he hated the financial transaction of prostitution and condemned the exploitation it involved and the two-faced attitudes that encouraged it, he found courage and generosity in Edinburgh bar and brothel life as well as degradation. And he had cause for gratitude, for the nature of his sexual initiation and early experiences was such that he retained a sensitive and generous attitude towards women that was far from typical of his time. He learnt to ignore the barriers of class and sex, a lesson of the greatest importance. When he insisted defiantly in verse, 'give me the publican and harlot', it meant more than the striking of a pose.[2]

Women found Louis's combination of charm and brilliance appealing, although the young bourgeoises often found him alarming. Sisters of his friends, for instance, tended to find him an attractive but formidable companion, whose behaviour in the drawing-room or at the dinner table could be precipitately unconventional. The slight and eloquent young man could suddenly erupt into a baffling force. One gets an impression of middle-class young girls as a wide-eyed audience for his performances. Flora Masson, another daughter of the David Masson household, described dinner at Heriot Row.

Our end of the table was, to me, almost uncomfortably brilliant. Mr Stevenson had taken me in, and Louis Stevenson was on my other side. Father and son both talked, taking diametrically opposite points of view on all things under the sun. Mr Stevenson seemed to me, on that evening, to be the type of the kindly, orthodox Edinburgh father. We chatted of nice, concrete, comfortable things, such as the Scottish Highlands in autumn; and in a moment of Scottish fervour he quoted – I believe *sotto voce* – a bit of versified psalm. But Louis Stevenson, on my other side, was on that evening in one of his most recklessly brilliant moods. His talk was almost incessant. I remember feeling quite dazed at the amount of intellection he expended on each subject, however trivial in itself, that we touched upon. He worried it as a dog might worry a rat, and then threw it off lightly, as some chance word or allusion set him thinking, and talking, of something else. The father's face at certain moments was a study – an indescribable mixture of vexation, fatherly pride and admiration, and sheer bewilderment at the boy's brilliant flippancies, and the quick young thrusts of his wit and criticism.[3]

Louis had not time for 'nice, concrete, comfortable things'. If Thomas Stevenson represented the best of what young women expected the Edinburgh older generation to be, Louis was certainly not representative of the younger. Most girls were probably more dazzled than attracted, although there was one at least who responded very positively, about whom Louis was to drop hints in a letter to his friend Mrs Sitwell. He felt he had behaved badly to her. He seems to have been attracted to Eve Simpson, Walter's sister (who could be the girl there referred to) and even to have entertained fleetingly the thought of marriage.

It may have been Eve with whom he skated on Duddingston
Loch, an experience he celebrated in a poem.

Certainly Louis was not without vanity and liked to think
himself attractive to women – stories are told of how he could
not pass a mirror without a look at himself – but it was clear,
even in his early twenties, that no conventionally brought up
and conventionally opinioned girl would deeply attract him. He
visited prostitutes not only because they provided the tacitly
accepted outlet of the time for curious and sexually uneasy
young men but because he found them interesting. They had
not been tamed by middle-class manners.

His wincing at the exploitation of women recurs throughout
his life. He referred to one prostitute with whom he was
familiar, 'the robust, great-haunched, blue-eyed young woman
of admirable temper and, if you will let me say so of a prostitute,
extraordinary modesty',[4] and claimed, vanity coming to the
fore, that 'I never saw one who could resist me'.[5] In a letter,
written after his marriage, to an anxious young man who had
written for advice, he reflected on the tricky problem of chastity,
but could not resolve it, given the custom and expectations of
society, for men or for women.[6] In his plea that prostitutes
should be regarded with greater respect and not treated as
outcasts, the implication is that he considered prostitution
acceptable. He was more than ready to acknowledge that he had
benefited from the buyable women of Edinburgh, and even to
romanticise them in some of his early poetry. He was clear that
there were some, at least, who had no regrets about the way they
earned a living: his father, committed to rescuing the fallen
from the streets, would have profoundly disagreed. But much of
Louis's respect for women he learnt from his father.

Louis's romanticism was bound to idealise his anticipations
of love, *la grande passion*. Much of his early poetry is, usually
insubstantially and often artificially, the result of his mode of
versifying, about love:

> Let Love go, if go she will.
> Seek not, O fool, her wanton flight to stay.[7]

The word is much more concretely and convincingly used when
he is not talking of romantic love at all, but of an earthier, more
immediate response:

I walk the street smoking my pipe
And I love the dallying shop-girl
That leans with rounded stern to look at the fashions.[8]

The best of Stevenson's early poetry has such straightforward
statement and images of everyday reality, although his free verse
is often rhythmically lax. There is a striking genuineness of
feeling here which is lost when Stevenson sets out to write a
deliberate 'love poem'. This poem, probably written in the early
seventies, and clearly showing he had been reading Whitman,
maintains its convincing directness.

I love night in the city,
The lighted streets and the swinging gait of harlots.
I love cool pale morning,
In the empty bye-streets . . .

Was there a woman, he must have often wondered, of his own
class and background who could share, or at least sympathise
with, this kind of thing? A woman as companion, as lively
participant in his volatile ways, as sharer of jokes and thoughts
and opinions, awake to his sense of adventure, he was not to find
in Edinburgh. When he did find someone near to this, twice and
elsewhere, he went overboard, in different ways. It is revealing
that the two women who meant most in Louis's life were both
older and more experienced than himself, had both been
exposed to unhappy marriages, had both lost a child, and were
both unconventional and independently minded. In both cases
their suffering was part of the attraction. Stevenson, though
incorrigibly unable to express this in his own fiction until the
end of his life, had infinite sympathy for the sufferings of
women.

Louis had to communicate; to his friends in letters and
conversation, to his notebooks, to his parents argumentatively
and provocatively. In his adventures in the Edinburgh underworld he explored physical sensation and emotional feeling;
through writing, he explored language and expression. In 1873
two events occurred which strained his capacities for both
feeling and expression to their utmost. Since the spring of 1871
he had been dividing his working time between writing and
fulfilling his commitment to the legal profession. In May of the

next year he joined the office of Messrs Skene, Edwards and Bilton, Writers to the Signet,[9] but he was hardly challenged by the work there. A lot of tedious learning had to be done to qualify for the Bar, and Louis's commitment to the legal profession was never more than formal. He completed his work out of a sense of duty rather than conviction. (However, his studies did provide him with material that he later found useful in his writing.) In the following November he passed the preliminary examination for the Scottish Bar. He was over the first hurdle.

He pressed on with his studies, but spent long periods at Swanston too, struggling with his writing, though not productively. He was without encouragement, the encouragement of those in a position to read and comment on what he was doing, and the more concrete encouragement of actual publication. He did not flee the Edinburgh winter during these two years, except for brief stays at Bridge of Allan and Dunblane, and his health consequently suffered. He can't have been helped by the deaths of two young Balfour cousins. But his friends were sustaining. By September 1872 Bob had initiated an exclusive little club, the L.J.R. (Liberty, Justice, Reverence), which brought the little group of friends – Louis, Baxter, Ferrier, Simpson – together for meetings in a pub, and was perhaps intended to reflect the glorious heyday of Edinburgh drinking and debating clubs in the eighteenth century. It seems not to have got very far, though there was a written constitution, which was apparently blasphemous and thoroughly anti-establishment. The band of stalwart rebels scarcely needed the formality of a society to articulate their objections to the status quo. But the getting of their general tenor down in black and white was to have drastic consequences.

In January 1873 Louis returned to Heriot Row after a stay in Great Malvern with his mother. He had been previously very unwell, and this time it was necessary to escape to the south. Shortly after he got back he spent a pleasantly convivial evening with Charles Baxter. He got home late, and came in from the gas-lit street to be accosted by his father. He had been cheered by his evening with Charles. In Great Malvern he had been thoroughly depressed, and had written to his friend morbidly, talking of seeking escape from a burdensome life through

RLS aged about twenty-six, by T. Blake Wirgman after a drawing by Fanny

brandy, or laudanum, or suicide. 'I give up my chair to whoever wants it: here gentlemen is the refuse of what was never a very good hand and the one or two counters still left to me – share them and adieu!'[10] he had written rather wildly. Illness and his sense of imprisonment had had their effect. But now he had even more cause to complain of the hand that had been dealt him.

Thomas had been waiting for him. The two of them sat late into the night while Thomas distressfully questioned him about his religious and moral beliefs. He had found the constitution of the L.J.R. and could not rest until he had assured himself that it represented some passing aberration on the part of his son, that it was some kind of game, that he did not really hold such atheistical iconoclastic opinions. Louis could not give him this assurance. He was precipitated into profound and agonised disagreement with his parents on issues that were of the most supreme importance to them. In reply to his father's insistent questioning Louis confessed his agnosticism. He badly wanted

to be honest. The results were shattering, as he described in an
outpouring of his difficulties to Baxter.

> The thunderbolt has fallen with a vengeance now. You know
> the aspect of a house in which somebody is still awaiting
> burial: the quiet steps, the hushed voices and rare
> conversation, the religious literature that holds a temporary
> monopoly, the grim, wretched faces; all is here reproduced in
> this family circle in honour of my (what is it?) atheism or
> blasphemy. . . . My father put me one or two questions as to
> beliefs, which I candidly answered. I really hate all lying so
> much now – a new-found honesty that has somehow come
> out of my late illness – that I could not so much as hesitate at
> the time, but if I had foreseen the real Hell of everything
> since, I think I should have lied as I have done so often before.
> I so far thought of my father, but I had forgotten my mother.
> And now! they are both ill, both silent, both as down in the
> mouth as if – I can find no simile. You may fancy how happy it
> is for me. If it were not too late, I think I could almost find it in
> my heart to retract, but it is too late; and again, am I to live my
> whole life as one falsehood? Of course, it is rougher than Hell
> upon my father, but can I help it? They don't see either that
> my game is not the light-hearted scoffer, that I am not (as they
> call me) a careless infidel. I believe as much as they do, only
> generally in the inverse ratio. I am, I think, as honest as they
> can be in what I hold. I have not come hastily to my views. I
> reserve (as I have told them) many points until I acquire fuller
> information. I do not think I am thus justly to be called a
> 'horrible atheist'; and I confess I cannot exactly swallow my
> father's purpose of praying down continuous afflictions on
> my head.[11]

What made it all doubly painful was this feeling that if he had
lied it would have been preferable, that his parents actually
wished that he had lied to spare them having to confront the
horror of the fact that Louis could find no proof of the existence
of God.

For months the rift dominated the household. Thomas
Stevenson tried over and over again to bring Louis back into the
fold, plied him with literature, insisted on discussions of
fundamental points, harried him with anxiety, all of which

Louis found scarcely bearable. (Much later his mother told him they had no idea he found it so distressing.) The situation deteriorated desperately when Thomas decided that the cause of all the trouble was Bob. Another cousin had on his deathbed warned Thomas of the evil influence of the dissolute and irreligious Bob. If briefly Bob, as scapegoat, diverted attention from Louis, the atmosphere of anger and hysteria at 17 Heriot Row was no less intolerable.

Louis was badly shaken. The intensity of his father's anger and self-torture, his mother's hysterics, the accusations against Bob, his dear companion, as his corrupter, the cause of the ruin of the Stevenson household and the Stevenson heir, and the condemnation of Louis himself for being so weak and degenerate as to entertain Bob's society and influence, were profoundly disturbing. For all his criticisms and rebellion and his open disrespect at times Louis dearly loved his parents, and he was agonised at their distress. When his father hysterically declared that he wished he had never married, had never had a son, or wished his son dead rather than an atheist it was amazing that Louis's own distress remained tempered by affection. Although there were times when he felt it best to keep his distance, he did not turn his back on his parents.

Louis expressed the pain and disruption in his letters, but he is not bitter. There is more than a hint of bitterness in a much more abrasive piece of writing he produced at this time, which he clearly sat down to as a source of relief for his pent-up feelings. In a brief and unpublished manuscript are contained 'The Edifying Letters of the Rutherford Family', a fictionalised account of what was going on in the Stevenson household. The 'Rutherfords' are the Stevensons. The younger Rutherford writes to a friend describing what has been going on, while the elder approaches a colleague for advice on how he should handle his worrying son. The young William Rutherford's letters give a vivid and unequivocal account of relations between an errant son and over-anxious parents.

I may come in when I please, they are up and broad awake; I apply my stealthy pass key in the small hours, and behold the dining room is lighted up like day, and there is a domestic group about the fireplace, waiting in rosy respectability for the prodigal. This a sort of anti-climax that my soul cannot abide. I may have been out all night climbing the heavens of invention, drinking deep, thinking high; go home, with my heart stirred to all its depths and my brain sparkling like wind and starlight, I open the door, and the whole of this gaudy and light-hearted life must pass away in a moment, and give place to a few words of course and a pair of formal kisses. The sky-raker must give some account of his evening, if you please; and the spirit which has just been reconstructing the universe and debating the attributes of God, must bring down its proud stomach, and screw up its somewhat hazy eyes, to read a chapter from the authorized version of the Bible! To be thus knocked off the apex of apotheosis, and sent to bed with a renewed sense of all one's troubles and sober after all, is as Butler [Baxter] would say, a sheer waste of drink.[12]

There is more hostility here than in any of the letters Louis wrote in his own name, but he did indeed bitterly resent having to account for himself to his parents. He cared too much to allow himself in real life to be as hostile as the Rutherford letters suggest.

But like his fictional persona Louis longed to get away. William Rutherford describes an evening he spent with his friend Butler:

. . . we pleased ourselves . . . with elaborate pieces of childishness; making believe that we were going to start with all the trains, and looking forward to the pleasant waking in a new place with new air to breathe and a new accent in people's speech . . . making believe, in short, in all sorts of ways, that we had slipped the leash, and were gotten clear away out of our old life and out into the world as young men ought to be, among their rivals and their aspirations.[13]

The need was deep, not only to escape from Heriot Row, to 'slip the leash', but to get out into the world, to test himself in new situations and with new people, to find out if he really amounted to anything.

Circumstances were in his favour, and allowed him an eventful respite. In July 1873, a long six months after the initial explosion but before Bob had been identified as the culprit, Louis, with the encouragement of his parents who considered it entirely suitable, went to visit a Balfour cousin, Maud, who had married the Reverend Churchill Babington. The Babingtons lived in Cockfield, Suffolk, near Bury St Edmunds. Louis combined his visit with some walking in Suffolk. To be alone in the soothing, very gently undulating, green and ripening summer landscape must have done him good. He arrived at Cockfield Rectory, an attractive, Georgian house on a slight rise (as high a rise, though, as is to be found in that part of England) with a view across to the church spire at Lavenham, with his knapsack on his back. He was twenty-two years old, glad to be away from the suffocating atmosphere of Heriot Row, liberated by the open fields and sunshine, restlessly anxious to be active and creative, but not very sure how to go about it. Maud Babington had a friend staying with her, Frances Sitwell, wife of another cleric, and her young son Bertie. They saw a lanky, uncouth figure cross the lawn, and a rather awkward, apparently shy young man presented himself. Bertie volunteered to show him the garden and especially the moat, which arched round three sides of the house. With Bertie, Louis was comfortable at once. For the time being he was happier in the boy's company – lawn, shrubbery, trees and moat were rich territory for boyish exploration. He was a success with Bertie, but very soon was to find he was scarcely less so with Bertie's mother.

Louis arrived at Cockfield on 26 July. Frances Sitwell was thirty-four years old, beautiful, vital, intelligent and sympathetic. She was married to 'a man of unfortunate temperament and uncongenial habits', possibly an alcoholic, undoubtedly a man of uncertain temper who seems to have physically abused his wife.[14] She was at Cockfield Rectory partly to get away from her husband, from whom she was to become formally separated. She had had two sons, but one had died a few months earlier. Bertie was to die of tuberculosis in Switzerland when Louis himself was there in an effort to control his own lung disease. Mrs Sitwell had suffered, and had borne it courageously, not allowing her own troubles to diminish her sympathy for the problems of others. She was pictured by contemporaries as a wise and experienced woman who knew how to handle with affectionate tact the impulsive young men who tended to fall in love with her. But it is worth emphasising, too, that she was a woman who had been starved of generous and stimulating love. The involvement of Louis and Mrs Sitwell was not one-sided, however graciously maternal her image.

To a young man whose intellectual, spiritual and sexual responses were full of expectancy, Mrs Sitwell's radiance and sympathetic understanding were irresistible. He was ready for anything that might lift him out of the Heriot Row morass. One suspects that Louis did not know quite how to behave with girls of his own age and background: his reluctance to become involved was not only an anti-bourgeois reaction. He had learnt how to handle Edinburgh's female underworld, but regarded the task of acting the gentleman to young middle-class girls with awkwardness. But Frances Sitwell was a woman of experience, considerably older than Louis in years and in suffering. He was struck by her beauty, and he was curious. He was highly aware of the vulnerability of women, of the fact that economics and social mores were against them, and that if life treated them badly their means of escape or reversal were slight. Frances Sitwell like Fanny Osbourne, the woman he married, had been given a rough time by her husband without becoming defeatist. The combination of vulnerability and courage which both displayed, was immensely appealing to Louis. He would never have been attracted by a passive woman in the conventional Victorian mould, but he did want to be able to pity and protect the woman he loved. He wanted to be her champion. Frances Sitwell might almost have been a character in the grand opera he rather wanted life to be.

The relationship developed rapidly. They walked and talked and read poetry together. Mrs Sitwell was soothing. She literally smoothed the brow that had frowned in anguish over the Heriot Row troubles. The lovely garden was a constant invitation to intimate walks and exchanges. The moat was just big enough for boating. The Babingtons smiled on the relationship, so it is certain that Louis at this stage made no overt sexual advances, but that he was falling in love and rejoicing in it there was no doubt. The stay at Cockfield was blissful.

Like Ann Jenkin, Frances Sitwell saw an electrifying current of genius darting from the extraordinarily thin and tautly-strung young man who walked into her life through the french windows on that summer afternoon. She at once summoned her close friend and admirer, the man whom it was tacitly understood she would marry if she could, to share the remarkable experience. Sidney Colvin arrived from Cambridge, where he was Slade Professor, with high expectations, and he was not disappointed.

The most robust of ordinary men seemed to turn dim and null in the presence of the vitality that glowed in the steadfast, penetrating fire of the lean man's eyes, the rich, compelling charm of his smile, the lissom swiftness of his movements and lively expressiveness of his gestures, above all in the irresistible sympathetic play and abundance.

He was immediately enthusiastic about the effervescent personality and the signs of real talent. His response was intellectual, spiritual and physical. It is noticeable again and again, in men who may well have had no hidden homosexual tendencies (and also in men who did – Edmund Gosse, for instance) that the male appreciation of Stevenson was often intensely physical.

If you want to realize the kind of effect he made, at least in the early years when I knew him best, imagine this attenuated but extraordinarily vivid and vital presence, with something about it that at first struck you as freakish, rare, fantastic, a touch of the elfin and unearthly, a sprite, an Ariel. And imagine that, as you got to know him, this sprite, this visitant from another sphere, turned out to differ from mankind in general not by being less human but by being a great deal more human than they; richer-blooded, greater-hearted; more human in all senses of the word, for he comprised within himself, and would flash on you in the course of a single afternoon, all the different ages and half the different characters of man, the unfaded freshness of a child, the ardent outlook and adventurous daydreams of a boy, the steadfast courage of manhood, the quick sympathetic tenderness of a woman, and already, as early as the mid-twenties of his life, an almost uncanny share of the ripe life-wisdom of old age. He was a fellow of infinite and unrestrained jest and yet of infinite earnest, the one very often a mask for the other; a

poet, an artist, an adventurer; a man beset with fleshly
frailties, and despite his infirm health of strong appetites and
unchecked curiosities; and yet a profoundly sincere moralist
and preacher and son of the Covenanters after his fashion,
deeply conscious of the war within his members, and deeply
bent on acting up to the best he knew.[15]

Colvin paints the picture of a remarkable man, perhaps the
fullest portrait we have of Louis as a young man. When Colvin
met him he had done nothing of any significance, he had
nothing tangible to back up his literary aspirations. Yet Colvin
was absolutely sure that he had found a young man of striking
talent: the talent was in the personality. It is the most vivid fact to
emerge out of a study of his life. His genius lay in who and what
he was, rather than in the products of his pen.

Colvin himself was twenty-eight when he met Louis that
summer, exactly half way in years between Louis and the woman
they both loved. He cannot have been unaware, even at that
early stage, of the intensity of Louis's feelings towards Frances
Sitwell, and of the affectionate interest and sympathy that she
showed towards him. For all her striking attractions she was
probably flattered that this marvellous young man found her so
compelling, and he must have provided a welcome diversion
from her own personal problems. Colvin could scarcely have
been more different in personality from the man whom he
apparently did not see in the position of rival: he was reserved,
cautious, meticulous, a worrier. There are in the evidence that
remains of the three-cornered relationship the merest hints of
difficulties, but no tangible indications of real differences. But
Colvin was certainly aware that it was dangerous ground. When
he edited a carefully selected edition of Stevenson's letters after
his death he left out the bulk of the correspondence with Mrs
Sitwell. He commented on how she helped and encouraged the
aspiring writer, but he clouds the fact that Louis was intensely in
love with the woman it was understood he himself would marry
when she was free.

His own friendship with Louis developed rapidly. He seems
never to have censured his young friend or tried to intervene,
although Louis was clearly from time to time behaving with a
distinct lack of propriety. His need for a sexual affair with Mrs

Sitwell radiates from his letters. We can assume that the women he had slept with had all been prostitutes, although he may not always have had to pay for their favours. Here was the dizzy prospect of a full-blooded affair with a mature but respectable woman. It was, after all, the other traditional way of young men of good family gaining sexual experience – with older, married women. It was so well understood that it had begun to appear in popular fiction. Louis had probably read Ouida's *Under Two Flags* where the phenomenon is made very explicit. To what extent Colvin was aware of all this it is hard to say. He recognised Louis's 'strong appetites'; one would guess that he realised that Louis at times had difficulties controlling them in respect of Mrs Sitwell. His own love for Louis remained unshaken.

Sidney Colvin, photo by E. O. Hoppé

Colvin was a man of established professional achievement when he met Louis. His sober, scholarly character was an apt foil to Louis's volatile ways, and his commitment to Louis's literary abilities was crucial in getting him started. Colvin took Louis under his wing. It was through him that Louis made contact with the journals and their editors, with the men of influence and ideas whose interest was virtually a necessity for literary success. Colvin was to work hard on his behalf, gave him solid, steadying advice, thought of his best interests continually. At this stage, at least, he was invaluable. And meanwhile Louis was passionately pursuing his relationship with Mrs Sitwell, and after his return to Edinburgh pouring out letters to her.

He returned north full of his English experiences, but he found Heriot Row in fresh ferment over his religious defections. Throughout September Louis was coping with the switchback of feelings and behaviour on the part of his parents at home, and pouring out his problems and his passion to Mrs Sitwell almost daily. The quarrel with Bob, which brought the whole affair to a new pitch of intensity, disturbed him deeply, and he tried hard and genuinely to regain common territory with his parents. There were improvements. On occasion the endless, distressing talks with his father and mother seemed to bring some understanding on both sides: at least Louis seized on any sign that that might be so.

> To night my father was talking of how he feared to do what he knew he ought [that is, disown his son); and I did I think some good to our deplorable situation in this home of ours by what I said. I spoke to my mother afterwards: telling her how I felt with my father and hoped all good from anything he could do; and only hoped in that, that every man should do what he thought best, as best he could. But I had to stop as she was getting hysterical. I hope I have done something tonight.[16]

But he was fighting continually with profound depression, and even allowing for the tendency to dramatise – and he did not feel constrained in his letters to Mrs Sitwell, of which this is one – we can sense this. He goes on in the same letter,

> . . . indeed I do think things are going a little better with us; my father I believe has some of the satisfaction consequent

upon a good auto-da-fé now he has finally quarrelled with Bob and banished him. And although it seems mean to profit by what my own heart feels anxious to resent, I am only too glad of any peace between us. . . . You will understand the wearying, despairing, sick heart that grows up within one, when things go on as they sometimes do; and how the whole of life seems blighted and hopeless and twilight. . . .[17]

The pull of divided loyalties was heartbreaking. Louis understood his father's sense of helplessness, the sense that nothing he could say or do could change the situation, the feeling that he had lost his son for ever, that he should perhaps cast him out of the house. Thomas was torn in two by the contradiction of faith and love. Louis was in the same situation, although his father denied his 'faith', and was further torn by the conflict implicit in his love for Bob and his love for Thomas. Somehow he retained his balance, probably because he was able to pour out his difficulties to so sympathetic a receiver, and if his understanding of his parents took on a new dimension, his feeling for them survived. The experience strengthened him, and helped to prepare him for later periods in his life, when love survived against all the odds, and his understanding of what love demands as well as grants was tested to the utmost.

There were times when he was attacked by despair. His father's self-torment was relentless. In late September, Louis was writing to Mrs Sitwell telling her how Thomas had said, ' "I would ten times sooner have seen you lying in your grave than that you should be shaking the faith of other young men and bringing such ruin on other houses, as you have brought already upon this." '[18] He considered leaving home, but could not bring himself to do something that would have so strongly underlined his parents' sense of failure. It is possible that Louis's loyalty to his father and mother was too strong, that they all might have suffered less in the long run if Louis had felt able to take himself away rather sooner from Heriot Row, not to some parentally approved destination but quite independently. But like most people he found it very difficult to act independently. It was not only his illness that was to imprison him at intervals throughout his life, but his commitments, to friends, to women, especially his wife, to his parents, to dependants. This highly developed and warmly expressed sense of responsibility was to cause him some of his acutest problems. When he did get away from Edinburgh, in November, he had the authority of his doctor, who insisted that his parents should not accompany him.

The correspondence with Fanny Sitwell flourished. She replied to his letters, and on one occasion at least caused him wild dismay when nothing arrived from her for days. It transpired that the porter at the Speculative, the postal address which for obvious reasons Louis used, had carelessly failed to hand over Mr Stevenson's mail. Louis's letters vary in mood and content, much preoccupied of course with events at Heriot Row, but quietly tender too, sometimes, and frantically romantic at others. He thought about her all the time, worried about her health (she too was often unwell), admired with a kind of awe her courage in dealing with her difficult marital situation, and underlying everything there is his physical longing. 'I just write to let you know I am thinking of you, although it is scarcely necessary now; you are the very texture of my thought, I am never an hour without you slipping in somewhere, dear.'¹⁹ He clearly enjoyed the *idea* of his relationship with her. He was after all a romantic young man, and here was a grand passion, enhanced by secrecy and difficulty. But her letters to him have not survived. On 15 September he wrote to tell her that he had burnt her letters, excepting the first and the last, which can only suggest that he considered them compromising. He may well have been over-sensitive on this point, and over-dramatic in his action, but it does imply that Mrs Sitwell reciprocated his feelings to some extent and that her letters were not in a distant or maternal vein.

There are those who have seen the relationship as the infatuation of a young man for an older woman which was tolerated but not returned, and have argued that the fact that Stevenson fell twice for a woman considerably older than himself indicated his need for a mother figure, and therefore an element of immaturity in his affection. The surrogate parent will almost always feature in some form in any love affair, but to isolate this as the dominant characteristic in Louis's love for Frances Sitwell and Fanny Osbourne is misleading. It is true that it is in a letter to Mrs Sitwell that Louis specifically talks of the excluding nature of his parents' love for each other and his need for a mother substitute who could be more than his own mother was to him.[20] But this is a part of his later rationalisations. In the early months the character of things is rather different. Mrs Sitwell seemed to embody a potential response to all his current needs. To love a woman who had already experienced a sexual relationship, who had borne children, released Louis from a basic inhibition. He could not think of love in the respectable drawing-room terms of the Victorian middle-class. His letters to Mrs Sitwell do not express a polite, conventional interest, but an urgent need. She gave him encouragement, comfort and commitment, all of which were immensely important to him. But the awareness that that was all she could give him is the more vivid for Louis's honest recognition that he wanted more. In her he found a woman who was prepared both to champion his career and to respond warmly and affectionately to his personality. On her part, she received the passionate admiration of a gifted young man, a dazzling companion and correspondent, at a time when her own marriage caused her much pain, when she had lost one of her children, and when perhaps she just occasionally grew the tiniest bit impatient with her own only too cautious official admirer. If she was too sensible and too wise to allow herself to be compromised, which for a woman in her position at that time could have been disastrous, we can guess that she valued Louis's love and did not discourage it.

The relationship lasted with intensity for about two years, although Louis went on writing to her occasionally for the rest of his life. And through those two years it changed, or at least Louis's overt attitude changed and his struggle to come to terms with it produced different results. In December, when he had at last been able to get away from Edinburgh and was in the South of France, he could write calmly acknowledging the crucial influence of Mrs Sitwell in bringing him peace of mind.

> I want to tell you how thoroughly everything in my life has fallen into order, and how *everything* seems for the best. The prospect looks so quiet and happy, in spite of all, that I have sometimes a little shudder lest it should be a mirage. My own heart is reconciled to itself, that is perhaps the great thing and that no one can take away from me. How much this has been

your doing, Consuelo, I can never tell you, for I can never explain it to myself; only as I said, you came to me as it were the point of day and I began to see clearly.[21]

As often as he was able he made trips to London to see her. By the summer of 1874 he was resolving to be less of a burden to her. Possibly she had been reproving his more importunate requests.

Try to forget utterly the RLS you have known in the past: he is no more, he is dead: I shall try now to be strong and helpful, to be a good friend to you and no longer another limp dead-heavy burden on your weary arms. I think this is permanent: try to believe it yourself, that is the best means to make it so.[22]

He was probably talking of his general state of mind as much as anything, his efforts to take a more positive attitude to life and work. But shortly afterwards he is writing,

I don't know what to write either that will be agreeable to you, except the one fact that I have been and am very content. I do think the passion is over; I would not be too sanguine or fancy there would never be any momentary relapse; but in the meantime, I am quite strong and satisfied.[23]

And again,

The storm is over. I believe in the future faithfully, I am not sad nor angry, nor regretful. I am fully content and fear nothing, not death, nor weakness, nor any falling away from my own standards and yours. I shall be a man yet, dear, and a good man; although day by day, I see more clearly by how much I still fall short of the mark of our high calling; in how much I am still selfish and peevish and a spoiled child.[24]

This is scarcely the language of the rebellious scoffer. It is important to be clear that Stevenson's bohemianism had always a very positive quality: whatever he was against, there was a great deal that he was for. He was no nihilist, although he could be scornful of most established systems of ideas. The crucial year of 1873, with his falling in love and his religious break with his family, draws attention to the morality of his feelings and the sensitivity of his morality. He did indeed want to be a good man.

As the years went on he applied to himself a more rigorous set of standards of behaviour than society or even religion would have wished to apply.

It seems clear that Louis and Mrs Sitwell had agreed as to what their relationship should be, loving but non-sexual, mutually supportive, but not passionate. The above passages are taken from a letter written in June 1874. He had stayed with Colvin in Hampstead during the early part of that month, and had seen Mrs Sitwell. During their talks she probably made it unequivocally clear that she was still theoretically married and that she had no wish to wreck her relationship with Colvin. (An ambiguous reference to Colvin in an earlier letter is the only indication that Louis felt any rancour: 'You need not have written to me about SC, I knew all along there was nothing in it, but my mauvais coeur and all I said was that I wasn't going to write until the impression had died out and I could write nicely.'[25] There is no clue as to what Louis is referring here, but possibly he was offended at Colvin objecting to his closeness to Mrs Sitwell.)

From this time the language that Stevenson uses to describe his feelings for Mrs Sitwell changes. He begins to refer to her as 'mother' – 'you were the mother of my soul as surely as another was the mother of my body' – which suggests a deliberate and conscious attempt to cast his feelings into a different mould.[26] If he was forbidden to love the object of his affections as a man loves a woman, then he would do so as a son loves his mother. If one pattern wouldn't do, he would find another, and that was clearly the only appropriate alternative. In December he first uses the word 'madonna' in addressing her; in 1873 his favourite word had been 'Consuelo', a direct reference to the novel by George Sand, of the same name, which Louis much admired. 'Madonna' indicates a compromise, suggesting as it does a respectful and spiritual passion for an untouchable woman, but it may have a further reference. In May 1875 Louis performed the part of Orsino in the Fleeming Jenkins' production of *Twelfth Night*, and in that play the jester Feste ironically addresses his mistress Olivia, who rejects the love of men, as 'Madonna'. Could Louis have been reading *Twelfth Night* the previous December, and could there be a touch of irony, of humour, in his use of the word? It is important to

remember how flourishing was Louis's sense of fun. It seems
probable that he gleaned the word from his reading, as he had
gleaned 'Consuelo', and *Twelfth Night* is a likely source.

At Christmas 1874, Louis wrote to Mrs Sitwell a letter that
suggests very strongly a self-conscious attempt to reinterpret his
feelings.

> God knows [the letter] comes from a good heart. And now I
> think of you reading it in bed behind the little curtain, and no
> Bertie there, I do not know what longing comes over me to go
> to you for two hours and tell you, you have another son. This
> letter will not speak to you plainly enough; and you must eke
> it out with what you know of me, madonna – and you do
> know that I love you dearly – ; and think of what I would say
> to you if I were there; and what I should look like as I saw you
> again, out of the body with delight; and how childish I should
> be for very pleasure; and so, if you love me this letter shall be
> to you as a son's Christmas kiss. And I do think, madonna,
> that you love me; and, believing this, I am not out of hope
> that I may make this day something more joyful than it would
> have been without me: which is my best hope in this world, so
> help me God.[27]

But the mother and son roles could not contain his feelings, and
a week or so later he is writing a letter desperately reiterating his
character as her son but expressing instead an outburst of
intense physical need.

> I am to be a son, you must be a mother; and surely I am a son
> in more than ordinary sense, begotten of the sweet soul and
> beautiful body of you, and taught all that I know fine or holy
> or of good report, by the contact of your sweet soul and lovely
> body – transmuted and transfigured and made a new
> creature, even though at times I may still stumble, by the
> knowledge of your goodness and beauty: if this is so, and it is
> so my mother, in a real mild way, that is more real than
> commonplace realities, you have your duties to me as
> certainly as ever a fleshly mother had, and for these duties you
> must be true to me, and happy for me, and the brave, good,
> beautiful, happy mother I want.[28]

The tone here is so exaggerated that he may have written this letter under the influence of opium, which he took in various forms for his health, or of wine. But even so, the spiritualised sexuality, or the sexualised spirituality, is vivid, and echoes certain features of Catholic worship, with which he would have become acquainted in France.

Louis's attempted transformation of Mrs Sitwell from lover to mother, does raise again the relationship with his parents, particularly with his own mother. To some extent, and inevitably, his filial affections were diverted to Cummy. In some ways she was the more obvious counterpart to his father's stern but excitement-loving nature. The quarrel with his parents had made him acutely sensitive about his feelings for his mother, for here she was so radically on Thomas's side, and appealing to him in a way he found it almost impossible to respond to. The Oedipal jealousy that underlies that cry of exclusion, 'my mother is my father's wife', is only too understandable in such circumstances. Yet when he goes on, in the same letter, to describe what he thinks a mother should be, he exposes his romantic idealism, 'someone from whom I shall have no secrets; someone whom I shall love with a love as great as a lover's and yet more; with whom I shall have all a lover's tenderness and more of a lover's timidity; who shall be something fixed and certain and forever true'.[29] An idealisation of motherhood, certainly, but surely also a confusion: in attempting to convince himself that he loves Mrs Sitwell as a son he transforms 'mother' into someone very like 'lover'. It would probably be a mistake to see Louis's revealing mention of his 'orphan' state because of his parents' closeness, as a clue that he was indeed searching for a mother. Certainly there is little doubt that he really wanted in Mrs Sitwell a woman he could love fully, whose mind, spirit and body were equally attractive. In all his protestations of a son's love something quite different flares brightly. The pose of son was a scarcely adequate disguise of his real feelings.

In April 1875 there is another letter that suggests a moment of crisis has been passed. Louis refers to being in London, suggesting that he got carried away. Was he rebuked again? 'I will be as good as I can for your sake,' he writes. 'I know I must be good for the love of you, and my oath's sake.'[30] All the time the switchback of his emotions drives through his letters, with his fight to control them, to identify them, not to offend.

'Nobody loves a mere mother as much as I love you,'[31] he writes in the winter of 1875–6, after trying to reinforce the filial self-image, and in the process contradicting its viability. The urgent longing for moral and spiritual 'goodness' can be seen partly as an effort to make Heriot Row loom less overwhelmingly in his life. Mrs Sitwell could not be all he wanted, and his passion inevitably dwindled, though not his affection. But he was primed for passionate response, and he was soon to find another to let it loose on.

1873 had been a climactic year. The differences with his parents, and therefore to an extent with Edinburgh and his entire background, seemed to be total. At the same time he had fallen in love with a woman whose connections with the literary and intellectual world of the south heightened its temptation. Colvin and Mrs Sitwell both encouraged him in his writing and advised him on where to place what he wrote. The easiest entry into the literary world was through writing short pieces for journals, and this was what Louis began to concentrate on. He worked on his essay 'Roads' during that summer, a pleasing though self-conscious reflection on the joys of exploring English landscapes on foot. He was working on it during August and September, in the intervals between writing to Mrs Sitwell and interminable discussions with his mother and father. It was rather astonishing that he was able to work at all, and he did so by totally abstracting himself from his immediate surroundings, even his own existence: there is no *personality* in the essay. It was published in *The Portfolio* in December, having been rejected by the *Saturday Review*. It was Louis's first paid contribution to a journal, and the princely sum of £3 8s. that he received for it must have cheered him immensely.

Inevitably his health had suffered under the stresses of that summer. The prospect of a Scottish winter was not encouraging. In the October of 1873 Louis slipped away. He told his mother he was going to Carlisle: she must have thought he was bound for some walking in the Lake District. She was rather taken aback to receive a letter from him in London, announcing that he had seen Dr Andrew Clark, a specialist in lung disease, who had advised an immediate retreat further south. She and Thomas went post-haste to London. They found Louis very unwell, staying in the same house as Mrs Sitwell and in the care of her and Colvin, both of whom the Stevenson parents liked. Suspicious though they had been that the planned trip to the south was a put-up job, there could be no doubt about either the debilitated state Louis was in, or about Dr Clark's advice – which included the stipulation that Louis should travel without his parents. They accepted the inevitable. Louis made good his escape, to Menton, to sea air and sunshine, and solitary hours of reflection.

Chapter 4

THIS DAMNED LIFE

> O, I do hate this damned life that I lead. Work – work – work;
> that's all right, it's amusing; but I want women about me and I
> want pleasure.
>
> Letter to Mrs Sitwell

It was November. Louis had turned his back on 'the gloom and depression' of an Edinburgh winter, 'the bleak ugliness of easterly weather', 'the unrefulgent sun going down among perturbed and pallid mists',[1] but walking the esplanade alone in Menton was scarcely inspiriting. He was psychologically and physically at a very low ebb. Soon after his arrival he was writing dismally to Baxter.

> I am awfully weary and nervous, I cannot read or write almost at all, and I am not able to walk much; all which put together leaves me a good deal of time in which I have no great pleasure or satisfaction. However, you must not suppose me discontented. I am away in my own beautiful Riviera, and I am free now from the horrible worry and misery that was playing the devil with me at home.[2]

Whatever the state of his lungs, it is clear that Louis was suffering as much from something in the nature of a nervous breakdown as from anything else.[3] The emotional extremities of the previous nine months more than explain it. It was all the harder to bear as he was beginning to feel he was getting somewhere with his writing – '. . . I am out of heart at this knock-down blow just when I was beginning to get a possibility of good work and a livelihood. It is beastly to have a bad head like this, and have to pay for half an hour's thinking with a bad night or an hour or two of miserable nervousness.'[4]

He tried hard to cheer himself. 'I cannot be a heretic to my own favourite gospel of cheerfulness altogether,' he went on, but it sounds as if he were trying to convince himself. He began work on a piece, 'Ordered South', which was to win much admiration. It was probably some relief to be writing again, but the immediacy of personal experience is not really present in the essay, although he is writing about an invalid's responses to things, jaded most of the time, unexpectedly vivid occasionally. He was still, as he was to continue to do for some time, deliberately distancing himself from his material, from his own experience. He writes in a slightly aloof third person, as if he felt it were in some way improper to be directly personal.

His letters convey much more of what it was like to be lonely and unwell in a pleasant Mediterranean town, full of delightful vistas and tantalising incident, which he had neither the strength nor spirit to enjoy. After a few weeks he is writing again to Baxter. 'I must say straight out that I am not recovering as I could wish. I am no stronger than I was when I came here, and I pay for every walk beyond say a quarter of a mile in length by one, or two, or even three days of more or less prostration.'[5] 'Ordered South' was admired for its stoical, accepting attitude towards his condition, and it is usual to praise Stevenson for his lack of self pity. But I feel the underlying vein of self-pity in 'Ordered South' is not hard to detect, and in the letters of this time, however hard he is trying to conquer it, he is feeling very sorry for himself. Only too understandably, he badly needed reassurance and moral support. He was exhausted and depressed, and he was thinking that his writing career might well have ended before it had really begun. A letter to Mrs Sitwell, written at the end of November, reflects his mood, but can also be read as an appeal.

> I have given up all hope, all fancy rather, of making literature my hold: I see that I have not capacity enough. My life shall be, if I can make it, my only business. I am desirous to practise now, not to preach, for I know that I should ever preach badly, and men can more easily forgive faulty practice than all sermons. If Colvin does not think that I shall be able to support myself soon by literature, I shall give it up and go (horrible as the thought is to me) into an office of some sort: the first and main question is, that I must live by my own hands; after that come the others.[6]

Louis periodically agonised over money. His father of course was paying for his stay in Menton. The problem wasn't that Thomas couldn't afford such things, but that Louis hated to be morally chained to his father by money. In fact Louis was not to be financially independent of Thomas until his father's death brought him an inheritance, which came soon after Louis's first popular success. Louis quite frequently resolved to cease his reliance on his father's money, but the next dozen or so years of his life were beset with emergencies, and to some extent delinquencies, which made that reliance necessary. At this time, though, at the end of 1873 in Menton, he badly needed to prove to himself that his survival need not be due to his father's generosity. It was painful. He felt in himself that he could write ('capacity' in the above quotation refers to physical strength, not ability) and Colvin and Mrs Sitwell were telling him that he could. But how long would it take before he could prove it – and make a living by it? In spite of his deeply discouraged state he worked away at 'Ordered South', which was eventually published in *Macmillan's Magazine* in the following May, and tried to resign himself to making slow progress in health and work. After a time he discovered that life in Menton had more to offer than had first appeared.

Louis found he could cure his depression and suppress his cough by taking opium, and sometimes relished the effect it could have on him. 'I had a day of extraordinary happiness; and when I went to bed there was something almost terrifying in the pleasures that besieged me in the darkness.'[7] In the form of morphine and laudanum, opium was widely used medicinally as a painkiller and sedative. It was no secret that it could also be hallucinatory, addictive and lethal. There is no evidence that Louis experimented extensively with drug-taking, although addiction to laudanum and morphine was quite common in the Victorian period, and many victims were unaware that they were in effect addicts. The infamous 'Gregory's Mixture', administered to fractious infants, contained laudanum. There are occasional letters written by Louis whose delightful incoherence suggests the possible effects of opium, but they could just as well be the effects of alcohol in immodest quantity or of sheer high spirits. But Louis took both his work and his health too seriously to risk seriously jeopardising either.

Much more of a tonic than opium was his discovery of lively

company. Colvin came to join him, and while he was there Louis changed hotels. It was certainly a change for the better: his new fellow residents were far more to his taste. There were three little girls and two rather older ladies whom Louis found particularly enticing. At first he was writing, 'kids are what is the matter with me' to his mother, as he described the winning antics of two little Russian girls aged two and a half and eight, and an eight-year-old American, who danced and sang and teased.[8] He was entranced. But to Mrs Sitwell he was describing, with some confusion and embarrassment, his embroilment in the curious and complicated lives of the two older Russians, sisters, one of whom was the mother of the little girls. The sisters were both married, both in Menton without their husbands, and both seemed to find Louis a thoroughly attractive young man.

Louis wasn't sure of exactly the right way to behave. There was something of a hot-house atmosphere in the hotel community, an atmosphere of heightened feelings, with just a suggestion that the rules of conventional society might not apply. The difficulty helped him to draw away from some of his depressing preoccupations, but it also caused him some problems. One confusion caused him no embarrassment, but struck him as highly poignant. The two little Russians were sisters, but thought they were cousins, for their mother, Mme Zasetsky, gave her second child, 'dedicating it before it was conceived', to her childless sister. But Bella, an impish two and a half year old, 'is the curse of the poor adoptive mother's existence. She loves her devotedly and has spoiled her without limit, and Bella repays her with disobedience and drives her into hysterics every day or two.'[9] Louis was fascinated by the drama of the situation – the uncontrolled child, the real mother regarded as a 'crossgrained aunt', the adoptive mother tormented by her inability to discipline the child she had so much wanted. 'God knows what a tragedy lies before the family,' Louis was writing to Mrs Sitwell.[10]

Other developments brought acute awkwardness, the more so as Louis could not detect the motives that lay behind them, and was afraid of making a youthful fool of himself. Mme Garschine seemed to be out to entrap him. He confided in Mrs Sitwell, and tried to explain his own behaviour, while assuring her that his affections were not engaged. But his interest was. 'I don't know what Mme G's little game is with regard to me. Certainly she has either made up her mind to make a fool of me in a somewhat coarse manner, or else she is in train to make a fool of herself.'[11] Mme Garschine was, it appeared to Louis, more or less openly inviting him into an affair, and he cared enough about her susceptibilities to wish neither to take advantage of her nor to expose her, though he was obviously pleased and flattered at her attentions. He employed all the delicacy and tact he could muster to avert the difficulty. He reacted warily to each new development in his dealings with the ladies: part of the problem was that he liked their company, and he needed friendship. Ultimately the consequences were happy. Mme Garschine became his confidante, and both sisters became warm and sympathetic friends. They were volatile and emotional, delightfully un-Anglo-Saxon, and he thoroughly enjoyed their conversation. The experience caused him considerable embarrassment, but it was also good for his morale.

Colvin's visit had been a tonic, too. He arrived in Menton in December, and the fact that he made the visit indicates how much he cared about Louis. He wrote a meticulous report to Mrs Stevenson, whom he had met when the Stevensons had hastened to London in October; Thomas and Margaret had both been very taken with both Colvin and Mrs Sitwell.

> He is certainly better in all ways, both bodily and mental, than when he passed through London. As certainly, there has been no development of any organic disease, such as for a moment seemed to be feared if he had not been able to get south. But he has gone only a little way towards recovering proper nervous strength. He is very easily tired and very easily agitated, and a little fatigue or agitation tells upon him for some time. On days when these are not encountered in any form, he is quite like himself, and gets abundant enjoyment out of the Mediterranean climate and scenery.[12]

This sober report does not reveal what was clearly the case, that he and Louis had quite a merry time. Louis was avid for the kind of comradeship Colvin could provide. They spent a little time in Monaco, and although Colvin was never the boon companion that Bob and Baxter were, they enjoyed themselves. After

Colvin's return Louis teased him in a letter, retelling with glee a rumour to the effect that 'we were both drunkards – came down screwed to dinner – and when you did not come, it was because you were dead drunk and unpresentable, at least. Theory? Curious how, wherever I go, I come trailing clouds of dipsomania.'[13] Colvin was probably not too pleased that this was the reputation he had left behind him.

So eventually the time was passing interestingly for Louis in Menton. He took his daily dosage of fresh air and sunshine, often in company, did some writing in his room, enjoyed the children, spent the evenings talking or playing cards with his fellow residents. In January he was working on an essay on Walt Whitman, having got Baxter to send him *Leaves of Grass* and *Democratic Vistas*. He found Whitman's poetry exciting and liberating, although the essay he produced is a little cautious in its opinions. The influence on his own poetry is distinct, but he never managed the stylistic audacity of Whitman. It was his energy he admired, the bold assertions, and the faith. His interest in American literature must have implanted in him an interest in America itself. There seemed to be the tantalising prospect of a fresh and vigorous society on the other side of the Atlantic.

Winter came to an end, and the return to Edinburgh could not be put off. On the way back he met Bob in Paris. Bob had been studying art in Antwerp but had now moved on to Paris. He introduced Louis to Parisian bohemia, to the casual, unhampered world of art students and young struggling writers. Louis got a taste of a scene he would revisit frequently, before making his way on to sombre Edinburgh. By May he was in Swanston, trying to write and trying not to be depressed. The parental environment was calmer now, but the anxious watchfulness of Thomas and Margaret was hard to live with.

Stevenson never had any doubts not only that he wanted to write and be published and known, but that he wanted to earn a living by writing. He began his career as an essayist. It seemed the best way to insert himself into the journals, and Colvin, and later Leslie Stephen, would have advised him to try his hand. He may also have had ideas of becoming a latter-day Montaigne, whom he avidly admired. But it was virtually impossible to make a living out of essay-writing and occasional publication. The few guineas Louis earned would not keep him in beer, let alone in burgundy, his favourite tipple. One might perhaps, after serving a suitable apprenticeship, achieve the editorship of a journal, like W. E. Henley, who was to become an intimate friend of Louis, or like Leslie Stephen, who assisted the careers of both Henley and Louis in their early stages. But even then success depended on a fickle public. Louis was not an academic. He did not, like Stephen or Colvin or another literary friend, Edmund Gosse, have a university or establishment post to provide some financial security, although he did apply later for an Edinburgh professorship which he must have known he had no hope of getting.

He began to get to know the world of literary competition. The young aspirants Louis became acquainted with, Gosse, Henley, Andrew Lang, were poets and essayists, not fiction writers. They also, although Lang was a Scot and Henley spent some time in Scotland, assumed that London was the centre of literary life. It is interesting that Louis chose – and was encouraged – to cultivate the more polite area of literary endeavour. With his childhood immersion in story-telling, and his youthful attempts at writing fiction, one might have thought that he would naturally have turned to the production of short stories. It is interesting that it was a few years yet before he turned to writing stories. He seems to have started on a novel at some point in 1876, but it was clearly abandoned, and the first distinct evidence that he was writing stories does not come until the following year.

There are possible explanations. His Calvinist upbringing may have still had enough hold on him to be making him uneasy at the idea of publishing fiction. He may well have been advised against it by Colvin. He was not getting to know fiction writers. But there was possibly a much more profound difficulty, and that was the question of what he was to write fiction about, what *kind* of stories should he tell? He had had a try at historical fiction. He clearly needed to come to terms imaginatively with the Scottish past and his own background. He had looming behind him the monumental figure of Sir Walter Scott who had with such striking effect done both – it is a mistake to compare Stevenson with Scott, which can only be to the former's disadvantage, for Stevenson's stories set in the past are

quite a different kind of thing from Scott's historical novels.
This difficulty, the problem of what he should write stories
about, he was only beginning to solve at the end of his life. At
this stage it may not have troubled him too deeply, though he
was developing distinct ideas on the kind of fiction that should
be encouraged. He had plenty of other projects to keep him
busy. Through 1874 he was hard at work on a number of essays
and reviews, and the rewards were coming in the shape of
publication, and some favourable comment. It was a highly
romantic notion, this idea of actually feeding and keeping
himself through the published word. Novelists had done it, but
for the genteel essayist – and Louis's writing was pretty genteel –
the prospect was not promising. Henley had an idea, to try their
joint hands at drama, but although they had a serious try success
was elusive. Stevenson's was not the bohemian struggle for art in
a cold garret, because his father had money, and although there
were profound disagreements and long periods of dissension,
and he wasn't over the hump yet as far as these were concerned,
Louis did not withdraw himself from his family. He was perhaps
too cushioned, in fact, by his doting and worried parents in
Edinburgh, and his admiring literary friends in London. It was
when he was at a distance from both and faced with difficulties
more drastic than anything he had been able to anticipate that
his search for worthwhile subjects for his art began to yield more
promising results.

Thomas, however deeply it troubled him that Louis was
embarking on such a risky career, must have found the idea of
an author son exciting. Thomas loved tales, and he had
communicated his love of melodrama and his love of invention
to his son: though we can guess that he had many painful
wrestlings with his conscience over his enjoyment of make-
believe. Louis never pretended he was taking the law very
seriously, although he fulfilled his side of the bargain with
reasonable goodwill, and was delighted when he passed his final
exams for admission to the Bar. When he received the news of
his success in July 1875, he paraded through the streets of
Edinburgh in an open carriage clowning and waving and
embarrassing members of his family, and a brass plaque was
duly put up on the door of 17 Heriot Row announcing his new
professional status as advocate. But having achieved this he now

felt free to turn his full attention to writing and doing the kinds of things that fed his writing. His father must have rapidly become aware, if he had not guessed before, that his son was no lawyer. But he gave him a thousand pounds, an acknowledgement of his good faith, perhaps, and although he could not accept his son's religious apostasy, deep down he may have been glad that Louis was exploring roads he himself found tempting but had never ventured on. The imagination was a dangerous weapon on Presbyterian ground, but perhaps the best and kindest thing Louis could have done for his parents was to allow it to glitter in the foreground.

Without his father's financial support and faith in him Louis could scarcely have stuck it out during those first uncertain years. He needed more than that, of course. He needed the support and encouragement of his friends in the south, Colvin and Mrs Sitwell, Leslie Stephen – a chieftain of the literati – Gosse and Henley. He needed literary friends to argue and joke with as well as literary advisers to help him place his manuscripts. And he needed some success, in the shape of the gratifying experience of seeing his words in print. By the time he was admitted to the Bar he had published some substantial pieces. Essays on Whitman and Victor Hugo admitted him into the ranks of literary critics, and a long piece on 'John Knox and His Relations to Women' marked his first attempt at handling highly pertinent Scottish material. (He seems to have planned something on the Covenanters and another essay on 'Four Great Scotsmen', which may have included Knox and Burns, but neither materialised.) There were disappointments too, of course. A piece on Burns, which bluntly drew attention to his moral failings – scarcely a popular way to treat Burns – was turned down by the *Encyclopaedia Britannica*.

Louis worked on his writing assiduously, not yet sure of his style, not yet sure what it was he really wanted to write about, yet taking great pains, and anxious. Was his career likely to amount to more than that of genial essayist and 'vagrant' critic, as he himself described his critical wanderings from one author to another?[14] He admired Hugo and Whitman because they were robust talents, who courageously faced 'the materials of life' and handled them vigorously.[15] The self-consciously self-obliterating style Louis was evolving at this stage hardly suggests that he thought of himself as another tough, comprehensive spokesman for real life, but it is likely that he always had something like that in mind. He talked often of literature as entertainment, of the writer as a performer who was obliged to please his public, yet beneath this we can always detect his sense of a deeper obligation, the need to come to terms with life in all its aspects from fun to tragedy, and to find the right language to communicate this engagement.

His seriousness communicated itself to at least some of those who interested themselves in his career. There was generated a feeling of immense expectation. Literature, many considered, was at a low ebb at this time. Dickens and Thackeray were dead. George Eliot was no longer young, and her last novel, *Daniel Deronda* (1876) most critics considered disappointing. George Meredith was publishing steadily, but few liked him. There seemed to be no major poetic voice of a younger, or even a middle-aged, generation. The new school of naturalism in fiction, which flourished in France and seemed to be taking effect in Britain, in the novels of George Gissing for instance, was disturbing. Perhaps young Louis Stevenson could revitalise contemporary literature. To understand the attitude of many of his friends and acquaintances to Louis it is necessary to understand this – the feeling that in a number of ways literature, and culture in general, had grown demoralised, and needed to be rescued. The expectations of some of the younger literary generation began to centre around Louis. The disappointment, when he appeared to turn his back on the English literary world just when he was gaining some success, was proportionately profound.

In June 1878, when he had seen the earliest of Stevenson's short stories, Leslie Stephen wrote to Louis:

It has occurred to me lately that you might help me in an ever recurring difficulty. I am constantly looking out rather vaguely [?] for a new novelist. I should like to find a Walter Scott or Dickens or even a Miss Brontë or G. Eliot. Somehow the coming man or woman has not yet been revealed. Meanwhile I cannot help thinking that, if you would seriously put your hand to such a piece of work you would be able – I will not say to rival the success of Waverley or

Pickwick but – to write something really good & able to make
a mark in the *Cornhill* [of which Stephen was editor]. Of course
you must have thought of this, but a little push from outside
may help the thought to develop itself. Will you turn the
matter over in your mind & let me know whether you are
prepared to make the attempt? You might start a few chapters
& then let me see whether I thought them available for *Cornhill*
purposes. But of course I do not want to push you, only to
throw out a hint with wh. you can deal as you please. I have a
strong persuasion that if a good subject struck your fancy, you
could make a good piece of work.[16]

This letter is a remarkable statement of faith in a young writer
who had barely proved himself. Stevenson's first book, *An
Inland Voyage*, had been published a couple of months earlier,
but there was little there on which to base such a hope. It was
probably, and once again, the magic of Louis's personality that
was working on Stephen, rather than specific literary achievement. Louis Stevenson was effervescing with ideas and spirit. He
seemed to colour everything he set eyes on or reflected on with
freshness.

Louis had come home in the summer of 1874 to the old life in
Edinburgh. There were periods at Swanston, theatricals with the
Jenkins, who had moved from the lowest east side of the New
Town to the upper west, law studies off and on, much writing,
and also quite frequent spells away. He was adding to his
experience of independence and exploring new territory in his
relations with other people. That summer there was a cruise in
the inner Hebrides with Walter Simpson, with whom Louis also
canoed on the Forth, and a holiday with his parents in Wales and
the West of England. In October he was walking in the
Chilterns. That summer, too, he was elected a member of the
Savile Club, which was to become a favourite haunt when in
London. The Savile was then one of the newest of London clubs,
founded in 1868 not as an environment of silence behind
newspapers but as a place where conversation, wit and
argument were considered necessities of existence. At the Savile
Louis met many of the period's liveliest minds, and later his
wife, trying to protect her frail husband from over-excitement,
would learn to curse it.

He went south for periodic immersions in London life, which meant time spent with Mrs Sitwell as well as long evenings of drink and discussion at the Savile. But he always returned to his top-floor room at Heriot Row. And although new friends were stimulating old ones were no less important. During these years Louis's reliance on Bob remained considerable. It was Bob who introduced him to bohemian life in Paris and the Fontainebleau artists' colony; it was Bob above all who dissolved the inevitable loneliness of his position as anxious rebel and apprentice author. In the summer of 1874 Bob was in Edinburgh, and he became ill with diphtheria. The thought that Bob might die was unbearable. He walked out to Portobello, where Bob was staying, to see him, having heard that he was seriously ill – and diphtheria was a killer. He half expected to see the curtains drawn, the signal of death, as he approached the house. Bob survived, but Louis was shaken.

These were active years, and most of the time Louis was well enough to live them fully. The tensions and dramas of his relationships with his parents and with Mrs Sitwell may at times have been profoundly depressing, but they also gave his life a substance, helped him to feel that he was fully involved in life, even when writing away in his room in Heriot Row, or out at Swanston, or reduced coughing to his bed. He was deeply and personally involved in two of the major late Victorian storm centres. Both in his conflict with his father over religious belief and in his questioning of conventional love-and-marriage he embodied the wider problems of thinking and sensitive late Victorians. His friend and contemporary Edmund Gosse was to write gently and understandingly the story of father and son unable to agree on religious belief. It was a book Louis never read, published after his death, but we can imagine that the two friends must have covered the same territory in conversation. Gosse was also an only child, but had the added loneliness of losing his mother when he was very young. Louis would have recognised every note of the chords of solitariness, self-reliance and affection that support the theme in Gosse's *Father and Son*. Elsewhere we find the conflict of the generations more rebelliously and angrily expressed. But however it emerged there is no doubt that this conflict was a major element in the culture of the last quarter of the century. It was part of the

*Edmund Gosse, photo by
E. O. Hoppé*

late Victorian effort to come to terms with Victorianism.
Changing attitudes to love and marriage were a part of this
too. Most of Louis's friends accepted the convention ultimately;
Bob, Henley, Gosse, Baxter all married and set up orthodox
middle-class establishments. Louis chose for his wife an
American divorcée, and not yet divorced when their affair
began, ten years his senior, who would be criticised by
acquaintances for her sloppy housekeeping. For only one
period in their married lives did they reside in what could really
be called conventional middle-class circumstances. Louis
rejected the idea of a marriage of unassuming respectability. He
was troubled by the subordination of women, which the
accepted style of Victorian marriage implied. He had much
sympathetic curiosity about the lives of women and attitudes to
women. In some quarters the whole idea of marriage was being
challenged and rejected: Louis questioned the accepted basis.
In his article 'Virginibus Puerisque', which he was writing in
1876, he had some trenchant and somewhat cynical remarks to
make upon the subject. Marriage, he decided, required an

impossible compromise and inevitable duplicity. Given the usual moral imperfections of young men, he saw it as 'inexcusable that they should draw another's life into their own'. He went on,

> What! you have had one life to manage, and have failed so strangely, and now can see nothing wiser than to conjoin with it the management of someone else's . . . You are no longer content to be your own enemy; you must be your wife's also. You have been hitherto in a mere subaltern attitude; dealing cruel blows about you in life, yet only half responsible, since you came there by no choice or movement of your own. Now, it appears, you must take things on your own authority: God made you, but you marry yourself; and for all that your wife suffers, no one is responsible but you . . . you have eternally missed your way in life, with consequences that you still deplore, and yet you masterfully seize your wife's hand, and, blindfold, drag her after you to ruin. And it is your wife, you observe, whom you select. She, whose happiness you most desire, you choose to be your victim.[17]

The very idea of marriage, as the approved institution of society and the state, he seems to suggest is the height of hypocrisy. And far from being prepared by education and experience to live together, men and women, he felt, were encouraged to be as different as possible, with the result that the idea of sharing their lives together on common ground becomes ridiculous.

> . . . it is the object of liberal education not only to obscure the knowledge of one sex by another, but to magnify the natural differences between the two. Man is a creature who lives not upon bread alone, but principally by catchwords; and the little rift between the sexes is astonishingly widened by simply teaching one set of catchwords to the girls and another to the boys. To the first, there is shown but a very small field of experience, and taught a very trenchant principle for judgment and action; to the other, the world of life is more largely displayed, and their rule of conduct is proportionately widened. They are taught to follow different virtues, to hate different vices, to place their ideal even for each other, in different achievements. What should be the result of such a

course? When a horse has run away, and the two flustered people in the gig have each possessed themselves of a rein, we know the end of that conveyance will be in the ditch.[18]

Stevenson wrote this before he met Fanny Osbourne. He must have been thinking, with the dwindling of his relationship with Mrs Sitwell, that it was unlikely that he would marry. There is a ring of personal engagement here that enters his writing for the first time, although the vein of clever irony enables him to keep his distance from his own susceptibilities. He was not yet able to shed his protective colouring. The debate about women and the debate about marriage attracted much attention in the 1870s and '80s. Louis was responding to the currents of the times as well as levelling his ironically aware gaze at what he saw around him. But significantly, and in a way that was not characteristic of the debate at that time, he emphasises the results of the differences in the education and upbringing of the sexes. His sense of the practical realities of life, and their influences, is very acute.

In 1873, when still in the middle of parental storms and as yet without the consolation of Mrs Sitwell, he made out a list of desiderata.

I. Good-Health.
II. 2 to 3 hundred a year.
III. O du lieber Gott, *friends*![19]

Two years later he was without the first two, and the thousand pounds his father gave him on his admission to the Bar was soon dissipated, lent or given away, cheerfully spent, but on the third point he had become well off. In the winter of 1875 he gained a new focus of interest and commitment. That February Leslie Stephen came to Edinburgh to give a lecture, and on Colvin's advice visited the budding Scottish writer, some of whose work he had already seen. While in Edinburgh he visited another young writer whose work had struck him, the poet W. E. Henley, who lay immobilised in the Infirmary. Henley had come to Edinburgh in search of a cure for a tubercular foot, having already had the other amputated. He came to the Infirmary to consult Joseph Lister, whose development of germ theory and use of antisepsis had turned the hospital into one of the most progressive in Britain. Lister saved Henley's foot, but it was a long and painful process. Leslie Stephen became interested in Henley after he had sent him, as editor of the *Cornhill*, a collection of lyrics written in hospital. He found Henley in desperate need of books and entertainment to while away the long months in the Infirmary, and took Louis to meet him, in the hope that he might be able to provide either or both of Henley's needs.

The two young men had a great deal in common, physical disability being the most obvious. Louis admired immensely Henley's courage in the face of pain and boredom, and his determination to carve himself out a literary career under adverse circumstances. He admired the energy of his personality, which gave him, a large, bearded, noisy figure in his hospital bed, power and substance. They were a splendid contrast. Henley large, with a shock of red hair and beard, Louis slight, lank-haired, but well matched in the verve of their talk. After their first meeting Louis visited him frequently. He brought him books, French novels that were devoured eagerly, talked to him, later took him out for doses of breezy air and blue sky. When Henley was allowed to sit up Louis brought him an armchair; not able to find a cab he carried it on his head up the Mound from Heriot Row. When he was allowed carriage rides Louis lifted the bulky man in and out, and carried him up and down stairs. There was no doubt that Henley, his tuberculosis kept at bay only by Lister's frequent and hideously painful scraping of the bone, was much worse off than he himself; with Henley his sympathy, his sense of comradeship and adventure, his commitment and his humour were all totally engaged.

It was the spirit of adventure that they shared most genuinely, with its ingredients of rebellion and irreverence. It was a spirit that they encouraged in themselves and each other certainly partly because of their respective disabilities. It was a conscious effort sometimes, a deliberate compensation, as well as the natural bubbling over of excitement and a belief in action. A determination to survive and to make an impression was part of it too. 'Survival' had become a key word of science. Herbert Spencer and Darwin had made most of the literate population familiar with it. Henley and Stevenson were determined to prove themselves amongst the fittest, not physically perhaps, but

in spirit and intellectual action. Although this attitude was
tinged with rebellion, certainly in the minds of these two, it had
in fact become intellectually respectable. 'I would exhort
you . . . to scorn base repose – to accept, if the choice be forced
upon you, commotion before stagnation, the leap of the torrent
before the stillness of the swamp. In the one there is at all events
life, and therefore, hope; in the other, none,' challenged a
professor in an address to the British Association for the
Advancement of Science. These may have been the words of an
advanced thinker, but the attitudes behind them were not
outrageously new. Stevenson and Henley, the one to become
genuinely popular, the other to draw around him a very
committed following, chimed in their mood with currents of
excitement and belief that were already eddying. Their
popularity and their following owed, of course, a great deal to
this.

The friendship flourished, and they began to talk of
collaboration. They felt themselves in agreement over literary
objectives; they both needed to make money from what they
wrote – and Henley's need was greater than Stevenson's, for not
only was he without a solidly well-off father to back him, he had
heavy medical fees to pay, although Lister's services were free. It
was to be some years before actual literary collaboration came
to fruition, but in the meantime there was plenty of mutual
support and encouragement, and the making of an advantage
out of disability. 'The challenge of life lies not in the possible
victory but rather in the inevitable defeat,' Henley wrote to
Louis.

Satisfaction of desire means the death of the spirit. Growth,
struggle, assertion – these are their own rewards. Pain is but a
goad to the restless soul, driving it away from the bypaths of
indolence, prodding it ever on towards complete, but
unattainable, realization. Happiness ceases to be the object in
living.[20]

The friendship did not survive the collaboration, partly because
the resulting plays did not succeed and partly on account of
Louis's marriage. If Louis's wife was jealous of the demands
made on her husband by over-enthusiastic comrades, Henley

was jealous of the love and time Louis gave to his wife. For it is
clear that Henley was, in a sense, in love with him.

Henley was to draw round him a group of devoted admirers –
and he needed admiration. 'I disagreed with him about
everything,' Yeats wrote in his autobiography, 'but I admired
him beyond words.'[21] Henley was older then, and Yeats a young
man, and Henley was for him and others 'leader and . . .
confidant.' 'I think we listened to him, and often obeyed him,
partly because he was quite plainly not upon the side of our
parents.'[22] Henley referred to the young men he encouraged as
'my lads'; Louis, for all the enthusiasm and energy of their
friendship, for all the advice he sought and got from Henley,
was never one of his lads. Henley was admired for the heroic
independence he expressed in his poetry, and his forthright
style.

> I am the master of my fate:
> I am the captain of my soul

are lines that have lasted more ringingly than most of the poetry
Stevenson wrote.[23] Henley was to feel later that Louis deserted
the heroic anti-establishment struggle through his marriage and
his escape to the South Seas. The route to this belief was to be
painful for both of them.

But in their twenties they could both believe that the effort to
captain their own souls should be pre-eminent. We can sense
Louis's restlessness during these years. He is always on the
move, making a ritual of it almost, writing gaily and a little
defiantly to his mother on the subject of her having a vagabond
for a son, and rather self-consciously dismal when he is
stationary at Heriot Row or Swanston.

> . . . I can just manage to be cheery and tread down
> hypochondria under foot by work. I lead such a funny life,
> utterly without interest or pleasure outside of my work:
> nothing, indeed, but work all day long, except a short walk on
> the cold hills, and meals, and a couple of pipes with my father
> in the evening.[24]

The periods of inaction did not last long. Friendship and travel,
and his last performance in the Jenkins theatricals, as Orsino in
Twelfth Night, kept him busy. There was a visit to France with Bob

in the spring of 1875, and a longer trip in July, after his final examinations. With his admission to the Bar accomplished he could legitimately escape for a while.

It was during this summer visit that Louis was first introduced to Fontainebleau, to the little town of Barbizon where, at the Hotel Siron, a group of artists spent the summer sketching, painting, eating and drinking, walking in the forest, and just lazing in the sun. Bob was one of the group, and Louis was made welcome by his friends. The generation of the Barbizon School as such had really passed, with the deaths of Corot and Millet in 1875. But Barbizon had stayed on the map of landscape painters, and the little colony that Louis got to know was lively. It was a multi-national, multi-lingual group. Louis became close to one in particular of the painters there that summer. He met Will Low, an American, first in Paris, introduced of course by Bob. Low fell at once for Louis's personality and his talent. 'It was not a handsome face until he spoke, and then I can hardly imagine that any could deny the appeal of the vivacious eyes, the humour or pathos of the mobile mouth, with its lurking suggestion of the great god Pan at times, or fail to realize that here was one so evidently touched with genius that the higher beauty of the soul was his.'[25] Bob, Louis and Low spent hours and days in each other's company. Louis was held by most of the group to be second to Bob in terms of vivacity, wit and sparkling conversation, but they were an irresistible duo. And the special nature of Louis's charm was not lost on Low.

> Louis, quite unconsciously, exercised a species of fasci-
> nation whenever we were together. Fascination and charm
> are not qualities which Anglo-Saxon youths are prone
> to acknowledge, in manly avoidance of their supposedly
> feminizing effect, but it was undoubtedly this attractive power
> which R.L.S. held so strongly through life; and which, gentle
> though it may have been, held no trace of dependence or
> weakness . . .[26]

This 'feminine' quality was one of the things men and women most loved in him, although not everyone identified it in the way Low did. Louis responded gleefully to lively companionship and good wine and seemed to have little trouble in fitting into the group of, mostly serious, artists. He was, as many pointed out, in gestures and conversation, more Gallic than Anglo-Saxon. He was not afraid of emotion; he would burst into tears or express excited joy if he felt so inclined. Although he believed in survival and making the best of things he had little use for stiff upper lips and the negation of feeling. Feeling and expression were as much as action what made life worth living. 'Feminine' sensitivity was as important as 'masculine' aggression.

Siron's Hotel at Barbizon was a companionable environment. Barbizon was at the edge of the Fontainebleau forest, leafily picturesque, full of temptations to the eye. Siron's was well adjusted to providing for the needs of the easy-going and unconventional, whom it thoroughly suited. Will Low described it.

Siron's hotel was built around a court, a rambling structure giving evidence of gradual growth and added construction as necessity had arisen. The dining-room looked on the village street and was panelled with wood, on which all my and the previous generation had painted rather indifferent sketches. Long tables ran round three sides of this room, a piano which

Siron's Inn, Barbizon, c. 1875

was inured to hard usage was in one corner, and a fireplace in the other. For the modest sum of five francs a day augmented occasionally by 'estrats', as the mysterious spelling of our host had it, we were furnished with very good food and lodging.[27]

This room saw much conviviality and friendly argument, but if the participants were bohemian and free-living in some ways, there was yet a kind of conformity required of them. The apparently easy-going environment of Siron's had its rules, as Stevenson himself described in his essay on 'Fontainebleau'.

Theoretically, the house was open to all comers; practically, it was a kind of club. The guests protected themselves, and, in doing so, they protected Siron. Formal manners being laid aside, essential courtesy was the more rigidly exacted; the new arrival had to feel the pulse of the society; and a breach of its undefined observances was promptly punished. A man might be as plain, as dull, as slovenly, as free of speech as he desired; but to a touch of presumption or a word of hectoring these free Barbizonians were as sensitive as a tea-party of maiden ladies. I have seen people driven forth from Barbizon; it would be difficult to say in words what they had done, but they deserved their fate. They had shown themselves unworthy to enjoy these corporate freedoms; they had pushed themselves; they had 'made their head'; they wanted tact to appreciate the 'fine shades' of Barbizon etiquette.[28]

The components of what Louis called this 'random gathering' were diverse in character and nationality but it was no crude conglomeration. For Louis an atmosphere that depended on natural courtesy and sensitivity towards others was blissful. He returned to Barbizon, or to Grez-sur-Loing, another Fontaine-bleau village not far away, as often as he could, and took deep breaths of the unburdened air. The fact that it was in such an atmosphere that he met his future wife had a great deal to do with his falling in love and his marriage.

At this time Louis's health was good enough to allow him to indulge in two of his favourite recreations, walking and canoeing. Low says, 'He never seemed ill . . . it never occurred to us that his slender frame encased a less robust constitution than that of others.'[29] He explored the Fontainebleau forest on

foot and the waterways by canoe. It was canoeing that led to the
exodus to Grez, for Grez was on the river. An impulsive
expedition set out one day to explore the possibilities. With
Louis there were Bob, Will Low and Simpson, Louis's favourite
canoeing companion, with whom he was to share his inland
voyage. Grez did not make a good first impression. The rain
washed out intentions of swimming and boating – a 'very
melancholy village' wrote Louis to his mother, 'such an
atmosphere of sadness and slackness'.[30] But, after an unpromising start, Grez was to become the centre of much
pleasurable activity: '. . . to awake at Grez, to go down the green
inn-garden, to find the river streaming through the bridge, and
to see the dawn begin across the poplared level. The meals are
laid in the cool arbor, under fluttering leaves. The splash of oars
and bathers, the bathing costumes out to dry, the trim canoes
beside the jetty, tell of a society that has an eye to pleasure.'[31] It
was a superlative tonic to exist in such a society after long
stretches of Calvinist-weighted Edinburgh.

Late in the summer of 1876 Louis and Walter Simpson set off
on the canoe trip that he was to describe in *An Inland Voyage*, his
first book, published in 1878. The staidly quiet impression that
Simpson gave, so unlike the volatile Louis, was partly deceptive.
But he was deeply respected by Louis and many of his friends. In
some ways he was a sad character, something similar to the
'superfluous man' of nineteenth-century Russia. Low described
him as a man with 'a sincere desire to do something in the world
for himself, without apparently any very definite idea as to how
he should apply his not inconsiderable abilities', and in fact,
though he qualified as a lawyer, he never did very much with his
life.[32] (He also quarrelled with his brother and sister, and
made a rather dubiously-regarded marriage.)

Louis and Simpson made a complementary pair. They began
their trip on the Scheldt at Antwerp, paddled along canals and
navigated the Oise, returning to the Loing. It was a gentle
pastime but, unfortunately for the book, remarkably un-
eventful. Although many people have enjoyed it, the book is
about very little. Not very much happened. There is a lack of
distinct individuality in the sketches of towns and people.
Occasionally there is a spark of excitement – at the end of the
account, for instance, when Louis, travelling then on foot, was

arrested as a suspicious vagrant by the gendarmerie of Chatillon-sur-Loire. Otherwise the little scraps of comedy are insubstantial. The two odd-looking and ill-assorted companions lived a fine holiday but an uninspiring book.

But Louis was fascinated by life on the river, and particularly by the barges that made a slow and dignified passage through French and Belgian waterways. He so fell in love with a romantic idea of barge-life – he was invited on board by a barge-living family and was much impressed by the directness and simplicity of his hosts – that the following year he, Simpson, Bob, and a fourth of the company at Grez clubbed together to purchase a vessel of their own, which they named the *Eleven Thousand Virgins of Cologne*. But ambitious plans for the barge never materialised. It languished on the riverside for lack of funds to complete the necessary conversion, until it was finally sold.

Chapter 5

THE MOUNTAINS OF THE MOON

. . . it's such fun just to give way & let your pen go off with you
into the uttermost parts of the earth & the mountains of the
moon.

Letter to Sidney Colvin

On an early summer evening in 1876 Louis arrived at Grez to
find everyone already seated and eating in the dining-room of
Chevillon's hotel. Characteristically, he jumped in through the
window, to be greeted with shouts and cheers by the assembled
company. There was a family of newcomers who looked on with
curiosity, a Mrs Fanny Osbourne, her husband Sam, her almost
grown-up daughter, and her young son Louis Stevenson, of
whom they had heard so much, twin spirit, they had been told,
to the irresistible Bob who already had them spellbound, had
arrived. As the commotion subsided Louis was introduced to a
small, dark-eyed woman, a blossoming young girl who had
already caused some havoc in the community, and a fair, short-
sighted little boy.

Fanny Vandegrift Osbourne had arrived in Paris earlier that
year. She had come from California, where she had left her
husband after nearly twenty years of erratic marriage. He had
now temporarily joined her. Fanny Vandegrift (later she
'improved' the name into Van de Grift) was born in 1840, in
Indianapolis, in the middle of the North American continent.
The town was then in its second, post-pioneering phase of
existence, a rough, rapidly-growing town, and those who
thrived in it required a fair measure of self-reliance and
enterprise. Fanny's father Jacob had enough of both to make
some success out of real estate and other dabblings to establish
himself in a brick house, which meant something in a town of
shanties and other less stable structures, and eventually in a
sizeable Indiana farm. Their Indianapolis house was next door to
the church of Henry Ward Beecher, who was to become famous

as an abolitionist preacher, and notorious when he had an affair with one of his flock.

Fanny as a little girl was a lively and intrepid tomboy, her boyish talents perhaps increased by repeated female attempts to improve her unfashionable dark hair and complexion. Dark was ugly, according to the tastes of the times, and it can't have done Fanny any good to be told so. If Indianapolis could no longer be described as a frontier town, Fanny's upbringing had a frontier hardiness, and Fanny herself learned a frontier independence. Whatever she lacked she had qualities, of looks and spirit, that were to strike Louis Stevenson immensely when he met her that summer at Grez. At seventeen, small, dark and curly-haired, and scarcely out of the tree-climbing stage, Fanny married. Her husband was twenty-year-old Sam Osbourne, a tall, personable young man, whose career was to swing wildly through the army, prospecting, clerkships, but who was at the time of his marriage secretary to the Governor of Indiana, and a man with prospects.

The Civil War caught up with Sam Osbourne, and in 1861 he had a captain's commission in a local regiment. Indiana fought for the Union. But he gave it up after six months, having seen no fighting and lost interest. By this time he and Fanny had a baby daughter, Isobel. In the winter of 1863 Sam set out to accompany his severely tubercular brother-in-law, George Marshall, married to Fanny's sister Josephine, to California. But George never made it. He died on the way, and Sam continued to the West coast, and then on to Nevada, alone. He was bitten by the prospecting bug, and Fanny joined him in a Nevada silver camp, where what frontier skills she had were much required. In a mining camp shack she cared for little Belle, cooked ingenious meals out of limited and unvarying ingredients, learned to roll her own cigarettes, and tried to maintain her composure when Indians peered curiously in at the windows. Then there was a move to Virginia City, the boom town of Nevada silver-mining, thriving on the lustrous Comstock lode. Perhaps the atmosphere of excitement went to Sam's head; it was in Virginia City, anyway, that Fanny discovered that Sam had other female interests.

Sam sought fresh pastures not only in women but in places, and set off with a friend on a hunt for gold in Montana.

Montana in the 1860s was untamed territory, where the Indians resented white intrusion and the scattering of mining camps were lawless. When a report came that Sam had been killed by Indians it seemed only too likely to be true. By this time Fanny had left Virginia City for San Francisco, where she settled down in modest rented accommodation with Belle and earned some kind of a living by needlework. Sam reappeared. In 1868 their son Samuel Lloyd, who was later known always as Lloyd, was born – Lloyd, after a Welshman, John Lloyd, who was devoted to Fanny and had been of considerable support to her in coping with mining camp rigours. Their baby son may have celebrated Sam's return from the dead, but it did not cement his return to the marital fold. He was unfaithful again, and this time Fanny took her children and returned to her family in Indiana.

Sam had great charm. He was handsome, good-humoured, generous when he had any money. Fanny returned to him. He was unsettled, as so many were after the disruption of the Civil War and by the galloping pace of the last stages of frontier development, and found it impossible to stick to one job or one woman. That Fanny was hurt and exasperated we can guess, but to what extent she continued to love her husband, or to feel committed to him, is harder to establish. His daughter adored him, and was to write about him with unwavering affection.

> I cannot remember ever hearing a cross word from my father. If he would ask me to sew on a button, or darn some socks, and it wasn't done, instead of scolding, like most fathers, he'd stick a notice on my mirror: 'Miss Handsome's attention is directed to her Papa's socks' or 'Miss Osbourne's Papa is now buttonless'.[1]

Sam must have been easy to live with in some respects, and it was curiously difficult for Fanny to make the final break, even with her intended second husband on the doorstep. Divorce of course was not easy then, but Fanny had already demonstrated that she could be decisive and courageous. Sam could clearly look after himself, only too well. Louis needed looking after. Neither man, as Fanny discovered, perhaps sooner rather than later, was likely ever to have looked after her – 'I have always wanted to be taken care of,' she was to write to Charles Scribner, the publisher, many years later.[2] But in 1869 Fanny returned to

Sam, and in 1871 a third child was born, a rather frail little boy called Hervey.

Fanny found life interesting in San Francisco. The town had grown to a substantial size at an incredible speed, in the wake of the 1848 gold rush, and by the 1870s was full of life and activity. Fanny and Belle began to study art with Virgil Williams, and through him became acquainted with San Francisco's artistic set. She had friends: the Williamses, who were to provide steadfast assistance through her divorce and second marriage, John Lloyd who was now also in San Francisco, and Timothy Reardon, a lawyer, with whom she indulged in a thoroughly enjoyable flirtation. She enjoyed, probably needed, the attentions of men, perhaps especially as she had grown up being told she was unattractive, and had an errant husband whose activities were pretty well known. Both Lloyd and Reardon seem to have come under her spell, although she could scarcely have got away with an affair with either even if she had been so inclined. And neither in the end proved sufficient compensation for Sam's inability to reform.

Finally she could take it no longer, and decided, adventurously, to make a trip to Europe, with her children, in order to continue her art studies. She was never a painter of any great talent – Belle had more – but a purpose for the trip, other than escape was necessary as was, psychologically, the belief that she had useful skills. The discrepancy between Fanny's awareness of life's possibilities and her actual achievements was at the core of her difficulties in life. Unhappily the discrepancy was in some ways heightened by her marriage to Louis, although at the time of their marriage it must have seemed as if she were on the point of eliminating it altogether. The train trip from the West Coast across the continent to the East Coast for embarkation to Europe was Fanny Osbourne's first step towards taking her life into her own hands.

The Osbourne family, accompanied by a friend, 'aunt' Kate, who insisted on being with them, arrived in Antwerp in November 1875. That was where Bob Stevenson had begun his art studies. They had little money, and what they had was provided erratically by Sam. In Antwerp there were setbacks. Fanny and Belle found that women were not accepted as art students in conservative Antwerp. And then little Hervey became ill. A doctor recommended Paris. In Paris they found acceptance as art students, but Hervey grew no better. He was suffering from what was called 'scrofulous tuberculosis'. Money was scarcer; Sam couldn't or simply didn't keep up the monthly payments. 'We were miserably poor', Lloyd wrote, looking back, 'it seems to me that I was always hungry; I can remember yet how I used to glue myself to the bakers' windows and stare longingly at the bread within.'[3] Fanny denied herself and the older children so that she could afford medicines and delicacies for Hervey, but there was nothing she or the doctors could do. Sam was summoned. In the last days of his life the little boy's bones were breaking through his skin and he oozed blood. In April 1876, the golden-curled Hervey was dead.

It was a terrible blow for Fanny. She had sat helplessly for weeks beside her beautiful youngest child and watched him die. Her effort to make a constructive, independent life for herself, though it may have been unrealistic and romantic, was now savagely blighted. The family endured some weeks in Paris, stunned by their loss, until it became clear that some effort had to be made towards recuperation. A fellow art student suggested a stay at Grez. In Fontainebleau, with the trees and the river, and an undemanding atmosphere, they would be able to relax, and Lloyd, who was not well, would get the benefit of country air. The four of them went to Grez and settled in at Chevillon's Hotel in the midst of the assembled company of artists. 'Aunt' Kate left them to take up a post in Paris. But Sam did not stay long. There was no suggestion that the shared loss might have brought the two together again. Sam had missed his children, and would continue to do so, but he must have felt that Fanny had moved out of his world, if he had not long before moved out of hers.

Company was perhaps what Fanny needed most of all. There had of course been loneliness since she had left her old life, although she didn't like to admit it. She had had one or two brief flirtations in Antwerp and Paris. She wrote arch, teasing letters which demonstrate the least attractive side of her character to Timothy Reardon, and to which he replied. But she needed much more radical support than this kind of thing, or her husband, could provide, perhaps especially as she had an attractive seventeen-year-old daughter who was receiving

Fanny Osbourne

considerable attention on her own account. Her work clearly had not made any great impression, although she was awarded some praise and encouragement. She was no more than competent as an artist. Even before Hervey's illness her letters home read like exercises in boosting her own morale. She could not help feeling that she had perhaps done the wrong thing in coming to Europe, in leaving Sam who, to her surprise, was feeling her absence, in taking such a risk, in bringing her delicate little four-year-old son who was missing his father. Friends in California had tried to dissuade her from making the trip. It would have been a hard thing for Fanny to admit failure, but after Hervey's death she must have been haunted, possibly unconsciously, by the thought that she may have, in a sense, killed her son. She went to Grez in a state of extreme emotional and psychological vulnerability, which she was only partly aware of.

The artists at Grez were not at first too sure about the presence of the Osbourne family. Women, at least of the respectable kind, were not customarily a part of the artists' colony. The female presence was only known in the form of models, who may or may not have done much modelling, who were acknowledged as a necessary part of the painters' life and work. Writing from Barbizon, probably in 1874, Bob had told Louis, 'Everyone keeps a woman now. I begin to see the intrusion of Latin Quarter life.'⁴ Bob was scarcely puritanical in his relations with women (in a later letter he describes his 'Paris girl' – 'the most sensual party I ever met')⁵ but he is not sure if he likes the intrusion. The further intrusion at Grez of a woman with claims to being a fellow artist, with a husband who was obviously out of place, and with children, was regarded by the inmates of Chevillon's with some concern.

But once Fanny was established she and her children were accepted with the good will and courtesy that were a part of the code. They all three found the atmosphere restorative. The grief, the strain and the undernourishment were mitigated. And as well as being restorative Grez was exciting. Fanny and Belle became centres of attention, while Lloyd relished opportunities for exploration and riverside discovery. There were walks and freedom and boats, and there was the drama of encounters with unconventional personalities.

> . . . I can recall my mother and myself gazing down from our bedroom window at Isobel, who was speaking in the court below to the first of the arriving Stevensons – 'Bob' Stevenson as he was always called – a dark, roughly dressed man as lithe and graceful as a Mexican vaquero and evoking something of the same misgiving. He smiled pleasantly, hat in hand, with a mocking expression that I learned afterwards was habitual with him, and which reminded me of the wolf in *Little Red Riding Hood*. I suffocated with terror and suspense.⁶

Belle was to receive a great deal of 'wolfish' attention from Bob, and from others.

There was much talk of Louis, but it was hard to believe there could be another like Bob. His strange dress – striped stockings, wide brimmed hat, casually knotted neckerchief – and sparkling mockery combined with real kindness, his zest for talk and foolery, added up to a man wholly unlike anyone Fanny or Belle had met before. It was Bob who, even after Louis's arrival, commanded her interest, though it was Belle with whom Bob become emotionally involved. Bob was the dominant personality at Grez. Like the others he did some sketching and painting, spent a great deal of time in and on the river, walked and talked. Into all this activity Fanny, Belle and Lloyd were absorbed with little difficulty.

Fanny flourished in such an atmosphere, and loved the attention she received, though her grief and guilt over Hervey was still sharp. While the men flirted with Belle they coddled Fanny, and she bloomed under such treatment. 'Mama is ever so much better and is getting prettier every day,' her daughter reported in a letter home.[7] Louis met her at a time when she was bound to interest him. Her experience of life, unlike anything Louis would have encountered in a woman before, her suffering, her courage were all apparent. So was the fact that she had scarcely a thriving relationship with her husband, who had not yet left Grez when Louis arrived. Her looks were striking, but not conventionally attractive. She was described by an American member of the colony.

> . . . a grave and remarkable type of womanhood, with eyes of a depth and sombre beauty that I have never seen equalled – eyes, nevertheless, that upon occasion could sparkle with humour and brim over with laughter. Yet on the whole Mrs Osbourne impressed me as first of all a woman of profound character and serious judgment . . . in no sense ordinary. Indeed she was gifted with a mysterious sort of over-intelligence, which is almost impossible to describe, but which impressed itself upon everyone who came within the radius of her influence.[8]

It was not only Louis who felt the impact of the looks and presence of this woman who was 'in no sense ordinary'. She was a woman to be noticed. She had a strength, a forcefulness, something to do with the 'over-intelligence' commented on here, which was not at all conventional, and which many did not like, but which always made an impression. It was not surprising that some of those who knew Louis as an invalid and with qualities that could be described as 'feminine' were alarmed at the sturdy toughness of the woman he loved. But the toughness was only one aspect of Fanny, part of a well-developed instinct for survival, again something that Louis admired. She was in fact full of uncertainties, needed, as she said herself, to be looked after, and wanted to be admired. To become an object of interest in the eyes of an attractive, gifted, much loved young man was just the mighty boost to her morale that she badly needed.

Louis was drawn by Fanny's circumstances – he must have been to some extent aware of the echoes of his first meeting with Frances Sitwell – but no less by her personality. He found her stalwart and forthright, her physical qualities reflecting her personal attributes. She was tough, but there were hints of fragility. Will Low described her 'delicately moulded features and vivid eyes gleaming from under a mass of dark hair'.[9] Her hair was already beginning to grey. Louis responded to both the toughness and the fragility. The toughness stood him in good stead in the years of illness and crisis that were to follow, but the fragility was to become ultimately a burden he could not have foreseen.

At Grez they passed the time pleasantly together, but not

In the garden of Chevillon's Inn at Grez, 1877: Bob Stevenson is in the striped stockings, with Frank O'Meara on his left.

exclusively. Louis was just one of a circle of concerned admirers who were happy to spoil Fanny. Fanny was attractive, unusual and good company. She had a lively sense of humour, and was prepared to enter vigorously into the fun and games at Grez without affectation. She messed about on the river with the others, and wasn't afraid to get wet. At whatever point Louis admitted to himself that he was in love he was clearly drawn to Fanny this first summer. The development of an intimate relationship would have been difficult. Fanny had two children, Lloyd still very young, and the spirit of Grez was communal; that was part of its charm. Belle in a letter home suggested the atmosphere.

> We generally congregate down in the garden by the big tree after dinner. Mama swings in the hammock, looking as pretty as possible, and we all form a group around her on the grass, Louis and Bob Stevenson babbling about boats, while Simpson, seated near by, fans himself with a large white fan.[10]

It was a fertile atmosphere for dalliance. But Fanny does not seem to have given Louis any special attention at this time. She wrote to her erstwhile companion in flirtation, Timothy Reardon, describing Louis as 'the wittiest man I ever met' but comically professed herself nonplussed by his habit of bursting into tears unexpectedly.[11] Louis, although it was hardly possible not to be intensely aware of him, was no more than one element in an environment in which Fanny flourished.

Fanny took her children back to Paris, to a small apartment in Montmartre, and there both Louis and Bob were frequent visitors. She was fascinated by both cousins, 'the two mad Stevensons . . . so filled with the joyousness of mere living that their presence is exhilarating', but was also convinced that the chances were they would both come to some kind of a bad end, either through insanity or their excesses.[12] Louis was exhilarating company, but he also could be terrifyingly unpredictable. Behaviour that might be amusing at a distance became something rather different at close quarters, as Fanny described in another letter to Reardon.

> When he begins to laugh, if he is not stopped in time, he goes into hysterics, and has to have his fingers bent back to bring

him to himself again; and when his feelings are touched he throws himself headlong on the floor and bursts into tears; and you never know when either thing is going to happen. I like him very much but there are times when it is a little embarrassing to be in his company; and sometimes, I imagine, not altogether safe. Once we were going over to the other side in a cab when he began laughing, and couldn't stop, and asked me to bend his fingers back. I didn't like to do it, so he laughed harder and harder, and told me that I had better for if I didn't he would bend my fingers back and break every bone in them, which he proceeded to do, and I only saved them by suddenly biting his hand till he bled, when he immediately came to his senses and begged pardon, but I couldn't use my hands for more than a day afterward.[13]

There was clearly an element of self-dramatisation in this, the kind of thing that Bob and Louis encouraged in each other, but Louis was confident enough of his friendship with Fanny to feel that restraint was not needed. It was not so much that such behaviour was self-induced as that in certain situations there was no compulsion to control his impulses.

At what stage Fanny and Louis recognised and acknowledged that they were in love it is impossible to establish. Louis spent a great deal of time in Fanny's company. The following summer they were again at Grez together. Again, when precisely they became lovers is difficult to guess at, although there is no doubt that they did. Belle many years later was to deny it fiercely, pointing out that she herself was around all the time and it would have been scarcely possible without her knowledge.[14] But in fact Belle had interests of her own to pursue. She had become involved with an Irish painter called O'Meara, and also seems to have given some encouragement to Bob Stevenson. Bob was certainly deeply smitten by her, and even after her marriage, to a third, could not give up the hope that she might want him. Bob's passion for Belle was a complicating factor in Louis's relationship with Fanny.

Finding time to be alone together may have been a problem, but it was not insurmountable, and Fanny and Louis did not attempt to hide the nature of their involvement from their friends. As long as they were in Paris there was little need to.

Belle, incidentally, must have been perfectly aware of the fact that Louis Stevenson shared her mother's bed. But complete indiscretion was something to be guarded against. Fanny was still, after all, a married woman, and was risking everything, even her chances of a divorce, by becoming the acknowledged lover of another man. And Louis did care for her reputation. But he also hated hypocrisy, and their need for each other was powerful. Fanny had lived for years with the knowledge that her husband persistently had affairs with other women, with inevitable damage to her sense of herself. The love and passionate need of a much younger man must have been hard to resist, however strongly she may have felt she should. All the signs are that her moral sense was pragmatic rather than spiritual, but even on that basis she was taking a supreme risk. Louis, whatever the rewards of his relationship with Mrs Sitwell, which by this time had dwindled, must have been deeply anxious for an honest sexual union on equal terms. It was the only honourable kind of relationship. The fact that both of them were on neutral ground, as it were, at a distance from home territory and the climate of Victorian social opinion, must have made it easier. They were cushioned by the bohemian artistic life of Paris.

There are numerous hints to suggest that Louis worried seriously about how an honest sexual relationship might be achieved. The kind of relationship that was open to him, with a Parisian grisette perhaps, like Bob's 'sensual party', he appears to have rejected. And Bob wasn't very happy about it either. In the summer of 1874, two years before Louis met Fanny, he had written to Louis about how affairs with 'slavies and "hoc genus omne"' were tempting but meaningless.[15] What both young men wanted as much as anything was stability. The qualities Bob seems most to have admired in his Paris girl were her de-pendability and considerateness, and he felt bad that he could not offer her more in return. He valued these qualities without finding her, he admitted, particularly attractive, although, he wrote with something like awe, 'she is a burning fiery furnace really'.[16] Although Bob doggedly insisted that pleasure was what he would like to live for – 'female flesh, old wines, conviviality, foods, fires, with exercise, expeditions in the sun and snow' – he was as unable as Louis to free himself from restraints.[17] It was one of the things that made them both so likeable.

Louis's sense of moral commitment to Fanny, which was to lead to an acutely difficult journey of six thousand miles to reach her, was cemented by his sexual commitment. His feelings about women were highly scrupulous. He could not have tolerated having to accuse himself of taking advantage of Fanny. She was an older and more experienced woman, but in sexual matters Louis seems to have believed, in an age when it was common for men to escape guilt by invoking the female temptress, that the initiative and the responsibility were the man's. The sexual victims were the women. There is little doubt that he considered himself fully committed to Fanny at an early stage. The possibility of marriage was fraught with difficulties of vast dimensions; Louis may have thought of the relationship and its implications as a challenge of heroic proportions, which could only have increased its attractions in his eyes. He certainly wasn't going to retreat from any of the demands it made on him, and he was thinking seriously of marriage before Fanny left Europe. Louis told his parents about Fanny, that he was in love with an American who hoped to divorce her husband, and they were aghast. Thomas came to Paris to try to get a better idea of what was going on, but he probably didn't meet Fanny. Louis had a separate address, though by early 1878 he may well have been in effect living with her. It all seemed highly dubious: Fanny, the circumstances, Paris, Grez. Louis's friends were not sure how seriously to take it, and tried very hard to dissuade Louis from the mad dash to California that he made in pursuit of Fanny in 1879. They felt he should be consolidating his work and reputation on known territory. A bit of fun with a woman old enough to look after herself was something none of his friends would blame him for, but marriage with an American not-yet-divorcée with quite a bit of pioneering rawness still in her was quite a different proposition. It looked dangerous. Even the adventurous considered it best to play safe if a literary reputation was at stake.

Louis had now a much stronger magnet to draw him to France. The attraction had always been strong. He loved the French language, which he spoke fluently, and French culture,

French habits and freedom from prudishness. He was more excited by the French literary scene than by the English, and his reactions to French literature helped to shape his own writing. His expressive nature was more at home on that side of the Channel. Paris and Fontainebleau were for him areas of liberation, places where he could loosen the hold of the Calvinist stronghold of his birth. Bohemianism in Edinburgh was always overlooked by the gaunt images of religious conviction. In 1877 and '78 Louis made as many trips to join Fanny as he could. Fanny soon discovered that the man with whom she had involved herself was not robust. Although to his other friends at Grez Louis had appeared perfectly healthy, Fanny noticed what she interpreted as signs of tuberculosis, though this was before the doctors were suggesting the possibility. When Louis was in Paris in the autumn of 1877 he developed an eye infection which made him seriously ill. Fanny was so worried that she sent a telegram to Colvin announcing their arrival and transported Louis bodily to London.

It was her first close acquaintance with the experience of nursing Louis. There would be many more times when she felt she just could not cope on her own. Louis was not always easy to handle. On this occasion she made a move that brought not only relief to herself and Louis but the friendship of Sidney Colvin and Mrs Sitwell. She herself had an injured foot that needed surgery. She stayed in Mrs Sitwell's home and was, as she said, petted like a kitten. They even tolerated her smoking, which Louis predicted would scandalise them. Her introduction to the literary world of London, in which Louis had a place, was friendly. She was liked and treated considerately, and although she did not feel at all at home there, and never would, she was gratified to be favourably received. At this stage Louis's friends were not yet worried about what would seem to them later a very curious relationship with this rather rough and ready American woman.

Both Louis and Fanny had money problems. It is clear that Louis was at least partially financing Fanny. Supplies from Sam were still unreliable and sometimes dried up completely. The situation was helped somewhat by Fleeming Jenkin, who employed Louis as his secretary in the summer of 1878 while he was attending the Paris Exhibition. But there had to be an end.

Fanny, who had planned to return to California long before, had finally to make up her mind to go. She and Louis went first to London, where she had another taste of London literary life. Henley was embarking on the editorship of the magazine *London* and inevitably Louis and Fanny were drawn into the turmoil that this involved. Louis was providing copy for a desperate Henley and running around with a certain degree of self-importance. Fanny had an opportunity to see at close quarters the literary lion cubs in action, and she may well not have liked very much what she saw – a lot of excited and well-lubricated talk (Henley was a devout whisky drinker) and much rushing about in cabs, neither calculated to improve Louis's health. But Fanny's European adventure was nearly at an end. In August 1878 Louis accompanied Fanny and Belle and Lloyd to the station and saw them off on the boat train. As the train steamed out he walked away down the platform and would not look back to catch a last glimpse of the woman he loved. Suddenly, after the weeks of bustle and excitement, he was alone.

Louis was left to savour his loneliness, and to make a famed trip with another lady friend, Modestine, the recalcitrant donkey. There was time for reflection. Six thousand miles away Fanny was going to have to sort out her problems without his presence and without his aid. Sam was waiting. It is difficult to know what hopes Fanny and Louis could possibly have had of a happy resolution. Louis's plans for the immediate future were sensible. He was going to get on the move again, though at a slow pace and with sometimes a heavy heart. Within a month he was in the mountain village of Le Monastier preparing for his walking tour in the Cévennes.

He resisted self-pity, as he had done on previous occasions. During an absence from Fanny earlier that year he had written to Henley, to whom he described himself as a '*positively*, not negatively lonely man', and went on:

I'm a miserable widower; but so long as I work, I keep cheerful, and I find I have no tendency to reproach God or disown the highly respectable solar system on account of my irritations. . . . And do I not love? and am I not loved? and have I not friends who are the pride of my heart? O, no, I'll have none of your blues; I'll be lonely, dead lonely, for I can't help it; and I'll hate to go to bed where there is no dear head on the pillow, for I can't help that either, God help me; but I'll make no mountain out of my little molehill and pull no damnable faces at the derisive stars. . . .[18]

A major resource in coping with his deprivation was work. These years of dashing to and fro between Paris, London and Edinburgh had been productive. He was now being regularly published in journals and magazines. He had completed his first book, *An Inland Voyage*, which came out in 1878. It did not do well – Stevenson's own verdict on it was 'not badly written, thin, mildly cheery and strained' – but was nevertheless a landmark. And he had started writing fiction.

As early as 1875 he had been telling Bob about his efforts at writing stories, and it was clear that it did not come easily.

I have been working like Hell at stories and have, up to the present, failed. I have never hitherto given enough attention to the buggers speaking – my dialogue is as weak as soda water. . . .[19]

He gave up an attempt at a novel. It seems he also wrote a deliberately outrageous long story as part of a collective enterprise with Henley and others to compete in depravity. Louis seems to have won; the manuscript was kept for some time by Baxter, masquerading as a *History of Mexico*, until it was finally destroyed. Whatever the content it was all part of the practice that was to lead him further into fiction. In January 1878 his first story, 'Will o' the Mill' was published by Stephen in the *Cornhill*. It is a puzzling story, part fable, part impression of an unfulfilled existence, not perhaps the most promising indication of a career that would be chiefly remembered for its fiction. But the grasp of character is there, the interest in the interactions of personality and circumstance, and subsequent stories of the 1877–8 period, that came directly out of Louis's stays in France, demonstrate this also. Stevenson's early stories show how the writing of fiction became an essential means of handling these interactions. People and places, character and circumstance, the essential qualities of existence that were beyond the shaping of *specific* moments in history, these were what interested Stevenson, and these were what led him to write stories that were much closer in character to the romances of the American writer Nathaniel Hawthorne than to anything in British Victorian fiction. Timelessness is a striking quality of most of Stevenson's stories; although it might seem to be a contradiction it is also a quality of his so-called historical romances. It is the quality that has always caused problems for those who have tried to compare Stevenson with Scott.

It was a fertile time for Louis. He was full of ideas and projects. Many came to nothing, but it mattered more that the ideas were flowing, that the mind and imagination were creative even if the pen couldn't always keep up. It was a testing time. The guineas came in a trickle, mostly in single figures – he received £20 for 'Will o' the Mill', which was an encouragement to try more fiction – but he was a long way from financial independence. He was borrowing money from Baxter. Relations with his parents, which had quietened considerably since the stormy days of 1873, were still troubled. Their knowledge of the existence of Fanny prevented complacency. When Fanny left he was nearly twenty-eight years old and he had not accomplished a great deal. His commitment to Fanny made it doubly important that he should persevere with his writing, and this brought into focus what would be for the rest of his life an agonising problem, the problem that is deeply embedded in the existence of most writers: to what extent he should deliberately attempt to write for money. It was splendidly exhilarating to allow fancy to transport his pen to the mountains of the moon, but he needed to strike gold there if such indulgence was to be tolerated.

Around him were crystallising the hopes of a number of figures who were very concerned about the current state of literature. Leslie Stephen wrote that remarkable letter. Knowing this Louis was bound to have felt it as a distinct pressure on his work. The generation of writers just a little older than himself tended to be unsure and half-hearted in their attitudes towards writing. Andrew Lang, for instance, a fellow Scot, six years older than Louis, was associated with a group of poets whom John Gross has described as 'born too late for one literary generation, too soon for the next. They half rose to embrace aestheticism, and then sank back; if they hankered fitfully after bohemia, it was from a respectable distance. . . . The whole movement was

wistful, enervated. . . .'[20] Louis became friendly with Lang, a
useful friendship as Lang was an influential literary journalist,
and was to make and break, in a not always entirely responsible
way, literary reputations. He certainly helped to make
Stevenson's. Lang was keen that there should be good, clean
popular fiction, and became very enthusiastic about Rider
Haggard when he began publishing in the 1880s. If Louis at any
stage discussed with him the possibility of writing adventure
stories, which he very likely did, Lang would certainly have
encouraged him: he was delighted with *Treasure Island* and
Kidnapped.

Andrew Lang has left behind him a reputation that is not
without acrimony, but to Louis he was friendly and generous,
although he affected disapproval of some of Louis's wilder
bohemianisms. He had an energy and a sense of humour that
chimed well with Louis – 'garrulous like a brook', was the way
Louis described him[21] – although he cultivated a languid pose
which some people found irritating. He plied Louis with ideas,
one of which, the suggestion for a Charles Edward story with the
outline of a plot, Louis had begun to make use of when he died.
His letters to Louis in Samoa are entirely without the resentful
note that tended to creep into those from other friends, who
found it hard to reconcile themselves to his departure. And he
sparkles with ideas and plans and a wholly enthusiastic
immersion in literature of all kinds. 'Haggard and I have
written a novel which borders on the slightly improbable,' he
was writing to Louis in 1888, 'especially when the hero, having
gone to bed with Mrs Jekyll, wakes up with Mrs Hyde. It is a
moral work.'[22]

Lang, being aware that he himself was not going to supply
what was required to boost the currency of the novel, was quick
to champion those who he felt might do it. Another whose
friendship Louis valued, and who also occupied a position in
the world of literary journalism, was Edmund Gosse. He met
Gosse at the Savile Club in 1877.

> We went downstairs and lunched together, and then we
> adjourned to the smoking-room. As twilight came on I tore
> myself away, but Stevenson walked with me across Hyde Park,
> and nearly to my house. He had an engagement, and so had I,

but I walked a mile or two back with him. The fountains of talk had been unsealed, and they drowned the conventions.[23]

Talk was of the essence in Louis's friendships. The material circumstances did not matter. He would visit Gosse and his wife in their almost unfurnished house – 'the one person who thoroughly approved of our great, bare, absurd drawing-room was Louis, who very earnestly dealt with us on the immorality of chairs and tables' – and undeterred by the absence of conventional comforts carried on talking. As armchairs slowly appeared, when Gosse could afford to buy them, he 'handsomely consented to use them, although never in the usual way, but with his legs thrown sidewise over the arms of them, or the head of a sofa treated as a perch'.[24] Louis in conversation rarely stayed in the same place for long. When he was not actually reduced to his bed or at his desk writing he was in motion, incessantly smoking, pacing and prowling the room that caged him.

These friendships were sustaining, but they also in a sense concentrated the pressure. The problem of what he was going to write about intensified, although the attempts at fiction diverted it a little. For a time the answer seemed to be to set up deliberately situations which he could then translate into writing. He had done this with his inland voyage, but the book did not sell well, and the literary qualities are not striking. He wanted to write about human experience, but not about *ordinary* human experience. He wanted to write about a life of heightened interest and challenge, but first he wanted to live that life. The odds were against him. He was physically not strong. His moral and emotional commitments were such that he could not readily disengage himself from them. The usual routes to an active and challenging existence were not open to him; he could not become a General Gordon, whom he greatly admired, or a Richard Burton, and perhaps he could not even stand the rigours of life as a literary journalist, and become an Andrew Lang.

His adventures had to be constrained, or they had to come out of his own imagination. And although he sometimes talks as if this were not so, he sought adventure not for its own sake, but for his pen's sake. When Fanny left he turned his head to the mountains to find something to write about, for the one thing he could *not* write about was his sense of loss. He took with him to the Cévennes a large notebook and writing materials in order to keep a journal of his trip, a journal for publication, for public consumption. He would rewrite it and polish it before publication, but even in the original journal there is only one passage in which we are made aware of the fact that he was missing Fanny intensely. Although he was to say later that *Travels with a Donkey* was full of 'mere protestations to F.' one would never have guessed it.[25] Even in the journal he suppressed most of his real feelings, and disguises the fact that, alone in the mountains, he was savouring Fanny's departure undisturbed.

He spent some weeks in Le Monastier preparing for the journey. He designed a somewhat cumbersome sleeping-bag, capacious and lined with sheepskin, and negotiated the purchase of a small donkey. She cost him sixty-five francs and a glass of brandy, and he called her Modestine. For twelve days Louis and Modestine struggled together across the mountains. Although he describes in light tone his equivocal relationship with Modestine, their painfully slow progress, the villages and the people they encountered, and the grandeur and sometimes wilderness of the mountains, and makes out of this something more distinctly characterful than the *Inland Voyage*, one is never so aware, knowing the circumstances of the journey, of the effort he has made to distance himself from his writing. It was of course excellent therapy, to have taken on a professional exercise at a time of emotional disruption. But it emphasises once again the striking fact that there are few writers whose personality is so intimately involved with his writing, and whose feelings are so little revealed.

One of the chief interests of the trip for Louis was to set eyes on the country of the Camisards, the French parallel to the Scottish Covenanters. His attention to the landscape brightens when he reaches the 'confused and shaggy country' where 'in that undecipherable labyrinth of hills, a war of bandits, a war of wild beasts, raged for two years between the Grand Monarch and all his troops and marshals on the one hand, and a few thousand Protestant mountaineers upon the other'.[26] His fascination with fanatical guerilla warfare breaks out, a fascination with a dedicated, heroic minority in a struggle against established power. He could not resist the combination of banditry and intense belief, of conscience and cruelty. Hackston of Rathillet was at his shoulder again as he speculated on the episodes and the personalities of the Camisard struggle.

Frontispiece of the first edition (1879) of Travels with a Donkey, *illustrated by Walter Crane*

As they neared the end of their journey both Louis and Modestine reached a point of total exhaustion. Modestine, her legs rubbed raw, was sold for thirty-five francs, and with some relief Louis made the last leg of his journey in the diligence. It had in some ways been a Quixotic undertaking, but it had given Louis time to himself. It is clear he would have found it hard to face family and friends, all secretly if not openly wondering what would happen next, if anything, between Fanny and himself. And it had given him the makings of a book. He went back to Edinburgh, to work, to prepare *Travels with a Donkey* for publication, and to write *Picturesque Notes*, where he records his ambivalent feelings about Edinburgh, which he had started earlier that summer, and to allow his pen to wander a little into the mountains of the moon.

He wrote to Sidney Colvin to dedicate *Travels with a Donkey* to him. 'Every book is, in an intimate sense, a circular letter to the friends of him who writes it,' he said. 'They alone take his meaning; they find private messages, assurances of love, and expressions of gratitude, dropped for them in every corner.'[27] But Colvin, like most of his other friends, was not aware, or did not want to be aware, of the true nature of his commitment to Fanny, or the depth of feeling that the impersonality of the book disguises. Louis's appreciation of his debt to Colvin, and to others who had helped and encouraged him, was probably what he wished the book's hidden messages to convey. But there is the beginning of an impression that there were very few people in whom Louis could genuinely and fully confide. There was no one person, and his wife was not to become that one person, with whom Louis felt he could share all aspects of his intimate life. This reinforces the sense that grows powerfully in his later years that the major dislocation in his life and career was that his art, his marriage, his love for friends, his parents could never coalesce. It would have been a great deal to ask, more perhaps than any individual has a right to expect, but we are all the more aware of its absence through Louis's expression of a deep need and longing for such a coalescence. He was far too sensitive and idealistic a man to be content with less than seemed right and possible, and far too generous to complain when the possibilities did not materialise to match his hopes.

Chapter 6

IN EXTREMIS

It was not bliss that I was interested in when I was married; it was a sort of marriage in extremis.

Letter to P. G. Hamerton

Fanny Osbourne had been gone a year. It was early August 1879, and Louis Stevenson was a passenger on a river boat dropping down the Clyde from Glasgow's Broomielaw to Greenock. Off Greenock lay the *Devonia*, the ocean-going steamer that Louis was about to board. A very few days of desperate activity and emotional intensity had brought him to the point of taking passage for New York, the first leg of a six thousand mile journey to join Fanny in California. A year of separation had been enough. Fanny was suffering. She sent a cable to Louis, and whatever it said it contained such force that Louis had no hesitation in deciding what to do. Without allowing himself time to reconsider he had within days found passage on the *Devonia* and made hasty financial arrangements with Charles Baxter, who from that time became a very necessary agent handling most of Louis's sources of income.

He said not a word to his parents, who had been hoping that Fanny Osbourne would gently fade out of his life. Only Baxter had a forwarding address. He saw friends briefly in London, but found no sympathy in their reaction to his intended departure. To them this precipitous journey was at best ill-considered. Louis's health was not up to it. He was prejudicing his career, his future, and they strongly suspected that Fanny was a dubious if not a dangerous companion. Colvin, Henley and Gosse attempted vigorously to discourage him, but having made up his mind Louis was not to be dissuaded. Fanny needed him, and he needed Fanny; besides, there was the sheer adventure of the thing. In fact he must surely have entertained the idea of going to America before the momentous cablegram. He had been intrigued and attracted by the country and by American writing.

He had been tantalised by what he had grasped of the American experience. However strongly he wanted to see Fanny, and felt he should go to her, he also wanted to see her country.

Fanny had been writing to him, and it was clear that she had been having a difficult time coping with Sam and her own position. The extreme stress of the situation had made her ill. Colvin, worried as always about Louis and deeply concerned that he should do nothing rash, had written to Henley early in 1879.

> Louis has been to pieces, and was together, or nearly together, again, when he went away yesterday week. He had got a quite sane letter from an intelligible address in Spanish California, where, after wild storms, intercepted flights, and the Lord knows what more, she was for the present quiet among old friends of her own, away from the enemy [Sam] but with access to the children. What next, who shall tell? Louis had eased his mind with a telegram, without, however, committing himself to anything. He won't go suddenly or without telling people – which is as much as we can hope at present.[1]

It is clear from Colvin's letter that Louis was thinking about the possibility of going to California several months before he actually left. Fanny's cable presumably indicated that the situation had reached a new crisis; Louis's departure may have been sudden, but the decision must have been half formed in his mind for some time. The rapid and dramatic uprooting was almost certainly the easiest way to tear himself away from friends and family, quickly and cleanly. A year of separation from Fanny was unlikely to have improved his patience. His journey has been interpreted as the impulsive undertaking of a romantic lover, but it is hard to find much of romance in Louis's commitment to Fanny, however idyllic was the dalliance at Grez. Louis was nearly twenty-nine years old. He may not have outgrown youthful enthusiasms, indeed he tried hard not to, but he had too much respect for women in general, and to much knowledge of Fanny in particular, to take a romantic view of love and marriage. He was unlikely to have been entirely optimistic and innocent in his contemplation of a future with

Fanny Osbourne. He had shared her problems as well as her bed, her emotional convolutions, her uncertainties and her determination. He knew this was no simple or complacent personality with which he dealt. He was aware of the emotional and psychological risks involved in the barriers they had broken, and also of the barriers that divorce and remarriage were yet to present, and had already written of his views of marriage – 'the man who should hold back from marriage is in the same case with him who runs away from battle'.[2] He had also written about falling in love, 'the one illogical adventure'. The lover 'has to deal with commanding emotions instead of the easy dislikes and preferences in which he has hitherto passed his days; and he recognises capabilities for pain and pleasure of which he had not yet suspected the existence'.[3] Commanding emotion was sending Louis on a long and exhausting journey. When he sailed on the *Devonia* on 7 August 1879 he was responding to a challenge. The outlook was not promising. 'I have a strange, rather horrible sense of the sea before me, and can see no further into the future,' he wrote to Colvin before sailing.[4]

It had been a hard writing year. He was ranging through a number of different forms; we can sense how the more he wrote the nearer to himself his writing became. He had tried his hand at plays in collaboration with Henley – they worked away at *Deacon Brodie* intermittently for several years, at fiction, at essays on a variety of subjects. It was important for him to be working hard. It helped to fend off brooding about Fanny, and if they were to have any future at all together it was clear that money would need to flow in more steadily. To his friends it may have looked as if he were conscientiously following up a good beginning. He might settle down, dividing his time between London and Edinburgh, and produce inoffensive literature that the public liked to read. Colvin especially may have felt that Louis owed it to him to stick to the route that had been virtually mapped out for him. Henley had ambitious ideas about writing plays that would make a lot of money, and this would satisfy the more energetic aspects of Louis's talent.

In spite of the progress of his work the year had been a struggle. Depression conquered him sometimes, and he was lonely, 'a poor, lone, penniless man of letters', as he wrote to

Gosse.[5] He was torn by his happiness in Fanny and his distress in separation. He confided in Colvin.

> I want you to understand that with all my troubles, I am a happy man and happier than often of yore. I have mastered my troubles; they are under my hand; they are now a part of me and under where I sit and rule. And one thing I proclaim, that the mere act of living is the healthiest exercise, and gives the greatest strength that a man wants. I have bitter moments, I suppose, like my neighbours, but the tenor of my life is easy to me. I know it now; and I know what I ought to do for the most part and that's the important knowledge.[6]

It is quite clear that there was no thought of retreating from his involvement. It must have been an immense relief, after a year of misery and minimal support from friends and parents, to board the *Devonia* and prepare for the ten-day crossing. There was a certain satisfaction to be gained from so firmly turning his back on both London and Edinburgh.

Louis travelled second class rather than steerage, the cheapest, because he had to be able to carry on writing. The voyage, of course, contained the makings of another book. Now, more than ever, he was desperate for money, and it was worth paying the eight guineas for second class rather than the six for steerage, to give that next book a better chance. Not that he gained much in comfort for his extra two guineas, apart from a table to write on. The food was terrible, tea 'with a flavour of boiling and dishcloths', 'chicken-bones and flakes of fish' often making the evening meal, and twice a week 'a saddle-bag filled with currants under the name of a plum-pudding' were amongst the offerings.[7] Louis kept going on porridge, soup and bread, but lost fourteen ill-spared pounds in the course of the voyage. Of course his health, which had not been in too good a state when he left, suffered.

He was determined to adapt himself without complaint to his new circumstances. The majority of his fellow passengers were emigrants, Scots, Irish, some Scandinavians, the odd Russian and German, and Louis found his encounter with emigrant experience depressing. He probably remembered the summer trip with his father when he had watched Highlanders boarding an emigrant ship in a West Highland sea loch, torn by hope and sorrow. On the *Devonia* the contrast between the boldly adventurous idea of the pioneering newcomer to the new continent and the pathetic reality struck Louis forcefully. He saw around him 'family men broken by adversity, elderly youths who had failed to place themselves in life, and people who had seen better days'.[8] Louis learned something. He experienced in an immediate way the plight of men and women without work and without prospects whose last hope lay in beginning again in the new world. 'We were a company of the rejected; the drunken, the incompetent, the weak, the prodigal, all who had been unable to prevail against circumstances in the one land, were now fleeing pitifully to another; and though one or two might still succeed, all had already failed.'[9] His participation in this was not just picturesque. Although he was not actually travelling steerage he shared to a great extent the discomforts and difficulties of the emigrants. He had very little money. His dress did not distinguish him from the steerage passengers, and first-class passengers did not recognise him as a 'gentleman'. And some of his feelings about his departure chimed with those of his fellow passengers. If he had not exactly failed in the old country he had certainly felt himself rejected. There had been times when there seemed no place for him there. There had been deep divisions with his family, who were unsympathetic towards his liaison with Fanny; his friends were equivocal; he had struggled without much public appreciation; and, though he had no inkling of this yet, it was to be in America that the first really enthusiastic response to his books was to arise.

Louis associated himself with the emigrant experience and wrote about himself as one of a community, something which he had not done before, but he never forgot his role as observer and recorder, and the style in which he wrote of his journey, in *The Amateur Emigrant*, retains this self-awareness. Although there he was, so immediately engaged in a rigorous and demanding experience, he writes not without feeling but with a tinge of self-conscious irony that has the effect of preserving his distance. It still seemed to him the only appropriate style, as if he were describing events that were being played out on a stage and he himself were actor-manager. The bad food, the impossibility of keeping clean, the games, the singing and dancing with which the passengers sought to pass the time, the sea-sickness, the

blunt inhumanity of some of the crew, the characters of his
fellow-travellers, are all there, but in a sense Louis himself is
missing. He is more narrator than character in his own drama.
The alert and suffering young man defends himself from his
own experience with gallant self-mockery.

But the gap between writer and experience was to close as the
journey became more demanding. This trip, indeed the whole
American experience, was a landmark in Stevenson's writing as
well as in his personal life. The coming to grips with so naked a
challenge on his physical and mental powers had an inevitable
effect on the style and substance of his writing. Not a dramatic
effect, not a sudden change of direction, but a toughening of
sinews, the development of a more muscular style, and a
modifying of the posed stance of the writer himself. On the
morning of 18 August, New York was sighted. Louis and a
companion of the voyage called Jones, who had tutored him in
how to roughen some of his gentlemanly angles, disembarked
into pouring rain and made their way along West Street, hard by
the dockside, where they found lodging in the Reunion House
for a dollar a day. Jones knew the place. They were welcomed in
friendly fashion, and Louis's adventure in the new world
commenced. It was, initially, a wet adventure. In *The Amateur
Emigrant* Stevenson reflects on the romantic attraction America
held for Europeans, the energy, the movement, the cheerful
spirit, the weapons that 'seem more connected with courage
than with cruelty', the wide-open optimism that he found so
invigorating in Whitman.[10] His first experience of America was
to suggest little of these. The rain poured down. New York
seemed much like Liverpool. The welcome at the Reunion
House may have been warm, but not warm enough to dry out
the rain that kept him comprehensively soaked. In his one day in
New York Louis had numerous errands to accomplish, and he
went from bank to post office to bookseller dripping pools of
water on to a succession of floors. He was so wet when he got
back to the Reunion that he had to abandon his clothes.

> I had simply to divest myself of my shoes, socks, and trousers,
> and leave them behind for the benefit of New York city. No
> fire could have dried them ere I had to start; and to pack them
> in their present condition was to spread ruin among my other

possessions. With a heavy heart I said farewell to them as they lay a pulp in the middle of a pool upon the floor of Mitchell's kitchen. I wonder if they are dry by now.[11]

It was not the best state in which to emark on the next stage of his journey. At five o'clock he was at the ferry depot. Four ships had docked and disgorged their load of immigrants, most of whom were to travel on the same train as Louis. The crowd, the confusion, the rain, the noise were all appalling. 'Cold, wet, clamour, dead opposition to progress, such as one encounters in an evil dream, had utterly daunted the spirits. We had accepted this purgatory as a child accepts the conditions of the world. For my part, I shivered a little, and my back ached wearily; but I believe I had neither a hope nor a fear, and all the activities of my nature had become tributary to one massive sensation of discomfort.'[12] The seething mass first had to cross the river by ferry to Jersey City, and then there was a long and harried wait before the train was boarded. It was a desperate experience, a nightmare. Louis waited, numbed by exhaustion and cold, and watched families struggling with their worldly goods, lost children, individuals reduced to total wretchedness and panic, half-crazed, totally selfish in their fear and ignorance of what was happening to them, as inept officials only exacerbated the misery. Whatever encounters Louis had had with the destitute and downtrodden of Edinburgh, whatever moments of fellow feeling he had experienced, nothing in his past could compare with this vast mass of stricken, helpless humanity.

It was the start of a journey that all but killed him. It was thirty hours before he was able to find a meal, and the discomforts scarcely diminished. The immigrants were on the whole treated with contempt. 'Equality, though conceived very largely in America, does not extend so low down as to an emigrant' was Stevenson's comment.[13] Louis was sometimes able to buy meals at stations along the way, but often went without, either because he was too ill to eat or there was nothing available. Already exhausted by the sea voyage, and having suffered the weight loss dreaded by all those with weak lungs, drenched and chilled by rain, subject to the anonymous tyranny of railroad officials, he was then cooped up for hour after hour in an airless and crowded train where rest, let alone sleep, was almost impossible. He was feverish, and probably had some form of dysentery. The acute discomfort of suffering from diarrhoea in such circumstances was almost unbearable. The stink from unwashed bodies and primitive toilet facilities was overwhelming. He wrote to Colvin, 'I had no idea how easy it was to commit suicide. There seems nothing left of me; I died a while ago; I do not know who it is that is travelling.'[14]

The immigrant train made its slow way westward. Any lingering sense of adventure was trickling away, though it was only three years since General Custer had been defeated at the Little Big Horn, and they were traversing untamed territory. The hostility of the country as they crossed the plains and climbed into Wyoming wearied Louis, mile after mile through 'the same broken and unsightly quarter of the world . . . not a tree, a bird or a river. Only down the long, sterile cañons, the train shot hooting, and awoke the resting echo. That train was the one piece of life in all the deadly land; it was the one actor, the one spectacle fit to be observed in this paralysis of man and nature.' And he reflected on the construction of the railroad, the turbulence of 'gold and lust and death' that accompanied it. Both the 'epical turmoil' and the fact that it was 'conducted by gentlemen in frock-coats, and with a view to nothing more extraordinary than a fortune and a subsequent visit to Paris' made it in Louis's eyes a striking image of modern America.[15]

There was something to be gained by reminding himself of an older generation of immigrants who had crossed the plains and the mountains 'at the foot's pace of oxen'.[16] But on the frontiers of civilization Louis was seeing both civilisation and nature stripped to unlovely nakedness. Another memorable image of his journey was the Indians he saw.

. . . now and again at way-stations, a husband and wife and a few children, disgracefully dressed out with the sweepings of civilisation, came forth and stared upon the emigrants. The silent stoicism of their conduct, and the pathetic degradation of their appearance, would have touched any thinking creature, but my fellow-passengers danced and jested round them with a truly Cockney baseness. I was ashamed for the thing called civilisation.[17]

This could only add to the failure of America to measure up to romantic expectations. The frontier period was already drawing to a close, but Louis must have hoped to encounter something of pioneer nobility. Now he was seeing humanity at its worst, civilisation at its most decrepit, all the more sordid aspects of frontier expansion. It can only have helped to weaken his resistance to sickness and exhaustion. Whatever he was still able to hope from his destination, as he made his way painfully across the continent, he was deeply stricken in both health and spirits.

There was an end. Louis arrived at Monterey ill and weak. Always thin, he now looked skeletal. His exhausted condition marred the joyousness of his arrival. Fanny may have had second thoughts about the wisdom of taking on the shadow of a man who now presented himself at her door. Lloyd Osbourne remembered 'the brilliancy of his eyes [which] emphasized the thinness and pallor of his face. His clothes, no longer picturesque but merely shabby, hung loosely on his shrunken body; and there was about him an indescribable lessening of his alertness and self-confidence.'[18] It was hard to believe that this was the same exuberant, colourful young man who had been such good company in Grez and Paris.

While still on the train Louis had been able to write cheerfully to Baxter, 'I keep in truly wonderful spirits . . . right side up and smiling all the time', in spite of discomforts and the almost insupportable continuation of a skin irritation that had developed on board ship.[19] But even the relief of reaching Monterey and Fanny could not sustain him now, and his next letter to Baxter makes no pretence of cheeriness. 'This is not a letter, for I am too perturbed. . . . My news is nil. I know nothing . . . and now say good-bye to you, having had the itch and a broken heart.'[20] It must have looked at first as if he had made the trek for very little. His presence in Monterey seemed to make things more rather than less complicated. He did not linger with Fanny, who was boarding with her children in a Mexican household in Monterey, but headed straight for the mountains in the hope of achieving physical recovery and perhaps also an emotional perspective on the whole situation.

With a horse and pack, alone, and clearly depressed, Louis made his way into the unfamiliar mountains. He could hardly have stayed with Fanny; any prospect of a divorce necessitated extreme discretion on the part of both of them. Fanny explained his arrival by saying that he was a Scottish author on a lecture tour. Anyone who saw him, ill, exhausted, dirty and itching, must have been surprised. To find, as he did, that there was really very little he could do in California, that in his present state he could scarcely be even a moral support to Fanny, was the final devastation. The trip into the mountains was probably a necessary escape as much as a quest for health.

Escape perhaps he did find, but at an enormous cost. He almost did not survive. Weaker than he had realised, or had wanted to admit, he collapsed miles from human habitation, and was just able to drag himself far enough to find water for his horse and himself. For three days he kept alive on coffee. By lucky chance he was discovered by a bear hunter, who took him to his goat ranch and nursed him somewhat roughly back to health. He had never been quite so near to death. He was not to recover his health even half securely until after his marriage. From his sick bed in the mountains he wrote again to Baxter.

> I write you from an Angora goat ranch where I live with some frontiersmen, being fallen sick out camping. I am not yet recovered up to the point of being good for much; indeed I am pretty well dished in the meantime; but my fever has gone, and though I cannot yet walk about at all, I both eat and sleep, and if you come to that, work . . . I am lying in an upper chamber nearly naked, with flies crawling all over me and a clinking of goat bells in my ears, which proves to me the goats are come home and it will soon be time to eat. The old bear hunter is doubtless now infusing tea, and Tom the Indian will come in with his gun in a few minutes.[21]

Though one can detect Louis's relish for his frontier experience, he was full of anxiety. His collapse in the mountain wilderness had been a shock, and he was forced to ponder the possibility that he might not surive to marry Fanny even if the divorce went through, and that Fanny might be worse off than she was now. He worried about his parents as well as Fanny. He was not in direct communication with them. He relied on Baxter for news and also for money, but the supply of cash was limited and the problem of economic survival was monumental, especially if

Louis's health was to go on letting him down, and making it hard, if not impossible, to work.

But a degree of strength returned and he got back to Monterey, the Spanish capital of California, which he found still attractively un-American. (It was not to remain so long. When Stevenson wrote about Monterey he lamented the passing of its old character: 'It is not strong enough to resist the influence of the flaunting caravanserai, and the poor, quaint, penniless native gentlemen of Monterey must perish, like a lower race, before the millionaire vulgarians of the Big Bonanza.'[22] He found quite pleasant lodgings and visited Fanny regularly but discreetly. He began to feel more confident that he had been right to come. Fanny's health was better and a decision on the divorce had been made, although Sam continued to equivocate for some time. In the middle of October, Louis was able to tell Baxter that the divorce would go through in January. He was working and he was happier.

He was not fully aware, though, of what was going on at home. His parents were shamed and shaken by their son's sudden departure, without an explanation, without a goodbye. He had at last, it seemed, deserted them and rejected them. For months Margaret Stevenson did not mention his name in her diary. Thomas, with no way of getting directly in touch with Louis, tried frantically to persuade him back. He wrote to Colvin begging him to intervene and get Louis home. His friends exchanged anxious and angry letters deploring the whole escapade and wondering how they could dislodge him. Henley and Colvin both had no doubts that the enterprise was a terrible mistake, but as time passed advised each other to accept the inevitable. Colvin deplored the trip, the divorce, the marriage, the effect on Louis's health, and was convinced that his writing was deteriorating. When Louis sent him the completed *Amateur Emigrant*, which he had been working away at in California, he was worried.

What disturbs me most of all about him is that the work he has sent me from out there are *not good*. I doubt whether they are saleable, and if so, whether they could do anything but harm to his reputation, this is more particularly true of the account of his voyage in the Emigrant Ship, on which I had built, and

so had he, considerable hopes. But now that I have read it, I
find it on the whole quite unworthy of him. . . .[23]

And as Louis was desperate for money (at this stage his parents
refused to send him any) Colvin was doubly worried – 'if his
work is no good, how is he to live?', was his question, and he
shuddered at the thought of Louis 'settling to some cadging
second rate literary work out there', about which he felt Fanny
would be quite happy.[24]

Colvin's anxieties were exacerbated by the behaviour of
Thomas Stevenson, whose exaggerated reactions to his son's
departure were too much for Colvin's patience: 'When he talks
of being obliged, by a purely private step of Louis's in regard to
his own life, to leave Edinburgh and set up somewhere in
England where he is not known, he seems to me to be talking
unreasonably,' he complained to Baxter.[25] Letters were sent to
Louis telling him his father's standing in Edinburgh was ruined,
telling him that his father was seriously ill, insisting that he
should return. In November, Thomas was writing to Colvin,

> My wife & I have exhausted all our powers of persuasion to
> get Louis to return home but without success. It is possible he
> may listen to you who have throughout been so good a friend
> to him. For God's sake use your influence. Is it fair that we
> should be half murdered by his conduct? I am unable to write
> more about this sinful mad business but I do most earnestly
> entreat you will use what influence you have with him. Our
> case is painful beyond expression.[26]

Two months later he is still writing in the same vein. 'I see
nothing but destruction to himself as well as to all of us.'[27] But
Louis, as his friends recognised, had gone too far to come back
to Edinburgh without Fanny.

Louis had stirred up one hornet's nest by his departure, and
had jumped into another by his arrival in Monterey. Fanny was
in a highly nervous state and had clearly been finding it
impossible to take any firm decisions during the preceding year.
Sam, who could be friendly and co-operative, could also be
truculent and difficult. He was meant to be supporting Fanny
and the children, but most of the time failed to do so. Louis
found himself having to keep going a household consisting of

Lloyd Osbourne

Fanny, her sister Nellie, Belle and Lloyd. There was emotional turmoil too. Nellie and Belle wanted to get married, both to impecunious gentlemen. Louis must have begun to wonder if he were expected to support them as well. Belle in particular was a problem, for Fanny disapproved of Joe Strong, the young artist she hoped to marry, though Louis seems to have liked him, and was having his mail directed to his address. That Belle should be difficult at a time when Fanny and Louis had their hands full of their own problems was a particular trial. Precisely what the complications were with Belle and Joe Strong are unclear, but in October, Louis was cryptically telling Colvin not to send his mail to Strong any longer. 'No more to Strong, difficulties about Belle having hurt me a good deal. More hell with that young lady.'[28] Eventually Belle and Joe took matters into their own hands and with Sam's connivance and without Fanny's knowledge got themselves married. There is a possibility that there was a shot-gun factor involved.

Nellie too was married, to Adolpho Sanchez, before Fanny

and Louis managed it, although there was no acrimony here. Her son was to be named after Louis, and was to be the recipient of a poem, 'To My Name-Child', which must have brought to the author's mind more than little Louis Sanchez 'on the beach of Monterey',

> Watching all the mighty whalebones, lying buried
>   by the breeze,
> Tiny sandy-pipers, and the huge Pacific seas.[29]

For Louis himself, hagridden by the heaped-up complications of his life, walked often along the shore, alone, or with Fanny, and Nellie as chaperon, giving himself to the roar of the surf and the mingled smells of salt and pine that the wind brought. It was during a walk on the beach with Lloyd that Louis told him of the hoped-for marriage. He must have been relieved when Lloyd put his hand into Louis's as token of his acceptance. He would have been deeply disappointed if the boy he had grown so fond of had rejected him as his mother's husband.

Other people's plans and activities intruded drastically into their own lives. Fanny's family in Indiana were upset about the divorce. One thing after another occurred to drag the business out. From the very start Fanny and Louis were unable to disentangle their own lives from the lives, and usually the emotional and practical difficulties, of others. They very rarely had anything of a life alone together. Years later Louis was to look back at some months spent at Hyères in the South of France as the happiest time of his life: it was the only period he and Fanny had time to themselves. Louis became an instant father, supporter, adviser to an extended family, and Fanny had to achieve the challenging task of being accepted into the loving stringency of Heriot Row as well as facing the scrutiny of Louis's friends. Perhaps neither of them were quite aware of what they were undertaking. Rarely can a marriage have taken place in more difficult or unpromising circumstances.

In Monterey Louis found a room in an adobe house which was perfectly pleasant though barely furnished – there was a bed, but he chose to sleep on the floor – and took his meals at a little restaurant run by a benign Frenchman called Jules Simoneau. The atmosphere and the clientele at Simoneau's were alike soothing. The modest food and the multilingual talk were a delight, but most of all Louis valued Simoneau himself, 'my papa Simoneau', who fathered him and spoiled him and looked after him when he wasn't well.[30] His meetings with Fanny were circumspect. After a month she went to the cottage in Oakland Sam had found for her. Louis stayed in Monterey until just before Christmas. He worked systematically, spending the mornings writing in his room. He made progress with *The Amateur Emigrant*, and was writing *A Vendetta in the West*, a frontier adventure story that he never finished – 'only remarkable for the heroine's character', was his comment, and perhaps abandoned because this character was based on Belle;[31] it is surely to be regretted that one of his earliest attempts at a real heroine has been lost. He also started his essay on Thoreau and was working on 'The Pavilion on the Links', one of the pieces that Colvin shook his head over, but which was accepted for publication by Leslie Stephen. It is a story distinguished scarcely at all for what it is, but full of interest for its indications of much of Stevenson's future fictional material. He was also at this time probably writing some articles for the local paper, the *Monterey Californian*, which brought him a couple of dollars a week, and which, without his knowledge, was subscribed by collection from fellow diners at Simoneau's. After his morning's work he joined the company at Simoneau's, refreshed himself with food and friendship, and returned to work. But his health remained shattered. He could not sustain long periods of writing, had to lie down frequently. His digestion never seemed to recover from the rigours and irregularities of travel, and the itch on his hands which he had acquired on the *Devonia* would not go away.

Monterey was friendly but curious. There was no way in which Louis and his relationship with Fanny could not be the subject of public speculation. 'To live in such a hole, the one object of scandal, gossip, imaginative history – well, it was not good,' he wrote to Henley.[32] Monterey did not know quite what to make of this shabby literary character who could be seen wandering around and looking about him in his accustomed fashion. Nobody, fortunately, witnessed an idle experiment with fire which blazed within seconds into a forest conflagration which sent Louis scurrying from the piny slopes that faced the ocean. Such moments of irresponsibility were rare. Louis's situation was stark. He was keeping a tight, if somewhat tenuous, hold on life.

While Fanny remained in Monterey, with Nellie, Belle and Lloyd, Louis visited decorously in the afternoons and sometimes read them the results of his morning's work. They sometimes walked on the beach; Fanny and Louis must have cherished any moment of intimacy they could snatch. But there were few opportunities to allay the strain that was building up in all of them. Louis had to use all his tact and understanding to handle her emotional and psychological tensions. How or when Fanny told Sam she wanted a divorce we don't know. He had little grounds for defence, although he knew Fanny and Louis had been lovers, but he was truly sorry to lose her, and very unhappy at the prospect of losing his son. Belle clearly resented Louis, which was understandable, and possibly her hasty marriage to Joe Strong was partly an attempt to gain independence from her stepfather. The fact that Louis must have been a continual reminder of Bob can't have made things easier for her.

Louis arrived forlornly in San Francisco in late December. He was not to find the friendliness or attractive atmosphere that had cushioned him a little in Monterey, though he was lucky in the Bush Street lodging he found. His landlady, Mrs Carson, was caring and attentive, but in both health and finance Louis was now in almost desperate straits. Medical attention cost money, and he could not afford to buy it. Doctors turned him away when he made it clear that he could not afford to pay for their services immediately. His worn clothes and gaunt look scarcely helped to create a favourable impression. His modest midday meal at a nearby café had to be cut down as the money dwindled. Mrs Carson did her best, tactfully supplementing his diet and not mentioning the rent, but then her own child, four-year-old Robbie, fell ill, and Louis dropped everything to help care for him. He could not bear to see a child ill and suffering, and surely driven by memories of his own long, feverish, wakeful nights sat with the little boy through the night and devoted himself to his care. Robbie survived, but inevitably the effort took its toll on Louis. Illness laid him low completely yet again. It turned out to be malaria that had been causing so much trouble since his arrival in California, aggravated obviously by weak lungs, fatigue and lack of proper meals. But at least once diagnosed the malaria itself could be treated with quinine.

At this point Fanny, across the bay in Oakland, threw propriety to the winds and insisted that Louis was moved nearer to her, first to a nearby hotel, then into her own home. It was the dramatic appearance of Bluidy Jack, a presence that was to become all too familiar to both of them, that prompted this drastic move: Louis had apparently began to bleed from the lungs. The years of bronchial infections, of fevers and coughing, now erupted in blood that filled his mouth so that he could not speak. Fanny and Louis were both shaken. It was, to say the least, an ill omen. Fanny must have had little doubt in her own mind by this time that the signs pointed to tuberculosis, which even when it did not kill debilitated drastically. If his ill health in California could at first be explained by the rigours of the journey and generally weakened state, it now looked as though Fanny was pledged to marry a tubercular and enfeebled man who might not live long and who, if he did survive, would need constant care. But in January the divorce had come through and there was no thought but of marriage.

By this time Louis was fully supporting Fanny's household – 'a wife, a sister-in-law, five cats, two dogs, three horses . . . and occasional descents of a son-in-law'.[33] The 'son-in-law' was Lloyd, his stepson, who was away at school; before long Louis would be helping to support Belle and her husband too, though in the meantime Belle's marriage meant one less mouth to feed. During these months Louis's letters to Baxter were full of money, requests, receipts, panics over misdirections and confusions, and his contorted efforts to somehow lay hands on more.

Baxter without fail and without criticism supported and helped him. Without Baxter the travelling and the stay in California, the marriage even, would scarcely have been feasible. Colvin and Henley finally accepted the inevitability of Fanny entering Louis's life, but then began to worry that he might not come back. Colvin worried about his health. Henley was writing to Colvin in January, 'It is absolutely necessary that he should be brought to see that England and a quiet life are what he wants and must have if he means to make – I won't say a reputation – but money by literature.'[34] Their concern was genuine, but there was also a degree of jealousy. Louis was *their* charge. He had no business to be gallivanting off independently, beyond their care and help, and perhaps allying himself to one who would then have a greater claim on his affections and company than they would ever be able to have again. They had been assiduously cultivating his talent and his career, and here he was taking impossible risks, undoing, it seemed, all they had helped him to.

A resentful tone crept into their letters. They told him he should never have gone, and that he should come home at once. They continued to be harsh about the work he was sending back, and they backed each other up, and both were reluctant to believe that Louis's motives were deeply felt. 'He has gone too far to retract,' Henley wrote impatiently to Colvin, 'he has acted & gushed and excited himself too nearly into the heroic spirit to be asked to forbear his point.'[35] But, Henley added, and it almost appears as a punishment, they shouldn't hold back on the severe criticism of his work. Such attitudes, though they were not communicated so explicitly to Louis himself, made him acutely unhappy. When he received a friendly letter from Gosse he was very touched, and wrote back:

My boy, I am having a rough time here; as indeed I begin to think it is my way to have. Some people are so made, I fear, that their ahem brings down the avalanche; and step where they please, they must always tread on other people's hearts. A combination of lapsing money, horrid feuds with threatening letters, telegrams requesting me to come home right away because my father was ill, sleepless nights waiting to run for the Doctor here, Doctors telling me that those who are most dear to me would not pass the night [Fanny clearly ill again]. . . . Your letter was like a warm shake of the hand in the midst of all these concerns. I try to tell myself that I am indifferent to people's judgements; but it is partly a pretence. I give you my word of honour, Gosse, I am trying to behave well, and in some sort, which is as much as one can say, succeeding . . . your kind letter, coming when it did, was an act of friendship of a far greater import than you could have dreamed when you wrote.[36]

Gosse replied, 'Why do you write such letters to wring my

heart?' but even he could not refrain from pleading that Louis should come home.[37] He thought of Louis lonely and miserable in California, but neglected to remember that though this was partly true Louis had, or very nearly had, Fanny.

It was Thomas Stevenson who took the first leap of commitment, as distinct from grudging acceptance, to the new direction in Louis's life. Weak and penniless in San Francisco, despairing as to how he was ever to fulfil the new responsibilities that were suddenly his, Louis received from his father a cable, which informed him that he, Thomas, was ready to provide him with £250 a year. Louis was profoundly relieved and immensely grateful. He was ready to work unremittingly to make the money he so badly needed, but he knew that he might indeed work himself to death. Without his father, he wrote to Baxter, 'I should have been trying to work and succeeding in dying, I fancy.'[38] Now marriage seemed less like a burden, or a last desperate gesture, and promised something more like rest and at least a temporary ease. Earlier Colvin had offered to lend him money. 'I must support myself,' Louis had written back; 'this is a test.'[39] But the offer from his father meant more than just money; it meant his father's blessing.

Nevertheless months were to pass before the wedding was possible. The needs of Belle and Nellie pushed Fanny's wants into the background. There were problems with her family. There was sickness at home as well as unhappiness about their daughter's divorce and remarriage to a strange Scottish writer they had never met. Whenever the way before seemed to clear, fresh obstacles rose before them. During this time Fanny was much helped and supported by her friends Virgil and Dora Williams, who extended a warm welcome to Louis when he came to San Francisco. He got to know some of their friends, a welcome diversion as on the whole he did not much enjoy San Francisco. There was something feverish about the city, which was not just the product of his often fevered brain.

The streets lie straight up and down the hills, and straight across at right angles, these in sun, those in shadow, a trenchant pattern of gloom and glare; and what with the crisp illumination, the sea-air singing in your ears, the chill and glitter, the changing aspects both of things and people, the

fresh sights at every corner of your walk – sights of the bay, of
Tamalpais, of steep descending streets, of the outspread city –
whiffs of alien speech, sailors singing on shipboard, Chinese
coolies toiling on the shore, crowds brawling all day in the
street before the Stock Exchange – one brief impression
follows and obliterates another, and the city leaves upon the
mind no general and stable picture, but a profusion of airy
and incongruous images of the sea and shore, the east and
west, the summer and the winter.[40]

It was 19 May before the wedding took place, performed by a
Scots Presbyterian minister resident in San Francisco. Dora
Williams was the only other person present. Such was the
reticence about Fanny's divorced status that she described
herself as 'widow' on the marriage certificate. After the wedding
Fanny and Louis spent a few days in rooms in the same building
as Belle and Joe Strong's apartment, and then made their way
north to the mountains. Louis was still in a fragile state, 'a
complication of coughs and bones' he was to write to a friend
some years later,[41] and he was laconically aware of the fact
that he didn't make a very impressive bridegroom. But the
mountains held promise of revitalisation; just to get away
from the coastal sea-fogs would help him. The Williams's
recommended the Napa Valley, fertile wine-growing country,
and Fanny and Louis duly set forth. The railroad took them to
Calistoga, at the mouth of the valley. At its head rose Mount
Saint Helena, their destination, but for the rest of the journey
they had to rely on horsepower.

Louis must have remembered his last venture into the
mountains, under such different circumstances. Now was a fresh
beginning and a new adventure. With his usual flair for making
the most of necessity, for translating it into acceptable and often
appealing terms, Louis made out of his health-seeking
honeymoon a frontier escapade. Fanny's frontier experience,
her flair for improvisation and, at her best, her real enjoyment
of the unconventional made her an indispensable aid as well as a
loving sharer of these first challenging weeks. It was a stretch of
uncluttered time together, and they badly needed it. They had
no very clear idea of where they would take up their abode once
they reached Calistoga, a small community which was the result

of a stillborn attempt to establish a health resort (California's version of Saratoga Springs), although they were prepared for rough living, and couldn't afford much else. The Napa Valley was rich in vines. With his enthusiastic palate Louis was not likely to forgo the chance of tasting the local product. He was intrigued by the vineyards, by the whole idea of wine growing in California – 'a California vineyard, one of man's outposts in the wilderness' – and saw it as a significant aspect of pioneering.[42] The fact that it was still in its experimental stages and hindered by marketing problems did not deter Louis from sampling and enjoying the wine.

They were not, however, going to take things easy in the Napa Valley drinking wine. With local help, tempered by local self-interest, they decided to make their stay at a disused mining camp way up the mountain – Silverado. The journey itself was quite an undertaking. They made their way by wagon and on foot, assisted by a cheerful Jewish family, who had clearly made a lot of money out of Silverado in the bonanza days, and by Rufe Hanson, a local hunter, and finally reached their destination. Louis described what they found.

> Fanny and I dashed at the house. It consisted of three rooms, and was so plastered against the hill, that one room was right atop of another, that the upper floor was more than twice as large as the lower, and that all three apartments must be entered from a different side and level. Not a window-sash remained. The door of the lower room was smashed, and one panel hung in splinters. We entered that, and found a fair amount of rubbish: sand and gravel that had been sifted in there by the mountain winds; straw, sticks, and stones; a table, a barrel; a plate-rack on the wall; two home-made bootjacks, signs of miners and their boots. . . . The window . . . was choked with the green and sweetly smelling foliage of a bay; and through the chink in the floor, a spray of poison-oak had shot up and was handsomely prospering in the interior.[43]

Undeterred, Louis and Fanny took possession and settled in. They occupied the rough wooden bunks, built a fire in the abandoned forge nearby, and improvised some pieces of furniture. Stores and books were brought up by wagon by Rufe

Hanson. Lloyd joined them, and there was also a dog, a setter called Chuchu. A few repairs accomplished by Fanny made the house slightly more habitable, but life in it remained pretty much exposed to the open air – 'we enjoyed, at the same time, some of the comforts of a roof and much of the gaiety and brightness of *al fresco* life' was the way Louis put it.[44]

Fanny perhaps remembered the Indians who had peered through the window of another mining shack fifteen years earlier. Many of the boom camps were now, like Silverado, ghostly with odd traces of what had once been hives of frenzied activity. But Louis and Fanny were prospecting for some peace, some happiness. To be together, to have momentarily at least shed some of the burdens that had weighed so acutely – this was precious. Louis rapidly established a routine. He was up early, and made the breakfast of porridge and coffee. Moving about on the steep slope was difficult. They had not only the mountainside to deal with but the mine dump, which encroached on their habitation, though a space had been levelled out on the gravel heap and to this most of their activities were confined. Louis spent considerable time resting, but he also gave lessons to Lloyd, now twelve, read, wrote a little, and gently explored the mountain. His pleasure in their existence at Silverado is readily sensed in the pages of *The Silverado Squatters* in which he described it. The writing is more robust than his previous style, suggests a more direct encounter with experience, more personal in many ways, although Fanny features in the narrative more as companion than as wife; he certainly wanted a wife who *was* a companion. And with Lloyd there, and Joe Strong too for a while, the open-plan nature of their living quarters must have curtailed intimacy. Above all, Louis's whole involvement in the experience of the moment, and his satisfaction with it, is apparent.

Once he was feeling stronger, morally and physically, Louis had begun to wonder if he had not been too impatient with his friends back home, too resentful of their criticisms. With the way clear to marriage and feeling calmer than he had for months he was writing apologetically to Colvin shortly before the wedding. He wanted to be sure of his standing with his old friends.

. . . I am afraid you fellows over in the dear old country are not only a little hurt, but despise me into the bargain. I think the last a mistake; I have come through a severe illness on my feet and without ceasing to work; I have had great anxieties to make things worse; and if I wrote carelessly and in any painful or unkind way to you, it was because I wrote to you without forethought. That was wrong, I now see; and I will try to be more kind in the future. Do not suppose that glumness hurts me; it is not an assistance, that is all; and I am now so well and strong and have so good a prospect of happiness, that I require none. I have come through the physical and moral tempest, and I do not think I am a hair the worse.[45]

He was apologising, but it is clear that he still felt that his friends had not been as much of a support as they might have been. But that chapter of his life was over. Silverado opened a new one.

Louis and Fanny began their married life living primitively on a mountainside. Edmund Gosse was to comment on the a-

Woodcut frontispiece by Joe Strong of The Silverado Squatters, *showing Louis and Fanny in their shack at Silverado*

materialism of Louis's attitudes. He was not interested in possessions. As long as he had a few books and writing materials and could keep the weather out he was satisfied. Although in the last years of his life he was to establish himself on an extensive property he never enjoyed the responsibilities of ownership, and although there were of course facets of his Vailima existence that he did relish he was by nature profoundly not a man of property. Silverado was in many ways more characteristic of his wants than Vailima.

Fanny and Lloyd became ill, however, and it was necessary to retreat down the mountain, back to Calistoga. Fanny's health was always to be a problem. But they returned to Silverado, bringing with them this time a Chinese cook (Fanny was not devoted to domestic chores) for more weeks of life perched high up, the steep slope of the mountain studded with tall pines rising above them, and the valley spread below, often swimming in fog. Louis was stronger. When his parents anxiously expressed their wish to see their son and daughter-in-law it began to look realistic to contemplate the trip to Scotland. They had a great deal to thank Mr and Mrs Stevenson for.

Fanny's role in making this possible was crucial. She had been writing to Thomas and Margaret, showing a warmth and a concern for the anxieties of the parents-in-law she had not met. But more than that, is was she who made life possible at Silverado, for Louis's pioneering scarcely went beyond lighting fires and fetching water. She wrote to Louis's mother,

> You wonder at my allowing Louis to go to such a place. Why, if you only knew how thankful I was to get there with him! I was told that nothing else would save his life, and I believe it was true. We could not afford to go to a 'mountain resort' place, and there was no other chance. Then, on the other hand, the next day I put in doors and windows of light frames covered with white cotton, with bits of leather from the old boots (miners' boots) for hinges, made seats and beds, and got things to look quite homelike. We got white and red wine, dried peaches and fruits which we kept cool in the tunnel and which we enjoyed extremely.[46]

So with Fanny's ingenuity, their wine, tinned and dried food, clement weather, and clean mountain air, their rugged honeymoon was not without comforts. It was important that Thomas and Margaret should understand what Fanny was doing for their son. The combination was right for Louis. He flourished, and they decided to risk the return home.

They descended the mountain, paused briefly in San Francisco, and set off, Lloyd with them. This time it was not necessary to suffer the indignities and depredations of the immigrant train. They could afford some comfort. The trip made no alarming demands physically, but emotionally they must have been needing all the support they could give each other. Fanny was leaving her native America, having committed herself to an ailing Scot whose parents had been fiercely antagonistic to the marriage. She was forty years old. She had so far led a life that had been notably without emotional and physical security. Now she had married a man of uncertain profession (although he had confidently written to Fanny's brother that it was quite possible to make a fortune from writing),[47] of unreliable health and of dubious financial prospects. She had not gained what a nineteenth-century wife most commonly looked for, stability, a home, comfortable and sustaining routines, an ordered life. She was a divorced woman, and therefore suspect in polite society. She had lost a child, and had reached an age when child-bearing was increasingly dangerous. Did she see her future entirely in terms of caring for the body and nurturing the genius of her husband? Probably not. Fanny was a determined woman, and a self-interested woman. We can guess that however deeply committed she was to achieving good health and success for Louis, she wanted much for herself also. Life with Louis was not going to be easy, because although he knew what he wanted, she was never to reach any clear idea of what was right for her.

It is difficult to know how self-aware she was, but she must have reflected on some of this as she and Louis made their way eastward. She clearly did not look for conventional stability. Middle age was not cooling her adventurous spirit. Yet an essential element of her character, as with most of us, was a profound need for approval. She flourished when she was thought well of. In the old days in San Francisco with her gentlemen friends, a centre of attention at Grez, loved intensely and exclusively by a brilliant younger man, these things brought

out the best in her. It was going to be very important that her
husband's parents should like her and approve of her, should
acknowledge how well she had done in her care and concern for
Louis. She was ready to try her hardest for this.

For Louis too the return home must have been a time for
reflection. He had not been able to tell his parents when he left –
he could not face it. He had run away. But he knew it had been
an act of cowardice and that he had caused them terrible
distress. This had clearly weighed heavily on him during the
westward journey and his stay in California. He had never been
so conscious of his love for his father and the pain that was a part
of it – this he had written to Baxter, whom he reproved for
taking it upon himself to inform Thomas of Louis's
whereabouts before Louis had been in touch himself. His
parents had overcome the immense barriers that divided them
from the acceptance of Fanny. They were prepared to accept
her as she was, American, divorced, ten years older than their
son, so entirely different from any woman they might have
imagined as their son's wife. It must have been almost as difficult for Louis to face them again in their generosity and forgiv-
ingness as it had been for him to explain to them his intentions
before his hasty and furtive departure down the Clyde.

Thomas and Margaret came to Liverpool to meet the
steamer. They did not venture to the dock, as Colvin somewhat
waspishly told Henley in a letter – Colvin himself did. It was
August 1880, a year since Louis had left. The reunion was warm.
Fanny was embraced. They all had lunch in a Liverpool hotel
and Lloyd ate as if he had gone without food since leaving
California. There was no question but that Louis and Fanny
would travel on to Edinburgh with the elder Stevensons. First
impressions were promising all round.

Colvin was rather less happy. He had travelled to Liverpool
from London especially to meet Louis and Fanny,
predominantly Louis, of course. He was there in the early
morning on Liverpool dock to welcome them. He may have
hoped to bring Louis back to London with him, although he
must have known that a reconciliation with his parents had been
achieved. But perhaps it was curiosity as much as friendship and
concern that prompted him. Here Fanny was as Louis's wife. He

wanted to get some impression of Louis as a married man. He wrote to Henley,

> . . . it is quite clear that he likes his new estate so far all right, and is at peace in it; but whether you or I will ever get reconciled to the little determined brown face and white teeth and grizzling (for that's what it's doing) grizzling hair, which we are to see beside him in future – that is another matter.[48]

A grudging letter. Colvin dwells on Fanny's physical appearance, but of course it was not really that that troubled him. It was hard to accept that Louis was no longer one, independent, spontaneous, delightfully irresponsible. For him and Henley and some others Fanny was potentially a threat. Louis was not free in the old way, free to entertain them, theirs, perhaps, to mould as they best saw fit. They were unwilling to acknowledge that in fact Louis's independence could be seen in some lights at its most courageous in his arduous and painful journey across an ocean and a continent and his commitment to marriage. Marriage need not be the end of an adventure, but the beginning. Henley was to say later that marriage tamed Louis, changed him, killed the spark of defiance and unconventionality that had lit his life. But for Louis marriage, especially in those circumstances, was a challenge, a challenge he felt, returning to Scotland, his family and his friends, that he could rise to. He was ready now for fresh contingencies. He may have found himself accepting aspects of bourgeois behaviour that in the past he had railed against, but he had had a crucial experience in coming to terms with life's realities, which had fortified him. We can see it in his prose. The man emerging in the pages of *The Amateur Emigrant* and living in *The Silverado Squatters* has a substance, an acquaintance with sorrow, an engagement with life, that the companion of Cigarette and Modestine had not yet discovered.

Chapter 7

TOO LITTLE IN LIFE

I perceive I have grown to live too much in my work and too little in life.

Letter to W. E. Henley

Fanny was introduced to Heriot Row. For the first time she occupied as her home an upper middle-class residence, with its unmistakable tone of money and security. These were the things that she had never had. In marrying Louis it must at first have seemed as if she were taking on a more ominous risk than ever Sam Osbourne had been. A frail, still tentative author was not the choice for a woman looking for permanence and security. That cable of Thomas Stevenson's that guaranteed financial support for his son and his son's wife was an immense relief, but it must have been an even greater one to enter the handsome residence in a handsome street in a solid, deeply-rooted city and see for herself the signs of prosperity and propriety. She and Louis had gambled against convention; Heriot Row was a good place to forget that. Fanny's acceptance by Thomas and Margaret Stevenson was the seal of approval she had clearly been longing for.

Another journey was over. It was a relief to be comfortable, and well fed, and well looked after, to be in a household with solid furniture, to shop for good and pretty clothes. But most of all it was a relief for both Fanny and Louis to have achieved the coming together of parents and son and daughter-in-law. The rift between Thomas and Louis would never be so deep again. Fanny got on especially well with Thomas. 'Fanny fitted into our household from the first,' Margaret wrote in her diary. 'It was quite amusing how entirely she agreed with my husband on all subjects, even to the looking on the dark side of most things, while Louis and I were more inclined to take the cheery view.'[1] Once the elder Stevensons had decided that Fanny was acceptable there seemed to be no problem on their side. They realised that Fanny was capable, a strong character, and promised well for the role of nurse and adviser, which it seemed likely she would have to undertake.

For Louis, after the most difficult and demanding year of his life, it was good to be home, although it is unlikely that he thought seriously of staying there. For a while it was irresistibly pleasant to relax amidst the comforts of Heriot Row. There was the excitement of showing Fanny his 'precipitous city',[2] as he would describe it in a poem to her years later, and the real and profound pleasure of being reunited with his parents, of discovering that they liked Fanny, and that Fanny was coping admirably with the new situation she found herself in.

On her side Fanny liked her parents-in-law. After a month of getting to know them she was writing to her friend Dora Williams,

> The father is a most lovely old person. He is much better looking I fear than Louis will ever be, and is hustled about, according to the humour of his wife and son, in the most amusing way; occasionally he comes in with twinkling eyes and reports a comic verse of his own making with infinite gusto. Mrs Stevenson is a much more complex creature, much more like Louis. She is adored by her husband who spoils her like a baby, both I can see, have spoiled Louis. Mr S. has just come in to shake his head in solemn protest over Louis who has begun work too soon in the morning. He is a most delightful person; anybody else seems so sodden and dull at this hour, while his eyes are sparkling and he comes in with a sprig of heather in his hat looking so pert and wholesome that it does one good to see him.[3]

Thomas found Fanny both sensible and amusing. She was a good talker. There was nothing flimsy about her conversation, or her appearance, or her attitudes. Margaret set out to spoil Fanny, which both clearly enjoyed though Fanny was rather overwhelmed. Gifts were showered on her, especially of clothes. Writing again to Dora Williams she described how Mrs Stevenson bought 'everything she can find in the shops for me' and gave her things of her own. 'When everything else is exhausted she puts on her dressing gown and has a good time trying her own things upon me from jewelry to caps, just as a child plays with a doll.' Fanny discovered quantities of fine clothes belonging to Louis which he had never worn (his parents had always been buying him respectable clothes which he had ignored) and persuaded Louis into them. 'The tramp days are over, and this poor boy is now, for the rest of his life, to be dressed like a gentleman.'4 Louis added his comment – 'She married a beggar with no seat to his trousers; presto – behold, a gentleman with an elaborate wardrobe, herself arrayed in the most elaborate toilettes.'5

They did not stay long in Edinburgh, but made their way north, the four of them, first to Blair Atholl in Perthshire and then to Strathpeffer in Ross. The northern air was recommended for Louis's health. After the California illnesses the fear was more intense than ever that the Scottish climate might kill him. But if Strathpeffer and the Ben Wyvis Hotel were healthful for the body the latter was not at all congenial to the spirit. The atmosphere and the company Louis found heavily depressing. It was a resort hotel, of the kind that began to flourish in the latter half of the century, and the residents were, Louis wrote in a set of comic verses he sent off to Baxter, ogres.

> They had at first a human air
> In coats and flannel underwear.
> They rose and walked upon their feet
> And filled their bellies full of meat.
> They wiped their lips when they had done,
> But they were Ogres every one.6

Louis found himself back in the bosom of the bourgeoisie with a vengeance, and however beautiful the mountains and clear the Highland air he rapidly became exasperated and chafed to be off. By the middle of September they were back in Edinburgh. But it was out of the question that Louis should spend the winter there. Fanny was tempted by the comforts of Heriot Row, and probably wanted to prove to herself and to others that she could lose her rough frontier ways and adapt to those of genteel Edinburgh, but the doctors' opinions were categorical.

The Swiss Alps were the currently approved locale for the tubercular or the potentially so. (There remains some doubt as to whether Stevenson was in fact ever tubercular. It was difficult to diagnose with any certainty at that time, but modern opinion of the evidence suggests that he may have suffered from a chronic bronchial condition brought about by repeated attacks of bronchitis and pneumonia as a child. The haemorrhaging which was to be a constant feature of his illnesses until he settled in the South Pacific could have been a symptom of this rather than of tuberculosis.) To avoid prostrating attacks of fever and blood spitting and long periods of incapacitating listlessness was worth going some distance. On 7 October Louis and Fanny, with Lloyd and a black Skye terrier presented to them by Walter Simpson, whose name transmuted from Wattie through Woggs to Bogue, left for the south.

A pause in London was irresistible. Louis was keen to catch a few whiffs of London life before moving on, and to have passed through without seeing Colvin, Henley, Gosse and other frequenters of the Savile Club was unthinkable. They were all curious about Louis, and more curious about Fanny, wondering perhaps whether Louis's old habits were gone for ever, and certainly dubious about future relationships with Fanny. Fanny herself was well aware that she was likely to be regarded somewhat suspiciously. But Colvin was always courteous to her, though he had privately expressed his reservations on the marriage, and others found her intriguing. Gosse commented later,

> She was one of the strangest people who have lived in our time, a sort of savage nature in some ways, but very lovable extraordinarily passionate and unlike everyone else in her violent feelings and unrestrained ways of expressing things picturesquely, but not literary. I think R.L.S. must have caught some of his ways of feeling from her. . . .[7]

The comment is intriguing. Fanny's rich and passionate nature, her exoticism – she was so dark there were those who thought she must have had one Creole parent – attracted Louis, but disturbed others. The tensions and contradictions between her unconventionality and her longing for bourgeois acceptance made many find her prickly, as well as causing considerable unhappiness to herself. Few of Louis's friends were prepared to be generous in their attitudes towards her. Gosse suggests that Fanny's influence on Louis was enriching. Certainly his writing was becoming more robust, less refined. Whether this was due to Fanny specifically, or to the American experience as a whole it is impossible to say, but of course Fanny was an essential part of the American experience. Others saw Fanny's influence as confining, limiting. Henley especially was to become bitter about this.

During those two weeks in London, when Louis and Fanny stayed extravagantly at the Grosvenor Hotel, and then had to write to Heriot Row for more money as they had in their carelessness and inexperience run up large bills, the inherent confrontation between Fanny as Louis's nurse and protector, and the more boisterous of his friends became apparent. Long evenings of wine and heated talk did not please her, partly because she was genuinely worried about the effect they could have on his health, and she had seen him almost dying, an experience denied to his friends, but also because of a certain amount of jealousy.

She was guardian of a man who at times refused to be guarded. She had dedicated herself to keeping him alive and writing, but he was reluctant to trade his pleasure in the present for the imponderables of the future. In pledging herself to make a success of this marriage, she was pledged to making a success of Louis, as man and author. She had married a man who had always said that writing was his life, and she was ready to take him literally. But there were times, and always had been, when writing seemed to Louis, although he was reluctant to admit it, incompatible with living. It was one thing to justify experience by thinking of it as vital material for the author, another, Fanny thought, to waste time and squander strength in the company of men who were insensitive about Louis's state of health.

Fanny felt her own authority and significance in Louis's life challenged, and she was always to be sensitive about this, just as a number of Louis's friends were sensitive about their position in his life. Henley's jealousy rivalled Fanny's: sooner or later a clash with irreversible consequences was inevitable. Henley was not a patient man, and his impatience often emerged petulantly. The clash was likely to be sooner rather than later. Like many others Henley loved Louis. He hated to think that he might have lost him to a wife and to the institution of marriage, in spite of the fact that he himself was now married and adored his wife. His erratic career, his frequent quarrels with those who were in a position to forward it, and his addiction to the whisky bottle did not help to soothe him. Of the close friends in London only Gosse seemed to be able to retain balance and generosity and regard the marriage without rancour. It would have been much easier for Louis's friends if he had married an unimposing personality content to play a negative role.

Not only was Louis loved, he loved in return, and the strongest commitment to a woman was not going to restrain him from a heady plunge back into the old glorious company. Fanny herself was to say later, though perhaps slightly less than honestly, that she believed Louis's love for Colvin to equal his love for her. Colvin himself was not above jealousy. The people Louis gathered around him were a refuge as well as an inspiration, and he gloried in the good talk, the good wine, the exciting fellowship he had been without for over a year. It was splendidly familiar territory. He was reacting against Edinburgh too; the familiar pattern of pent-up thoughts and feelings of the north being released explosively in the south established itself again. But for Fanny it was trying, and she resisted adamantly any suggestion that they should stay longer than planned in London. To Louis's mother she wrote,

> For no one in the world will I stop in London another hour after the time set. It is a most unhealthful place at this season, and Louis knows far too many people to get a moment's rest. . . . Company comes in at all hours from early morning till late at night, so that I almost never have a moment alone, and if we do not soon get away from London I shall become an embittered woman. It is not good for my mind, nor my body either, to sit smiling at Louis's friends until I feel like a hypocritical Cheshire cat, talking stiff nothings with one and another in order to let Louis have a chance with the one he cares the most for, and all the time furtively watching the clock and thirsting for their blood because they stay so late. . . .[8]

Fanny was not only unused to literary society, she was unused to English middle-class society, and however unconventional some of Louis's associates were they were also accustomed, unconsciously, to certain norms of gentility. Fanny's appearance, her speech (though she seems to have tried to eliminate the more powerful aspects of her Middle-Western accent), her directness, were unlikely to appeal to unadventurous gentlemen. She did not fit into any established categories of English-women.

Her awareness of this did not make it easier to cope with what she saw as excesses. They were spending far too much money. Neither of them was careful with money and both could be cheerfully profligate. London hotel bills and London entertaining were both expensive, and Fanny, in a situation where she felt she did not have to count the pennies, was no better than Louis at being cautious about spending. It was nice to have £250 a year, but it was a very modest portion and would not support an extravagant lifestyle, and ahead of them was a winter in Switzerland, with hotels and travel and medical attention to be paid for. Louis wrote to his parents confessing in some puzzlement that they had run out of money. Colvin had to provide £10 to get them on their way.

It was well into autumn, and for this reason too Fanny was anxious to leave. It was an arduous and slow journey, 'creeping towards Davos in the midst of wind, rain, coughing, and night sweats'.[9] Davos Platz, their destination, was high in the Alps and inaccessible by train. To get there required an eight-hour journey by sleigh up the steeply sloping valleys at the end of two weeks of slow stages through France. The white silence of the Alps made sleighs and horses and people seem at any distance like mimers on a stage, colour and movement sparkling clear in the mountain air and sound muffled by snow. At first Louis responded with his usual curiosity and sense of discovery to this fresh environment, but after a while it became impossible to deny that there was a dreariness about a snowbound Alpine village, a tedium in the unchanging white of snow and ice, and a sense of morbid imprisonment that life in a cut-off community of the sick inevitably brought.

They settled down in the Hotel Belvedere. A hotel community did not much appeal to Louis and Fanny, and to some extent they kept themselves to themselves. Louis was of course under doctor's orders, those of Dr Ruedi, who presided over the Davos tubercular. In November, Louis was writing to his parents, 'The whole of life here is one vast chronic swindle. Ruedi says I have chronic pneumonia, infiltration and a bronchitic tendency; also spleen enlarged; says I am just the party for Davos.'[10] He was put on a diet, with a lot of milk, and his smoking was restricted. Exercise in moderation was good for him; he skated and did some toboganning, although generally his exercise was confined to walking and he soon got tired of covering the same unchanging white ground over and over again. It was a restless time. He was writing very little, indeed had written little since his return to Europe, although he had always prided himself on being able to write under the most adverse circumstances. 'I can't work,' he is reported as having said at Davos. 'Yet now I've fallen sick I've lost all my capacity for idleness.'[11] He sat on the hotel veranda and read. He put together the collection of essays that became *Virginibus Puerisque*, which was published the following spring. He sporadically took part in some of the entertainment the hotel had to offer, readings and concert parties in the evenings, and occasionally ventured on a game of billiards.

> . . . one could often chance upon Stevenson in the billiard-room, though not often with a cue in his hand. Only once do I remember seeing him play a game, and a truly remarkable performance it was. He played with all the fire and dramatic intensity that he was apt to put into things. The balls flew wildly about, on or off the table as the case might be; but seldom indeed ever threatened a pocket or got within a hand's-breadth of a cannon. 'What a fine thing a game of billiards is,' he remarked to the astonished onlookers, – 'once a year or so!'[12]

But on the whole it was not an environment he could be happy in. Fellow residents at the Belvedere were scarcely stimulating company, in fact some of them he took pains to avoid, and so he was much reliant on Fanny, Lloyd and Woggs for company. (Wogg's change of name to Bogue seems to have been due to his disrespectful treatment of foreign carpets – 'bogging' is the word Louis used). Lloyd especially became a great companion in entertainment.

Louis and Lloyd planned together numerous schemes during their two long stays at Davos, though there was more scope for them in their second year when they were able to rent a chalet and were independent of the hotel. Lloyd had been given a toy theatre, and all three participated in preparing productions. He also had a printing press, and that kept Louis as well as Lloyd busily occupied. Lloyd at first seemed content with printing hotel menus and concert programmes, but of course it was inevitable that Louis would try his hand at something printable, and by the second Davos stay he and Lloyd had become quite ambitious. Louis engraved woodcuts and wrote verses to accompany them. The results were delightful and the fun of it palpable. 'I enclose all my artistic works,' Louis wrote to Bob, 'they are woodcuts – I cut them with a knife out of blocks of wood: I am a wood engraver; I aaaam a wooooood engraver. Lloyd then prints 'em: are they not fun? I doat on them.'[13] *The Graver and the Pen* or *Scenes from Nature with Appropriate Verses* by Robert Louis Stevenson, was duly announced in a leaflet, 'a most strikingly illustrated little work',[14] and advertised for sale at ninepence a copy. Louis also produced *Moral Tales* –

> Come lend me an attentive ear
> A startling moral tale to hear,
> Of Pirate Rob and Chemist Ben,
> And different destinies of men.

The story tells of respectable Ben who turns out to be a cheat and a hypocrite and Pirate Rob, of course the hero, who conquers evil –

> Out flashed the cutlass, down went Ben
> Dead and rotten, there and then.[15]

A major production was *Black Canyon*, a Western yarn attributed to Lloyd, but which clearly bears the marks of a more experienced hand.

This collaboration was a great pleasure to both of them. Lloyd had loved and admired Louis from the first, and the fact that Louis delightedly treated him as an equal could only increase their pleasure in each other's company. For Louis, it was wonderful to have a companion with whom he could indulge his boyish interests, and to have an excuse for them. Louis was always able to relate to children, always took them seriously and always approached them as equals. The illness and isolation of his own childhood clearly had something to do with this, as if he were trying to give to children something that he himself had missed. His sheer pleasure in the company of children is readily detectable, in his early essay on 'The Movements of Young Children', in his letters about the two little Russian girls at Menton, in the way he was always eager to make sharers and fellow-conspirators of the children he met. Childhood was for him not simply a transition to adulthood but a state of existence valid and valuable in its own right. The preoccupation with youth is more complex than this, but the belief that childhood is not something that is sloughed off and left behind but that the child remains a part of the man, was a large part of it. The child was also an enigmatic, agonising figure, a constant reminder of ageing. The Victorian period had brought a new awareness of childhood, and a host of equivocal and contradictory feelings, but Stevenson was quite clear that childhood was to be respected and enjoyed. It became the more precious as the complexities of the modern world ravelled adult life. There is a sense in which Barrie's *Peter Pan* is a direct result of the Industrial Revolution.

The relationship between Lloyd and Louis reached its heights in the elaborate and protracted war games they played on the floor of the attic in the Davos chalet. Louis had been re-enacting great moments of military confrontation since he was a small boy and marshalled his troops on the dining table in Colinton Manse. He had always had a great interest in strategy as well as heroics, and he had always been given to announcing from time to time that his true calling was military rather than literary, and only his health kept him out of the army. In playing the carefully worked out games with Lloyd on the attic floor, manoeuvring lead soldiers and firing printer's 'quads' out of miniature cannon, Louis wasn't just indulging in boyish fantasy. He was enacting just that combination of fact and imagination that we find in his best fiction. The planning was precise and the rules were exact; in other words, the imagination worked on and was fed by just those limits the player and writer chose to impose. Stevenson's most impressive literary achievements were to be those where his imagination was active but controlled.

The game was fully absorbing. It was a splendid way of allowing scope for invention, but there was no satisfaction without sticking to the rules. Lloyd described it – it involved no less than six hundred lead soldiers and the entire attic floor.

The attic floor was made into a map, with mountains, towns, rivers, 'good' and 'bad' roads, bridges, morasses, etc. Four soldiers constituted a 'regiment', with the right to one shot when within a certain distance of the enemy; and their march was twelve inches a day without heavy artillery, and four inches with heavy artillery.[16]

It was a splendid way, also, of cementing his relationship with Lloyd, for the games were clearly more a question of collaboration than of opposition, and like the printing prepared the ground for a more creative collaboration later. Perhaps above all it gave Louis something to do in a situation that became difficult and trying. He exhausted the possibilities of Davos fairly quickly, but without exhausting the need to be cautious about where he spent his winters.

Hotel life did not suit him, and the constant company of other invalids, the air of mortality, were heavily oppressive. From time to time a familiar face disappeared, but no one talked of death. He did make one acquaintance, though, who helped to alleviate the situation, and that was J. A. Symonds, a man whose reputation was well known to him. Symonds had come to Davos to live out the rest of his tubercular life there, and occupied with his wife and daughters a chalet close to the Belvedere. There Louis and Fanny visited him, and Louis had an opportunity for lively literary conversation and an exchange of ideas. Symonds was an essayist and literary journalist of the kind that Louis might well have thought he himself would become. His interests were eclectic. By the 1880s he had published, fairly considerably, travel sketches, popular studies of the Classics and of Italian art and literature, and his writing about Switzerland itself did much to encourage interest in the Alps (Leslie Stephen also contributed to this), an interest that became very evident in late Victorian literature: many of Meredith's characters, for instance, have firm convictions of the physical and spiritual value of Alpine mountaineering.

Symonds was ten years older than Louis and appeared in some ways, in spite of his consumption, to have had a more conventional and more obviously successful career. A Harrow and Oxford education, a winner of prizes and fellowships: Symonds' road to literature must have seemed much smoother than the route he himself was on. But Louis seems to have been unaware of the signal and agonising fact of Symonds' existence, which was that he was a homosexual who felt himself forced to deny his real sexual nature. He had been advised to marry when he confessed his inclinations to doctors. The marriage had become, inevitably, a wasteland, although it had produced four daughters. By the time Louis and Fanny met the Symonds's they had no sexual life together at all, and Symonds' wife was aware of her husband's needs. Symonds was desperately torn, for he felt that he should not be secretive about his sexuality, that he should communicate to others like himself – he *needed* to – but he spent most of his life fighting against his instincts. He was not an easy man to know. His biographer writes,

In middle age Symonds was embittered by the conviction that his talent had been blighted by the strain of accommodating himself to conventional morality. Passionately aware of the possibilities he thought life could offer, he believed that he had never been able to attain complete self-fulfilment because of the constant façade he was forced to maintain. A man hidden behind a mask, a writer who never attained first-rank, he suffered the tormented struggle of a homosexual with Victorian society.[17]

Stevenson's struggle with society was not quite the same, but they had more in common than they were able to recognise. They both occupied rather uneasy positions in the conventional world.

There was probably a touch of envy in each of them. Louis was a bit of an upstart – Symonds knew of his reputation in London. Was all the promise of the next generation of writers really contained in this attractive but insubstantial man who seemed to lack intellectual depth? 'I have apprehensions about his power of intellectual last,' Symonds wrote to a friend. 'The more I see of him, the less I find of solid intellectual stuff.' And he added rather patronisingly, 'He wants years of study in tough subjects. After all, a university education has some merits. One feels the want of it in men like him.'[18] Of course, Louis had had a university education, of sorts, but there is a touch of resentment here in Symonds' feeling that perhaps Stevenson's reputation and promise were not so well-founded. Louis on his side, in

John Addington Symonds

looking at Symonds' conventional progress, must have reflected on his position as a Scot and an outsider, which he had intensified by marrying Fanny. The last quarter of the nineteenth century was a time when writers outside the literary establishment were acutely sensitive and aware of their position: Meredith, Hardy, Gissing, to mention only three of the greatest, all had to fight for readership and reputation. Stevenson was lucky – perhaps. He had good friends only too anxious to bring him within the establishment, who encouraged him to write in a way that was both respectable and refreshing. He had come in from the outside with every chance of success, but he clearly felt himself at times no less an outsider for all that, and this may have been something that his literary friends in London found difficult to understand.

Meanwhile he was in Davos, cut off physically and intellectually from sources of stimulation, and Symonds couldn't wholly compensate. Their evenings together were not always easy. Fanny was prickly. Symonds' wife had good reason for unhappiness, and seemed out of her depth in literary company. When the Symonds's visited the Stevensons in their own chalet they were horrified by the untidiness and Fanny's carelessness in house management. But Symonds liked both Fanny and Louis, 'so full of innocent jollity and beautiful bohemianism . . . the beautiful companionship of the Shelley-like man, the eager, gifted wife, and the boy for whom they both thought in all their ways and hours'.[19] The four of them made an ill-assorted group. There is no hint that Symonds found Louis sexually attractive, although he had always been very circumspect in his approaches to men, but there were tensions, exacerbated by the long, confining Alpine winter.

Dr Ruedi's prescriptions for Louis were rigid, covering when and what he ate, his rest, his exercise, and it did not please him to be thus controlled. The thrills of tobogganing were only possible on good days. The limited cigarettes and the tedious pedestrian exercise, back and forth on an unvarying stretch of mountain path, the nagging necessity of being polite to his fellow invalids, the difficulty in working, all told on Louis's patience. Fanny tried hard to keep him to the rules, and Ruedi seems to have been satisfied with his progress. But Fanny herself was often not well. The altitude did not suit her, and affected her heart, and sometimes she had to leave for lower slopes. Especially during their second stay Louis's letters are full of references to Fanny's poor state of health. In spite of Fanny's difficulties in many ways life in Davos must have suited her quite well. Louis was beyond the reach of his obstreperous friends and he was making good progress. The frightening haemorrhages were kept at bay. With luck, a substantial improvement would mean they could turn their backs on Davos and find a more congenial environment for their life together.

By the spring Louis was finding Davos life increasingly irksome. Although he and Fanny tried hard not to get too involved in hotel life there were inevitable animosities they could not escape in that closed little community, and Louis yearned for some action. He wrote to Colvin,

. . . since I have known you, already quite a while, I have not, I believe, remained so long in any one place as here in Davos.

That tells on my old gipsy nature; like a violin hung up, I
begin to lose what music there was in me; and with the music,
I do not know what besides, or do not know what to call it, but
something radically part of life, a rhythm perhaps, in one's
old and so brutally over-ridden nerves, or perhaps a kind of
variety of blood that the heart has come to look for.[20]

Some of his restlessness was due to the fact that he was not
writing systematically – and this letter suggests that he felt he
couldn't, confined and restricted as he was. But with the warmer
weather escape was allowed, and he and Fanny were able to
return for a summer in Scotland. They went down the mountain
in April. To be on the move again, even on the tedious and
protracted journey to Edinburgh and with the customary mixed
feelings attendant on the prospect of a period in Scotland with
the older Stevensons, revived Louis's spirits. At all events, it was
to be a productive summer.

In June and July they were all in a small cottage just outside
Pitlochry. The little stone house looked out over the town, with
hills and Ben Vrackie rising behind and a burn rippling within
earshot in front. A few miles away is Loch Tummel, edged with
bracken and birch woods, a treasured spot for connoisseurs of
the picturesque. But the weather was terrible. The rain poured
down. Louis was forced to ignore the temptation of hills and
lochs. They decided to make a move, to try to escape the rain
and mist. They found a cottage, slightly larger, at Braemar,
north and east from Pitlochry. A long, bleak journey by carriage
took them through wild Glen Shee, Grampian terrain at its
barest, and into the Dee Valley, in the heart of what had become
one of the best known areas of the Highlands owing to the
proximity of Balmoral, where the dumpy, black-clad queen
spent her summers. But the rain came with them. Louis had
been ill at Pitlochry, and got no better at Braemar.

Perhaps stimulated by his return to Scotland, and perhaps
more open to his country's influences after a sterile winter,
Louis was writing again, and writing fiction, fiction whose
origins and atmosphere were profoundly Scottish. In Kinnaird
Cottage, Pitlochry, he wrote 'Thrawn Janet', a story he had first
thought about many years earlier and was now finally getting

down on paper. It was his first piece of Scottish fiction, in maturity at least, a story that uses the fears and prejudices of a devil-conscious national imagination with great effect. His touch was sure, style and atmosphere deftly consistent, and he was confident enough of the result to send it straight to Stephen for the *Cornhill*. Stephen liked it, and it appeared in the magazine the following October.

Louis had had a longstanding interest in witchcraft and the supernatural. He had been brought up on stories of the devil, he had soaked himself in aspects of Scottish history in which superstition was a powerful element, and he was well aware of the close relationship between the satanic and the romantic. That there were aspects of humanity that somehow only the existence of the devil could explain was a thought that had entered his mind in primitive fashion in earliest childhood. It was to emerge in his writing in several ways. But here was Satan's first entry on the scene of Stevenson's writing. He had written before of the corruptibility of human nature, he had seen the process, taking his cue from Victor Hugo, as a product of time and place and circumstance, but he was now to write of the susceptibility to the devil as inherent in human nature itself. Two more stories in similar vein followed 'Thrawn Janet', though one 'The Body Snatchers', was not completed that summer. It has a lighter note than either 'Thrawn Janet' or 'The Merry Men', the third and the most striking of the three stories, which was probably the most difficult for Stevenson to write. He was revising it later in the year. For 'The Merry Men' Stevenson drew on vivid and precise recollections of his summer visit to Erraid in 1870.

'The Merry Men' has the effect of a sinister folk ballad. The savage and mysterious nature of the sea, almost human in its deceitful ways and terrifyingly inhuman in its power, is absorbed into the madness of the man who vies with and gains from the ocean's cruelty. Stevenson starkly and with the minimum of explanation presents an elemental conflict, within human nature, between man and nature, between, literally, black and white. For the first time with full success Stevenson was to manage in these two stories, 'The Merry Men' and 'Thrawn Janet', a complete reconciliation of style and subject.

That they should both dig beneath the prickly, ominous, dark logic of Calvinism to the more primitive devils that fed it is of course significant.

For the first time Stevenson was using the traditions he had absorbed as a child. There was nothing second-hand about such writing, as there is in his earlier fiction, the French short stories which so patently owe their existence to Victor Hugo and Balzac. Now he was handling more intimate material. That the emblematic nature of the stories he now began to produce chimes most closely with those of Nathaniel Hawthorne, who also wrote about a deeply superstitious and high principled society, who also admitted the devil on to his stage, does not detract from their effect. Stevenson had read Hawthorne. Their similarities owe more to recognition than imitation. He had also read Poe, though the likenesses there are more superficial. We can see Poe's presence in a story like 'Markheim', written later.

The summer would have been memorable if it had only produced the stories. But it is more obviously memorable for the fact that one late August day, with the chill of autumn in the air, Louis began to write the story for which he is inevitably most remembered, the story that was to be published as *Treasure Island*. There were problems at Braemar, which the weather did not help. Louis's illness was not improved, may even have been caused, by the frictions and difficulties that developed within the cottage. 'If you knew all that I have had on my hands,' he was writing grumpily to Colvin, 'what with being ill myself, having other people most *painfully* ill, living in an atmosphere of personal quarrel, apologies and (God save the mark – what has become of all my themes) imminent duelling . . .' Life in such proximity to his parents was clearly not easy. 'I am in a great hurry to leave this hell of a place,' he added.[21]

Some distraction needed to be found. From time to time Louis dabbled with Lloyd's paint box, and on one such occasion the two of them produced a map. Out of that map, too insistently present to be ignored, there grew a story.

> . . . as I pored over my map of *Treasure Island*, the future characters of the book began to appear there visibly among imaginary woods, and their brown faces and bright weapons peeped out upon me from unexpected quarters, as they

passed to and fro, fighting and hunting treasure, on these few square inches of a flat projection. The next thing I knew, I had some paper before me and was writing out a list of chapters. How often have I done so, and the thing gone no further! But there seemed elements of success about this enterprise.[22]

Lloyd records that he was the first to draw the map, and Louis improved it. He watched him writing in names and then 'he put the map in his pocket, and I can recall the little feeling of disappointment I had at losing it. After all, it was my map, and had already become very precious owing to its association with pirates, and the fact that it had been found in an old sea chest which had been lost and forgotten for years and years.'[23]

The following day Lloyd was summoned. Louis spent his mornings in Braemar in bed, writing. This time he had produced something for Lloyd's ears, something of which Lloyd was the best possible critic, the opening pages of an adventure story for boys. Louis read the story aloud with much dramatic emphasis. Lloyd listened. But perhaps the most entranced listener, as the story progressed and was read in the evenings to the assembled company, was Louis's father. It was a story out of Louis's childhood, a story that Thomas himself might have told standing in the doorway of a dimly lit room where a feverish small boy lay sleepless, absorbing himself as he attempted to absorb his son. 'His own stories, that every night he put himself to sleep with, dealt perpetually with ships, roadside inns, robbers, old sailors, and commercial travellers before the era of steam,' Louis was to write fondly.[24] Fanny described Thomas's pleasure as he drank in his son's words.

My father-in-law would sit entranced during our daily chapter, his noble head bent forward, his great glowing eyes fixed on his son's face. Every incident of the story could be read in his changing countenance. At any slip in style, or taste, or judgment he would perceptibly wince. I shall always believe that something unusual and great was lost to the world in Thomas Stevenson. One could almost see the creature of cramped hereditary conventions and environment, and the man nature had intended him to be.[25]

The writing of *Treasure Island* in the little house at Braemar was

Illustration from Treasure Island, *serialised in the magazine* Young Folks, *July 1881 to June 1882*

the final stage in the reconciliation of father and son, and whatever the inspiration of Lloyd's map, and the exigencies of a chill, damp Scottish summer, and the importance of a youthful audience, it is hard not to see the story as written in grateful and affectionate tribute to the father who had done so much, mostly in spite of himself and his beliefs, to nourish Louis's teeming imagination. He was appealing to the side of his father's nature that had been most neglected.

The new focus of interest improved spirits at Braemar. It was taken for granted that the elder Stevensons would share the life of Fanny and Louis whenever possible, but it was hard to pretend that it wasn't trying for both of them. Now each day Louis wrote briskly and each evening the next instalment of *The Sea Cook*, as Louis at first called it, was read aloud for the approval or criticism of all; he could take the criticism as long as there was enthusiasm there too. The abysmal weather weighed heavily. Louis advised Gosse, who was planning a visit, to equip himself for the Arctic. But *The Sea Cook* alleviated things.

Gosse did visit, as did Colvin, and they too were listeners to the early chapters. There was also a visit from a man Louis had not met before, Alexander Japp, who had been in correspondence with him over his article on Thoreau. Japp arrived, at Louis's invitation, expecting to carry on an exchange of ideas on Thoreau, but found himself listening enthusiastically to Jim Hawkins' encounters with Pugh and Billy Bones and Long John Silver. Japp knew editors. It was his suggestion that the story should be tried with a boy's paper, and he undertook to show the manuscript to the proprietor of the *Young Folks' Magazine*, a man called Henderson. 'He carried in his pocket, not a horn or a talisman, but a publisher,' was the way Louis put it.[26] Japp took his leave with the first chapters of *The Sea Cook* in his luggage. Henderson liked the story, and undertook to serialise it in his paper, but he suggested a change of title. The change was certainly for the better.

Louis had run out of steam. After the first fifteen chapters the writing came to a halt. Perhaps if publication had not demanded its completion *Treasure Island* would have gone the same way as *The Vendetta in the West*, which he had begun and abandoned in California. It was time for Louis and Lloyd and Fanny to make the long trip back to Davos for another Alpine winter, and it was not easy to get back into the swing of the *Hispaniola* after the disruption of travel. Davos was in spirit a far greater distance from the Spanish Main than Braemar. But the sea and pirates were a natural subject for Louis. Since childhood he had lived with the sea, and sea adventure was in his blood. He had not forgotten his two forebears who had adventured and died in the West Indies, or the sea voyages he himself had made, the sound of the waves and the wind and the creaking ropes and the smells of salt and tar. Solitary inns, blind pirates and gold doubloons may have come out of his imagination and his childhood reading, but much of what he was writing arose directly out of real experience. There is a photograph of Louis Stevenson braced on a schooner's bowsprit. It captures something essential about his relationship to the sea.

An island suggests a perfect territory of the imagination, especially a distant, barely charted island. Isolated, hard to find, cut off, a world unto itself, it is the perfect territory to exclude, not necessarily reality, unless one chooses to, but any aspect of life that one does not want to intrude. An island was a place where child or adult could forget any part of the adult world that challenged or distorted fantasy. No man is an island, Louis might have said, but every man looks for one. And his Scotland was a country of islands, from the tiny island in the pond in Queen Street Gardens to the Bass Rock off North Berwick, to little stony loch islands, to the islands of the Hebrides and the treacherous rocks and shoals that his father studied and built on. Louis's experience of islands was extensive. He knew what it felt like to be surrounded by water.

It was not only the island that spelled magic to Japp. Like most people meeting Louis for the first time he was much taken with him, and described him in his velvet jacket and broad brimmed hat, the 'gentle radiance and animation' of his eyes, his nervous hands, and his incessant smoking. 'Faint suggestion of a hare-brained sentimental trace on his countenance, though controlled by Scotch sense and shrewdness,' he commented.[27] Japp much enjoyed the evenings of talk that followed dinner, dominated of course by Louis who made the most of his release from silent mornings in bed. It was clearly an enthusiasm for Stevenson as much as the *The Sea Cook* that led Japp to take the manuscript off with him in search of a publisher.

Louis was in good writing form, but he remained unwell right through the long damp stay in the Highlands. He was coughing badly, and most mornings was unable to move from his bed, where he was allowed to write but forbidden to speak. When Gosse visited they played silent games of chess together up in Louis's bedroom. Gosse remembered later 'those cold nights at Braemar, with the sleet howling outside, and Louis reading his budding romance by the lamp-light, emphasising the purpler passages with lifted voice and gesticulating finger.'[28]

The terrible Scottish summer, the coughing and the blood-spitting, did not deter Louis from thinking seriously about establishing an at least half permanent base in Scotland. The Chair of History and Constitutional Law at Edinburgh University was becoming vacant, and it seems to have been Thomas's idea that Louis should apply for it. Thomas was deeply anxious to retain Louis as close to him as possible. There was also a salary of £250 a year, and the only obligation was the delivery of some summer lectures. Louis could still spend the winters abroad, if necessary. Of course he had no chance of the post, but applied for it none the less, perhaps to please his father. He seems also to have thought rather cavalierly that he might do well at it. He canvassed for support, wrote around to friends and contacts for testimonials, but whatever pleasant things could be said about him no one could honestly point to any past achievement that suggested he could fill the Chair adequately. There was no surprise when he did not get it. But although the application was unrealistic it did reflect Louis's real and increasing interest in Scottish history. He had been thinking seriously of a book on the Highlands, beginning with the Jacobite failure of 1715. He probably would not have made a good historian. He was too attracted by the moments of vividness and intensity: it was with a novelist's eye that he looked at the drama of the past.

There remained a money problem, and a salary was tempting. The acceptance of the odd story or essay, even the serialisation of *Treasure Island*, was not going to bring in even a modest competency. *Virginibus Puerisque* was not a money-maker. The humiliating dependence on Thomas continued to be necessary, especially as Louis's survival required the payment for travel and hotels and medical treatment. He was acutely aware that he was extremely lucky in having the kind of freedom that lack of immediate financial worry allowed him, but he never thought of himself as an 'ivory tower' artist who needed to be protected from life's realities and did not need to concern himself with what people really wanted to read and would not be prepared to pay for. He frankly wanted to make money out of what he wrote. He did not want to compromise his art, which some thought he was doing with *Treasure Island*, but he had come a long way from those early days of scrupulous imitation. What were books without readers? For Louis *Treasure Island* eventually, though not at once for it was not very successful as a serial in *Young Folks*, became the first intimation that he could write what he wanted to write, and be read, and receive the approval of the literary opinion that he respected.

At first, though, his adventure story looked less promising. The judges in London were shaking their heads at publication in a paper like *Young Folks*. It began to look as if their pure and promising young man was prostituting himself. Hearing about this Louis wrote furiously to Henley:

To those who ask me . . . to do nothing but refined, high-toned, bejay-bedamn masterpieces, I will offer the following bargain: I agree to their proposal if they give me £1000, at which I value *mon possible*, and at the same time effect such a change in my nature that I shall be content to take it from them instead of earning it. If they cannot manage these trifling matters, by God, I'll trouble them to hold their tongues, by God . . . Let them write their damn masterpieces for themselves. . . .[29]

He must have been remembering Leslie Stephen's letter.

In September, Louis and Fanny, with Lloyd, left Scotland to make their way back to Davos. There was another pause in London, and a pause also in Weybridge, during which Louis spent some time with George Meredith, whom he had met some years earlier. He had great admiration for Meredith, who had had far from a smooth career as a writer, and Meredith, who was generous in his attitudes towards younger writers, thought highly of Louis, so highly, in fact, that he based the real hero of *The Amazing Marriage* on him, the unorthodox and independent Gower Woodseer. Louis embraced Meredith's influence on his own writing rather over-enthusiastically: the results were not to be happy. But the older writer was important to him, not only for what he had written but for what he was, a writer who had gone his own way and survived lack of popularity.

In Weybridge, Louis was able to add a few more chapters to *The Sea Cook*, but it was hard going. It was only after they were back in Davos and well settled, this time in the chalet and therefore able to order their own lives, that with considerable effort Louis was able to write himself back into the original enthusiasm for the story. By the time it was finished serialisation had already begun. It was a familiar situation for the Victorian novelist. Louis received £100 for it.

It was in more than one respect a breakthrough for Louis to have written an adventure story with a juvenile audience in mind. It was his first full-length piece of fiction. It was the first time he had finished something in the vein that he relished all his life, at the same time writing as an adult – and the style makes us very conscious of this. But most of all it was a breakthrough for him in terms of reputation. It did not make his fortune, but it established Stevenson as a writer who was able to produce a kind of story for which there was a hungry readership, a hungry readership of adults who had seen the Victorian age eat away at fantasy, at dreams, at romance, at heroics, and longed for a legitimate adventure fiction. Stevenson was lucky; not lucky that his talent should be recognised, for it was manifest and accessible, but lucky that his talent should coincide so creatively with a need of the time.

Treasure Island has lasted as a children's adventure story. It rests uneasily in that genre. It has always been a story that adults have relished perhaps more than children, in fact it may be adult favour that has kept it so very much alive. Stevenson was more concerned with writing out of his system certain elemental fantasies than in deliberately putting together a story that would appeal to boys, and it tends to be this aspect that attracts critical attention. A neutral, unformed hero (a borrowing from Scott) enters an anarchic world, uncovers but scarcely discovers some vivid truths about human nature, and returns none the worse but none the better either to normality. If the story is read by children sometimes with impatience it may be because the hero, the character with whom they are asked to identify, has so little personality. Jim Hawkins does not seem to be of any great importance. The memorable characters are those surrounded by moral ambiguity, Billy Bones and Long John Silver, and the characters in whom greed and deceit, fear and violence are an integral part of their substance. There is no doubt that Long John Silver, based with his loud flourishes and one-leggedness on Henley, is the hero of the book. Jim Hawkins slides out of the memory. Stevenson was to do much better with a 'neutral' character when he created David Balfour. Significantly, poor Jim fades through a superabundance of equivocal father figures. Did Thomas see himself as one of the adventurers on treasure island?

With a book on the boil Davos was more tolerable. The second winter had compensations which the first had lacked. Louis and Fanny took up residence in the Chalet am Stein, and set up house with a cook and other domestic necessities. But although things went better Louis was seriously ill again in November. Symonds found him 'lying, ghastly, in bed – purple cheek-bones, yellow cheeks, bloodless lips – fever all over him –

without appetite – and all about him so utterly forlorn'.[30] And
Fanny was ill also. Early in December she had to leave Davos to
seek treatment. She went to Zürich and Berne, and gallstone
was diagnosed. Davos, however beneficial it really was to Louis's
health, was a strain on both of them, and even their own chalet
could not protect them from the depression of the place, the fact
that they were surrounded by the sick and the dying. Mortality
was brought oppressively home when Mrs Sitwell had arrived in
the previous spring with her son Bertie, dying of consumption.
Fanny and Louis both watched the temporary rallying and then
the increasingly pitiful state of Bertie with deep distress. That it
should be the son of the woman Louis had once been so in love
with and a boy whose company he had so often enjoyed, who
was so closely associated in his memory with the summer days at
Cockfield Rectory, affected Louis intensely, although after his
death he was able to write a poem of consolation for Mrs Sitwell.
He was perhaps trying to console himself as much as her,
pointing out the compensations of dying young, at the peak of
expectation, before disappointment could cloud one's life.

Woodcut from The Bookman, *1913*

Louis worked at a number of essays, and also on *Prince Otto*, a strange and uneasy novel which candidly acknowledges the influence of Meredith but, unlike Meredith, strays rather too whimsically far from reality. He had his periods of depression, but there were few to whom he would admit this. To Baxter he always wrote frankly, though his moods were often submerged in gloriously extravagant epistolary impersonations of the two characters he and Baxter had invented, Johnson and Thomson, whose invented doings irrupted from time to time into the pages of Louis's letters.

> Ae thing, onyway: I dinnae ken muckle o' only comi*tee*, and I ken naething o' yours by ordinar, but my fegs, they arena gentlemen. A gentleman, to my thinkin' o't, 's a guid, plain, straucht, fine, canny, honest body, aye ready for a dram an' to be jolly wi' a freen; but the Lard safe us frae your Edinburry gentry wi' their gestcrin ways an markit sixpences. I've kennt mony a leery – aye and ne'er saw'm sober forbye – 'at wad hae skunnered at the thocht. But man, Tamson, that's life. I'll drink your bonny guid health, sir, an' wishin ye weel ower a' this bit clavers – it'll shune blaw by: I've had the like mysel – I'll jist awa to ma bed.[31]

But he could not always rise to the heights of Thomson and Johnson, and there were times when he gave way to delicious nostalgia for the old dyas.

> Ah! what would I not give to steal this evening with you through the big, echoing, college archway, and away south under the street lamps, and away to dear Brash's, now defunct! But the old time is dead also, never, never to revive. It was a sad time too, but so gay and so hopeful and we had such sport with all our low spirits and all our distresses, that it looks like a kind of lamplit fairyland behind me. O for ten Edinburgh minutes – sixpence between us, and the ever-glorious Lothian Road, or dear mysterious Leith Walk![32]

Later that month there was a dramatic, arduous and freezing sleigh ride, bringing Fanny back up the mountain, which was almost unbearable. Fanny and Lloyd were wretched in their discomfort. Louis kept his spirits up by singing, but when Lloyd remarked that he was the only one with any courage left he became quite incapable of maintaining the pretence. The cold, the isolation, Fanny's health and the dreadful monotony of the snow brought a longing for escape.

In the spring permission was granted not only to escape for the summer but to try the effect of the South of France. So April again found them making their way to Scotland, where the parental magnet still drew them. There followed another summer with the elder Stevensons, in Peebleshire and Inverness-shire this time, from June to August, and then again in the autumn the retreat southwards. Fanny stayed behind at first while Louis and Bob travelled together to Marseilles on the hunt for somewhere to take up quarters. Fanny joined Louis there, and they found what at first seemed a delightful cottage at St Marcel, just outside Marseilles.

It was the autumn of 1882. There was no reason to believe that Louis's love for France had changed at all; travelling with Bob he must have been full of thoughts of past adventures, with and without Fanny. Things were different now, and his life was no longer dominated by the tension between his independence and his parents' expectations, though it was still there. Life was, indeed, much more complicated than that. But in spite of the health problems of both Louis and Fanny, in spite of Fanny's desire to be settled, her longing for somewhere of her own to shape and look after which was growing stronger, in spite of Louis's continued difficulties in coping with the tug of loyalties, life was looking promising. The writing had been going well. He was widening his scope all the time, and in the process discovering things about his capability. In the congenial atmosphere of the South of France he and Fanny settled comfortably in a pleasant cottage, near enough to England for visits from friends to be a welcome possibility, with expectations of a fruitful existence. But Bluidy Jack and other unwelcome visitants were not far away.

Chapter 8

HADDEN DOON BY THE BUBBLYJOCK

Here's a bit checky, chuckie. It micht hae been mair; and it's His
Mercy its nae less. Hoots. Write to a buddy. Sair, sair hadden
doon by the Bubblyjock, and that's wark.

Letter to Charles Baxter

On his way south, with Bob and without Fanny, Louis had been
badly ill again. Bleeding and exhausted he made an enforced
stay at Montpellier. As he often did when he was physically in a
bad way he became depressed. He missed Fanny, yet hated her
to see him ill, and he must have said so, for he was having to
reassure her in a letter that he didn't really mean he did not want
her with him, only that, 'I don't want you when I'm ill – at least,
it's only one half of me that wants you, and I don't like to think
of you coming back and not finding me better than when we
parted'.[1] He reproved himself for not having more courage –
marriage had made him soft, he felt. 'I have neither pluck nor
patience and I must own I have wearied awful for you. But you
will never understand that bit of my character.' But it was
perhaps the side of his character she understood best, his at
times helpless need of her. It was certainly something she had to
respond to over and over again.

His self-pity deepened. 'I do not ask you to love me anymore.
I am too much trouble. . . . You cannot put up with such a
man.'[2] It was not a promising start for their trial of a new
environment for his health. But soon he was more cheerful, or
making efforts to be cheerful, and inditing comic verse
accompanied by comic sketches.

> Where is my wife? Where is my Wogg?
> I am alone and life's a bog.

He drew a very fat woman and a very thin man running to
embrace each other, and added,

The fat and lean
Shall then convene.[3]

The attractive and affectionate silliness that was an important part of Fanny's and Louis's relationship tells us a lot: Fanny's sense of humour was one of the things Louis most loved. To survive with Louis it was a necessity.

When Fanny joined him all seemed well. The house was found, comfortable and attractive. There was much work to be done, but a balmy climate, the sun and the sea air, and a pleasant home would make that possible. Campagne Defli, St Marcel, was a place they could make their own, a home for Fanny to preside over, for both to share and enjoy, released from the pressures of family and stressful acquaintances. But it wasn't long before certain doubts arose, the least important of them immortalised in verse by Louis's alias Thomson.

> Campagne De – fli:
>   O me!
> Campagne De – bug:
>   There comes the tug!
> Compagne De – mosquito:
>   It's eneuch to gar me greet, O!
> Campagne De – louse:
>   O God damn the house![4]

The insect life was not the only sign of disquiet. Louis's letters were full of enthusiasm for the house and its surroundings, and it was possible to joke about the mosquitoes, yet for some reason he did not seem able to apply himself as he had visualised.

Louis found he had no strength. The haemorrhages recurred, and fever accompanied them. He had no energy. He made some attempt at work, but was able to do very little. He was trying a French story again, 'The Treasure of Franchard', very much based on his knowledge of Fontainebleau. Even the pastimes of the sick had to be handled with care. A month of Campagne Defli found him writing to his mother, trying to be cheerful. Fanny wasn't well, and he had to make a great effort to disguise his depression. It was scarcely successful.

I do not go back, but do not go forward – or not much. It is, in one way, miserable – for I can do no work; a very little wood-cutting, the newspapers, and a note about every two days to write, completely exhausts my surplus energy; even Patience I have to cultivate with parsimony. I see, if I could only get to work, that we could live here with comfort, almost with luxury. Even as it is, we should be able to get through a considerable time of idleness. I like the place immensely, though I have seen so little of it – I have only once been outside the gate since I was here! It puts me in mind of a summer at Prestonpans and a sickly child you once told me of.[5]

Things dragged on for another month, though neither Fanny nor Louis was happy about the situation. They began to feel that something must be badly wrong with the place. When a fever epidemic broke out in the area Fanny, over-anxious as always about possible contagion, was convinced it was typhus. In something of a panic she despatched Louis to Nice while she stayed herself in Campagne Defli to pack up. When after several days she had heard nothing from Louis, who should by that time have been comfortably installed in a Nice hotel, she set off after him in some desperation. Enquiring after him at stations along the way she was assured by railway officials and police that Louis had probably died and the body hastily disposed of, with a suspicion of a corpse that had come from a fever area. In growing hysteria Fanny made her way onwards to Nice where she found Louis perfectly safe and calm: a strayed letter explained the lack of contact. In writing about the experience to friends Fanny probably over-dramatised – she always enjoyed dramatic recountings of her experiences – but she had clearly had an acutely distressing time. She had had to face the prospect of Louis's death many times, but to have him die without her, on a train, and buried anonymously, had been beyond her imaginings. Coming as it did at the end of two months of Louis's constant illness, which was depressing enough, the incident must have seemed that much worse.

They were not going to return to Campagne Defli, but this put them in the unsettled position of again living in hotels looking for a suitable home. It took them some time to find, and it was March before they were able to move into a cottage in the little inland town of Hyères. The cottage had an individuality that appealed to Fanny and Louis, although it was without the spaciousness of style of Campagne Defli. It was an imitation Swiss chalet, built on a small scale as an exhibit in the Paris Exhibition, the same that Louis had attended as Fleeming Jenkin's secretary while he and Fanny were at the height of their affair. The situation was pleasant and the view lovely. After their abortive start at St Marcel things began to look promising again. Much rested on what they could make of La Solitude, Hyères.

Early in March, Louis had been able to announce to his mother that he was 'off the sick list'.[6] He had put on weight and was feeling stronger. Settled once again he felt fit for work. *A Child's Garden* was almost ready for the press: he had gradually been putting the poems together for some time under the original title of *Penny Whistles*. It was a book he cared a great deal about; the form had to be right. He was finishing *The Silverado Squatters*, which had lingered on for a considerable time, working still on *Prince Otto*, and had started *The Black Arrow*. There were stories on the go too. The previous summer his first collection, *New Arabian Nights*, had been published. Most of the stories in it represented dead ends for Louis, although he was fond of it himself and the book has always had its devotees. But the whimsical convolutions of 'The Suicide Club' and 'The Rajah's Diamond' were in a vein that Louis was, fortunately, to abandon, for although it produced the memorable young man with the cream tarts, and the delightful logic of his enterprise, the stories rest uneasily in a limbo between fantasy and psychological realism. They had been mostly written for Henley's *London* in the summer of 1878; it is possible that the excitement of providing copy and the knowledge of Fanny's imminent departure had gone to his head. They owed much to Bob, who fed him with extravagant ideas. The second part of the volume, in the initial publication the second volume, included three French stories and the 'Pavilion on the Links', a bare, intense little drama, nothing like as good as 'The Merry Men' but with the same flavour. He employed a similar central character, akin to David Balfour too, alone, without family, detached from his background.

As always Louis was anxious about money, one of the reasons that he embarked on *The Black Arrow*, destined for *Young Folks*, but in April was writing happily to Mrs Sitwell, if somewhat ruefully expressing his preoccupation with cash.

I am going to make a fortune, it has not yet begun, for I am not yet clear of debt; but as soon as I can, I begin upon the fortune. I shall begin it with a halfpenny, and it shall end with horses and yachts and all the fun of the fair. This is the first real grey hair in my character: rapacity has begun to show, the greed of the protuberant guttler. Well, doubtless, when the hour strikes, we must all guttle and protrube. But it comes hard on one who was always so willow-slender and as careless as the daisies.[7]

If he was able to work, and work was going well, Louis was liable to be in good spirits. An offer for the book publication of *Treasure Island*, a modest £100, made him jubilant. During the sixteen months he spent at La Solitude, Louis accomplished a quantity of writing, and if he complained about the pressure of work it was usually with some confidence that he could cope. For a writer it was always better to have too much work on hand than too little.

Some years later Louis was to confide to an American friend that his time at Hyères had been the happiest of his life. For a great deal of the time he and Fanny were alone together, for the first time since their marriage, although Fanny was often not well and he had some of his most extreme bouts of illness. Lloyd was away at school, and they were the right distance from friends – visits were possible but not too frequent. La Solitude, both the house and the state, was good for them. Their first two years of marriage had been harassed by family and friends and acquaintances, but in France there were periods of respite. The period between houses had been discouraging, with Fanny ill and Louis beginning to feel that their hopes of finding a viable home in France were unrealistic. All they wanted was somewhere where he and Fanny could 'feel like people'[8] – and La Solitude really seemed the place.

But Louis's attacks were frightening, worse than anything that had gone before, and the price they had to pay for being on their own was that Fanny had to bear the brunt of the nursing. Louis was not always an easy patient. Although to others he may have seemed so often the courageous and cheerful sufferer, urging others to bear their pain optimistically, this was not the Louis that Fanny always experienced. Illness was for Louis frustrating and depressing. He needed to work, for money, and for his own peace of mind. Enforced idleness was scarcely tolerable. He hated to feel dependent on Fanny, and there were times when he felt he was ruining her life. His letters from Montpellier show how unhappy he was at being a burden on her, and yet how badly he needed her. As a child Louis had received the devoted and total attention of his nurse. When he was in a high fever and spitting blood and wretched there must have been times when he wanted Fanny to be Cummy, to bury her personality in his helplessness. Fanny's touchy, individualist personality resisted this, although she nursed Louis with care and tenderness. Louis had been in many ways protected all his life by people who were prepared to handle gently his volatile egocentricity. There were times when Fanny could not do this, and times when Louis was less than sensitive towards her needs. The fact that she was so often ill suggests an uncontrollable psychosomatic reaction to the demands that were made on her, although there was clearly a physical basis for her ill-health too. Her heart and stomach both gave her a lot of trouble; but she lived for twenty years after her husband's death. In principle Louis would never have asked a woman that she suppress herself for his sake. In practice it almost had to happen, although in so many ways Louis tried hard not to allow it. His encouragement of Fanny's not very talented writing was a part of this effort. A situation that was virtually built into the institution of marriage was exaggerated by Louis's special gifts and special needs.

In January of the following year, 1884, Louis and Fanny were in Nice when he became seriously ill again, and Fanny had a frantic time trying to cope alone. There was not only the anxiety and the mental strain, but the physical demands nursing Louis made on her. She had to be ready at any hour of the day or night to give Louis the ergotine that helped to control a haemorrhage. The blood suddenly filling his mouth, making him speechless, spilling on to his clothes, always looking much more than it really was, could be terrifying. There were complications this time with doctors and anxious parents writing to insist on a second opinion and misunderstandings which burdened Fanny further. Later that year a sudden rush of blood convinced Fanny that Louis had burst a blood vessel – 'the blood spurted all over everything in a moment, he was almost strangled with it – and she was quite sure he was dying.[9] Her frantic letters to Henley and Colvin were not sympathetically received: they were sure she was crying wolf, and with some irritation commented on her panic. But she badly wanted male assistance and asked that Bob should come out at once. She had to lift Louis herself, and sometimes to carry him when he needed to relieve himself, for he refused to use 'any of the invalids' appliances'.[10] He was often light-headed, truculent and very fussy about what he ate. Fanny tried every way to tempt his appetite, but what she produced was often spurned. Louis's temper was not improved by the fact that he hated to be so helpless. His impatience with his situation could so easily become impatience with Fanny. The demands that he made on her, much of which he was probably scarcely aware of, were heavy.

For the next five years, until he reached southern Pacific waters, Louis was liable to sudden illness at any time. Nowhere, neither in France nor the south of England, was he free from the likelihood of haemorrhage, fever and debilitation. Yet during those five years he was writing steadily, making some money and inching towards a substantial reputation. He wrote in bed. He wrote sometimes when he was forbidden to talk. He wrote with meticulous care and corrected proofs with meticulous attention. He wrote often when the physical and mental labour of carrying on was extreme. Fanny and some particular friendships kept his spirits up, but he often thought he was going to die, and developed a way of coping with the knowledge. He had of course lived with this particular reality for a long time. He had a childhood acquaintance with death, as so many Victorian children were bound to do. The heightened sense of mortality that his youthful illnesses brought about sharpened his visions of sin and damnation, and underlined the terrors of the night. As a young man he could be cavalier. There was something rather dashing about knowing that he was likely to die young. If he could burn with a brief, vivid flame like Fergusson life might well have been worth it, though when he had reached the age at which Fergusson died, twenty-four, he had scarcely begun. Now he had been overtaken by the immediate concerns that marriage had brought: responsibilities, and a commitment outside himself. It would be more to the point to forget about the bright, vivid flame and aim for a steady glow that would last and put forth real heat.

The importance of survival was underlined by the news, in September 1883, of the death of his old friend Walter Ferrier. Ferrier, perhaps, had been a more natural inheritor of Fergusson than Louis, although he never achieved much. He, too, was a lung sufferer, although it was drink that finished him rather than tuberculosis. Louis had always admired him, ever since Ferrier had asked him to join in the venture to produce a new college magazine all those years before. He had always been convinced that Ferrier would do something splendid, but there was little concrete sign of it. He was yet another son of middle-class achievement, another 'superfluous man' of the last quarter of the century, promising, charming, clever, and directionless. He had translated Heine, and Louis had urged him to publish, but he never did. Ferrier's energies seemed to be dissipated in some intangible way, yet Louis was sure that nothing of his life had been wasted, for his very presence had been beneficent. He was a gentle, courteous, patient man, without self-conceit, generous and encouraging towards others, handsome. A valued friend was lost, a pulsing strand of Louis's own life was broken. And he might well have felt grateful that he himself had avoided superfluity.

> . . . to think that he was young with me, sharing that weather-beaten, Fergussonian youth, looking forward through the clouds to the sunburst; and now clean gone from my path, silent – well, well. This has been a strange awakening. Last night, when I was alone in the house, with the window open on the lovely still night, I could have sworn he was in the room with me; I could show you the spot; and, what was very curious, I heard his rich laughter, a thing I had not called to mind for I know not how long.[11]

Part of the pain of Ferrier's death was Louis's awareness that few had acknowledged his real qualities, as his dissipation and apparent irresponsibility were so evident. It was to Henley that Louis poured out his feelings – 'If anything looked liker irony than this fitting of a man out with these rich qualities and faculties to be wrecked and aborted from the very stocks, I do not know the name of it,' he continued in his letter. He was deeply shaken. When he wrote to Walter's sister, Coggie Ferrier, who was to become a close friend herself, he 'could not see for crying'.[12] And there may have been a touch of guilt there too, for his closeness to Walter had laid him open to accusations of encouraging his weaknesses – and perhaps he had.

Certainly Walter's mother, the daughter of Christopher North, the pseudonym of John Wilson, that appealingly eccentric Edinburgh literary figure, thought so. Earlier that year she had written in furious distress, accusing Louis of, at best, collusion in her son's downward career. Her son had become degraded, hypocritical, self-indulgent. Everything had been done to 'save him from destruction and all to no purpose and he now exists among the number of those degraded ones whose society on earth is shunned by the moral and the virtuous among Mankind'.[13] Louis, the implication was, was also one of those degraded ones. Mrs Ferrier's hysteria was understandable. Her son was sick, an alcoholic, possibly addicted to opium too (he had certainly used it), but such recrimination could do Walter no good, nor Louis. And there was little Louis could have done, especially then. Her daughter, who shared her brother's gentleness and generosity, clearly bore no grudge against Louis; she became a much loved friend to both Louis and Fanny.

Louis accepted that Walter had long since reached the point where his life was useless. He was better dead, for his own sake and for the sake of his family and friends. But he was acutely conscious that what he called 'the tradewinds of death' had begun to whistle near him, and accustomed though he was to the nearness of death his reflections were sombre.[14] He wrote to his friend Will Low, the American painter, that he was preoccupied with 'new thoughts of death. Up to now I had rather thought of him as a mere personal enemy of my own; but now that I see him hunting after my friends, he looks altogether darker.'[15] He was worried about his father, who was not only unwell but in a more than usually gloomy state of mind, and about Henley, whose health had deteriorated. The prospect of losing more of his friends was agonising, especially as he had always assumed that it would be his friends that would lose him. And that, of course, was the way it turned out for most of them.

Death, the pressure of work, money, his own ill-health, and Fanny: these were the realities. In these months at Hyères he was trying to maintain a commanding vision of all of them. Illness rose up like a dragon in his path over and over again. The dragon was slain and the knight passed on his way. The goal was a double one: success and real achievement in his writing, and closely related to both, the articulation of a genuine, unhackneyed, unrestrictive, and above all positive, morality. Somewhere, Stevenson always hoped, was a Holy Grail that represented a true fusion of art and morality. In the meantime he wrestled with the problem like his own Bogue, still with them, with a bone. There were times when he flourished his ideas joyously, like Alan Breck his sword in *Kidnapped* – 'Am I no a bonny fighter?', but often he was airing them more cautiously, tentatively, enquiringly. His friendship with Henry James, yet to come, would help him on his way.

The work in hand gave him some opportunity for both the flourishes and the caution. *The Silverado Squatters*, which he had laboured at most in Switzerland, he was not happy about and made many revisions in proof. *Otto* he was not too sure of, and rightly so. It is an uneasy piece of fiction, at times intimately related to Prince Florizel and the cream tarts, but without the keen irony and fine vision that kept his mentor in this case, George Meredith, on the direct route. The morality of the story, which Louis himself considered to be at its heart, is lost in a dense whimsicality which fails to capture an authentic atmosphere, either imaginary or real. There are passages of sparkling prose, and the novel still has its attractions, but somewhere in the process the attempt to bring together the fantastical and the everyday, setting real personalities down in a 'scenery of dreams' (he used the phrase in his dedication of *Kidnapped* to Charles Baxter – he valued greatly the scenery of dreams), he loses his way. It was not the right form for him. It was probably just as well that he was distracted from further experiments of this kind by the pressing need to make money, which resulted in *The Black Arrow*.

The Black Arrow was a frank attempt to write for a younger audience, but initially had considerably more popularity than its predecessor. At first sight it might have looked as if it had less ambiguity than *Treasure Island*. Louis dismissed the enterprise as

Chalet La Solitude, Hyères, from The Bookman, *April 1912*

nothing more than 'tushery', as he cheerfully called it, but there was pleasure in the writing of it, and he went to some trouble to explore the background and character of his story. His interest in the character of Richard Crookback was lively, as was his continual interest in the confusions and moral dilemmas of history. In the characters and events of the past, in the workings of personality and conviction, cause and effect, there ought to have been some answers – that was the attraction of history for Louis as a novelist. However, he was not looking for historical answers, like Scott, but moral answers. Stevenson did not have the right kind of imagination to seek for historical answers, although he nearly triumphs in *Kidnapped*, and his great mistake was to think that moral answers could be sought in the past without the aid of an historical imagination.

The young hero of *The Black Arrow* is a courageous lad, but he is also a pawn and a victim, and the insistent message of the story, which seems to emerge in spite of all Stevenson's best efforts at tushery, is about moral ambiguity. The action and the suspense, the alarms and excursions, cannot disguise the fact that in a situation of civil war (and this applies equally to the Jacobite Rebellion, the Covenanting wars, the contentions between Free and Established Church in Scotland, as well as to the Wars of the Roses, the issue of *The Black Arrow*), uneasy alliances, uncertain allegiance, battle itself, prevent any kind of black-and-white interpretation. In *The Black Arrow* the problem is not that the morally dubious characters have their own kind of powerful attraction, like Long John Silver, but that it is hard to find any individual or any situation that is not morally dubious. It is possibly this that caused Stevenson difficulties in the telling of the tale, for having with some care explored a situation full of interest and intrinsic excitement, and utilising an attractive emblem – the numbered arrows – he does not ultimately know what to do with them. A love story extricates young Dick from his historical predicament. Scott does this all the time, of course, but in his novels the historical predicaments have their own rich life, which in Stevenson they do not. *The Black Arrow* has some splendid moments, but if by 'tushery' Louis was indicating a lack of historical imagination, he was quite right.

In *Kidnapped*, and it is perhaps the only novel in which he achieves this, he makes something incisively positive out of the dilemma of history and the individual, although in *Catriona*, the sequel, he removes the same hero, David Balfour, from history, because he knows of no other means of resolution. With *The Black Arrow* complete, and published serially in the summer and autumn of 1883, Louis began work on *Kidnapped*. He was on good ground, and he knew it. He chose an intriguing moment, five years after the Jacobite defeat at Culloden, which gave him both a specific time and situation, anchored firmly by his incorporation of the Appin murder, and great scope for action. Some critics consider *Kidnapped* is the nearest Stevenson got to Scott, almost suggesting that because it is good and historical and Scottish it must be like Scott, or should be like Scott. But this is to misconceive both novelists. Scott's novels burgeon out of his historical situations; character, action, circumstance have their common nourishment in time and place. Stevenson deftly – and *Kidnapped* is as deft as anything he wrote – weaves real characters and historical fact into his narrative. The narrative comes first. It is quite a different process, and a comparison is barely productive, especially if it begins with the assumption

that Scott was the master against whom Stevenson was meas-
uring himself. Of course he could not but be aware of Scott's
achievements, but probably he knew that he wasn't trying to do
what Scott did. In *Kidnapped* Stevenson produced something
like a fable, and in essence and shape it is in fact a long short
story, the form that there is little doubt was Stevenson's best.
There were times when he clearly felt he should try to master the
multi-charactered novel spread over a large canvas, like Hugo,
or Balzac, or Scott himself. But it was a mistaken urge, and he
never followed it up. His nature and his art leaned distinctly
towards fable.

The focus and perspective of the story, from its beginning
with the schoolmaster's son leaving the parish with the
minister's advice in his ears to its end with the same youth
heading for the British Linen Bank, is beautifully balanced and
sustained. David Balfour is a character of no great depth or
intrinsic interest, but the faint irony that is both a part of his view
of himself and the world, and of the author's view of him, is
delicately controlled. The success of the work largely rests on
this very delicate thread, which Stevenson preserves intact
throughout. We can simultaneously laugh and admire, share
the suspense and keep our distance, applaud and disapprove.
David's adventures lead him into encounter after encounter
with morally dubious characters, the dubiety both underlined
and confused by the sectarianism, but throughout he preserves
what might be called his rational innocence. He is not surprised
by what he finds, nor does it lead him to change his view of the
world. The young man who is making his way towards the
British Linen Bank at the end of the novel is the same young man
whose life up to the moment he left home had never led him to
question the world. David's adventure is quite properly
bracketed by the minister and the bank: they provide an
appropriate perspective. Yet if David is innocent, his rationality
means he can interpret what he sees. He does not lose his
innocence, but he has no illusions. He can outwit his uncle, he
can highlight the flaws in Alan Breck, he doesn't fall for the
romance of heroism, as Scott's Waverley does. He is a very
literal young man, and in this case we can see literal as the
opposite of romantic.

In the nature of things David Balfour would have survived

neither the plot nor the needs of the imagination without some help, and the help to both is provided by Alan Breck Stewart. It is almost too easy to see David Balfour and Alan Breck as the two irreconcilables of Louis's own character, the Stevenson character, the Scottish character, the 'war in the members' again. Alan is the self-dramatisation of romantic commitment, of individual courage – the egotism and self-display that is both entertaining and shocking.

> He came to me with open arms. 'Come to my arms!' he cried, and embraced and kissed me hard upon both cheeks. 'David,' said he, 'I love you like a brother. And oh, man,' he cried in a kind of ecstasy, 'am I no a bonny fighter?'[16]

This is Alan's triumph over three dead and one dying after the fight in the round-house. The extraordinary achievement of *Kidnapped* is the way in which a lack of judgment on either David or Alan is maintained. Alan Breck, outrageously cavalier, David Balfour, dourly rational, both ill-equipped to deal with some of the situations they find themselves in, are both seen as psychological facts, to be neither praised nor condemned. They both have their admirable qualities and their failings, their courage and their pride, their rashness and their canniness. They reveal something of great significance about Stevenson's moral drive. That his whole nature inclined towards the moralist there can be little doubt; but an intrinsic part of his morality was restraint. Not restraint from the pleasures of the flesh, not self-control in that sense, for its own sake, but restraint from damaging human nature, which he felt to be at least potentially creative and rich, and restraint from condemnation. In Stevenson's catechism to distort human nature and to condemn are the cardinal sins. To place any human being beyond the reach of fulfilment and salvation, which was precisely what Calvinism did, was intolerable and destructive. He tried to say this over and over again. At the same time there was a problem of evil to be dealt with, and although he confronts ambivalence he sidesteps that one in *Kidnapped*. Later, though, he was to come back to it uncompromisingly.

The bonny fighter and the rational innocent share experience and confront each other. Inevitably they quarrel, and the quarrel between Alan and David is one of the best moments in the book. As they exaggerate their differences they become most like each other. It may seem too neat to say that this kind of confrontation was happening all the time in Louis's life, but it is none the less apt. He was a fighter, and he longed to be more of one. He loved what he had created in Alan Breck. But he was close at David's side when he walked down the High Street to claim his inheritance. It wasn't so much a division between heart and mind, which in some respects operated in Scott's case, as sometimes a rather painful inclination of both to yearn in different directions. He wanted life to be an opera, yet realised the impracticalities of buying cigars in recitative.

The yearning operated graphically during this period in his life. In *Kidnapped* it was splendidly productive. The control, the delicate spareness of the narrative, the affectionate irony, these were valuable qualities, the best of Stevenson's middle phase of writing. They emerged from a period when the pressure to work was great, when Bluidy Jack was a frequent visitant, when the money problems were intensified by the fact that Thomas's failing health was exacerbated by business difficulties, which Thomas was at times fearful would be financially damaging. It is clear that there were times when Louis lost his grip. Although he had both courage and patience there were times when both evaded him. There were times when he was so ill that he had no control over his body, and scarcely over his mind. In July 1884 he and Fanny were in Royat, where they were to meet the older Stevensons. It was a health resort which it was felt could benefit both father and son. But haemorrhage, sciatica and ophthalmia struck. For a time Louis was both blind and speechless – whenever there was a serious risk of haemorrhage he was forbidden to speak. The myth that grew even as he lay in his sickbed was that Louis was never downhearted and always bravely faced the realities of his ill-health. Of course this was often true, but the qualities have that much more value when it is remembered that there were also times when he was truculent and depressed, and that if he was able to give a different impression this was often the result of a supreme effort. It did not necessarily come naturally. It was very important for Louis to avoid admitting defeat, to avoid saying that death would be preferable to the long periods of half-life. Except in occasional youthful outbursts, and later in one or two moments of intense personal pain, Louis, although he often assumed that he would die soon, never wished himself dead, nor deliberately invited an exit from life, as his friend Walter Ferrier had done. On paper, at least for publication, his message was: fight, whatever the adversities.

That summer of 1884, Louis could not pretend that he wasn't wretched. He was writing to Colvin, 'My life dwindles into a kind of valley of the shadow picnic.'[17] Even when he was able to see, there was not much joy to be derived from watching Fanny playing patience, which was all he was allowed to do. 'I am very dim, dowie, and damnable,' he continued to Colvin. 'I hate to be silenced; and if to talk by signs is my forte (as I contend), to understand them cannot be my wife's. Do not think me unhappy; I have not been so for years; but I am blurred, inhabit the debatable frontier of sleep, and have but dim designs upon activity.' For some time Louis was scarcely mobile, and remained a 'somnolent, superannuated son of a bedpost'.[18] It was always a good sign that he could maintain his sense of humour, but the effort can be sensed.

Fanny was now in her mid-forties. She too had times when she lost her grip and when panic overtook her, and not always on account of Louis's illnesses. In France she lacked close and supportive friends, although she and Louis benefited greatly from the loyal and devoted services of a French Swiss girl Valentine Roch, whom they had hired to help in the house. Fanny had often not got on with servants. She had never been accustomed to people working for her and possibly her difficulties with servants were due to her trying to behave as if she were. But Valentine was with them for six years, and was one of the few people who could be relied on to cope with Louis in his emergencies. She caused some talk when, in Fanny's absences, she slept in Louis's room to be on hand if the bleeding started. It was a measure of Fanny's faith in her that she sanctioned this: her over-sensitive nature was prone to jealousy which was later to reach distressing depths.

La Solitude gave Fanny an opportunity to preside over her own household. Although she had a reputation as an uncaring housewife, and several people comment on her domestic incompetence, she clearly enjoyed arranging her domestic environment and seems to have been rather good at it. She prided herself on her good taste, chose furnishings and decoration with some care. At La Solitude she experimented with the oriental styles then becoming popular with those of sophisticated taste. Her domestic incompetence was probably not the result of lack of interest in where and how she lived – the evidence suggests that she was keenly interested – but of sheer boredom with the more tedious chores of the domestic round. That kind of attitude was scarcely encouraged at the time, for even in the latter part of the century the ability to run a household efficiently was considered a priority amongst feminine qualities. Louis of course did not share such views. He himself could survive, and work, quite cheerfully amidst his own, and Fanny's, untidiness, and he seems to have cared little for his physical surroundings, except for valuing some pictures and books. As Edmund Gosse commented, Louis was that rare creature an a-materialist in an acquisitive society. As a younger man he had prided himself in his lack of concern for possessions, travelling light, and throwing away his shirts when they got too dirty to wear. Sheer improvidence for some, but for Louis a gesture of the low rating he gave personal possessions. His ability to work in all kinds of unpromising situations, on trains, on shipboard, in transitory rooms and camping places, was a part of the same outlook. If he had been meticulously demanding about his working environment he would never have been a writer.

Fanny also took pleasure in gardening, and she enjoyed being able to grow a few vegetables at La Solitude. Her experience was to be invaluable later on. But caring for Louis, arranging her home and tending her garden were not enough to satisfy her restless abilities. She did not keep up with her drawing and painting in any serious way. She had probably never been fully committed. Initially art must have meant for her an escape rather than a commitment. But she began to think of trying her hand at writing. Fanny's situation was that potentially tragic one of so many women of that time. Her abilities were striking, yet her talents were not in any particular distinct enough to carry her over the barricades of convention and prejudice. Louis almost certainly recognised this, and perhaps hoped that Fanny would achieve some success and fulfilment in her writing. He encouraged her, and if she had no real talent she had some gift for it, an energetic style and an almost apocalyptic imagination. But it is clear that without her association with Louis and without his help her writing would have got nowhere, and would have been yet another undertaking to be abandoned. She became involved in story-telling specifically when in order to keep Louis quiet during long periods of enforced silence and idleness she made up stories. Later she began to put them down on paper. She had tried her hand at writing for children before, but this time what she and Louis produced was 'The Dynamiter', which would appear in *More New Arabian Nights* and initiate a short-lived career as a serious writer for adults. It is possible that she might have made something more of her ability if she had persevered. Louis's increasing success may have had something to do with the fact that after a few years she did not carry on.

In the spring of 1884 Coggie Ferrier was with Louis and Fanny at La Solitude, and became a friend whom they were always to value. Her quiet intelligence and sense of humour much appealed to them, and for Louis, Coggie's presence helped the acceptance of Walter's death. They would not see a great deal of each other, but corresponded regularly, and Louis found himself able to write to her almost as if she were a male friend, falling into his Thomson personality at times, and venturing into a vein of humour that Edinburgh society would have frowned on. Coggie, though, had revealed a talent for telling somewhat risqué jokes, which had much delighted Louis.

In many ways Fanny and Louis did not have good luck in France, although there had been magic enough in these two years for it to remain for Louis a happy and special time. A final blow was a cholera outbreak at Hyères. For Fanny this was the definitive confirmation of her suspicion that the South of France was no place for Louis, and with the approval of doctors they made the decision to try the south of England. They headed back across the channel, slowly, for the summer of 1884 was a very bad one for Louis, and stayed for a while in Richmond. Lloyd was at school in Bournemouth and it was after visiting him there that they began to think it might be a suitable place for them to take up residence. It had gained some reputation as a health resort, indeed seemed full of the infirm. It had the right ingredients, sea air and pine trees, both medically approved for respiratory congestion.

They at first found rented accommodation and prepared to see if Louis could weather an English winter. They were to spend three years there, the longest Louis and Fanny would spend in any one place until they reached Samoa. They were on the whole three settled and productive years, the years in which Louis's reputation was unquestionably established; but they were also years in which Louis realised once and for all that he could not deny his restless nature the urge to be on the move. When he left Bournemouth, ostensibly yet again on the search for health, it was as clear as it had ever been that an environment of solid walls and solid bourgeois values could not hold him for long. His soul was as dependent on fresh experience as his body was on the drugs that pulled him out of his blood-soaked fevers.

Louis's parents were delighted to have him back on British soil. For the next three years he would be all too accessible. Thomas bought them a house, or rather bought Fanny a house – it was his wedding present to her. It is likely that he consciously hoped by doing so to root them firmly in one place. After some months in two different houses Louis and Fanny moved into the house they called Skerryvore, after Alan Stevenson's lighthouse on Dhu Heartach. (Their previous house, Bonallie Towers, curiously echoed the Bonally at the foot of the Pentlands.)

There was no question of expecting Bournemouth to be any better for Louis than Hyères, only of it not being any worse. Doctors were consulted before the choice was made, and they gave their approval. Medical opinion seemed fairly optimistic about Louis's chances. In France, after one of his worst bouts, Fanny had been told that if she could keep Louis alive until he was forty the chances were high that he would live out his natural life. But although doctors were optimistic, a definitive diagnosis was impossible. Louis's health did not improve in Bournemouth. The alarms of haemorrhage and fever and sudden collapse continued. He had to be protected from colds and infections – Fanny would allow no one with a cold anywhere near him. This was mostly instinct on her part, for the germ theory of disease was in its infancy. But the three settled years, in a comfortable home, without too much moving about, and with modest rations of good company (and some bad, or at least over-exciting) were probably necessary in terms of Louis's career. Fanny needed them, too. His friends were pleased and relieved to have him within easy distance of London, and within easy reach of their guidance. Colvin still overlooked Louis's welfare and his career with an anxious eye.

Skerryvore was a substantial middle-class villa, much like others that solidly fringed the town. The villa of recent construction was a distinguishing feature of Bournemouth. But it was attractively situated, on the top of Alum Chine, a cleft that ran steeply down to the sea, and in an area that was as yet sparsely built on. It had a splendid view, out to sea – the house had inevitably been called 'Sea View' before Louis's imagination got to work on it. The pine trees and heather on the cliff top had a fragrance of Scotland, and there was an acre of garden, sloping down in terraces, for Fanny to experiment on. It was from the beginning rather douce for Louis, without the sparkle of the Riviera, without the Mediterranean shimmer in the air, and without the rigours of the Scottish coast, the drama of wind and waves that literally takes your breath away. But he was ready to try it. Calling the house Skerryvore added a little more flavour to existence.

Fanny was busy, buying furniture and equipping the house. Part of her gift was £500 to spend on furnishing. She made trips to London to choose what she needed and took a great deal of care over it all. Such activity brought out her latent house-pride: Skerryvore was really her only chance to thoroughly indulge her tastes, which were slightly avant-garde, but with an individual flavour. She seems to have been happy with the current aesthetic trends. Louis, we can assume, cared not at all, and was willing to comply with her views.

Setting up Skerryvore was creative work for Fanny and she was busy and happy at it. Lloyd, who was now a short-sighted and slightly problematic teen-ager, looked back on Skerryvore with a conviction that Louis was never really at ease there. He had become, Lloyd said, on the surface exactly what he had always scorned.

The wanderers were now anchored; over their heads was their own roof-tree; they paid rates and taxes, and were called on by the vicar; Stevenson, in the word he hated most of all, had become the 'burgess' of his former jeers. Respectability, dulness, and similar villas encompassed him for miles in every direction.[19]

But in fact, at least initially, Louis quite enjoyed both owning and presiding over his own home. Settlement meant neighbours and new friends, visitors and spare rooms for them to occupy, and time and opportunity for the richness of conversation that he could so readily inspire.

Bournemouth was familiar territory to Louis in the sense that he was well used to being surrounded by seekers after health, and a large proportion of Bournemouth's population was just that. Bournemouth had grown up rapidly as a resort, offering healthful sea air combined with certain solid comforts. Skerryvore was, as described by William Archer, drama critic and translator of Ibsen, who stayed there several times, 'an unpretending two-storey house, its yellow brick peeping through rich growths of ivy'. Although the decoration inside was inherited from the previous owner, 'post-morrisian yet not ultra-aesthetic', Fanny's individual touch had given it its own character. Louis made his contributions; Turner's engraving of the Bell Rock lighthouse hung over the fireplace of the dining-

RLS, by Sir William Blake Richmond, 1887

room – the blue room – and a collection of 'buccaneering weapons' decorated the wall. According to Archer he was also partial to the currently popular blue-and-white china, produced in imitation of Chinese Ming. Archer commented on how uncluttered the furnishings were, worthy of note at a time when 'what-nots burdened with Japaneseries' were to be frequently encountered, but when more sophisticated tastes were leaning towards spareness. In the drawing-room there were wicker chairs and a yellow-covered window seat, a Rodin sculpture, photographs of Colvin, Henley and Fleeming Jenkin. Later Sargent's vivid portrait of Louis in mid-stride across the room with a teasing enigmatic glance straight out of the picture would be added.

Archer met Louis at Skerryvore for the first time, and like everyone else he was struck by his looks, his vitality, his grace.

> He now sits at the foot of the table rolling a limp cigarette in his long, limp fingers, and talking eagerly all the while, with just enough trace of a Scottish intonation to remind one that he is the author of 'Thrawn Janet' and the creator of Alan Breck Stewart. He has still the air and manner of a young man, for illness has neither tamed his mind nor aged his body. It has left its mark, however, in the pallor of his long oval face, with its wide-set eyes, straight nose, and thin-lipped sensitive mouth, scarcely shaded by a light moustache, the jest and scorn of his ribald intimates. His long dark hair straggles with an irregular wave down to his neck, a wisp of it occasionally falling over his ear, and having to be replaced with a light gesture of the hand. He is dressed in a black velvet jacket, showing at the throat the loose rolling collar of a white flannel shirt; and if it is at all cold, he has probably thrown over his shoulders an ancient maroon-coloured shawl draped something after the fashion of a Mexican poncho. When he stands up you see he is well above the middle height, and of a naturally lithe and agile figure. He still moves with freedom and grace, but the stoop of his shoulders tells a tale of suffering.[20]

Although illness and hard work continued to be dominant features of his life, Louis without his evenings of talk at the dinner table, and afterwards in the drawing-room with a glass of good whisky, Glenlivet perhaps, was not himself. He might be in bed most of the day, writing with slow difficulty with his dark red poncho keeping out the cold. The moment later in the day when he could descend and take his place amongst his family and friends was an essential part of what sustained him.

Chapter 9

A WEEVIL IN A BISCUIT

Remember the pallid brute that lived in Skerryvore like a weevil
in a biscuit

Letter to Henry James

There were times when even a gentle walk in the garden was
unwise, when Louis courted collapse if he strolled on the cliffs
and looked out to sea. Almost every time he gave rein to his need
for action or a change of scene he paid for it. There were facets
of restriction other than the physical. Although at first Louis
enjoyed the realities of ownership, enjoyed presiding over his
own home with its tangible indications of comfort and security,
he was also nervous about it. 'I am now a beastly householder,'
he wrote to Gosse shortly before moving in, 'but have not yet
entered on my domain. When I do, the social revolution will
probably cast me back upon my dung-heap.'[1] He knew he was
entering upon an existence that fundamentally went against the
grain.

Part of the pleasure that he did find in it may have been
concerned with a feeling that he owed something to Fanny. In
the first years of their marriage it looked as if he had lumbered
Fanny with an invalid husband and a vagabond life. The two
things did not go very well together. The security of Skerryvore
might make things easier for her. But of course the security was
elusive. Skerryvore was a home they could share, but they were
rarely left alone to enjoy it together, and however much Louis
loved his friends he valued the time he and Fanny could spend
alone together. Apart from the friends and professional
acquaintances who beat a path to the door the fact that the
house had been Thomas's gift gave him constant access to the
physical and emotional support of Fanny and Louis. At times
the burden of the elder Stevensons was almost beyond bearing.
A home was no insurance of good health. It was no insurance of
privacy. And Louis was still some way from independent

financial security. Skerryvore was an empty symbol in the sense that it did not truly represent that stage in his achievement. Later, when success and money arrived, he did not choose to spend his rewards on a suburban bourgeois residence, although he relished building a home and setting up his own particular kinds of household gods.

Friends were perhaps the most significant feature of life at Skerryvore. Fanny did her best to control the socialising, and often exhausted herself in the process. Because she constantly worried about the effect on Louis, and also because she was so often not sure of her own standing in relation to Louis's friends, these visits were a considerable nervous strain for her. But for Louis they meant the crackle of conversation, and at best a lightning exchange of ideas which could have fertile results. He was writing hard, but still neither making enough money to be self-sufficient – he was earning less than £400 a year at this time, and his expenses were substantial – nor finding yet a style and a subject that he could make fulfillingly his own. *Kidnapped* would provide the first claim to both. The friends streamed from London, and we can be sure they were not reticent in telling Louis what he ought to be writing. The bills flowed just as copiously, with their own particular message. And a regular visitor, quietly presenting himself in the evenings after dinner, was the most notable literary figure of the period. The affectionate and rewarding relationship that grew up between Robert Louis Stevenson and Henry James was of the greatest importance to both of them. James was perhaps the father that Louis was looking for, honest, acute and loving, and Louis the son that James would never have, adventurous, gentle and volatile. They were both more than that, for they saw themselves as professional colleagues exploring their craft, and it may be misleading to cast them in such roles. But certainly the idea of Skerryvore is as haunted by the shade of Henry James as it is by that of Stevenson.

The need to work was as imperative as ever. They had scarcely arrived in Bournemouth before Louis and Henley were hard at it together, re-engendering excitement over the play they had begun to work at some years before. They persuaded themselves, Henley doing most of the persuading, that the drama was the most direct route to financial gain, and as there was also a great deal of fun, if considerable argument, in working on it together it was hard to resist lavishing energy and time on writing plays. Fanny was at this stage enthusiastic too, tempted by the prospect of cash, and craving a lifestyle that required it. Her adventurous spirit was not dead, but Fanny had for a long time nursed an ambition for an upper middle-class environment. To start with she participated keenly in the excited planning of the dramas, although she got impatient with Henley, and especially with his addiction to the whisky bottle. Henley grumbled at her rationing of his drams.

The first play was certainly the best. The story of Deacon Brodie had been a part of Louis's childhood. This eighteenth-century resident of Edinburgh, respected in his trade of cabinet-maker, had lived a night life of daring criminality. The subject was a natural for Louis, for it contained the core of his preoccupations. Perhaps if he had handled it alone, and not for the stage, he would have made something memorable of it. He and Henley attempted to characterise a man who was conventionally bad, but whose attacks on the framework of a complacent, self-approving bourgeois society had a kind of heroic justification. It was a subject of natural drama, too. But although Henley at least convinced himself to the contrary, and Louis's love of play-acting beckoned, the drama was not the medium for either of them. Although both enjoyed the stage neither understood it in any practical sense. They were able to provide the audiences of the time neither with what they were accustomed to nor with something refreshingly and distinctively new. Louis's grasp of the dramatic was too much informed by a literary sense to allow for stage craft. The novelist who could describe action with such sparkling particularity on the page, and the poet who could invoke it so ringingly, could neither of them suggest it on the stage. All their plays read woodenly today, and must have done so then. In spite of frantic activity on Henley's part to get the plays read in the right quarters and to whip up interest, only *Deacon Brodie* was produced in Louis's lifetime, and it had little success.

Their other attempts were without exception though in different ways highly contrived. Louis could not resist the staginess of his childhood stories. *Macaire* and *The Admiral Guinea*, two further products of the collaborating pens, evaded their attempts to breathe life into them. It was as if Louis was trying to capture some distant adventure whose Skeltian colours had faded. There is little sparkle. *Beau Austin* is less wooden, with its crisper Regency setting, but its attempt to pose a genuine moral problem, concerning the reputation of the heroine, is checkered with uneasiness. They were not able to mix successfully a Regency setting and a message aimed at a Victorian public. Meredith's comment, when he was sent the play to read, was that he felt the British public would not accept a heroine who was obviously blemished. If the heroine were modified the play could achieve little more than pastiche. Henley and Stevenson were in fact roundly defeated by the demands of the medium they had chosen to work in. It was inevitable. Although the two shared much in belief and purpose and both can be so significantly identified with important literary trends of the time, from the very beginning of their association a wide gulf can be seen in what they actually wrote. In personality, the two friends clashed as much as they empathised – and enjoyed the sparks that flew. Significantly they instinctively realised that the only field in which they might possibly work together was one in which neither was proficient. Far from turning out an easy boost to their respective bank balances the immense amount of time and energy squandered on these dramatic enterprises were a terrible waste. And it is clear that Louis had doubts about it all even while he and Henley were debating most eloquently the twists of plot and character. Louis's doubts Henley would later interpret as a fatal lack of commitment, which undermined what would otherwise have been a productive achievement.

If the plays distracted Louis from other work, amazingly they did not draw him entirely away from it. The impetus that had really begun with the Scottish stories and with *Treasure Island* during that summer at Pitlochry and Braemar, was still carrying him forward. There was no stopping now. It was soon to be as if he had boarded a meandering little local train in his room at the top of Heriot Row which had transformed itself into an intercontinental express in the course of a decade. Failures in the drama would not hold him back; on the other hand the express, perhaps, never reached a destination.

During the Skerryvore years he was cushioned and protected.

Great writers thought highly of him, arguably the period's greatest, James and Meredith – though Thomas Hardy was not particularly impressed. In some ways the lack of critical hostility, even critical caution, was amazing. When *Treasure Island* appeared in volume form the response of established critics was delight. In his daily life he was cushioned too, cared for and protected by Fanny and Valentine who, although they could not always fend off importunate visitors, saw to Louis's physical comfort. There were friends who were eager to cosset him. Admiring articles were beginning to appear, he was receiving admiring letters through the post, and admirers came to his door. In spite of this at no time in his life did Louis became complacent. At this stage protection and admiration were good for him, engaged him, fed him, and helped him to keep going.

When the time came for Fanny and Louis to take occupation of Skerryvore they had had several months of rented accommodation in Bournemouth – and several years of not altogether settled occupation of rented homes in five countries. They were unpacking when they first encountered a young girl who was to leave a record of their time at Skerryvore. Adelaide Boodle came to call with her mother, and found Louis perched on a packing-case, 'emphasising his words with a brandished teaspoon'.[2] She fell in love instantly with both Louis and Fanny. Louis delighted her, Fanny she revered as his dedicated and tender protectress. She came frequently to the house, at first spending most of the time with Fanny, whose 'quiet heroism' impressed her greatly. Although hero-worship was part of her relationship with both it did not blind her to certain of the realities. In her memoir, *RLS and His Sine Qua Non* (the title itself reveals her assessment of Fanny) she comments on Louis's 'extravagant moods', often the result of a fever, and the difficulties of coping with them.

> . . . these erratic moods, in which all caution went to the winds, must often have tried her nerves almost to breaking point; but I doubt if ever she allowed him to know what agony she had to live through. To the utmost of her power, she guarded him from every risk; but when she saw that nothing would be gained by remonstrance, she quietly said her say, and then took refuge in silence.[3]

As an instance of Fanny's silent tolerance of certain of Louis's eccentricities she relates the story of the raspberry canes. In order to help her on a day that she was away, Louis carefully planted the raspberry canes she had bought. But Louis's ignorance of horticultural matters was total, and he made a complete hash of it. When Fanny returned she replanted the canes without saying a word, while Louis boasted to everyone of how useful he had made himself. His boyish pleasure in having accomplished something to assist Fanny, something of a practical nature, was such that she could not bear to destroy it.

Adelaide eventually plucked up enough courage to mention her literary ambitions, and tentatively asked Fanny if Louis might give her some advice. Fanny firmly said that Louis must not be bothered, and undertook to give Adelaide some instruction herself. Fanny was by this time a published author in her own right. She had written a story for children some time before, and had been collaborating with Louis. It must have done her good to feel she could help a young aspirant, and possibly she retained Adelaide as her own pupil for this reason. Her own literary abilities never became striking, but she clearly was well acquainted with the process of writing. In the end Louis too took a hand in Adelaide's education, for when he was asked to give some talks to aspiring writers at the British Museum he needed someone to practise on. Adelaide was the perfect listener, and as it happened the only one, for the British Museum proposal never came to anything.

Fanny and Louis were patient and kind with Adelaide, and Fanny enjoyed having a helper and, in effect, an acolyte. They regarded her with genuine affection, and certainly enlivened her existence, for she led what was otherwise probably a rather sterile life with her mother. When they left Skerryvore, Adelaide was asked to keep a watchful eye on the house and a number of pets who had to be left behind. This task earned her the name of 'gamekeeper', by which Louis referred to her in subsequent years.

There were other rewarding relationships. They became friendly with Sir Henry and Lady Taylor, who were amongst their neighbours. Sir Henry was a poet and civil servant in the Colonial Office, and he and his wife liked to include authors amongst their friends. She in particular became a kind and

caring friend for whom Louis had a real affection. To be taken
up by the moneyed upper classes did not do Louis any harm,
and was at times a great help. Louis and Fanny enjoyed their
evenings dining at the Taylors – they did not go out very often –
and also at the home of the Shelleys, other neighbours of note.
Sir Percy was the son of the poet. His wife regarded Louis as a
Shelleyan figure, which clearly rather flattered him, and her
admiration on that score was a little extravagant. But they too
were good friends and concerned themselves anxiously with
Louis's welfare. They added to the buttressing that was part of
Skerryvore life. In moments of crisis they proved, partly because
their caring was backed by money, rather more reliable than
some of Louis's older friends.

Although Louis's socialising was so circumscribed, for the
first, and only, time he and Fanny were in a sense established in
English society. If they had little to do with most of the local
population, and if later they were to be on familiar terms with
royalty, in Bournemouth their position was assured. This must
have allayed some of Fanny's insecurity. On both literary and
social terms Louis was confidently placed. True, there were
times when Skerryvore showed dangerous signs of sliding into
Bohemia, when Louis's more irrepressible friends descended,
and there were times when the household bristled with exposed
nerve ends, especially when the elder Stevensons were making
one of their prolonged visits. But there were antidotes to this.
The Taylors and the Shelleys helped to provide them. The
progress of the writing helped too. The complete strangers who
arrived on the doorstep to ask questions about Mr Stevenson
were signs that slowly and surely the reputation, even already
the legend, of RLS was growing. For a year or two his
movements and his illnesses were news. But most valued of all,
with little doubt, were the warmth and reassurance and
thoughtful stimulation that came with the quietly regular visits
of Henry James.

Louis had met James briefly some years before and had not
been much impressed. In fact he had been inclined to sneer.
James had not found much to admire in Louis either. They were
introduced by Andrew Lang, who was, interestingly, another of
the few who had not been much taken with Louis at first; Lang
had found Louis's style a little over-extravagant. James's

comment was, 'He is a pleasant fellow, but a shirt-collarless Bohemian and a great deal (in an inoffensive way) of a *poseur*.'[4] But he added that he found *An Inland Voyage* 'charming' – a judgment which rather devastatingly implies that he found it nothing more than that. Their relationship got on to a more substantial basis when they entered into a good-natured but intensely-felt literary controversy, the implications of which are of considerable importance in the development of ideas about the novel.

James's 'The Art of Fiction', provoked by a published lecture by Walter Besant on 'Fiction as one of the Fine Arts', was published in *Longman's Magazine* in September 1884. Besant was a novelist, well known in his day but not much remembered now, except for his *All Sorts and Conditions of Men* which had been published two years before, where his subject was London's East End. Besant argued that a novelist could not write about aspects of life he had not himself experienced. His view of the novel was business-like and limited: a novelist should write out of his own experience, with a moral purpose. His journalistic attitude to fiction (journalistic in spite of the fact that he was arguing the case for fiction to be regarded as one of the 'fine arts', like painting, or music, with similar acknowledgments and rewards) brought him close to Zola, who hunted verisimilitude in the streets of Paris, and whom James, like Stevenson, had begun by disliking and ultimately reluctantly admired.

James did not see Besant as in the same case precisely as Zola, but his verdict on Zola was of the greatest interest. As James became more closely acquainted with the French naturalists his dislike had been almost entirely drowned by his admiration. 'Zola's naturalism is ugly and dirty, but he seems to me to be *doing* something – which surely (in the imaginative line) no one in England or the United States is, and no one else here,' he was writing to a friend in 1896.[5] In a letter to William Dean Howells, the American novelist with whom he often exchanged ideas on fiction, James commented on the whole group of French naturalist writers:

> . . . there is nothing more interesting to me now than the effort and experiment of this little group, with its truly infernal intelligency of art, form, manner – its intense artistic life.

They do the only kind of work, today, that I respect; and in spite of their ferocious pessimism and their handling of unclean things, they are at least serious and honest. The floods of tepid soap and water which under the name of novels are being vomited forth in England, seem to me, by contrast, to do little honour to our race.[6]

After Zola's death James was to do him honour in more detailed fashion. It is interesting that to a great extent Stevenson shared this progress towards respect, and perhaps if he had lived longer might have become as unequivocal as James. But most important, he shared, profoundly, the view that the writer's responsibility was to be 'serious and honest'. Although his writing career and his insistence that literature should be 'entertainment' at times suggest otherwise, it was in his mind continually, and his involvement in this debate of 1884 indicates how deeply felt it was.

In 'The Art of Fiction' James was specifically challenging some of Besant's arguments. In particular he concerned himself with the problem of experience. Experience, he argued, was not a question of what the journalist observed and recorded in his notebook, but a continuing process of impressions, responses, guesswork, that evades a beginning and an end: 'It is an immense sensibility, a kind of huge spider-web of the finest silken threads suspended in the chamber of consciousness,

Henry James, photo by E. O. Hoppé

catching every air-borne particle in its tissue. It is the very atmosphere of the mind; and when the mind is imaginative – much more when it happens to be that of a man of genius – it takes to itself the faintest hints of life, it converts the very pulses of the air into revelations.'[7] In other words experience is as much a question of quality as of exposure to particular stimuli. The *quality* of the sensibility, the *quality* of the imagination, are vital. James insisted that, inevitably, the novel is 'a personal impression of life', and experience a highly individualised and personal business.[8] Reality has a myriad forms. But 'the air of reality' is what the novelist must aim to produce.[9] The novel cannot *be* reality, but it must produce an illusion of reality – 'the illusion of life'.[10] James was convinced that the great achievement of the novel was that it defied narrow definition and categorisation – it was the novel's 'large, free character of an immense and exquisite correspondence with life' that was its splendid quality.[11]

In spirit Stevenson shared intensely James's seriousness about his profession. As Janet Adam Smith has pointed out, there were perhaps no other two novelists of that generation who were so deeply concerned, and with such integrity, with their craft.[12] But it was on this question of reality that Stevenson felt compelled to enter the argument – especially as James had mentioned in his essay, and with praise, *Treasure Island*. James had talked of the novel competing with life. Stevenson's argument was that the novel could not begin to do such a thing. Fiction should be as truthful as history, James had said. Truth, Stevenson insisted, had nothing to do with it. He set his thoughts down with energy and commitment, entitled them 'A Humble Remonstrance', and sent them off to *Longman's*, which printed the article in the December issue. Between the two of them Henry James and Robert Louis Stevenson – and Walter Besant's provocation must not be left out – faced freshly and raised challengingly some radical questions concerning the novel and novelists. The debate, if it had existed at all, had never come to life like this before. A synthesis of their ideas, not impossible and perhaps what happened to both of them, provides rich and fertile territory for anyone at all interested in the art of the novel.

The secret of art, Stevenson said, was that it did *not* attempt to 'compete with life'. 'Man's one method, whether he reasons or creates, is to half-shut his eyes against the dazzle and confusion of reality.'[13] He uses a mathematical analogy. Geometry poses a perfect circle, an impossibility in the natural world. Art likewise idealises, and must idealise.

> Painting, ruefully comparing sunshine and flake-white, gives up truth of colour, as it had already given up relief and movement; and instead of vying with nature, arranges a scheme of harmonious tints. Literature, above all in its most typical mood, the mood of narrative, similarly flees the direct challenge and pursues instead an independent and creative aim. So far as it imitates at all, it imitates not life but speech: not the facts of human destiny, but the emphasis and the suppressions with which the human actor tells of them. The real art that dealt with life directly was that of the first men who told their stories round the savage campfire. Our art is occupied, and bound to be occupied, not so much in making stories true as in making them typical; not so much in capturing the lineaments of each fact, as in marshalling all of them towards a common end. For the welter of impressions, all forcible but all discrete, which life presents, it substitutes a certain artificial series of impressions, all indeed most feebly represented, but all aiming at the same effect, all eloquent of the same idea, all chiming together like consonant notes in music or like the graduated tints in a good picture. . . . Life is monstrous, infinite, illogical, abrupt, and poignant; a work of art, in comparison, is neat, finite, self-contained, rational, flowing and emasculate. . . . The novel . . . exists, not by its resemblances to life, which are forced and material, as a shoe must still consist of leather, but by its immeasurable difference from life, which is designed and significant, and is both the method and the meaning of the work.[14]

Stevenson's argument is that not only is fiction not an imitation of life, its essential character, its art, lies in its separate nature. Life is real, fiction is artificial, and the artificiality is the art. In fact he and James were not as opposed as, at this stage, Stevenson seemed to think. James was not arguing for an imitation of reality – that was Besant's claim – but for an *illusion* of reality. There is a crucial difference. Like Stevenson, James accepted that it was no part of the novelist's art to imitate narrowly, and that was why he had reservations about Zola, finally overcome by the fact of Zola's seriousness. Stevenson implicitly accepts that, although the novel is immeasurably different from life, it is life that provides the standard – without life there can be no art. It is the needs, the mood, the aspirations, the failures of life that both inform fiction and make it necessary.

James recognised at once that there was more agreement than disagreement, and wrote to Louis to say so. He had clearly revised his opinion of the bohemian *poseur*. He wrote, he said, 'with hearty sympathy, charged with the assurance of my enjoyment of everything you write. It's a luxury, in this immoral age, to encounter someone who *does* write – who is really acquainted with that lovely art.'[15] It had been good for Louis to set down his thoughts in an ordered fashion. He had been scattering letters with comments on art and realism for some time. James's provocation was timely. Now in correspondence they continued to exchange ideas which, when at last they met again, one can be sure constituted a substantial part of their conversation. Through their letters they established their great respect for one another, their real interest in each other's work, and above all the depth of their caring for literature, and their understanding of the value of the imagination. There were many who felt that the imagination had become debased currency. James and Stevenson, in their very different ways, brought it scintillatingly to bear again.

Louis invited James to call, if ever he should be in Bournemouth, and promised a bottle of decent claret and a bed. (It seems that by this time Louis's taste had graduated from burgundy, the favourite wine of his youth, to claret.) Early in 1885 James escorted his invalid sister during a prolonged stay in Bournemouth and had the opportunity to see a great deal of Louis. In spite of an unfortunate mistake on the first occasion he presented himself at the Stevenson home – the servants thought he was a tradesman – the warmth and creativity of the relationship were immediate. He came almost every day. He had his own special armchair, which remained vacant when James was not there to occupy it. Fanny liked him; although he was critical of Fanny later, he was obviously a courteous and tactful guest, something which some of Louis's more casual friends were not. For Fanny, perhaps James's most supportive quality was his real concern for Louis's health and his penetrating assessment of the circumstances that influenced it. James feared that Louis's life might come to an end at any moment. When his parents settled down for one of their extended visits James wrote in anguish to Colvin of Thomas and Maggie Stevenson's blindness to the effect their demands had on their son. Fanny found these visits exhausting, and Henry James was one of the few people who understood how she felt, and shared her attempts to protect Louis from such onslaughts.

The problem of Thomas was acute. His ill-health and increasing nervous strain meant that he and Maggie were increasingly inclined to make their way south. They spent some time at spas, at Great Malvern and Matlock, where Louis sometimes felt compelled to join them. It had been understood that the buying of Skerryvore was in effect the establishment of a residence on the south coast for whenever it seemed beneficial for Thomas to be there, which was increasingly frequent. Although Fanny had always got on well with Thomas clearly illness made him peevish and difficult, and Maggie was not accustomed to being the stronger of the two. The active, decisive Thomas had become weak and uncertain, worrying over the future of the business. By this time his brother's sons had unlike his own taken up the family profession. The situation was distressing for Louis and for his mother.

The tradewinds of death were blowing again. Not only was Thomas during the Skerryvore years ill enough to cause continual worry, but in June of 1885 Louis received word that Fleeming Jenkin had died. He had loved and respected Fleeming Jenkin, who had at moments of difficulty in Louis's life offered honest advice without letting Louis's charm erode his integrity. He was honest in everything he did, and his affection for Louis was no exception. He had refused to connive at Louis's attempt to get him to vouch for his attendance at the engineering classes from which he was conspicuously absent. When Louis was struggling towards marriage Jenkin had written to him in California, telling him that if marriage was what he really wanted he shouldn't let secondary considerations deter him. And he added, 'even when you acted more foolishly and worse than other men you did so from much wiser and better motives than their's'.[16] The fact that the Jenkins' own marriage was so positive a union meant a great deal to Louis. He wrote to Mrs Jenkin, agreeing to write a notice for the *Academy*. But soon he found he had much more to say about his friend than a short notice would allow, and was hard at work at *The Memoir of Fleeming Jenkin*. It must have had particular poignancy for Ann Jenkin that the youth she had identified as a Scots Heine was now writing about her dead husband with such warmth. And Louis, in writing about the man who had been something of a father-figure to him, who had written so calmly during that time of extremity in California, must have thought about how his own father had mortified himself on his account, and the undisguisable fact that his own father's life was drawing to a close.

Such things helped to root Louis more firmly into the wider realities of life. He was coming to grips with the nature of fiction. He was forced to face squarely not only the fact of death but some of the shaping influences and shaping experiences of his own past. *A Child's Garden*, a kind of catharsis, had been published in March. With what he said there about his childhood, with the evocation of the delights and of the fears, it became possible to refer specifically to his childhood as a time of pain and loneliness as well as of discovery and play. William Archer, who had not yet met Louis, wrote a piece on *A Child's Garden* suggesting that he must be of robust physique as well as of a robust nature to write as he did. He missed the clues that lie thick in the little book. Louis wrote to him mildly pointing out that he had spent a great deal of his childhood confined to his bed, and looked back on 'a very mixed experience, full of fever, nightmare, insomnia, painful days and interminable nights'. But Archer's was another piece of useful provocation. He published a longer article on Stevenson a few months later and Louis wrote again, and in a number of letters to him he articulated what came to be identified as the Stevenson philosophy, which he would state more objectively in 'Pulvis et Umbra', a later essay. He wrote to Archer,

> That which we suffer ourselves has no longer the same air of monstrous injustice and wanton cruelty that suffering wears when we see it in the case of others. So we begin gradually to see that things are not black, but have their strange

compensations; and when they draw towards their worst, the idea of death is like a bed to lie on. I should bear false witness if I did not declare life happy.[17]

We know of course that there were times when it was quite impossible for Louis honestly to declare life happy, but his insistence on a philosophy of optimistic cheerfulness was not specious: for him it was the right thing to do, the correct moral stance to take up in his position. If he had ever more than momentarily accepted negatively the bleakness of his situation, he would never have written himself into men's minds. His talent integrally involved his belief that it was always worth trying. But he knew better than anyone that he could not always live up to his belief.

He said a great many other things in his letters to Archer. His current life-style was still worrying him – he had now been living in Skerryvore for six months. 'Can you imagine,' he wrote of himself to Archer, 'that he is a backslidden communist, and is sure he will go to hell (if there be such an excellent institution) for the luxury in which he lives?' He went on,

> And can you believe that, though it is gaily expressed, the thought is hag and skeleton in every moment of vacuity or depression? Can you conceive how profoundly I am irritated by the opposite affliction of my own, when I see strong men and rich men bleating about their sorrows and the burthen of life, in a world full of 'cancerous paupers', and poor sick children, and the fatally bereaved. . . . In my view, one dank, dispirited word is harmful, a crime of *lèse-humanité*, a piece of acquired evil; every gay, every bright word or picture, like every pleasant air of music, is a piece of pleasure set afloat; the reader catches it, and, if he be healthy, goes on his way rejoicing; and it is the business of art so to send him, as often as possible.[18]

Seen thus in the context of Louis's uneasiness as to his own – he felt undeserved – circumstances, his insistence on the importance of the gay, bright word is not quite the shallow optimism that it sometimes appears. It is clearly a reaction to the darkness of Calvinism as well as to the shadow of sickness. The bright word or picture is seen as a moment of vivid humanity against the drab, grey stone of the environment of childhood and youth. His father's gloom, Edinburgh's biting wind, the rough, dark texture of the city and its life: with this behind him the pining for colour and vitality is not only understandable, but creative.

Literature, he says in another letter to Archer, should 'give joy';[19] it is the same argument that he uses in 'A Gossip on Romance', that literature should idealise. Certain facts of existence, he argued, should be left out of literature because they would be no help in the necessary process of making the most of life. 'To me, the medicine bottles on my chimney and the blood on my handkerchief are accidents; they do not colour my view of life . . . and I should think myself a trifler and in bad taste if I introduced the world to these unimportant privacies.'[20] But of course the medicine bottles and the blood on his handkerchief *did* colour his life; without them he would not have been quite so determinedly optimistic. They also coloured his view of literature. Between them, sickness and Calvinism and the heavy weights of the past sent Stevenson off on the wrong tack. It took forty-odd years for him to work around to the right one, and it was the enlarging of his experience of suffering and the dwindling of the necessity of preoccupation with his own health that was one of the favourable winds. But it can also be argued that he lost nothing by setting off on the wrong tack, that he gained all the time valuable writing experience. Part of his value as a writer was his frank acknowledgment that he had a long way to go. He was often excited by what he wrote, but he was never complacent.

He took pains to point out to Archer that to judge him by his early work would scarcely do him justice – 'You make no allowance for the slowness with which a man finds and tries to learn his tools.'[21] He could not, he said, pretend to say all, which was what Archer was asking. He had to be much more modest and limited in his intentions. 'We say each particular thing as it comes up . . . Words will not otherwise serve us.'[22] Archer was accusing him of failing to recognise the evil in life, and Louis attempted to defend himself. He could only write about 'what stands out, what takes on itself a presence for my imagination or makes a figure in that little tricky abbreviation which is the best my reason can conceive'.[23] To encompass the whole of life –

it was the same argument that he was engaged in with James – was beyond the craft and the imagination of the writer. Literature could not compete with life. It could, however, help to make life more bearable.

Archer became a good friend, visiting Skerryvore and, as we have seen, leaving a record of the Stevenson household. His little son, 'Tomarcher', was the recipient of several letters from Louis. It was of the greatest value for Louis to have someone on whom he could sound out his ideas, and the talk with Archer at Skerryvore must have pursued many of the arguments he suggests in the letters. For Louis the maintaining of a positive view of life was crucial. Without such as Archer and Henry James, more intellectually challenging than Henley, it is probable that such energetic statement would have evaded him. 1885 was an active year for publication, with *A Child's Garden* appearing in March, the beginning of the serialisation of *Prince Otto* in April and publication of *More New Arabian Nights*, including Fanny's 'The Dynamiters', in May. He was working on *Kidnapped*. During that summer his health crashed again. Fanny was writing desperately to Colvin, 'I had to lift Louis in and out of bed ten times in one night. [Louis was presumably still refusing to use 'invalids' appliances'.] He was quite off his head and would not be contradicted because he was bleeding at the lungs at the same time and got into such furies when I wasn't quick enough.'[24] To add to her difficulties Fanny had servant problems and endless visitors. Running the house, cooking, looking after Louis and attending to guests were often a severe strain on her, both physically and mentally.

There were times when Lloyd was also one of her problems. After a period of being educated at Bournemouth he went to Edinburgh University, staying at 17 Heriot Row. Thomas and Maggie seemed pleased to have him there, and there were plans to have Lloyd join the family firm. But it is doubtful whether Lloyd had any more enthusiasm for the work than his step-father. His studies were complicated by the fact that he had serious problems with his eyes. He had always been short-sighted, but it wasn't until now that the seriousness of his deficiency was realised. After a period of alarm adequate spectacles were found and Lloyd was at least able to see for most practical purposes. But close work was not easy for him. By this stage he was entertaining the idea of becoming a writer. It was natural that he should be drawn to the profession of his admired stepfather and influenced by the atmosphere of creativity that pervaded the household. Louis was pleased. Lloyd learned to type, as writing by hand was difficult for his eyes, and seemed prepared to work diligently during his apprenticeship. Louis was a patient and exacting teacher, but it is likely that his affection for Lloyd blinded him a little to the mediocre nature of his talent.

What constituted a more nerve-racking worry, especially for Fanny, was Sam Osbourne. Sam took a sporadic interest in his son. He saw much more of Belle, who was in California until she and Joe went to Hawaii to try to make their way as painters. Sam wrote to Lloyd and occasionally sent him money, though Fanny complained that he never gave her any concrete help in bringing up their son. And Sam came twice to Europe to spend some time with Lloyd; it was this that worried Fanny. After one of his visits she felt that Lloyd had picked up vulgar habits from his father. She was obsessively concerned that Lloyd should turn out a gentleman, and in describing him, which she did at length in a letter to her old friend Dora Williams, attributed to him an instinctive fastidiousness which may well have been wishful thinking. 'He is filled with a pained surprise when he finds himself in a house where a proper establishment is not kept up,' she wrote (he must often have been pained in his mother's house), and acknowledged, but we can detect the complacency, that he was 'something of a born prig'.[25] Although she may have thought her description of her son flattering it reads now like the characterisation of an impossibly narrow-minded and self-conceited young man. It is hard to believe that Lloyd was really like that, easier to believe that Fanny was describing what she thought her son ought to be rather than what he was. He may of course have been going through a stage that he quickly grew out of. The fact that Louis continued to find him good company suggests that this portrait of an anti-bohemian and lover of 'correct society in dress clothes where people talk about serious things, and there is not too much levity of manner, and the wit is very dry and refined and not too amusing' was something of a distortion, even allowing for the operation of Fanny's own sense of humour, which is present in her letter.

The problem of what Lloyd was to do with his life was a real one, and in a sense it was never solved. Louis was hardly in a position to discourage Lloyd from his literary aspirations, and he probably did not want to recognise that his would never be a major talent. Lloyd hero-worshipped Louis. From Lloyd's point of view the relationship was scarcely healthy, and the combination of it and the disruptions of his childhood did not promise well for the future. He would turn out to be singularly dependent, on his stepfather, his mother, and his stepfather's reputation, for most of his life. His eyes of course made life difficult, but as time went on it became clear that Lloyd was a dabbler, and that he had no very great inclination to strike out for himself in any particular direction. His acutely dependent relationship with Louis almost certainly contributed to his difficulties.

So Lloyd added to Fanny's worries, and to Louis's too, for his affection for the boy was very real, as was his sense of responsibility towards him, and he was probably unaware that his concerned involvement could do any damage. The Sam problem solved itself abruptly. Sam simply disappeared, in characteristic fashion. But this time he was never seen again. He had remarried, although his habits seem not to have changed, and one day he failed to turn up for his supper. It was never discovered what became of him. Fanny had never been at ease, knowing that Sam might re-enter her life at any time, and knowing that Belle maintained a close relationship with him. (She was often highly critical of Belle, and the fact that she continued to see and to love her father may have accounted for it.) Fanny had never really known how to cope with Sam, or with the fact of her divorce, something which should be borne in mind in view of Fanny's increasing psychotic difficulties. Sam's final disappearance, out of her life and everyone's, must have been a relief.

By the autumn of 1885 Louis was in better health, and he and Fanny set out on a trip into the West Country to visit Thomas Hardy. Louis's cousin Katharine, Bob's sister, about whom Louis had been much concerned since her short-lived marriage came to a painful and complicated end (with Louis inevitably trying to sort out some of the complications), went with them. They enjoyed meeting Hardy, who had not at that time produced any of the novels that are usually considered his greatest. Fanny found him 'modest, gentle and appealing', though she was less enthusiastic about his wife – '*very* plain, quite underbred, and most tedious', a verdict that was clearly at least partly the result of one of Fanny's snobbish lapses.[26] But the visit ended disastrously, with Louis taking ill suddenly in an Exeter hotel. In spite of the kindness of the hotel staff it was an especially traumatic time for both Louis and Fanny, and intensely depressing. It began to look as if Louis would never be able to stir any distance from Skerryvore without serious risk of collapse. Their horizons seemed to be continually narrowing.

It is understandable that this period in Louis's life is punctuated by a series of feverish enthusiasms. The dramatics with Henley were an aspect of this. The need for Louis to find ways of passing the time when he was too ill to write or do anything at all very much resulted in brief and vigorous concentration on things he could not do very well. He lay in bed modelling figures out of wax and convinced himself that this was a worthwhile and creative way of spending the time. He turned his enthusiasm to the piano, and although he kept trying – later it would be the flageolet – it was manifest that he had no great talent for music. He drove everyone crazy picking at the piano, even attempted to compose, but it is clear that he gave no one except perhaps himself any pleasure whatever. There were brief political enthusiasms too, notably the occasion when, mob violence in Ireland erupting, he resolved that he and Fanny should take up their abode with a family who were victims of the mob and thus, especially if they came to harm, focus the world's attention on the horror and immorality of that kind of violence. Louis's nature was not truly political. He at times described himself as a 'communist' and felt that morally socialism was the only decent route for mankind, but considered it totally impracticable. He was not able to reconcile his emotional responses to political realities, which he found highly distasteful. He was not concerned with taking sides in the Irish question and was not interested in thinking his way through political controversy. Politicians he distrusted, and radical politicians he considered no better than any others. In fact, he was seeking a soft option, a quietism that would allow him to avoid the need for political commitment but which would still be morally positive. For a while he thought he had found what he wanted in the later writings of Tolstoy. It was hard to resist the self-torturing message of that noble writer, who blamed himself for so much, and urged himself with such desperation into his highly individual interpretation of Christianity. Louis had always believed in moral self-sufficiency and Tolstoy was saying and living much that he respected. But it was also rather close to his father. Tolstoy lived out his years in agonised self-accusation for the sins of his youth. It is possible that Thomas Stevenson did the same.

Tolstoy's solution, retiral into a simple, active and self-denying existence, could scarcely be adequate in Louis's circumstances. And his gregarious instincts denied it too. His enthusiasms continued to flare, and his restlessness to act as an irritant. A story, too, might be said to be a product of these waves of feverish intensity. He was one night in the middle of a nightmare when Fanny, alarmed by his disturbance, woke him. Louis complained with irritation that she had interrupted a 'fine bogy tale'.[27] Seizing his pen the following day he began to write down the story he had dreamed. Initially it was the Gothic horror of the story that excited him, and he produced a first draft at great speed, reading the story triumphantly to Fanny when he finished. But Fanny wasn't happy with the story. She felt that it could be more than a Poe-like crawler, that it could be more morally pointed than Louis had fashioned it. Certainly in this case it can only be said that her comments did the story and Louis considerable good. Angrily the first draft was cast into the fire and he started again, this time producing the version of *The Strange Case of Dr Jekyll and Mr Hyde* that we know.

The story was written with speed in a white heat. Before Christmas of 1885, it was ready for the bookstalls, but publication was delayed until January, for it was feared the book would be lost in the Christmas rush. It was an inconspicuous little volume, and might have remained so if a chance review had not drawn attention to it in enthusiastic terms. After a slow start Dr Jekyll and Mr Hyde irrupted into public consciousness with striking impact. From this point Robert Louis Stevenson's reputation was assured. For Jekyll, Hyde and Long John Silver he would have been remembered.

Book-selling and book-advertising had become big business

by the 1880s. The surge of sophisticated adventure fiction, Haggard, Conan Doyle, Anthony Hope as well as Stevenson, owed a great deal to more streamlined methods of publicising, distributing and selling the product. The publication of Stevenson's 'The Body-Snatcher', one of the Pitlochry stories, in the *Pall Mall* Christmas Extra of 1884 had been advertised in London on sandwich boards. A year later Rider Haggard's *King Solomon's Mines* was advertised by fly-posters all over London. But *Jekyll and Hyde* had no need of such boosting. With amazing speed knowledge of the book grew. It was discussed everywhere, used as a pulpit text, inserted itself into the popular imagination with cryptic speed. Sending a copy to his old friend Will Low, Louis described it as 'a gothic gnome . . . but the gnome is interesting, I think'.[28] He knew in his heart the book was no great work, yet knew also that he had struck on an undeniable truth of human nature, a truth that had become a part of his very being at an early age. If the public read the book for thrills the absorption at the same time of a portrait of humanity that exposed the unavoidable grain of evil was inevitable.

Evil had been exposed before. Louis had dealt with it rawly in 'Thrawn Janet' and again in 'Markheim', in both of which the Devil appears in person. 'Markheim' came out just before *Jekyll and Hyde*; the dreaming of the latter clearly reflected current preoccupations. Louis's own uneasiness as resident of Skerryvore may have drawn to the surface again his preoccupation with the double life. 'Markheim' concerns the committing of a bloody and pointless murder by a man who is possessed overpoweringly by the need to kill. It is a brief, intense little story with a cathartic quality, drawn out by the murderer's relief when he is able to admit his crime and give himself into the sheltering power of the Devil. It is the acknowledgment that evil has won, and that giving oneself up to it is comforting. The theme is enlarged in *Jekyll and Hyde*, the theme that Louis spoke of, in a subsequent letter to J. A. Symonds, as 'that damned old business of the war in the members'.[29] It is the Calvinist view that man must maintain a constant struggle with evil, that the slightest lapse in vigilance will allow the Devil to triumph. The reality of evil, its ambivalence, its attractions, had always possessed Louis. The ambivalent characterisation of Long John Silver, so easily the most attractive character in *Treasure Island*,

reflects this. Louis's impatience with his father's anguished
guilt, his condemnation of Calvinist negativism, and his
absorption of the devil-ridden folklore of Scotland were all
operating in *Jekyll and Hyde*. The story, ostensibly set in London,
is redolent of the dark closes of Edinburgh's Old Town.

Stevenson had been arguing not long before that literature
should contain an optimistic message. But if *Jekyll and Hyde*
could provide a text to illustrate the self-destruction of evil it
could just as easily show how difficult it was for good to resist it.
The respectable Dr Jekyll cannot resist the temptation to
become the abominable Mr Hyde, not because he is himself
'bad' but because the chains of respectability weigh so heavily
on him. To shed them, to become 'pure evil', was to 'spring
headlong into the sea of liberty'.[30] Many reacted unhappily to
this aspect of the story. Symonds wrote in troubled admiration,
'You see I am trembling under the magician's wand of your
fancy, and rebelling against it with the scorn of a soul that hates
to be contaminated with the mere picture of victorious evil. Our
only chance seems to me to be to maintain, against all
appearances, that evil can never in no way be victorious.'[31] It is a
line of argument that Louis himself might have taken. But his
subconscious had been too strong for him. When it came to the
point, against all his surface inclinations, he had had to make
the attempt to come to terms with 'that damned old business of
the war in the members'.

Symonds drew attention to the ambivalence that is at the
heart of the story. Stevenson explores a situation in which there
is no doubt that evil is at least potentially more powerful than
good, and is suggesting that if it is allowed to break out, to come
into the open, it will inevitably conquer. Not only that, he is
saying that 'good' is restriction, and 'evil' is freedom, that
'good' forces human beings to deny certain urges that when
liberated burst out uncontrollably. Yet in order to come to
terms with evil it must be identified and understood. Symonds
found it hard to tolerate the necessity of exposing evil to the
public gaze, but it is just this problem that fascinated Louis, and
continued to do so for the rest of his life. Most pointedly of all he
was saying that it is when evil takes on a human aspect, the suave
devil and the gentleman murderer in 'Markheim', the decent
professional man Dr Jekyll who wants above all to be honoured

and respected but cannot curb his need for illicit pleasures, that it becomes most dangerous. The devils and spirits of the folk imagination, recognisable by the cloven hoof and the forked tail, are much less harmful than the gentleman in a dress coat.

It was hypocrisy that Louis was striking at. It is the bland but relentless outside of a hypocritical society that forces Jekyll first to hide his inclinations for what were probably relatively innocent pleasures, and then to free himself from his own sense of guilt by giving himself up to evil. In the form of Hyde he revels in violence for its own sake – Stevenson specifically makes the point that Hyde's evil is not to be seen in terms of excessive sexuality, although that is the way in which it has been frequently interpreted. As Jekyll, we presume though we are never explicitly told, he drinks and fornicates quietly out of the public eye, as Louis knew full well was Victorian custom. He had led a double life himself. The writing of *Jekyll and Hyde* may well have been a cathartic experience for its author.

Whatever it meant to him as a private experience, it precipitated him into the forefront of public consciousness. Rapid publication in the United States meant that there too he became suddenly successful. But his material circumstances did not alter overnight. Some eight months after the publication of *Jekyll and Hyde* Louis and Fanny made a trip to Paris to visit the Lows. It was the furthest afield he had been in two years. The trip had to be cut precipitately short because they ran out of money, and Louis did not like to admit as much to Will. Afterwards he found tucked into his pocket a cheque his father had given him to pay for the trip. He had forgotten about it. The story illustrates both Louis's vagueness about money and his continued dependence on his father. It was galling that this should still be so. Louis was now in his thirty-sixth year. Marriage had brought an end to his protestations that he would not be financially dependent on Thomas. But there were times when he longed to return to what he called a cave-dweller's life, and release himself from the financial chain that bound him to Heriot Row. The emotional chain could never be unlocked. It was not until Thomas's death that Louis could, and had to, operate without the knowledge that his father would put his hand in his pocket whenever necessary.

The serialisation of *Kidnapped*, again in *Young Folks*, in the

summer of 1886 brought solidity to Louis's reputation. The
published edition soon followed. The quality of the book was
recognised at once, though Louis was not entirely happy about
it and shook his head over public gullibility. If the public liked
something, he complained to Gosse, it was a sure sign that it was
bad. The following year saw the appearance of a collection of
short stories under the title *The Merry Men*, a volume of poetry,
Underwoods, his most substantial collection, Louis's piece on
Jenkin, *A Memoir of Fleeming Jenkin*, and *Memories and Portraits*.
The widening of his range was clear. The fruits of several years
'hadden doon by the Bubblyjock' at La Solitude and Skerryvore
were brought forth with general approval. He had mastered the
short story and the short novel; his style had mellowed, the
brittle, self-conscious edges had been smoothed. His poetry at
its best, though much of it remained mediocre, achieved a
memorable resonance. Certain moods, certain qualities of
feeling, he could catch with simple and felt precision. The best
were still to come, the poems of nostalgic longing written in
exile which still catch the throat. But he had learned a great deal
about life and about writing.

Music continued to absorb him, but that would never be a
success. He sent his efforts at composition to Bob for comment.
He and Lloyd – 'You should hear Lloyd on the penny whistle,
and me on the piano! Dear powers, what a concerto!' – were
sending their neighbours, he alleged, 'in quest of brighter
climes'.[32] It was all part of the need for expression. Thomas and
Maggie spent part of the winter in Torquay, and then returned
to Scotland. Louis and Fanny had contemplated a trip to
Scotland the previous summer, but it was too strenuous a trip to
undertake. For a while Thomas seemed better, the extremes of
absentness and irritation gone. But it was only temporary.
Thomas spoke to his little Lou as if he were a child again. Early
in May, Louis received a sudden summons from Heriot Row.
On 6 May he arrived in Edinburgh. 'Lou arrived this afternoon
and his father does not know him,'[33] was his mother's simple
entry in her diary. He did not recognise Louis before he died.

Chapter 10

TIMES ARE CHANGED SINCE
THE LOTHIAN ROAD

. . . times are changed since the Lothian Road. Well, the Lothian
Road was grand fun too; I could take an afternoon of it with great
delight. But I'm awfu' grand noo, and long may it last!

Letter to Charles Baxter

Louis and Fanny did not at first stay at Heriot Row. It seemed
best not to add to the stress there. They had telegraphed to
Charles Baxter asking if they could stay with him and his wife
Gracie. But the strain on Louis was intense. His father did not
know him in his last hours; perhaps he had never known his son,
refusing to recognise the echoes of his own uncertain youth.
Perhaps fathers could never know their sons, nor sons their
fathers. 'I cannot get used to this world,' Louis wrote later, 'to
procreation, to heredity, to sight, to hearing; the commonest
things are a burthen.'[1] How much of himself did he owe to his
father, who had tormented himself through so much of life?
That Louis remained preoccupied with his relationship with his
father, with procreation and heredity, with the burden of
common features of Scottish life, emerges powerfully in the
novel he began to write a few months later, *The Master of
Ballantrae*. The preoccupation was starkly present again in his
last, unfinished, novel.

Louis had scarcely arrived in Edinburgh before he was ill
again. Reading of his illnesses one begins to suspect a strong
psychosomatic element, and never does it appear so clearly than
at the time of Thomas's death. Louis 'caught a cold', but the
catarrh and the coughing may well have had other than
physiological causes. On doctor's orders, those of his uncle
Doctor George Balfour, he did not attend the funeral. While an
impressively large crowd accompanied the coffin Louis stayed
behind in the empty rooms of 17 Heriot Row, and for three
weeks, all the time he was in Edinburgh, he was ill.

Death had left its complications. In recent years Thomas had become less involved in the family business, and had allowed his two nephews, the sons of his brother David who had followed the profession that Louis had rejected, to take a larger share of the work and the profits. But it seems that this had not been achieved smoothly enough to avoid a degree of acrimony and distress. Thomas may well have taken it hard that there was no son of his own to inherit the business, and may well have resented the suggestion that he himself was growing too old and ill to cope. He retired entirely from the business some months before his death: one assumes that the arrangements entailed were accepted by all concerned. But Louis had the business of the will to deal with. Thomas had left much of his estate to the kirk, but it became eventually clear that, although there had been a period when Thomas had thought about disinheritance, Louis had been left £3000. It was money enough to launch him into some changes, but it is unlikely that he had any idea how radical the changes would be. In a wet Edinburgh May, wretched with cold and grief, he perhaps tried to cheer himself with thoughts of new possibilities, but there were too many other things to be dealt with to give himself up fully to dreams.

It was not a time, either, to revisit old haunts. Fanny and Louis could not linger in Edinburgh. They returned to Skerryvore, to bring to fruition plans for travel which had in fact been simmering before money brought them to the boil. Fanny had been away from her native country for seven years; their thoughts had been turning to America, and now there was a proposal that Louis's mother should accompany them. Fanny and Louis were carried by cab to Waverley Station. Countless times Louis had boarded trains at Waverley which took him south. Hindsight makes this particular departure of more moment than it could possibly have appeared at the time. Louis was never to see Edinburgh again. Lothian Road, Charles Baxter, the gaslights of Heriot Row in the small hours, father and mother in the drawing-room, the hills to the south and west, the Firth to the north – the present mysteriously became the past as the cab made its way along Princes Street and Louis looked up, as he must have done, it cannot be avoided, to the castle and the sloping outline of spires and gabled roofs. He was seen by Flora Masson.

An open cab, with a man and a woman in it, seated side by side, and leaning back – the rest of the cab piled high with rather untidy luggage – came slowly towards us. . . . As it passed us, out on the broad roadway . . . a slender, loose-garbed figure stood up in the cab and waved a wide-brimmed hat.

'Good-bye!' he called to us. 'Good-bye!'[2]

He would never see Edinburgh again, but it is hard not to see the death of his father as a liberation from the city that had gripped him so inexorably for so much of his life. It was only after this, and thousands of miles away, that he would write those moving, evocative poems of his native city.

Louis had frequently reprimanded his father for giving himself up to guilt, but in whatever other ways heredity had shaped him, guilt gnawed at Louis too. He wanted to be a good son. If his father's death freed him from the burden of struggling to be so (being a good son to his mother was a different thing) it left him with a pulsing vein of mixed guilt and anger which yielded *Ballantrae* and *Weir of Hermiston*. But for the time being depression and haemorrhage reigned. Only when plans for movement became reality were they diminished. Once on the move the former, at least, was conquered.

There was much to be done. Arrangements had to be made to let Skerryvore. When the will was sorted out they were sure that there would be money for the enterprise, and that Mrs Stevenson would be able to pay her share of the trip. After forty years of marriage, and sixty years old, she was amazingly spirited in her attitude to the proposed journey in a cargo boat from the Thames to the Hudson. With Maggie, Fanny and Louis, Lloyd and the faithful Valentine it was a large party, with a proportionate quantity of luggage. Louis's days of travelling light were over. It was an expensive proposition, even by cargo boat. But Louis looked forward excitedly to being on the sea again; salt water was his element, as he rediscovered during this trip. With money in his pocket he began to entertain ideas of sea-going yachts.

Before going on board the *Ludgate Hill* they spent two nights in London, in a little hotel in Finsbury Circus. There some of his friends came to say goodbye. For some of them this trip to America must have seemed ominous. Memories of the last time Louis had crossed the Atlantic must have crossed their minds: what would he bring back with him this time? Colvin came, and made his farewells on board ship. He and Fanny had quarrelled shortly before, probably the result of the combination of Fanny's touchiness and Colvin's disapproval of the whole enterprise. Louis had written despondently from the dismantled Skerryvore just before leaving, asking Colvin's forgiveness for himself and Fanny. He was aware of an ending, the ending of a phase of his life, and deeply anxious that his departure should be taken in an atmosphere of calm and goodwill. He, too, surely remembered the last time. 'This time of my life is at an end,' he wrote to Colvin. 'If it leaves bitterness in your mind, what kind of a time has it been?'[3] Colvin responded to the appeal.

Another of those who came to the Finsbury hotel – the 'real Todgers' as Louis delightedly described it – was Edmund Gosse, and he wrote about his farewell to a friend, almost with a sense that this would be the last time he would see Louis.

I have just got back, much excited, from saying farewell to RLS. I did not in the least expect to see him, but I had a summons last night . . . suddenly he came into the room, looking rather white, and a little dazzled in the eyes, but otherwise much better and less emaciated than I feared. I was allowed to be with him for a whole hour. He is in mourning for his father, and was quite stylishly dressed in a black velvet coat and waistcoat and black silk neck-tie and dark trousers, so that instead of looking like a Lascar out of employment, as he generally does, he looked extremely elegant and refined, his hair over his shoulders, but very tidy, and burnished like brass with brushing. He prowled about the room, in his usual noiseless panther fashion, talking all the time, full of wit and feeling and sweetness, as charming as ever he was, but with a little more sadness and sense of crisis than usual.[4]

On 22 August, 1887, they boarded the *Ludgate Hill*.

Maggie was clearly not too sure about it. She had taken a sad and rather lonely leave from Edinburgh. It was more exciting, and reassuring, to be with the bustle of company, but she had misgivings.

The ship looks dirty and shabby and has curious boards all round the deck. This rather disconcerts us & by & by we find out that it is a cattleship & that we are going to Havre to take in horses. We agree to look upon it as an adventure & make the most of it. Louis tells us that the stable smell is wholesome. It's very amusing & like a circus to see the horses coming on board.[5]

With the encouragement of Louis and Fanny, Maggie's gameness overcame a great deal. Louis himself relished every moment on shipboard. There was the sea, there was life full of incident – not only were horses taken on board, but monkeys also – and there was movement. Maggie was stoical, Fanny less cheerful. She did not enjoy sea travel at the best of times, and the crossing was rough enough to make her and numerous of the other passengers sick. Safely on the opposite shore Louis was writing spiritedly to his friends back home. To James he wrote,

> I . . . enjoyed myself more than I could have hoped on board our strange floating menagerie: stallions and monkeys and matches made our cargo; and the vast continent of these incongruities rolled the while like a haystack; and the stallions stood hypnotised by the motion, looking through our ports at our dinner table, and winked when the crockery was broken; and the little monkeys stared at each other in their cages, and were thrown overboard like little bluish babies; and the big monkey, Jacko, scoured about the ship and rested willingly in my arms, to the ruin of my clothing; and the man of the stallions made a bower of the black tarpaulin, and sat therein at the feet of a raddled divinity, like a picture on a box of chocolates; and the other passengers, when they were not sick, looked on and laughed.[6]

The joy in the incongruities sparkles. The world had come to life again for Louis. There were to be no tears shed over the loss of Skerryvore.

The world came to life in another way for Louis when the *Ludgate Hill* docked at New York on 7 September. He had no thought what a welcome would await him. He was greeted by journalists, hot for words from the lips of the author of *Jekyll and*

Hyde, which had been a stunning success in the United States, and by a representative of Scribner's, his American publishers, and by his old friend Will Low. There was a telegram for him also, from Mrs Fairchild, who had commissioned the Sargent portrait, informing him that hotel rooms had been booked for him and his party as the Fairchilds' guests. Journalists followed him there. Louis's arrival in New York coincided with the imminent production of a stage version of *Jekyll and Hyde*; it was exhausting, but it couldn't have given a heftier boost to this new phase of Louis's career.

After resting at the Hotel Victoria the Stevenson clan went on to Newport, Rhode Island, where the Fairchilds had invited them to stay at their summer house there. The Fairchilds were people with money who wanted to invest in culture. Friends of John Singer Sargent, whom Louis had got to know well while sitting for his portrait at Skerryvore, they were eager to take under their wing the up-and-coming, and charming, author who stepped off a cattle boat in New York harbour. Fortunately Louis liked them, and although he was somewhat embarrassed by the reception he received in New York, and did not trust that kind of popularity, he did not allow it or the Fairchilds' generosity to interfere with the rapid development of firm friendship. Louis had caught another cold, and it was a relief to be cared for and cushioned by Newport opulence. Lloyd and Aunt Maggie, presumably because there was not enough room for them at the Fairchilds', stayed in a Newport boarding house, where Aunt Maggie was much impressed by American cleanliness and cooking. She liked the coloured servants, 'pleasant and kind', and commented with some surprise on the fact that though they had nothing but iced water to drink, she did not miss her wine.[7] Louis, who was certainly well wined by the Fairchilds, would scarcely have been so tolerant.

The original plan had been to try the Colorado mountains for Louis's health. His Uncle George in Edinburgh had been insistent that a change was needed, and had suggested Colorado as having the dry, high, piny air that current opinion considered the best for lung patients. But an alternative solution presented itself, a place that was nearer to New York and less expensive, Saranac Lake, high up in the Adirondack Mountains near the Canadian border. In September Fanny and Lloyd set off up the

Hudson by steamer to reconnoitre, and by the end of the month the others were on their way to join them.

Saranac Lake was chosen because it was there that an eminent physician, who had himself suffered from tuberculosis, had established a clinic which was pioneering new methods of diagnosis. Dr E. L. Trudeau took on Louis as a patient and was soon pronouncing encouragingly on his condition. It was the beginning of a relationship that never seems to have become more than professional, although Louis was grateful for Trudeau's attentions and Trudeau was interested in his patient. Perhaps Louis found it difficult to develop cordial relations with the doctors who were inevitably associated with so much tedious misery. Throughout this winter Louis saw Trudeau regularly, and remained pretty well, although Fanny often was not. There was not much to the village of Saranac Lake at this time. It is still a town that has not quite lost its village flavour. There was Trudeau's clinic, a few patients scattered about, hunters, loggers, a post office. Fanny found part of a house to rent owned by the Baker family, who continued to occupy the rear premises. Lloyd described it as 'bald and isolated on a bluff overlooking the river and was the kind of house that a prosperous guide would run up in his spare time with the help of a local carpenter'.[8] Lloyd didn't like the cold – winter temperatures were habitually way below zero – and he didn't much care for the primitive nature of the household, and in fact spent part of the winter with the Fairchilds in Boston.

Fanny's experience of life reduced to basics stood her in good stead, and she set about making the house as warm and habitable as possible. Windows and the front door were sealed up to keep out the cold. Louis was cheerfully able to see resemblances to the Highlands – there was no peat and no heather, but the rivers, the lake, the pine trees and the hills still have a flavour of Scottish Highland scenery. As at Kinnaird Cottage, Pitlochry, the sound of running water could be heard from the house, always a point in favour as far as Louis was concerned. They prepared for the winter. Fanny went to Montreal to equip them all with fur and buffalo robes. Once the snow had come, keeping warm was a full-time occupation. When Valentine tried to wash the floor the water froze on the floor before it could dry. They had help from the Bakers with

cooking and the supply of wood and water, which had to be
brought some distance. Food was erratic – they were living on
bread and venison, Fanny wrote to Adelaide Boodle – but if they
were to get over-anxious about little things like that they would
never have survived the subsequent six years.

*RLS, Fanny and Lloyd on the verandah of the cottage at Saranac Lake,
1887–8*

For Louis, as always, the important thing was to get back to
his writing. Fanny was keen to see her family, so fairly soon after
she had got everyone settled in the Bakers' house she set off for
Indianapolis. Louis, after the New York and Newport interlude,
was in ebullient mood but anxious to work. New York had been
full of, if not inspiration, at least stimulus and encouragement of
rather overwhelming proportions. One of the first to greet him
as the *Ludgate Hill* docked was E. L. Burlingame, of Scribner's,
eager to tie Louis firmly to the Scribner imprint. But hot on his
heels was the irrepressible Sam McClure. McClure, a native of
Scotland, had come up the hard and fast way, in classic style, and

was by this time one of New York's chief literary entrepreneurs. Louis liked him, but was a little suspicious, and thought it outrageous that McClure should be offering him 10,000 dollars a year for a weekly contribution to the *World* magazine. He could not bring himself to accept it. But the more modest Scribner offer of 3500 dollars for essays on subjects of Louis's choice was realistically tempting, and this he accepted, although it meant promising all his writing to Scribner's. McClure, however, was not one to give up easily, and some time later extracted the promise of a novel to himself. There were ructions, of course, but the tangle was eventually sorted out, with profuse apologies in all directions from Louis who, as so often, had allowed good nature to banish all apprehension of business agreements. Without Baxter and Colvin cannily handling the British end of his publishing relationships, Louis would have countless times got himself into such difficulties. The American problems were resolved, but his future career in the United States was dominated by his relations with these two men, Burlingame and McClure, who came to wield perhaps more influence over him and what he wrote than was either reasonable or healthy.

Still, Louis could enjoy this splendid ending to his money problems. The Americans provided a public who wanted to read his books. He was establishing firm connections with publishers which meant an end to the pirating of his works which had gone on previously, although there were now legitimate editions of *Kidnapped* and *Treasure Island* on the market as well as *Jekyll and Hyde*. And they were publishers who were prepared to pay him on a scale he had never dreamed of on the other side of the Atlantic. But in some ways it went against the grain. It was the old problem. 'I am now a salaried party,' he wrote somewhat wryly to William Archer.

> I am a *bourgeois* now; I am to write a weekly paper for *Scribner's*, at a scale of payment which makes my teeth ache for shame and diffidence. . . . I am like to be a millionaire if this goes on, and be publicly hanged [on two counts, now, for this and for Skerryvore] at the social revolution: well, I would prefer that to dying in my bed; and it would be a godsend to my biographer, if ever I have one.[9]

But it is doubtful whether the putative consequences of an unlikely social revolution worried him too seriously, especially as plans for a yacht were very much alive, and yachts needed money. It began to look as though Louis would at last get 'all the fun of the fair', as he had predicted so confidently to Mrs Sitwell some years before.

Louis settled briskly to his work. The essays he began to produce for *Scribner's Magazine* were amongst his most provocative. He seemed less contrained now, more forthright in what he had to say. He was, he said of 'Pulvis et Umbra', frankly writing sermons. The stripped characterisation of humanity in this essay has echoes of *Hamlet*, both in cadence and in sentiment; he had not written in quite so straightforward and undisguised a fashion before, without the props of fiction. But the echoes of the Old Testament are even stronger, although his message was not quite a Calvinist one. He found it extraordinary and marvellous that man's life, though a 'tragedy of misconception and misconduct', should be so full of sincere struggle, that in the face of such enormous odds men still tried to do what they considered right.[10] If at the end the essay falls too drastically into his belief in the necessity of optimism, it rings more true here, perhaps, than in the jollier tones he sometimes used and by which he is most often labelled. Although he had communicated the gist of the message before, the sombre tones of 'Pulvis et Umbra' may have had something to do with his father's death.

The essays kept him busy, and he despatched them cheerfully to Burlingame. But the major task was another novel. He was contemplating a story in which he would portray family relations – between father and son, brother and brother, husband and wife – as painful and bitter, and doomed to be so by the nature of the family itself and by the particular features of the Scottish past that shaped it. In December 1887 he was writing to Colvin with an outline of the novel – it was *The Master of Ballantrae*. Choosing the territory of the 1745 Rebellion and its aftermath – *Kidnapped* territory, but only one of the major eruptions of Scottish history that split families and encouraged the belief that 'the war in the members' was both psychologically and physically native to the Scots – Louis started upon a tale of greater sophistication than anything he had attempted before.

It was not without problems. He chose to write it in the first person of one of his psychologically most convincing creations, Ephraim Mackellar, whose dour, dogmatic and unimaginative mind digests the story for us. The triumph of Mackellar's characterisation lies partly in the fact that while he gives an impression of being non-partisan and uncommitted he is in fact fiercely so, but committed not to a cause, nor even to a person, but to the preservation of the good name of the family he serves. Mackellar gives the novel its real distinction. It is when it strays away from him, either deliberately, when another character, the much less happily realised Chevalier de Burke, or unintentionally, when Stevenson's control over the personality and outlook of Mackellar slackens, that the novel falters. Stevenson was aware of the problems. At one point he contemplated recasting the entire tale in the third person, but he would almost certainly have lost more than he would have gained. The essential unpleasantness of the major actors could well have destroyed it. It started off well, though – the usual pattern. Louis was confidently writing to Burlingame from Saranac that he had in hand 'a howling good tale', and 'the public will like it perhaps, for it is picturesque and curious and dismal'.[11] The Adirondack winter provided a suitable environment for the writing of so stark a tale, and he couldn't resist setting the novel's closing chapters right there, perhaps with an eye to pleasing the American public. But the idea was not a happy one. The almost stern control that operates in most of the novel loosens and Stevenson finds himself with all the elements of a 'crawler' on his hands, but with no wish to develop them. The book was finished in the Pacific, at a distance from the mountains and forests of northern New York State where the story unsteadily ends. The last chapters were a serious obstacle, and when he finally brought the book to a conclusion, in a rush of enthusiastic writing in Hawaii, he wasn't at all pleased with the result. Neither was Burlingame, and both were right.

But Stevenson was also right, or partly so, in thinking that the only appropriate ending for his story of fraternal rivalry was the death of both brothers, and death in unhappy circumstances. There was no other possible resolution, and to have left it unresolved would have been more daring and experimental than the public were likely to have accepted. To have the two brothers causing each other's deaths was in the tradition of ballad and folk tale, though Stevenson robs the final contest of a real sense of climax, for in its particulars it is not a contest at all. To write a story in which the Devil features – and Stevenson made it quite clear that James Durie is in effect the Devil, his courage, his culture and his elegance an essential part of the characterisation – and avoid the business of retribution would have been, in Stevenson's terms, a failure of commitment. James Durie destroys his brother Henry as effectively as Hyde destroys Jekyll. But although the duality is equally inescapable and the opposition is stark, *The Master of Ballantrae* is a much more psychologically complex novel. Having established his theme in *Jekyll and Hyde*, prefigured it in *Treasure Island* and a number of short stories, echoed it in *Kidnapped*, in *The Master* he explores it more fully and deliberately.

At a small desk in a cramped corner of the Baker house Louis worked at the novel and produced his pieces for *Scribner's*. The magazine pieces were not all so weighty as 'Pulvis et Umbra'. He was in a mood for reminiscence and produced such essays as 'The Lantern Bearers', thinking back to summers at North Berwick, 'The Manse', about Colinton, and other scraps of memoirs. He provided an eclectic range for *Scribner's*, which also serialised *The Master*, much of it with a distinctly Scottish flavour which presumably went down well with American readers. Burlingame did not seem to be dissuading him from Scottish topics, in fact possibly the reverse, for when he came to read *The Wrecker*, Louis's next novel, written in collaboration with Lloyd, he complained about his characterisation of Americans. Although Louis had one or two notable successes in his descriptions of the American scene, particularly in *The Amateur Emigrant* and *The Silverado Squatters*, there were some significant failures too. One of the reasons that the last chapters of *The Master* do not hold is that he fails to communicate the ambience of eighteenth-century eastern America.

Lloyd was writing seriously now, with encouragement from Louis, who would hear Lloyd's typewriter rattling in the next room while he himself continued with his longhand. In so small a house Louis could scarcely be unaware of the activities of others, Valentine in the kitchen, Fanny discussing the dinner, Mr Baker bringing in wood and water. It was hardly surprising that towards the end of the long winter Louis was finding Saranac rather grim and bleak. Other things contributed to this. Fanny was often not well. On one occasion when both Fanny and Valentine were confined to bed Louis described with some pride how he managed in the kitchen, preparing meals and washing dishes, though getting a shine on glasses defeated him. In December there was depressing news of the lack of success of *Deacon Brodie*, which was touring the States. Contributory to this was the fact that Henley's brother Teddy was in the leading role, and Teddy was an embarrassment. He had a habit of drinking too much and getting involved in bar-room fights and other episodes that brought *Deacon Brodie* some bad publicity. He had always been an unreliable and difficult personality, and Louis and Fanny found their association with him trying.

Worse was to come, however, and it concerned the same family. Illness and bleakness and local difficulties with *Deacon Brodie* were all things Louis had coped with before, and to help him cope this time there was plenty of good news to sustain him. But in March he received a letter for which he was entirely unprepared. It was from Henley, beginning in characteristic vein, reproving Louis, with the touchy, tortuous humour that is so typical of Henley's epistolary style and always suggests that he means to be taken very seriously, for being so far away. It was a longish letter. The bombshell lay in what might have seemed an innocently expressed little paragraph.

> I read 'The Nixie' with considerable astonishment. It's Katharine's, surely it's Katharine's? The situation, the environment, the principal figure – *voyons!* There are even reminiscences of phrases and imagery, parallel incidents – *que sais-je?* It is all better focussed, no doubt, but I think it has lost as much (at least) as it has gained; and why there wasn't a double signature is what I've not been able to understand.[12]

'The Nixie' was a story of Fanny's, published in the March number of *Scribner's*. Some time before, when Louis's cousin Katharine de Mattos had been staying at Skerryvore, she and Fanny had discussed an idea for a story. Katharine had written it up but could not find a publisher. Dissatisfied with the outcome she had suggested Fanny should have a try. Fanny did, and 'The Nixie' was the result.

Louis reacted to Henley's letter as if a barb had struck his vitals. That Henley was aware of the explosive nature of the charges he'd laid was clear – 'Don't show this to anybody,' he instructed in the letter, 'and when you write, don't do more than note it in a general way, if at all,' and *'burn this letter'* he finished.[13] But perhaps he thought that what he had written was explosive only in respect of Fanny. If so, he entirely misjudged the depth and nature of Louis's loyalty towards his wife. His pained reaction, written after much struggle, is worth quoting in full. It helps us to avoid underestimating the effect of this episode, which brought to an end a rich and vibrant if at times unsteady friendship.

William Ernest Henley,
photo by F. Hollyes

My dear Henley,
    I write with indescribable difficulty, and if not with perfect temper, you are to remember how very rarely a husband is expected to receive such accusation against his wife. I can only direct you to apply to Katharine and ask her to remind you of

that part of the business which took place in your presence and which you seem to have forgotten. She will doubtless add other particulars which perhaps you may not have heard – such as that she refused to collaborate on my wife's version of the tale, and when she agreed it was to be written, asked that a copy might be sent her; she will also, I have no doubt, lend you a copy of her original story, from which you will be reminded how the matter stands.

I am sorry I must ask you to take these steps; I might take them for myself had you not tied my hands by the strange step of marking your letter 'private and confidential'. An accusation of this gravity, you must suffer me to say, should not have been made without leaving me free to communicate with Katharine. I wish I could stop here. I cannot. When you have refreshed your mind as to the facts, you will, I know, withdraw what you have said to me; but I must go further and remind you, if you have spoken of this to others, a proper explanation and retraction of what you shall have said or implied to any person so addressed will be necessary.

From the bottom of my soul I believe what you wrote to have been merely reckless words written in forgetfulness with no clear appreciation of their meaning, but it is hard to think that anyone – and least of all my friend – should have been so careless of dealing agony. To have inflicted more distress than you have done would have been difficult. This is the sixth or seventh attempt I make to write to you, and I will now only add that I count upon your immediately replying to Katharine for the facts, and await your answer with the most painful expectation.

You will pardon me if I can find no form of signature; I pray God such a blank will not be of long endurance.

Robert Louis Stevenson[14]

Louis's pain was not just huffiness. There were three elements in his response. First, that the accusation was false, second that it was a betrayal of friendship to have articulated it in the way Henley chose, third that there had been painful ructions before between the two friends, and Louis had felt some confidence that all their disagreements and quarrels, which he suggests elsewhere were largely Henley's fault – which was likely to be the

case as Henley was notorious for quarrelling with his friends –
were at an end.

   Louis also wrote to Charles Baxter, badly needing to share his
distress with someone who knew them both. He did not at first
share it with Fanny. In this letter, much longer, it is clear that
Louis had often before been pained by the instability and the
paranoid strain in Henley's personality. He attributed the fault
not entirely to Henley alone, but to the 'clique' of which Louis
felt he was a part, and it was all the more bitter to him as he had
tried to help Henley and his friends on numerous occasions –
and continued to do so, anonymously, after the quarrel.

> . . . what exasperates me in this clique is that they foment these
> things in my absence. Since I left (I would not say it to them – I
> may to you) I think not one of them has had anything but
> money from me; and here again they have sprung up one of
> their little bitter cabals in my absence and my silence. It is a
> process essentially weariful, and I perceive no possible end to
> it but a judicious distance – no longer in space, which avails
> me nothing, but in heart, which will at least save me from
> further lacerations.[15]

Of course, Henley was jealous of Louis's success and felt that
they were no longer on equal terms, and the fact that he was
receiving money and help from Louis only intensified the
jealousy. The failure of the plays was something that he always
held against Louis, suspecting a lack of commitment on his part,
and for a time relying heavily on the prospect of generous
remuneration from their success. Katharine, too, dabbling in
literature in much the same way as Fanny, was not without
jealousy. It became clear that she and Henley were in collusion
in their accusation. The discovery of this only rubbed salt into
Louis's wounds.

   Henley's jealousy had another dimension. He had never been
able to accept Fanny, and it is hard not to read his letter as a
possibly calculated, certainly at least unconscious, attempt to
diminish her stature in Louis's eyes. The urge to make another
see what appears so obvious to oneself is sometimes irresistible.
Henley was sure that Fanny was not only an insupportable
person herself, but was not good for Louis, interfering with his
writing and his life, especially his friendships, in an intolerable

fashion. The letter was perhaps a test of Louis's loyalty – would he choose to go with Henley, or with Fanny? His lack of understanding of the relationship between husband and wife in this case was gross, and that must have been part of what hurt Louis so profoundly. How could Henley ever have thought that in friendly male collusion Louis would, in however relaxed and unserious a fashion, have disparaged his wife? Later, when it was hard for Louis to disguise the fact that Fanny was a source of difficulties for them both, it was with the deepest reluctance that he intimated his problems.

Inevitably Louis suffered a backlash. No apology was forthcoming from Henley, who when he finally communicated blandly ignored most of what Louis had so painfully gone into, and Baxter was in the position of having to act as referee between them. It was not long before Louis was reproaching himself, 'counting up my sins against these friends of mine',[16] but the pain of Henley's offence against friendship did not ease – and he never went so far as to consider Fanny guilty. Friendship had always been of the greatest importance to Louis. When he said that even if Fanny had behaved in the manner ascribed to her (he entertained the possibility even though he didn't admit it) a true friend would have let it pass, this was not special pleading on his part but a genuine reflection of what he considered friendship to be. He was himself prepared to give a great deal and forgive a great deal, and had always done both. Friends would do the same for him; it was shattering to find they might not, that they could be unreliable, weak, even deceitful. It was the lesson he learned from the break with Henley.

Although he would correspond extensively with numerous friends, and would make many friends through correspondence, for the rest of his life, there was never again quite the same kind of spontaneous, self-generative, creative relationship that he had had with Henley, or the relaxed literary intimacy that he maintained with James. Although for the remainder of his life he would never be without an entourage of family and hangers-on, and had numerous lively acquaintances, Louis's crossing of the Atlantic westward for the second time initiated a very real exile. There were to be no more friends like Henley, Colvin, Baxter, and James. The loyalty of the last three remained unshaken; Baxter's walking of the tightrope between

Louis and Henley during the quarrel was sensitive and tactful. Colvin girned about Louis's absence and was often dissatisfied with what he wrote, and Louis was well aware of Colvin's limitations, but their mutual affection was deep-rooted. It wasn't just the distance that was responsible for the nature of the exile. It was also Louis's new stature. Louis was neither a young man nor a young writer any more. The sustaining paternal figures of Colvin and James were appropriately distant, for Louis, his father lost, needed father-figures rather less. He was in his turn becoming a father-figure, to young aspiring writers, and to members of his extended family. At Vailima, perhaps accepting the inevitable, he positively institutionalised the paternal role. He may have thought he needed some solid backing to preside over his wayward family. Some thought the role did not become him; he thought he could not shirk his responsibilities.

Louis never got over his break with Henley, although he was able to write to him later in friendly fashion again. All the time the break was in process he reiterated his belief in Henley's qualities, as if to remind himself of why he had admired him. Fanny, of course – and there was no way Louis could have kept it all from her even if he had continued to feel he should – was bitter, but for her there was not such a personal betrayal. She had never had much time for Henley. Louis's wretchedness about the whole business persisted; although Fanny was angry and scathing the hurt became a part of her general antagonism towards Henley. Henley nursed resentment too, which was to erupt with a certain viciousness after Louis's death, when he wrote his 'seraph in chocolate' article for the *Pall Mall Magazine*, accusing Louis of selling out his rebellious principles and becoming a darling of the conventional, bourgeois world. If Louis, who was always so quick to accuse himself on just those grounds, had seen it it would have cut him to the quick. But it is unlikely that Henley would have phrased it quite so uncompromisingly if Louis had been alive to read it.

Depression brought Louis close to self-pity. The fact that he could write at length to Charles Baxter was an essential outlet – Charles would understand both the depression and the self-pity. 'The bottom wish of my heart is that I had died at Hyères,' he was writing in the middle of April, harking back again to that period of happiness and severe illness, 'the happy part of my life ended there; since then I have never been well enough really to enjoy life, except for a day or two at a time, and I fear my character has suffered, and I know that troubles have grown upon me.'[17] He had forgotten, perhaps, the extremes of fever and sleeplessness and Fanny struggling to lift him, and the panics, and the overwork. Although he was right: he had lost something. Life would get increasingly complex, the troubles thicker; but there were to be compensations. Talk of yachts had materialised into concrete planning. Fanny at that very moment was on her way to California to explore the possibilities of chartering an ocean-going vessel that would take them into the Pacific. They had sat weaving extravagant plans in front of the fire in the Baker house, and now they were moving towards realisation. A few days after writing this depressed letter to Baxter, Louis left Saranac Lake for New York, and after two weeks went on to Manasquan on the New Jersey coast, where he was able to enjoy the sea and some sailing.

He found New York trying, although he met Mark Twain while he was there, and the two of them sat on a bench in Washington Square talking about writing: it presents a winning picture. Will Low suggested Manasquan as a suitable escape from New York, and came to visit him there. Augustus St

Medallion in bas-relief, by Augustus St Gaudens, 1887

Gaudens came too, another artist, who had worked on a medallion of Louis before he had gone to Saranac. The medallion, an enlarged copy of which is in St Giles Cathedral, Edinburgh, is in many ways one of the most striking portrayals of the bedridden author – although the St Giles version has replaced the characteristic cigarette with a pen. Louis had always savoured the company of artists, and Manasquan was one of those places where they congregated. His month there must have reminded him wistfully of days at Grez, with boating, picnics, sunshine, undemanding company.

In May there came electrifying news, a telegram from Fanny announcing the successful chartering of a schooner yacht out of San Francisco. All of a sudden the dream was reality. Louis was speedily writing to James about a trip to Honolulu, Tahiti, the Galapagos, Guayaquil, magic names they had rolled on their tongues at Saranac. He cabled 'yes' to Fanny and gathered his party together for the trip west – himself, Lloyd, Aunt Maggie and Valentine. Here at last was something that might convince him that the 'happy part' of his life was not yet over. 'It seems too good to be true,' he wrote to James, 'and is a very good way of getting through the green-sickness of maturity, which, with all its accompanying ills, is now declaring itself in my mind and life.'[18] Louis, reluctantly, was admitting that he had grown up. The excitement, then, of an adventure that smacked of youth was that much greater. The yacht *Casco*, lying in San Francisco harbour, contained his hopes for health and revitalisation, a tonic for the green-sickness, and food for fiction.

Chapter 11

BURGUNDY OR DAYBREAK

I loved a ship as a man loves burgundy or daybreak.
Edinburgh: Picturesque Notes

It was a day in December 1889 when the Reverend W. E. Clarke, missionary in Samoa, saw three 'Europeans' walking along the shore at Apia. Years later, when one of them was dead, he described what he saw.

> ... I met a little group of three European strangers – two men and a woman. The latter wore a print gown, large gold crescent earrings, a Gilbert-Island hat of plaited straw, encircled by a wreath of small shells, a scarlet silk scarf round her neck, and a brilliant plaid shawl across her shoulders; her bare feet were encased in white canvas shoes, and across her back was slung a guitar. . . . The younger of her two companions was dressed in a striped pyjama suit – the undress costume of most European traders in these seas – a slouch hat of native make, dark blue sun-spectacles, and over his shoulders a banjo. The other man was dressed in a shabby suit of white flannels that had seen many better days, a white drill yachting cap with a prominent peak, a cigarette in his mouth, a photographic camera in his hand. Both the men were bare-footed. They had, evidently, just landed from the little schooner now lying placidly at anchor, and my first thought was that, probably, they were wandering players en route to New Zealand, compelled by their poverty to take the cheap conveyance of a trading vessel.[1]

They were, of course, Louis, Fanny and Lloyd. The Reverend Clarke, Protestant, sent out by the London Missionary Society, which had established a strong foothold in the Pacific some decades before, observed with curiosity and described with affection. Later he would get to know Louis quite well – Louis enjoyed his company, and liked to argue out his equivocal feelings about the missionary presence in the South Seas. That Clarke was not particularly puzzled by this odd troubadourish group suggests something about the curious and drifting character of European life in the Pacific. It was something that Louis would write about, eventually with considerable insight.

When the trading schooner *Equator* dropped anchor off Apia, the main town on the Samoan island of Upolu, in a bay studded with the carcasses of German, American and British ships which had been driven on to the reef by the previous year's hurricane, Louis, Fanny and Lloyd had been in the Pacific for over a year. Louis was thinking about going back home, for a visit at least, even if he couldn't linger there. He was also thinking about where he might try next as a place of possible permanent settlement. They had been on the move, though with some long pauses, since July of the previous year. During most of that time Louis had been amazingly well. He hadn't lost his leanness – that would never go – but he was tanned and fit and active. There had been some illness, some relapses, but it is a pride in his new physical strength that radiates in many of his letters. 'My health has stood me splendidly,' he was writing to Colvin after two months at sea; 'I am in for hours wading over the knees for shells; I have been five hours on horseback . . .'[2] A year earlier this would have been inconceivable.

It may have been not only that the Pacific climate suited his body, but that ship and island life suited his psychological needs. Certain impositions fell away. Ships had always tantalised him. Under sail he was in touch with an elemental existence that was a part of his inheritance. The dependence on wind and weather, and the dangers, were real, and Louis was able to feel that the door was open on to areas of experience that it must often have seemed he would never encounter again. With this, there is a gentleness about a sailing ship, as well as vigour, and the pace of life confined to ship and island was slower. Although the mails reached him eventually, and he needed to be within their reach, the voices that urged, complained and demanded were that much further away. Scotland was far away. Edinburgh, Heriot Row, the memory of Thomas Stevenson, whose best and freest moments now lingered in his mind, were at a distance. The memory could be selective. London and Henley and Colvin, creating in their different ways enormous pressures, could be kept at bay. Money, at least for the time being, was no problem. There were other pressures that would grow and multiply but the dominant mood when Louis set foot on Upolu was liberation. While in Hawaii he had written to Adelaide Boodle of being 'oppressed with civilisation'³ – after some months at sea and in more primitive areas, a place of telephones with streets of trolleycars was too much. He could stroll through Apia in his shabby white suit, barefooted, odd, and undisturbed.

On 28 June 1888 the yacht *Casco* had slipped out of San Francisco harbour, under the command of Captain Otis, with Louis, Fanny, Lloyd, Aunt Maggie and Valentine on board. The first task Louis had had to accomplish on arrival in San Francisco was to meet and reassure the yacht's owner, a doctor called Merritt. Fanny's telegram had perhaps been a little precipitate. Dr Merritt had a deep distrust of literary people, and his first sight of Louis would scarcely have improved his feeling. But the charm worked and all was well. Dr Merritt was happy to complete the deal. Whatever misgivings Captain Otis may have had about taking on the literary vagabond and his following, it did not prevent the eventual growth of a good relationship between him and his passengers. However puzzling they were, they treated him with friendly respect.

Fitting out the ship took some weeks of activity, most of it undertaken by Fanny and Aunt Maggie. The getting together of stores and provisions for a lengthy voyage in unknown waters was a hefty enterprise. In the midst of the preparations Fanny underwent an unpleasant operation for the removal of a growth in her throat. Fanny and Louis must both have hoped that this would initiate a new period of good health for her, but although the operation was successful and there was no reappearance of the trouble, that was not the case. Louis himself, not well enough to take an active part in the preparations, did have a chance to taste of San Francisco life again. Dora and Virgil Williams, Fanny's old friends, introduced him to some of the artistic and literary figures, amongst them Charles Warren Stoddard who had travelled in the South Seas and written somewhat fulsomely of his experiences. It was Stoddard who introduced Louis to the books of Herman Melville, who had first brought the Pacific within literary perspective. Louis read him enthusiastically, whetting his appetite for the experiences that were soon to be his. He would have enjoyed the almost cryptic, eighteenth-century flavour of the style.

Before dawn, exactly a month after turning their backs on San Francisco, Louis and his companions were on deck trying to pick out the humped islands from the clouds that lay on the horizon. The uncertain light before the sun was up accentuated the excitement of their first landfall in the South Seas, in the Marquesas that Louis had been reading about in Melville's *Typee*. Half a century earlier Melville had had his encounters with the cannibals, and had later described an existence in which food and relaxation and beautiful women were to be had without effort. Louis was not disappointed to find that there were still a few cannibals about, though not currently practising, and the sight of his mother establishing a politely intimate relationship with an ex-cannibal chief was to cause him great amusement – and admiration. He had chosen the Marquesas, he said, 'as having the most beastly population', but found that 'they are far better and more civilised than we'.[4] Melville had been saying something similar. It was a useful first reaction to the Pacific islanders to have. Louis's openness to new experiences, his ability to refrain from judging according to the conventional standards, were to stand him in good stead.

The month at sea had done him good. He rediscovered the fact that the sea was his element. He feasted on sun, salt and wind, and on the unorthodox arrangements that life on board ship demanded. The unorthodoxy asked much of Fanny, and even more of Aunt Maggie, who nevertheless described the way things were on the *Casco* with some relish.

> From the deck you step down into the cockpit, which is our open-air drawing-room. It has seats all round, nicely cushioned, and we sit or lie there most of the day. The compass is there, and the wheel, so the man at the wheel always keeps us company.[5]

The *Casco* was rather superior in its appointments, a fact that was to cause vast interest amongst the native populations. The three women shared the after-cabin. At first Lloyd and Louis each had their own cabins, but Louis abandoned his because it was too stuffy, and joined the women in their quarters. There was no room for maintaining the conventional decencies. Fanny was soon to have accustomed herself to sleeping in numerous unlikely situations and with all kinds of unlikely company. When some time later she had to undress under the eyes of curious islanders, male and female, she managed with considerable aplomb.

As well as the five passengers there was the crew, Captain Otis and five men, Russian, Finnish and Swedish, and including a Japanese cook. A month at sea was a long time for eight men and three women crowded on to a schooner yacht, even though the weather meant that long periods could be spent on deck. Louis managed to carry on with his writing, but the landfall on Nukahiva was welcome. They set foot on the Marquesas, the name and the life both seductive, the mountains rising bright in the sun, promising, Louis wrote, 'a world of wonders'.[6] He was gaining strength, though he was still finding he tired easily. His curiosity and eagerness to find out were operating powerfully. He was alive to the anomalies of the islands, governed by colonial powers who were largely uninterested in the needs and wants of the native inhabitants, who at a distance toyed with Pacific islands in rather the same way that Louis had drawn his map of an imaginary island in the Spanish Main and then had made up a story to go along with it. Louis arrived in the Pacific at a time when the islands were moving into a final phase of disruption at the hands of French, Germans, British and Americans who plied their trade and their politics in that ocean. He was frequently disturbed and sometimes outraged by what he saw. It was this first-hand experience of colonialism in action that prompted him to be outspoken in print in a way that he would never have dreamed of ten years before.

When the *Casco* dropped anchor at Nukahiva the islanders swarmed aboard, as they always did when a strange vessel arrived, and examined every inch of the craft. The *Casco* travellers were a little taken aback at the ease with which the population assumed their right not only to come on board but to make themselves at home, but regarded it with considerable good nature. Louis was naturally a man of good manners, in the sense that he respected what others considered important, would not knowingly do anything to offend, and was prepared to do whatever was required of him in an unfamiliar situation.

This eased him through a number of awkwardnesses. It was all so new, so different. His delight, in accounts that are sometimes weighty with his determination to get the picture right, shines through. 'Bouncing Junos were never weary of sitting in the chairs and contemplating in the glass their own bland images,' he said of the women who came on board, 'and I have seen one lady strip up her dress, and, with cries of wonder and delight, rub herself bare-breeched upon the velvet cushions.'⁷

The Marquesan islands were in the hands of the French; Louis's fluency in the language was a help in establishing good relations. Their population had been a distinctive and dignified group of Polynesians, but their experiences with Europeans had been drastic. The Spanish, who had provided the name, had in their first encounters despatched them wholesale. It was a raw demonstration of what was to happen to the Marquesans more insidiously over the centuries. The white man's diseases took hold, as they did everywhere in the Pacific: smallpox, tuberculosis (ironically, as Louis's health improved) and venereal disease, the curse from which Captain James Cook had tried so hard to protect the Pacific islanders. Louis was very much aware of death and a dwindling population during his visit.

Disease was not the only encroachment. There were the governors and the missionaries, the traders and the entrepreneurs, the transients, white and Asian, who took what they could, successive intrusions that sought to implant or exploit or mould – inevitably to undermine, at the least, outrage at worst, the centuries old beliefs and traditions of the islands' populations. Thinking of such things Louis wrote, 'Bear in mind how it was the custom of the adventurers, and we may almost say the business of the missionaries, to deride and infract even the most salutary tapus.'⁸ Louis grasped quickly the deep-rooted importance of taboo, the prohibitions governed by superstition but essential to community harmony. Wherever he went he followed in the traces of Europeans who had blundered from island to island, shattering the susceptibilities of a people who were all the more vulnerable for their vivacious cheerfulness, their friendliness, their good-natured acceptance of the dangerous white man.

The Marquesans were impressed by Louis and the *Casco*. They summed him up as a man of substance – the mirrors and the velvet cushions demonstrated that. They named him 'Ona' ('owner') and he was treated by chiefs as a chief. He observed and made notes: these were things he was going to be writing about. Lloyd was taking photographs. Aunt Maggie and Fanny were going native. With half-worried, childish relish Aunt Maggie described the two of them.

> Fanny & I are dressed like the natives, in two garments, one being a sort of long chemise with a flounce round the edge, & an upper garment something like a child's pinafore, made with a yoke, but fastening in front. As we have to wade to and from the boat in landing and coming back, we discard stockings, & on the sands we usually go barefoot entirely. Louis wears only a shirt & trousers with the legs and arms rolled up as far as they will go, & he is always barefooted. . . . It is a strange, irresponsible, half-savage life, & I sometimes wonder if we shall ever be able to return to civilised habits again.[9]

Those back home in Edinburgh who read Maggie's letters must have wondered too, but in fact she returned to respectable Edinburgh life without, as far as we can tell, too much difficulty in adjustment. She had always given the impression of being resistant to anything that might have seriously changed the values and standards she considered important. It is hard to believe, though, that Louis could have found it anything but strenuously difficult to go back to New Town Edinburgh after even a few months of Pacific life.

He was working on *The Master*, writing on the *Casco* and making daytime trips to Nukahiva. He was also absorbing a myriad of sensations and impressions that were feeding his imagination and shaping his thoughts: not, perhaps, taking him away from Scotland, but affecting the way in which Scotland could be seen. The perspective was changing. He had five more years to live. They were to be full and productive years, during which he tried to write about Scotland vividly and unequivocally. When he died he was full of plans and ideas, some of which he had begun to put down on paper. There was so much he had yet to say about his own country, and he was never really, totally convincingly, to find a way of saying it. At the same

time the South Seas were insistently present to him, an
experience he was living more positively than he had been able
to live for years, an engagement with a pulsing, perhaps tragic,
situation which he could not ignore. His Pacific experiences
took him into a new area of writing, which was more than a
change of subject matter. He was moving into other ways of
writing about human experience, and they worked.

But for the time being *The Master* and crowded first
impressions dominated. He could not afford to relax too much.
His new life style required a productive pen. He had engaged to
write about the Pacific for *Scribner's*; he was writing long and
detailed (and Colvin thought, boring) letters to Colvin with a
view to publication. Every experience and every new sight had to
be made to work for him if at all possible. Fanny, Lloyd and
Valentine were dependent on him. Before long he was to take on
Belle and Joe Strong too.

When the nights were fine Louis slept in the open cockpit and
soaked himself in the cool, dry air. At times it probably seemed
to his friends back home that it was going to his head. 'This
climate; these voyagings; these landfalls at dawn; new islands
peaking from the morning bank; new forested harbours; new
passing alarms of squalls and surf – the whole tale of my life is
better to me than any poem,' he wrote enthusiastically to
Baxter.[10] The Marquesas were beautiful, richly greened and
boldly mountained, but touched with a tragic sense of loss.
Abandoned houses, the stone amphitheatre on Hiva-Oa, scene
of ceremonial cannibalism, the vestiges of a past life half-buried
in the luxurious undergrowth, some elements of dignity
retained, but vigour declining under the negative hand of the
French colonial presence. Some of these things reminded Louis
inevitably of the Highlands.

There were some problems. It took a while to learn and accept
the ways of Captain Otis who was not inclined to exclude his
passengers from shipboard discipline. Fanny was not a good
sailor, and long stints at sea did not please her. The confinement
must have exaggerated some of her already apparent difficulties.
Could she really cheerfully spend her days sitting in the cockpit
making island garments and chatting with Aunt Maggie or,
when the weather was bad, simply feeling unwell? The cook
took to drink. The next port of call was to be Fakarava, an atoll

in the Dangerous Archipelago, which would take some skilful navigation to reach safely. 'Dangerous' was not a misnomer. It was a mass of coral atolls, lying low in the swelling Pacific, inadequately charted, full of invisible hazards of rocks and reefs lurking below the surface. Before they left Nukahiva, Captain Otis engaged a new Polish mate who was familiar with that stretch of coral-strewn ocean, and a new cook, Ah Fu, Chinese, who was to become for a time an important and well-integrated member of the company.

They left the bold, volcanic, jungled Marquesas on 4 September. The voyage across to Fakarava was every bit as treacherous as they had feared. There were some near misses. 'I did not dream there were such places or such races,' Louis wrote from Fakarava to Colvin.[11] This time they were only five days at sea, but they were five stressful days, during which Louis had a curious vision. He was lying at night in the open.

There was nothing visible but the southern stars, and the steersman there out by the binnacle lamp . . . the night was as warm as milk; and all of a sudden, I had a vision of – Drummond Street. It came to me like a flash of lightning; I simply returned thither, and into the past. And when I remembered all that I hoped and feared as I pickled about Rutherford's in the rain and the east wind: how I feared I should make a mere shipwreck, and yet timidly hoped not; how I feared I should never have a friend, far less a wife, and yet passionately hoped I might; how I hoped (if I did not take to drink) I should possibly write one little book, etc. etc. And then, now – what a change! I feel somehow as if I should like the incident set upon a brass plate at the corner of that dreary thoroughfare, for all students to read, poor devils, when their hearts are down.[12]

How desperate was the vulnerability of his youth. Now a dream had come true: the dream had taken him, literally, into dangerous waters. He remembered the shoals that beset him in Heriot Row and the wynds and Lothian Road. In the warm Pacific night Edinburgh was present, and the days when all was hope and everything and nothing seemed possible were vivid. There was no turning back. Louis, looking up at the stars that night, was reflecting on his life; he might well also have been thinking of the *Casco* threading her way through half-submerged coral, under the fallible guidance of the helmsman by the binnacle lamp.

If the Marquesas were richly exotic, Fakarava was strange. The coral atoll can best be described in the words of J. C. Furnas.

> In a state of nature it is all sand, sun, and scrub. Where men have been it probably has coco-palms, as have most South Sea beaches. But the peculiarity of this outrageous setting is to be all beach – not a key buffering a continent nor a sand bar heralding a river, but an independent ring of coral detritus, continuous or broken into elongated islets, too low in profile to offer the security implied in the word 'land': too sterile to nourish much but pandanus and coconut; too dry to afford any but brackish water to which atoll-dwellers must specially adjust. Yet scores or hundreds of brown people have lived there for centuries.[13]

Aunt Maggie commented on the fact that these 'brown people' were darker and smaller than the Marquesans, whom she considered handsome, although, she said, 'it is only fair to add that they seem better behaved'.[14] They perhaps did not take such liberties aboard ship as the Marquesans, although they were entertained on the *Casco* from their limited stores with biscuits and jam. The men were offered rum to drink, the women syrup and water. Polynesian habits of hospitality were quickly learned by Louis and Fanny.

They were provided with a little three-roomed house to occupy while they stayed on the island, and it was refreshing to be able to expand a little and sleep on dry land. But Louis caught a cold, and in spite of the shelter it did not improve, although he was sure it soon would. He continued to be quite unwell during the trip onwards to Tahiti. When that next landfall was made there were those who thought he was near death. On Fakarava a cold could not prevent Louis from pursuing his endless enquiries about island life. Fakarava was spirit-ridden. Fascinated, he listened to stories of the supernatural, prompting his source with tales of his own. 'It is scarce possible to exaggerate the extent and empire of his superstitions,' he said of the story-teller, 'they mould his life, they colour his thinking; and when he does not speak to me of ghosts, and gods, and devils, he is playing the dissembler and talking only with his lips.'[15] Such tales were meat and drink to Louis. Although he was slowly absorbing – the process had to be slow, sifting, digesting the nuances of a Polynesian life whose outlines seemed so frankly vivid – he understood the power of the supernatural. It had since childhood operated so strongly in his imagination. When he came to write *The Beach of Falesá* the experience of Fakarava clearly informed his pen.

The quest continued – for that is what it was. Ostensibly Louis was in the Pacific to improve his health and to gain experiences that would feed his writing. But it is impossible not to think of him also both seeking and escaping. It is tempting to believe that he and Fanny were looking for somewhere they could be without the left-overs of the worlds they had had no choice but to bring into their marriage. There was nowhere. It was not only the physical bodying forth of the responsibilities that had attached to them that so solidly participated in their lives, but the ghosts and spectres of other times and other places. Louis must certainly at times have felt the need for himself and Fanny to have time alone. It was perhaps the most valuable of things he could have worked for. Yet to have allowed himself to want it too strongly would have been contrary to other impulses equally important, impulses towards caring for and providing for the clan that gathered round him. He and Fanny were not to have the opportunity to see their relationship solely in terms of each other. It was a real loss.

On the other hand Louis did successfully escape from certain pressures and distortions of the old life. A yacht on the Pacific was both a free spirit and a tiny, cramped prison. The outer space seemed limitless, the inner only too confining. Yet to be at the mercy of the elements and the unknown itself accelerated the adrenalin, sharpened the perceptions, made life that much more worth living and writing about. They threaded their way through the Dangerous Archipelago, on to Tahiti, were lost for twelve hours amongst the shoals, lay becalmed, rode out a squall by the skin of their teeth, and were left with a healthy repect for the realities of their new life.

Fanny was not so happy. It was not the opening-out experience for her that it was for Louis, and the fact that she was so much less clear about what she wanted from life burdened her experience of the Pacific. There is an impression that she simply could not fully respond; there were too many things that were not right for her. She seemed unclear about whether she was there because she herself positively wanted to be there, or there for Louis's sake. In her letters she leans in either direction. Certainly the next stage of their wanderings was not a pleasant experience for either of them. Louis had become quite ill, not in a state to appreciate the narrow shaves they had on the way to Tahiti, though he could write about them cockily to Baxter – 'We cam so near gaun head over hurdies that I really dinnae ken why we didnae althegither.'[16] He was having to admit that the trip contained 'incidental beastlinesses': it wasn't the first time he had had an intimate brush with the terror of the sea. To Colvin he wrote, 'The sea is a terrible place, stupefying to the mind and poisonous to the temper, the sea, the motion, the lack of space, the cruel publicity, the passengers. . . .'[17] He was perhaps suffering a little from Fanny's impatience as well as from what must have affected all of them, the living in each other's pockets. Fanny had liked the Marquesas, enjoyed the friendly admiration of the Marquesans, and could say confidently that they had done the right thing, feeling that for Louis this was the answer – 'Certainly we have found the right place for him: and we both love it.'[18] Up to that point she had had a fairly gentle initiation into shipboard and island life.

Papeete was not so prepossessing. 'It seemed to me a sort of halfway house between savage life & civilisation,' Aunt Maggie astutely observed, 'with the drawbacks of both & the advantages of neither.'[19] It was no accident that Louis opened his novel *The Ebb-Tide* on the beach at Papeete, introducing his readers to his three disreputable and demoralised characters in a scruffily corrupting environment. It was a seedy place, representing the worst of the colonial impact, which had been rapidly building up for more than a hundred years. The Tahitians had suffered from their readiness for friendly co-operation with the strangers who appeared ever-increasingly in their tall ships. Captain Cook, making his landfall in 1768, had treated the islanders courteously but firmly. His crew had lost no time in making the most of the Tahitians' willingness to co-operate – on every level. For the white man in many ways it was an idyll. A luscious and fertile coast, friendly men (although they would steal at any opportunity), beautiful women, an atmosphere of plenty and relaxation, a climate of feeling that brought, it seemed, no backlash to the women who took Cook's crew to their hearts and their mats. The idyll remained in men's imaginations. Tahiti, of all the islands of the Pacific, became the symbol of an exotic, unstressful life. Melville had been writing about the Marquesas, but in effect his images of young girls bathing, of gleaming brown flesh, of a slow-paced easy life, of food hanging in plenty from the trees, became absorbed into the idyll of Tahiti. If it had ever been like that, Cook, remarkable though he was for his ability to treat native populations with interest and respect, brought the seeds of destruction. It would have happened anyway – others had been there before him and no one was going to keep silent about the attractions of Tahiti. The demoralisation, the undermining of the complex social structures of Polynesian society, the exploitation, the venereal disease – all had eaten savagely into Tahiti by the time Louis, badly ill by this time, with haemmorhage incipient, disembarked at Papeete and convinced several that he was dying.

Papeete was the French colonial capital, and it was the place where misfits and degenerates, the floating white population of the South Seas who would never again find a place for themselves in the 'civilised' world, were cast up. Louis was not too ill to catch the atmosphere of the place and store it in his mind. But the priority was to get Louis somewhere where he could rest and recover. Medical opinion in Papeete feared the worst, but the worst did not happen, and being told of the beauties of the upper, and smaller, part of the island they decided to make a move and find if possible an attractive and comfortable spot at which to make a pause, for Louis to gain strength, and the rest to regain their spirits after the stressful trip.

Their quarters in Papeete did not tempt them to linger, although there might have been some point in staying near a doctor. As always, it was Fanny who busied herself to find a solution. They regained the *Casco*, that moved on around the coast and set them off again at Taravao, which wasn't much of an improvement on Papeete. There they encountered difficulties, again resolved by Fanny. She had to bargain for hours with a recalcitrant Chinese in order to hire a wagon that would take them on to Tautira. Fired by Louis's acute distress and need she refused to accept a negative response, and got them all through the strenuous journey over hopeless roads and dense vegetation to the village of Tautira. Captain Otis brought the *Casco* round the coast. Fortunately it turned out to be all that they wanted. They brought introductions from Papeete and were welcomed gently and hospitably by the local aristocracy, Princess Moe, a lady of considerable standing and authority. Through her a rather lesser member of the aristocracy, Ori a Ori, lent them a dwelling of his own and insisted on attending to all their needs – which shortly became rather more considerable than they had anticipated.

Tautira went to Louis's heart. He was cared for; Princess Moe herself, on finding that he would not eat, prepared a dish of raw fish marinated in lime juice and coconut milk to tempt him. He ate with relish and began to mend. Tautira and everything in it was at his disposal. Gaining strength he began to work again at *The Master of Ballantrae*. Yet it was at Tautira that homesickness struck, perhaps never kept quite at bay, and he sent to Baxter two revealing, if not entirely accomplished, stanzas. The first ran:

> Home no more home to me, whither must I wander?
>   Hunger my driver, I go where I must.
> Cold blows the winter wind over hill and heather;
>   Thick drives the rain, and my roof is in the dust.
> Loved of wise men was the shade of my roof-tree,
>   The true word of welcome was spoken in the door –
> Dear days of old, with the faces in the firelight,
>   Kind folks of old, you come again no more.[20]

It is a muddled poem, really, the curiosity lying in that he should have written it at a time when he was comfortably settled in a delightful South Sea village, in a house open to the sunlight, thatched with palm leaves, coconut palms shading the green lawns. But the contrary pulls could never relax. The joy of the sea, the adventure of it, the magic of wind, waves and the islands; the heavy depression of illness clutching yet again; the fiction imbedded in Scotland and his own past that came from his pen; the dangers of their last voyage; the sudden lump in the throat of sheer irrepressible nostalgia. Whatever Louis had escaped from, the world he was living in now was more complex, more layered with different levels of reality, more peopled with ghosts, than anything he had ever before experienced.

Tautira had a great deal to give him. There was friendship, always a prime necessity. Ori a Ori was six feet four and a personality of proportionate dimensions. Recovered enough to be on his feet again, Louis told Ori about Henley, another of large stature and personality, and imitated his walk, his piano-playing and his pipe-smoking — Henley incongruously brought to life in a Tahitian hut. Louis, by his own account, produced so successful a performance that Ori retired quite chastened, 'feeling that he was not the genuine article after all'.[21] Henley, in spite of everything, would surely have been tickled to learn of the impersonation in the Tahitian village of Tautira.

It seemed that no place and no person could put Louis off his stride. He was himself wherever he went, ebulliently international, or perhaps a-national, penetrating the barriers

Fanny Stevenson

of alien cultures and languages by straightforward self-dramatisation. His Edinburgh accent lingered, though he could clearly modulate his Scots at will. He never sought to cross barriers by defusing his Scottish identity. His self-dramatisation could have been disastrous – we know it didn't always work – for it might have suggested a lack of sensitivity towards just those differences that were important. But Louis managed to be uncompromisingly himself at the same time as maintaining an acute awareness of the manners and customs of the people he mixed with. While he spent evenings with Ori playing his flageolet, a more portable, practical and possibly less offensive instrument than the piano he had spent so much time at in Bournemouth, and telling him about friends back home, his curiosity about the essentials of Ori's life was manifest. And he was royally entertained and cared for, food, drink, songs, dances, stories all part of the feast that was set before him at Tautira.

Fanny and Aunt Maggie took their fill too. Church-going, of course, was an important item on Aunt Maggie's agenda. With admirable restraint she recorded her impressions. She felt that the minister wasn't quite up to the standard of the one at Fakarava – his garb, blue and white *pareu*, black coat and white tie, and bare feet, wasn't, she felt, as suitable as the 'proper-looking gown' of the latter.[22] But the service itself was not so different from what she was used to. She did not seem to be too badly distracted by the children playing ball and falling asleep amongst the congregation. If Aunt Maggie had to stretch herself to maintain her equilibrium at church, certain other aspects of Tahitian life demanded considerably more adjustment. She sat and watched while overtly sexual dances were performed for her delectation, and saw enough of the way things were to comment crisply: 'the more one sees & hears of what goes on here, the more one can understand the Indian system of early marriages!'[23] Pre-marital sexual activity was a cheerfully accepted Polynesian custom. Aunt Maggie commented on the practice of baptising illegitimate children, no questions asked, but did not register disapproval. She seems to have seen it as a practical necessity. The Pacific experience was allowing Margaret Stevenson an elasticity which could never have been possible at Heriot Row. The fact that her husband was dead and her son now unquestionably adult and beyond her authority perhaps had something to do with her relative ease in adaptation.

Certainly the South Seas did not seem to have the same loosening effect on Fanny, although the glimpses we catch of her are contradictory. There is increasingly a sense of Fanny needing space, of her vulnerable nature not reacting well to being cooped up in a ship's cabin or in a village hut, of confinement and long and close proximity to people increasing her abrasiveness. On a Pacific shore, barefooted, unconventionally clad, the ocean frothing at her feet, contentment is suggested. She would like to have thought of herself as a free spirit, soaring beyond the restrictions that would normally have surrounded a woman of her age. But she was never quite wholeheartedly bohemian. The pull towards security, towards the concrete representations of achievement, were understandably too strong. For Louis it had always been easier. He did not have an unsettled frontier existence in his past. Heriot Row stood firmly in the background, even as he braced himself on a dipping bowsprit or sat cross-legged and garlanded before the gracefully expressed sexuality of half-naked Tahitian girls. Fanny was never quite sure which were the symbols to be rejected, which to be revered.

There were friends of Louis who would suggest that it was Fanny who was keeping him away from them, preventing his return to Britain and standing in the way of their influence. Fanny would vigorously contend this, and protest that she disliked the Pacific, that she hated sailing and the sea, found it irksome and exhausting to be continually on the move, but that she put up with it all for Louis's sake. Probably the truth fluctuated, as truths so often do. She knew, as everyone knew, that the entire trip would have been impossible without her, for it was Fanny who had the practical sense and the determination to get the things done which were all the time necessary. Without Fanny, Louis would have been helpless. The old days of precipitately flinging himself into a journey and casting away his shirts when they got too dirty to wear, were over. The travels in the South Seas were the nearest he got to a repetition, but however bohemian an impression the spectacle of Louis the South Sea voyager presents, he would never have been there without the workings of Fanny. It was Fanny, too, who made Vailima possible. Without such a wife it could never have happened. In many respects it was Fanny who translated Louis's wild dreams into reality. Because there were so many who did not like the translation, her role in these years was perhaps not duly acknowledged. A lack of appreciation obviously added fuel to her discontent.

She seemed happy enough at Tautira. They were comfortable, although not without worries. They had not planned a prolonged stay, but discovered to their horror that the *Casco*'s masts had rotted, and must have been rotten throughout their voyage. She could have lost her masts at any point: they must have all thought back to the lurching squalls they had passed through. There was no way of making the necessary repairs at Tautira, so Captain Otis had to do the only thing possible and risk the schooner on a trip back to Papeete, where he hoped to find a man and materials for the job. It was a blow, for it meant extra expense of time and money. They had a problem of supplies, and a cash-flow problem too, for they had not equipped themselves for lingering at Tautira. The intention had been to proceed without delay to Hawaii where it was hoped a Honolulu bank would have money awaiting him. Now there was no way of going anywhere, and a big bill to pay for repairs. They were rescued from their embarrassment in one sense, though in another it was increased, by Princess Moe's insistence that they should accept her hospitality. She was happy to feed them. With no choice but to accept, the Stevenson party waited impatiently and anxiously for news of the *Casco*. It all took much longer than they had hoped, and would have taken longer still had Captain Otis not continuously chivvied the repairers.

The time was not wasted on Louis's part, though he could not stem his anxiety over money. He worked at *The Master* and assiduously carried on with educating himself on the subject of the Pacific islands. He collected songs and stories, fed himself on all that Ori and Moe could tell him and show him. Lloyd plied his camera. Fanny began to worry that Louis was not going to produce the right kind of book. She probably had in mind something in the vein of Charles Warren Stoddard, certainly something that would be bright and picturesque, but Louis intended his approach to be more scientific. Fanny felt the result would be over-serious and stodgy, and Colvin was inclined to agree. He did not like the long, detailed letters that arrived for him periodically, full of comments on life, society and politics. It was local colour that everyone was looking for, the exotic, the unusual. Louis was not blind to local colour, in fact he was revelling in it, but he was quite certain that a serious purpose of his travels was to make an honest and enquiring record of places and people and the facts that shaped them. The fact that in histories of the Pacific islands Stevenson's name occurs frequently, while Stoddard's does not, suggests the value of his approach.

The weeks passed. Communications with Papeete were not good. Bad weather increased the difficulty. Finally Ori, who shared the anxiety of his friends, volunteered to make his way in a Tahitian whaling boat round the coast to Papeete to find out what was happening. Louis was not happy at the undertaking as the weather remained treacherous, but Ori insisted, and was well rewarded, for he thoroughly enjoyed his stay at Papeete, entertained on board the crippled *Casco*, and was not in a hurry to return. When at last he did he brought money and provisions from Captain Otis, and, even better, reassuring news about the *Casco*'s progress and a case of champagne. Late in December the *Casco* was sighted and on Christmas Day 1888 Louis and Fanny, Lloyd, Aunt Maggie and Valentine were ready to set sail. The scenes were emotional. Louis and Fanny had exchanged names with Ori and Moe, a gesture symbolic of good will and mutual regard. They were tribal members. The tall well-built Ori wept, his wife wept, Louis and Fanny wept. Captain Otis fired a salute, and with a dip of the ensign the *Casco* leaned with the wind, north for Hawaii.

Chapter 12

FAR BETTER FUN THAN PEOPLE DREAM

> Life is far better fun than people dream who fall asleep among the
> chimney stacks and telegraph wires.
>> Letter to Sidney Colvin

It was to be another year before the travellers would be walking
barefoot on the beach at Apia, a year of calms and squalls, in the
weather and in other ways. With another stretch of the Pacific
before them they were first buffeted by the wind, and then it died
on them. The calm heightened Louis's anxiety about money –
he had no idea what, if anything, might await him in the mails at
Honolulu. It stretched out the voyage much longer than had
been anticipated, and food began to run short. The final
indignity occurred when the wind whipped up as they
approached the Hawaian islands and prevented their making
the harbour at Honolulu. They had to hang around, impatient,
reduced to salt horse for dinner. A priority, when the wind
changed and they ran into Honolulu, was a good meal at the
Royal Hawaian Hotel.

It had all been, Louis wrote to Baxter, a 'foolhardy venture'.
But now there was time to collect himself – 'If I have but nine
months of life and any kind of health, I shall have both eaten my
cake and got it back again with usury.'[1] The full horror of the
Casco having negotiated the Pacific in her unseaworthy state, the
impact of the luck they had had, struck him now. They had had
'every sort of minor misfortune . . . contrary winds and seas,
pertinacious rains, declining stores' and had survived in
remarkably good shape.[2] He was not regetting anything. It did,
however, seem a good time and a good place to be thinking
about the next move.

Louis talked of going back to Europe. It was the end of
January 1889. They would spend two or three months in
Hawaii, and with the spring and the gentler European weather
perhaps return. They talked about wintering in Madeira. The

Pacific experiment had been successful. He had fulfilled his longing for a life at sea, he was fit and well, and he had soaked himself in sun and experience. 'I never knew the world was so amusing,' he wrote to his cousin Bob.[3] He gloried in the impressions he had absorbed, 'the people, the life, the beachcombers, the old stories and songs I have picked up, so interesting; the climate, the scenery, and (in some places) the women, so beautiful.' Could he return home with these treasures and make use of them? The truth was, this was only the beginning. His stay in Hawaii, far from suggesting that he should turn his back on the Pacific, led him more deeply into Polynesian life and affairs. In this place of streetcars and telephones and electric lights Louis was soon impatient to be on the high seas again; the Pacific still tempted him with unexplored territory, and the more he talked about what he had seen already, and speculated about what there was yet to see, the sharper grew his appetite for fresh experience.

That last month's voyaging had been difficult for all of them. Fanny never would get her sea-legs, and was acutely seasick this time. They all had to spend most of the time below decks, and their diet during the last week or two left much to be desired. They could not help but be uncomfortably aware of the *Casco*'s frailty, in spite of the repairs. Honolulu was to mark the end of their relationship with her. Captain Otis was paid off and they said their farewells. Their journeyings in the Pacific would be henceforth in craft of a rather different kind. They said farewell to Valentine too, who had caused some embarrassment through an involvement with a seaman. The details are somewhat hazy and one wonders if Fanny   presumably it was Fanny – was not rather less than generous in dispensing with Valentine's services at that point, though it may well have been a relief for her to sever her connections with the Stevensons. Fanny had not been easy to work for. It is amazing that their relationship had lasted so long – Valentine had seen Louis and Fanny through Hyères, through Skerryvore and Saranac, and nine months of the Pacific islands – and that it did says a great deal for Valentine's devotion to Louis.

First to meet them as the *Casco* finally made it into Honolulu harbour with her hungry cargo was Belle and her young son Austin. Belle and Joe Strong had been for some time in

Honolulu, trying, without great success, to make their way as artists, and associating with the Hawaiian royalty. They had had nine years of somewhat uneasy marriage. Joe was not unlike Belle's father, restless, impetuous, unreliable, yet with a large helping of charm. They were both irresponsible with money. Joe may have been up to this time faithful to his wife, but he was not to remain so for long. He was also in a shaky state of health, and overfond of liquor and opium, which did not improve his prospects of regaining it. Belle's eagerness to board the *Casco* with her greetings may have had as much to do with her problems with Joe and with money as with the pleasure of seeing her mother and brother and stepfather again. Belle and Joe became immediately a part of the family; the invisible weights on Louis were piling up.

A house was found at Waikiki beach and Louis and Fanny moved in with their entourage. The immediate task was writing. Although Louis was amazingly adept at peripatetic composition, circumstances had not been conducive to the completion of *The Master*. And there were fresh ventures to pursue. Directly inspired by the stay at Tautira, Louis was beginning to work with Pacific material. Finally reassured about money, though there was a further wait before Louis learned that he was solvent, he settled energetically to commuting experience into words. He had already at Tautira been working on two long ballads, written with a Tennysonian flavour, one of which, 'The Feast of Famine', he had sent at once to Colvin. It is the less successful of the two, 'a patchwork of details of manners and the impressions of a traveller', as Louis himself described it, and in his notes to the poem he indicates its lack of authenticity – '. . . Indeed I am far from claiming the credit of any high degree of accuracy for this ballad. Even in time of famine, it is probable that Marquesan life went far more gaily than is here represented. But the melancholy of today lies on the writer's mind.'[4] He was relying on sheer narrative pace to carry the poem, but it falters too often to allow it to counteract the evident lapses in authenticity. His other South Sea ballad, 'The Song of Rahero', works better. It is based on a story that Louis heard from Princess Moe, and he had some of it written before he left Tautira. He said of it later, '*Rahero* is for its length a perfect folk-tale: savage and yet fine, full of tailforemost morality, ancient as the granite rocks.'[5] It is easy to see why it appealed so strongly to Louis. He felt that through 'Rahero', and 'The Feast of Famine' too, he was getting at the roots of Polynesian life. From Ori and Moe he had learned to understand something of island culture. From his own background he drew an instinctive feel for the balladic mode, the starkness of the ballad tale – 'savage and yet fine' – which seemed to him an appropriate form to convey a flavour of the Polynesian oral tradition. There were moments when Stevenson experienced the coming together of South Pacific and Scottish elements: such a coming together produced the ballads. The result was interesting, if not entirely happy. It showed, above all, his concern to absorb and communicate aspects of an alien culture.

Many other seeds had been flung broadcast in Louis's fertile mind, but they would take time to grow. They needed the nourishment of a new adventure. That there would be a new adventure soon became clear, but in the meantime Louis had plenty to keep him busy. There were family affairs and problems to be coped with. There was fraternisation with royalty, there was walking, riding and swimming, and there was a trip, typically undertaken by Louis who relished the inevitable risk for his soul's sake, to Hawaii's leper colony.

Hawaii was in many ways an unsettling place to be at that stage in its history, particularly unsettling for anyone thinking he had had a good taste of the Pacific and was about ready to return home. More so than any other group of islands, all of which were in process of cultural disintegration, Hawaii had been overrun, by the Americans. For the United States it was a last stage in nineteenth-century frontier expansion. The agricultural potential, which had been unexploited by the islanders, had tempted them – the best land was now theirs. And this brought little economic spin-off to the Hawaiians, for the land was mostly worked by imported Chinese labour, cheap and malleable. In a last-ditch attempt to preserve a sense of Hawaiian identity King Kalakaua was trying to revive a traditionalism which was bound to be uneasy at such a time of transition and, more dubiously, to see himself as a leader of Polynesian consciousness. His political meddlings to this end did little but complicate affairs which were already thoroughly confused, especially in Samoa, which was the prize in a three-cornered tussle between Germany, Britain and America. If the Berlin Conference carve-up of Africa now seems outrageous the jostling for position in the Pacific was perhaps one of the seediest imperialist operations ever. And it threw up a quantity of problematic personalities.

Lloyd, Fanny, Louis, King Kalakaua and Margaret Stevenson in the cabin of the Casco

Kalakaua was one of them, although he was impressive in his own way. Before Louis's arrival Belle and Joe had established a relationship with him, and Louis too was soon on easy terms. He was a large and portly gentleman, fond of jollity and champagne, and Louis, who had done his share of imbibing, was a little astonished at his capacity. Apparently Kalakaua's pre-prandial drinking could consist of five or six *bottles* of champagne in one session. 'You should see a photograph of our party after an afternoon with H.H.M.', Louis commented dryly, 'My! what a crew!'⁶ The champagne parties punctuated the writing. 'I have been toiling like a galley slave: three numbers of *The Master* to rewrite; five chapters of *The Wrong Box* to write and rewrite; and about five hundred lines of a narrative poem to write, rewrite, and re-rewrite.'[7]

Louis had reservations about Kalakaua's character, but he could not resist being drawn into an involvement which, if it wasn't exactly political, was certainly felt by Louis to be a matter of moral commitment. It was from Honolulu that Louis despatched the first of his indignant letters to *The Times*, hotly condemning German activity in the Pacific and the lack of reaction on the part of the other powers concerned, Britain and America. Samoa was the centre of this. Louis would soon be much more deeply embroiled in Samoan affairs but this was the beginning, before he had ever been there. Samoa was the first target in Kalakaua's plans, and it was with Kalakaua's eyes that Louis first looked at Samoa. It is clear that his letter to *The Times* was somewhat hasty, and that he discovered this afterwards. He had been fed with information by those who were not exactly disinterested and had reacted, as he so often and splendidly did, with more emotion than political acumen. But in spite of this his instincts were right, and his closer acquaintance with events in Samoa would bear this out.

Even at this early stage he was thinking of writing a book about political manipulations in the Pacific, centring on Samoa, with Joe Strong taking photographs to illustrate it. He could not resist the seepage into his ways of thinking and feeling of impressions and information that were demanding he should take up his pen. It was another motive for further travels. By March it was decided that there would be no return to Europe for another year. It was not easy to explain himself to those at home. 'I am outright ashamed of my news, which is that we are not coming home for another year,' he began to Colvin, who fretted as always at Louis being beyond his reach.[8] Louis's letters were disturbing, not because of what he said, or the state of mind and body they expressed, but because they were so preoccupied with events and experiences that were beyond the frontiers of Colvin's world, and that of Louis's other friends and associates in the south of England. Even Henry James was perturbed, though relieved that Louis was so much stronger in health. Louis wrote to James, too. While to Colvin he emphasised how much he would continue to miss him and visits to the 'Monument' – as he had always called the British

Museum, where Colvin had been resident for some years – and how his travels would produce a fine book. To James the sheer fun of his past and anticipated adventures conquered.

I have had more fun and pleasure of my life these past months than ever before, and more health than any time in ten long years. And even here in Honolulu I have withered in the cold; and this precious deep is filled with islands, which we may still visit; and though the sea a deathfull place, I like to be there, and like squalls (when they are over): and to draw near to a new island, I cannot say how much I like.[9]

If he withered in Honolulu, what would be the effect of Britain? He could not bear to take himself away from the places where he had felt fit, where he could walk on the shore outside the Waikiki house with his sleeves rolled up on his brown thin arms. He could participate in life as he had not done, or had the illusion of doing, since before his marriage, and life was fun and adventurous and serious, and all three things nourished his writing. 'Fine, clean emotions; a world all and always beautiful; air better than wine; interest unflagging: there is upon the whole no better life.'[10]

He was eager to be away, but it was not an easy matter finding a ship to take them. The party had diminished a little. Aunt Maggie had returned to Edinburgh and they had lost Valentine. But they had gained Joe Strong, a doubtful asset, and Belle and Austin were to go direct to Sydney to await them there. At first there were plans to join the American mission ship *The Morning Star*, although it wasn't a very alluring prospect as life on board was to be full of prohibitions. Louis, accustomed as he was to travel with copious supplies of tobacco and wine, would not have found it easy. Fanny with her scorn for conventional dress and habit of rolling her own cigarettes would also have been an awkward customer aboard *The Morning Star*. They were saved from such a fate, however. One day Louis, full of excitement, returned to Waikiki from a morning in Honolulu. He had just made arrangements with the Captain of the trading schooner *Equator* for his party to join the ship on her return from her current voyage. The *Equator* would carry on her normal business, and her passengers would have the opportunity to visit certainly the Gilbert Islands, with a possibility of the further afield Micronesian islands, the Marshalls and the Carolines. Samoa and Tonga were also on the list of possibilities. To celebrate, the company broke open the champagne and sat drinking it in the sunshine. There was great excitement when the *Equator* herself was seen, her sails filling, bearing out of the bay. It would be June before she would return to pick up her passengers, but the prospect was well worth waiting for, and well worth a toast.

In a letter to Adelaide Boodle, Louis described their Waikiki residence. Imagine, Louis wrote, coming out from Honolulu, 'all shining with electric lights', a convenience that certainly most of Edinburgh was at yet without:

The buildings stand in three groups by the edge of the beach, where an angry little spitfire sea continually spirts and thrashes with impotent irascibility, the big seas breaking further out upon the reef. The first is a small house, with a very large summer parlour, or *lanai*, as they call it here, roofed, but practically open. There you will find the lamps burning and the family sitting about the table, dinner just done: my mother, my wife, Lloyd, Belle, my wife's daughter, Austin her child, and tonight (by way of rarity) a guest. All about the walls our South Sea curiosities, war clubs, idols, pearl shells, stone axes . . .[11]

Louis led Miss Boodle's imagination to himself, not present with the company lingering at the dinner table, but hidden away in a little hut which he had made his work place, 'a grim little wooden shanty', inhabited by mice and cockroaches and scorpions and mosquitoes, and by Louis Stevenson, busily inditing a letter to Miss Adelaide Boodle, his old companion at Skerryvore.

The Master was finished, but not without effort and self-doubt. It had begun at Saranac as 'a howling good tale'[12] but was finishing in Waikiki with the problem of 'that damned ending' evading a solution. 'I fear it – I fear that ending,' he was writing to E. L. Burlingame, impatiently awaiting the final instalment.[13] Burlingame too had reservations about the ending, which lifts the book so suddenly on to a different level of narration and loses the dry, nervous, authoritative tone of voice that had carried it, but on the whole he approved the novel vigorously. It must have been a curious experience for Louis, to bring the book to its climax at such a distance from the Adirondack landscape that inspired it. The character of McKellar was shaped at sea, writing on deck and in cramped quarters below, on coral atolls and lush islands, with the sweat dripping on to the page.

It was now that Louis decided to make his visit to Molokai, the island to which Hawaii's lepers were confined. It was an enterprise which he was the first to admit was quixotic, though it proved a salutary experience. He made the voyage out with a party of nuns who were joining the colony to give their services, and with a fresh consignment of the sick to life imprisonment. They arrived at the settlement of Kalawao at daybreak, and in one of Louis's rare letters to his wife he described his feelings of 'fear and disgust' as they approached. His first sight of their destination was not prepossessing. 'Presently we came up with the leper promontory: lowland, quite bare and bleak and harsh, a little town of wooden houses, two churches, a landing-stair, all unsightly, sour, northerly, lying athwart the sunrise, with the great wall of the pali cutting the world out on the south.'[14] The frailty of the sisters, seasick on the way out, and their courage, moved him. It would have been impossible for him to prepare himself for what he would find. He came ready to admire any who took the risk of working with lepers, and primed by the story of Father Damien, a Catholic priest who had dedicated his life to the care of Molokai's lepers, and had died of leprosy.

The Damien story highlighted one of the many distasteful aspects of the white presence in the Pacific, the rivalry between Catholic and Protestant missions. The Protestants were sensitive about the fact that service to the lepers had been led by Catholics. There had been something like a campaign to damage Father Damien's reputation – he was, it was alleged, ignorant, dirty, coarse, and slept with the leprous women of the colony. The contrast which the settlement of Kalawao offered was stark. Here were nuns, heartrendingly inexperienced, 'one of them was crying . . . quietly under her veil', arriving to devote themselves to caring for those who were literally the physical detritus of the islands, the decaying remnants of human beings who had to watch their own and each other's flesh rot.[15] 'No stranger time have I ever had,' Louis wrote, 'nor any so moving.'[16] For more than a week Louis was amongst them. He refused to wear gloves, he refused to do or say anything that would draw attention to the gross abnormality of the people he was with. He was testing himself in a way he would never have to again, the only time, perhaps, that he had to look at and live and communicate with such suffering, such inevitable awareness of the mortality of flesh.

He did whatever the lepers did. He talked with the elderly and played with the children and tried to make himself open and available to all. He learned more about Father Damien, and the more he learned of his possible defects, the higher mounted his admiration. He was 'dirty, bigoted, untruthful, unwise, tricky, but superb with generosity, residual candour and fundamental good humour', the more of a hero for all his too human weaknesses.[17] The lingering personality of Damien deepened the emotional intensity of the experience. In a sense Damien was what Louis had always been looking for, the man who on conventional social and moral terms was to be condemned, but who in the terms that really counted – that counted for Louis and, he was sure, for humanity – was a true hero. There had been other heroes, a few, for Louis, but Father Damien was perhaps the only one who could be measured honestly and entirely according to what Louis himself had learned about life and humanity. Years ago it would not have occurred to him that heroism might be found in a leper colony rather than on the battlefield. Even if all the worst rumours concerning Damien were true, he could still be seen as a man of heroic dimensions. Molokai and Damien seemed to lurk beneath the surface of some of Stevenson's most memorable later writing.

The most direct consequence was the famous Damien letter. He was in Sydney many months later when he read a published letter from one Reverend Dr Hyde, which stated that not only was Father Damien all that the uncharitable had said he was but also that his presence on Molokai was unproductive. Louis was pained and furious and impetuously wrote at once to redress the balance. He did not actually defend Father Damien: the great appeal for Louis lay just in the fact that he had been both disreputable and splendid. But all his feelings of disgust at the hypocritical and the complacent, which had boiled up so often in the old Edinburgh days, seethed again. If Damien achieved little in the leper settlement, why were others not there to help him? There was no attempt to tame the virulence of his attack; Louis was writing straight out of the white heat of his feelings – 'When we have failed, and another has succeeded; when we have stood by and another has stepped in; when we sit and grow bulky in our charming mansions, and a plain uncouth peasant steps into the battle, under the eyes of God, and succours the afflicted, and consoles the dying, and is himself afflicted in his turn, and dies upon the field of honour . . .'[18] The rhythms are strikingly biblical. It is revealing, though unsurprising, that the combination of a sense of wrong and a need for rhetorical emphasis brought out the earliest influences, the Old Testament and the writers of the Covenant.

After consultation with the family Louis decided to publish, although the *Open Letter to the Reverend Dr Hyde of Honolulu* was probably libellous. He refused to accept any payment for it. 'I do not stick at murder,' he announced, with a dramatically ironic awareness of what the letter amounted to, 'I draw the line at cannibalism.'[19] It was rash, of course, to publish, though fortunately Dr Hyde took no action, perhaps feeling that the fury of a Scottish fiction writer was unimportant. But publication in a sense sealed Louis's commitment to the Pacific. He had not so publicly taken a stand on any issue in Scotland as he now found himself doing in Polynesian affairs. His letters – more followed that first one from Hawaii – to *The Times*, the Damien letter, the content of his correspondence home, they were all signs that he had found a place and a function, perhaps illusory, but convincing enough for him, in the Pacific which he had never been sure of in Scotland or England. Sensing this, his friends at home could only become more uneasy. It must have appeared that not only was he changing his commitment, he was changing his identity. Exile was working on him too thoroughly.

The *Equator* took them onward. Louis was not sorry to say goodbye to Honolulu. Now the party consisted of himself and Fanny, Lloyd and Joe Strong, and the Chinese cook Ah Fu, whom Fanny described as 'civilized just so much as we should like to have him, and a savage just so far as it is useful'.[20] There had been a confrontation with Joe, who was physically and psychologically in a poor state. When Louis reached the point where he couldn't take Joe's behaviour any longer, and threatened to throw him out, Joe talked of suicide. Louis, of course, gave him another chance. There is some evidence to suggest that Belle, too, either attempted or talked of suicide. Whatever was going on, events immediately before the departure of the *Equator* were traumatic. Fanny wrote to Colvin about Joe.

> Those who know him best say that there will be no further trouble now. I trust not, no one can help loving the creature; yet I would push him on to his death sooner than he should harm Louis. There I draw the line at philanthropy. There are many things to the poor soul's credit. I fully expected that he would fly to what has been his solace in the past, either drink or opium, but he has kept away from both. He has signed a paper drawn up by a lawyer in terms so frank that Louis was shocked by them, placing himself and his affairs absolutely in Louis's hands, and binding himself to obedience.[21]

One can understand why it was that Colvin heartily wished both Joe and Belle at the bottom of the ocean. Louis was propping up the two of them financially until the end of his life.

Louis wrote rather dramatic letters home as they prepared for the *Equator* trip, telling his friends not to assume that lack of news meant they were lost at sea. They were entering latitudes where the mails were few, if they existed at all, and life was beset with unknown quantities. After months of being 'oppressed by civilisation' in Waikiki Louis looked forward to a taste of danger again, to exploring the not much known Gilberts and Carolines, roughing it on a trading schooner which had not been built for passengers, although the Captain gave over his own cabin for the use of Fanny and Louis.

It was an eccentric group with eccentric equipment, including a magic lantern with slides and an assortment of musical instruments, to which King Kalakaua ceremonially made his farewells after being entertained on board. Captain Reid, a fellow-Scot, seems to have accepted the motley collection of people and things with unflustered good nature. Having a woman on board would have been difficult under any circumstances, but having a woman like Fanny, nearly fifty, tough but taut-nerved, could justifiably be seen as a mixed blessing.

Louis on the bowsprit of the Equator

It was the end of June 1889. The *Equator* was trading in copra, the staple of South Sea commerce. The coconuts were gathered and the meat dried by the islanders, then stored to await collection at trading stations. Copra trade was the third element in the three-cornered white presence, the element that Louis was seeing at close quarters for the first time. It found its way, like everything else, into his writing. *The Beach of Falesá* is the story that most directly expresses what Louis had learned about the trade-shaped relationship between white and islander, and the situations that were so ripe for abuse on either side. He was seeing now much of the worst of Pacific disintegration.

Their first stop was at the trading station at Butaritari in the Gilberts. Here the revolvers with which they had taken care to equip themselves proved their usefulness. There had been a lengthy July Fourth celebration at Butaritari. Normally the two trading stores were not allowed to sell spirits to the natives, but there had been a Fourth of July dispensation, and when the party landed from the *Equator* the effects were only too evident. They cannily performed some public target practice to demonstrate their handiness with weapons, for the mood was getting ugly. Drink and frustration had combined with their usual lethal effect to produce hung-over aggression. The store managers were cheerfully piling up their profits on the sales of spirits. After a time of witnessing the tension seething around them Louis decided something had to be done. If the local chief could not be persuaded to re-impose the taboo on liquor sales the store managers themselves would have to refuse to sell. The problem was to persuade them both. Louis took the initiative and handled the situation with some coolness. Both managers were persuaded, and the island was restored to sobriety.

Captain Reid was a young Scot, experienced in the islands, happy to enlighten Louis whose appetite for information had not abated. Louis spent instructive hours in the Sans Souci bar, talking with Reid, and Mr Rick the manager, and others who congregated there. In the movement from island to island, unloading trade goods, cheap cotton cloth a staple, in exchange for copra, Louis had the chance of absorbing the ambience of a relationship that rested on the morally sordid facts of exploitation that could so easily have a degrading effect on all concerned. He learned the possibilities of cheating, on both sides, the watering of copra, the fiddling of the weights and measures. The Gilberts were low islands, exposed to vast expanses of sky and sea, no hills, not much more than coral and scrub, little to mitigate the stark outlines. It was a raw experience, and living at such close quarters with the *Equator*'s crew, of them more or less, underlined the unprotected aspect of this existence. There was nothing between Louis and the unburnished human nature he was encountering. Yet he found many of the traders he came across 'simple, genial, gay, gallant, and obliging'.[22]

They moved into a house at Butaritari belonging to the local minister. Louis may have thought back to the padding of Heriot Row and middle-class Edinburgh, the inward-turning of the comfortable New Town homes, the ease of escape from both fact and conscience at which the Victorians had proved so adept. In the Pacific he was coming face to face with other aspects of

Victorian reality. There was a special satisfaction to be had in turning over for himself the underside of Victorian prosperity. Here, where the traders and the missionaries and the strategists gathered, was one of the areas of the world on which it all depended. He had probed deeper than his explorations of the Edinburgh underworld had taken him. And no one else, at least no one else with the ability to write about it, had done it before. Louis moved from his daylight view of 'the low horizon, the expanse of the lagoon, the sledge-like rim of palmtops, the sameness and smallness of the land, the hugely superior size and interest of sea and sky',[23] to evenings spent in the neatly appointed Sans Souci, where the glass sparkled in the lamplight and the interior 'glowed with coloured pictures like the theatre at Christmas'.[24] Real life and the story book came together still in all kinds of unexpected ways.

The *Equator* left them next at Apemama, still in the Gilberts, under the equivocal protection of the local tyrant, 'the Napoleon of the group',[25] Tembinoka, while Captain Reid voyaged further afield for trade. Louis did not know that Tembinoka's hospitality was, initially at least, reluctant. He was persuaded by a man called George Murdoch, who had long been resident in the Gilberts and acted as a factor for Tembinoka. Louis was rather dismissive of Murdoch, to whom he refers, but not by name. But Murdoch had also been a lung sufferer, cured by the islands, and it was on that account that he persuaded Tembinoka, who, it seems, sometimes whiled away the hours by shooting his subjects out of the trees just for fun, to set up for the Stevenson party a compound of huts, and to provide food and entertainment. Louis probably did not grasp to its fullest extent the real character of his host, though he described him as 'the last tyrant, the last erect vestige of a dead society';[26] he might have been less willing to accept his hospitality if he had. George Murdoch many years later reflected sadly that Stevenson might have changed his attitude if he had known that he was legally married to his island wife, which was scarcely usual at the time.[27]

The plans for fiction were stirring again. The *Equator* had generated new ideas, and while on Apemama Louis and Lloyd were collaborating further, this time more felicitously. *The Wrong Box* had been finished in Hawaii but there can be few who can find much to say in its favour. It is clumsy and heavy-handed, and certainly it is hard to believe that Louis and Lloyd had laughed themselves into paroxysms over the writing of it. Now the enterprise was *The Wrecker*, inspired directly by the Pacific, though Louis was reaching back to French experiences too, in fact writing directly about his times in Paris as he never did elsewhere. It is an uneasy assemblage, the uneasiness probably partly the result of collaboration, for Lloyd's areas of sensitivity bore little relation to Louis's and the sheer mechanics of the business were not easy, partly the result of *The Wrecker* being a necessary stage in the bridging that had to take place between Europe, America and the Pacific. The plot itself attempts to accomplish this bridging, but only succeeds in providing the story with an unnecessary preamble. Louis has tried to provide a plausible means of drawing Loudon Dodd, a young man of respectable middle class background, into the shadier Pacific ambience where fraud and murder have their own kind of inevitability. He was trying to explain too much. It is only when the Pacific ambience takes over, and explanation emerges with the reader no longer aware of the machinery grinding, that the narrative takes hold. Later, in *The Ebb-Tide* and even more so in *The Beach at Falesá*, he was able to dispense with explanation, much to these two stories' advantage. In *The Wrecker* Stevenson tried to preserve the adventure yarn, where convention demanded the provision of an acceptable route for the hero from respectability into adventure, the classic Scott mode, amidst the communication of fresh experiences. Imbedded in *The Wrecker* is a powerfully sinister story. The plot had suggested itself aboard the *Equator*. The novel was a necessary bridge in literary terms as well as geographical.

By this time *The Ebb-Tide* was also already begun, and a third story, *The Beachcombers*, which never materialised, was being contemplated. *The Ebb-Tide* began as another collaboration, but was not finished, suggesting that the usefulness of such joint working was now exhausted. Louis was to take it up again in Samoa, and rewrite and complete it himself. As parts of *The Wrecker* indicate, the process of absorption and production was working well, the balance of doing and writing was, in the Pacific as it hadn't been for years, right for him. In the *Equator* he talked with Captain Reid and his crew, got to know them well, absorbed their personalities, their habits, their modes of speech, their attitudes. On shore he drank with the station managers, the beachcombers, the drifters of the South Seas, often with a life of crime behind them (Louis reckoned he was on familiar terms with three murderers), listened to them, met their island wives, and learned that love and loyalty could exist in the most unpromising circumstances, more fuel for his belief in the survival of human nature.

Fanny's fear of the sea had not lessened after her Pacific experiences. She wrote to Mrs Sitwell that the problem was that as she stayed cool in a crisis no one would believe that she really did hate to be at sea in bad weather. But at least her boys were happy, living, writing, taking pictures. Life for Fanny on board the *Equator* lacked something of the style of the *Casco*; for a start she was one woman amongst fifteen men, although she may well have enjoyed that. They were at the mercy of Captain Reid's trading schedule, although even on the *Casco* plans had depended on factors of wind, weather and seaworthiness that were beyond their control. For two years now they had been on the move. There had been lengthy pauses, six months at Saranac, another six at Honolulu, just long enough to adapt to new circumstances and take breath before packing up again. They were a long way, hopping from one Micronesian island to another, from what either Louis or Fanny could call home. Did Louis, who wrote so feelingly of 'the hills of home', who was readier to commute his ideas of home into those fringe areas which were not so intimately associated with his upbringing and his parents, Swanston and the Pentlands above all, really believe that he would return to his native city, or did Fanny seriously envisage setting up house with her husband in California perhaps, scene of her most difficult years with Sam Osbourne, though probably the only part of the United States where she could think of growing roots? (It was to California that she did return, after Louis's death.)

At last they left the low coral atolls of the Gilberts behind them. Louis was tired of living on a 'diet from the pickle-tub or out of tins'. He was dreaming of food. 'I had learned to welcome shark's flesh for a variety; and a mountain, an onion, an Irish potato or a beef-steak, had been long lost to sense and dear to aspiration.'[28] They had been at Apemama long enough for the vegetables Fanny had planted to come up, but that did not reconcile Louis to a longer stay. 'A low island, except for cocoanuts, is just the same as a ship at sea', Louis grumbled to Colvin; 'brackish water, no supplies, and very little shelter.'[29] He was pining for 'an island with a profile'[30] as well as for steak and mangoes. When at last the *Equator* reappeared to pick them up the voyage proved disappointing.

> Rain, calm, squalls, bang – there's the foretopmast gone; rain, calm squalls, away with the staysail; more rain, more calm, more squalls; a prodigious heavy sea all the time, and the *Equator* staggering and hovering like a swallow in a storm; and the cabin, a great square, crowded with wet human beings, and the rain avalanching on the deck, and the leaks dripping everywhere.[31]

During a storm the *Equator*'s passengers had been for a while resigned to abandoning ship. Clothes, medicines and manuscripts were parcelled up and ready, but the emergency passed. Fanny spent the night with the ship's cat in her arms, afraid that otherwise she might be forgotten.

After narrow escapes from reefs 'of doubtful position' on the charts, there was a final indignity of a calm, a day's sailing from Apia. Louis was primed – although he did not know it, for he planned to stay only long enough in Samoa to complete work on the South Seas book, now well under way – to fall for the place, to be enticed. Within a few days, possibly after only a few hours, Samoa had come to mean more to him than just the final chapter of a book. It was indeed the final chapter for Louis, but a final chapter that contained a multitude of new beginnings.

Becalmed, they were frustrated. Lloyd, Joe and Fanny had all been unwell, Lloyd with an ulcerated foot. Yet they managed to keep up their spirits. Louis celebrated his birthday on board; he had entered his fortieth year. Mr Rick, the trading agent from Butaritari who ran the Sans Souci, had accompanied them on the voyage, and the party was also celebrating his birthday, on 12 November. A two-day festival was clearly called for. Shark and champagne were added to the menu in Rick's and Louis's honour. But a cause for greater celebration was their arrival at Apia. There had not been a wreck, but there might have been, and the relief of Apia was great.

Apia had established its importance in the island scene by developing as a provision port for the whaling vessels that by the early nineteenth century were crowding the South Pacific. Like all other such Pacific ports it had become a collecting place for the uprooted, a place with a temporary feel which inertia tended to convert into a reluctant permanency. It was part of the character of the Pacific; once a man had been around that ocean for a time it became almost impossible to go anywhere else. Stevenson was to communicate this feature strikingly in _The Ebb-Tide_. Men who anywhere else would be despised outcasts found a means of survival, and half a century before Louis's arrival this had been easier. Moral and social dividing lines scarcely existed. The children of missionaries went native, and often picked up the sexual habits of the islanders. Beachcombers settled down with native wives, perhaps a series of them, and fathered half-caste children who would grow into a generation of unsettled allegiance. Deserters, convicts, criminals on the run, adventurers in the sandalwood trade, or the copra trade, or the tortoiseshell trade, provided plenty of beachcomber material. Thirty-odd years before Louis and Fanny and Lloyd were seen wandering barefoot in Apia, the town had been described by an American official.

> A state of society existing that beggars all description; composed of a heterogeneous mass of the most immoral and dissolute Foreigners that ever disgraced humanity: principally composed of Americans and Englishmen, several of whom have been Sidney convicts. Responsible to no law for their conduct – certainly none that the Natives have the power or disposition to enforce against them – there exist anarchy, riot and debauchery which render life and property insecure.[32]

International squabbling over consular control of Samoa had proved demoralising for white and native and half-native populations alike, and had left the way open for anyone with energy and a thick skin to exploit an anarchic situation. By the 1880s it was Papeete that was notoriously the sink of the Pacific dispossessed, but Apia remained stamped by the distinctive features of the beach communities. Hard drinking, cheating and sexual carelessness had become a habit.

Yet, for Louis, Apia was a tonic. Vaea mountain rose behind the port. The Tivoli hotel promised a good dinner. A priority was the making of a feast for all the passengers and crew of the *Equator*. The menu was splendid, especially after weeks at sea: oyster soup, chicken, sucking pig, 'Cakes, Pie and Fruit', with punch, sherry, claret, Sauternes and, the final flourish, in capital letters on the menu, 'SCHLITZ MILWAUKEE BEER' for liquid refreshment.[33] It was an occasion of much jollity and good cheer

There was no plan to linger in Apia. Rather, below-decks conversations on the *Equator* had led Louis into, inevitably, quite another scheme, a seriously discussed proposal to buy his own yacht and install Reid as skipper. A first consideration once established in Apia was the arrangement of passage to Sydney. There was as always work to be done, more research, more writing, and then they would be off. Within a few weeks, though, Louis had become the owner of four hundred acres of land on the slopes of the mountain they had seen grow out of the sea as they approached Upolu, the summit of which would have a significance Louis would never know. Louis and Fanny had become, almost overnight, certainly without much in the way of thoughtful planning, excitedly, landed proprietors. It was not now a yacht they would buy but a house they would build and acres they would farm. They were going to settle down. For the first time in his life Louis had bought property.

Hindsight suggests that he had been preparing himself for the role of proprietor. In Waikiki he had described himself as 'Squire'.[34] As his nomadic ménage increased he must have begun to feel that the best way of handling them was to settle them in some permanent residence. The idea of returning to Britain with Belle and Joe Strong as well as Lloyd in tow was scarcely practicable, and none of them showed any signs of satisfactorily looking after themselves. It is clear that Louis did not necessarily fret at these responsibilities. He liked to be chief of his clan, to feel that he was able to care for his people. And perhaps he felt also that he was indirectly repaying his father for all those years of support while he himself must have looked very like the irresponsible sower of wild oats that Joe Strong now appeared. So however the idea of Vailima suggested itself, it came naturally. There were other considerations that emphasised its suitability. Apia was on the main sailing route to San

Francisco, and keeping in touch with the United States and
Europe was vital for Louis. His livelihood depended on it. There
was land available. And there were useful people there, notably
one Harry J. Moors, store manager of Apia, who was in-
strumental in the purchase of the land and the building of the
house. Without him, or someone like him, it is unlikely that it
would ever have happened. He turned out to be a mixed
blessing, but initially it was Moors who set things going, who
advised Louis on how to acquire what he needed and how to
organise the labour required, and who supervised operations in
Louis's absence.

There may have been another factor at work too. Louis was
primed not only to realise his proprietorial and paternalist
instincts, but to enter into some kind of commitment to Samoa.
In Hawaii he had seen Samoa as a key to the struggle for power
in the Pacific. The emotional commitment was already there,
too, for it was impossible for Louis to get to know as much as he
had about people and the facts that shaped their lives without an
emotional involvement. There had been talk of trying out
various European locales for wintering. They were still planning
to make a trip back to Britain via Sydney, and Vailima did not
appear at that stage to amount to a final cut-off from the old
world. But in the short term the indisputable fact that Louis was
better in health than he had been for many years, and therefore
in better psychological trim, indicated that it would be unwise to
be in a hurry to leave the Pacific. Hawaii had not been so good
for him, but the voyage south again had made it clear that sun
and sea air and low humidity were what Louis needed.

Accident played its part, of course. There just happened to be
land available, three miles out of Apia, uphill all the way, an
area of land so large that they could not be aware of all it
contained – or didn't contain. Fanny was enthusiastic. If Louis
fancied himself as landed proprietor, Fanny was certainly not
displeased at the prospect of being mistress of an extensive
estate. She wrote to Colvin describing what they had acquired.

> This tract consists of between three and four hundred acres,
> part of it table land of the richest deep virgin soil; more
> than enough for a large plantation. The rest is wild and
> picturesque; great cliffs, deep ravines, waterfalls, one some

two hundred feet deep and everywhere gigantic trees of different species. The whole lying some four hundred feet more or less above the sea level, and commanding magnificent views of the harbour, the sea outside, and the surrounding country.

Vailima would, initially at least, give Fanny a sense of purpose, which she badly needed. Over the last year, although her practical sense had been invaluable, the fact that Louis was writing hard and was fit and well, the fact that her son had grown up and had established his own independent relationship with his stepfather, had eroded what had at the time of her marriage been the main object of her life, to care for her husband and to help and support him in his writing. She still had strong views about what he should be writing, and they didn't always coincide with his. A major area of contention, over the South Seas book which Fanny thought should be light and pic-turesque, was due to the fact that she had not realised the changes that had taken place in Louis's approach to writing. She underestimated the seriousness of his attempt to educate his potential readers about the South Pacific. It was one of the dangers of the disparity in their ages. Louis had changed. Fanny was finding it difficult to adjust to the fact that she was no longer married to a vulnerable young man on the brink of a bright career.

Fanny elicited the support of Colvin, who hadn't been happy anyway about the effect Louis's drifting around in schooners in what seemed like an unreal quarter of the globe was having, he felt, on his writing. To hear that Louis was prolonging his stay, first, as he wrote from Honolulu for another year, then the news of the purchase of Vailima, was a heavy blow. Henry James shared Colvin's concern. He was sure, too, that the effect on Louis's writing was inevitably for the worse, although he took comfort from the fact of Louis's improved health. No one wanted to recognise the salient fact that Louis was changing. He had entered his fortieth year. He had come face to face with realities that were probably beyond the imagination of Colvin entombed in the British Museum, which housed, ironically, amongst its countless artefacts objects from the South Pacific. Even Henry James who eyed so acutely the world of upper-class mores and who always responded so sensitively to Louis could not see that the good recent years had done Louis was more than simply an improvement in bodily well-being. Louis was at last finding challenging and important subjects for his pen that were insistently a part of contemporary life. His search for real life and his search for a real literature looked as though they might be coming to a highly productive end.

Meanwhile arrangements were made for their passage to Sydney, still thought to be a stage on their route home. They left Moors in charge of their affairs. The house had been begun, a temporary residence to begin with, to go up quickly so that they could move in while work proceeded with a larger and more ambitious residence. In February they boarded the S.S. *Lübeck*, bound for Sydney and thinking of the affairs that awaited tidying up at home. Apart from the visiting of old friends there was Skerryvore, let all this while, to dispose of. They would have a house to furnish, somewhere where their varied and scattered possessions could find a resting place. Belle and Austin were waiting for them in Sydney, and shared the indignation when a smart Sydney hotel refused admittance to the disreputable looking party that turned up. They had long since abandoned the effort of dressing in conventional style and had possibly underestimated Sydney's claims to being beyond the Pacific frontier stage. In fury they went elsewhere, but the hotel must have had deep regrets, for as soon as it was discovered Robert Louis Stevenson was in town the Sydney press made much of his presence.

Louis made himself at home at once, unerringly sniffing out the congenial places and people. To get back to a civilisation of restaurants and bookshops was invigorating. He received a lot of attention, was made much of; that kind of thing was always a stimulus for him. It was during this stay in Sydney that Louis got to work on the Reverend Dr Hyde, but that was about as much as he did manage in a creative – or destructive – line, for Sydney proved nearly a disaster. He had ventured too far south. Suddenly he was ill again, struck once more by fever and haemorrhage, reduced to the old helpless feebleness and drastic loss of appetite. He was as bad as he had ever been. It was a bitter disappointment, for it meant the abandoning of any idea of making their way on to England, and for Louis to have to accept that himself, and then break the news to those back home was almost unbearable.

Until now the commitment to Samoa had not seemed to add up to a renunciation of home. Now it did. But a more immediate problem was simply Louis's survival. His condition got worse. The only possible remedy seemed to be to get him out to sea. It could not have been a worse time for such an undertaking, for the port of Sydney had been immobilised by a strike which affected all white seamen. Vessels lay untenanted in Sydney harbour. Desperate, Fanny haunted the dock area in her attempts to seek out a ship that would sail, and then to persuade the captain to take Louis on board. She found at last a grubby little steamer with a crew of kanakas, a general term covering all native islanders, and therefore untouched by the strike, and set about convincing the captain that taking a sick man and a determined woman on board was a feasible proposition. It was not an attractive prospect. The *Janet Nichol* was a cramped little craft, her rough-and-ready crew not used to the niceties that it looked as though a woman like Fanny would insist on. Louis could well be dying. Somehow, though, Fanny succeeded in talking the *Janet Nichol*'s captain into accepting them. They did not want to go anywhere in particular, just to be at sea.

For four months the *Janet Nichol* nosed from island to island with Louis and Fanny amongst the handful of passengers housed in her cramped quarters. The ship rolled prodigiously. The magic worked, and Louis began to get better, and more than that, completed another stage in his Pacific education. One fellow passenger, whom they first encountered drunk and wet after immersion in Sydney harbour, was written directly into *The Wrecker* as Tommy Hadden. Others filled in some of the gaps in his understanding. In several respects experience was being fed straight into writing, and Louis was living the novel as he wrote it.

The *Janet Nichol* visited the Gilberts and the Marshalls, and gave Louis a first, and depressing, taste of Melanesia when she put in at Noumea in New Caledonia. In spite of the discomforts, the dirt and the smells of the little tramp steamer, it was an eventful and often a jolly voyage, with surrealistic overtones: on one occasion a cargo of fireworks exploded with awesome effect and nearly involved the consignment to the deep of a burning trunk that happened to contain Louis's manuscripts. Such excitement did not prevent the tropic seas from performing their function. Back in Sydney in August, though, it all happened again. Louis relapsed into coughing and the spitting of blood. This time, turning their backs firmly on Europe, with regrets that Louis felt he could not put strongly enough to those who cared and were anxiously awaiting news of his return, they headed back to Apia on the *Lübeck*. In October 1890 Fanny and Louis took up residence in what there now was of Vailima, named for the five streams that flowed through their four hundred wild and demanding acres. Life was going to be strenuous.

Chapter 13

HARD WORK AND SHORT COMMONS

Hard work and short commons; but the commons are less short
now, thank providence.
Letter to Lloyd Osbourne

Shortly after his first arrival in Apia, Louis lay on the balcony of
Harry Moors' house and wrote to Charles Baxter.

The ink is dreadful, the heat delicious, a fine going breeze in
the palms, and from the other side of the house the endless,
angry splash and roar of the Pacific on the reef, where the
warships are still piled from last year's hurricane, some
underwater, one high and dry upon her side, the strangest
figure of a ship was ever witnessed.[1]

They had tried the hotel, but Moors had been insistent that they
accept his hospitality. Samoa, Louis was saying to Baxter, was
not as beautiful as Tahiti or the Marquesas, but it had its own
attractions.

. . . a more gentle scene, gentler acclivities, a tamer face of
nature; and this much aided for the wanderer by the great
German plantations with their countless regular avenues of
palm. The island has beautiful rivers, about the bigness of our
waters in the Lothians, with pleasant fords and waterfalls and
overhanging verdure, and often a great volume of sound, so
that once I thought I was passing near a mill, and it was only
the voice of the river. I am not specially attracted by the
people: they are courteous, pretty chaste, but thieves and
beggars, to the weariness of those involved. The women are
very attractive and dress lovely; the men purposelike, well set
up, lean, and dignified. As I write, the breeze is brisking up;
doors are beginning to slam, and shutters; a strong draught
sweeps round the balcony . . .[2]

We can see already the underlying appeal of the place, not in the overall impression so much as in the details, the rivers, the reminder of the Colinton mills, the gentle hills, the sound of the sea, the wind. On the way to Sydney on the *Lübeck* Louis was writing to Charles again, this time enclosing a poem he had written in Apemama. His closeness to Baxter was his most lasting bond with Edinburgh. All this time, and until the end of his life, Charles Baxter handled his affairs, cared for his needs, acted as go-between in dealing with publishers and often, as in the case of Henley, with friends. The poem celebrates that friendship, and others of his youth, but without a hint of a wish to return to that time, that place. Edinburgh is 'our scowling town', 'grimy', 'haggard'; youth 'the bitter hour before the dawn', a time of fear as much as of hope, of disillusion as much as of dreams.[3] It was a mark of Louis's confidence that he could write now unequivocally, without sentiment or nostalgia (although these would reappear), and without regret, of that period of his growing up when he was so anxious and so angry, and so painfully aware that things were badly wrong with the world, and so sure that something could be done about it. The poem suggests that he felt, in the year 1889, that he got a great deal of reward and happiness out of life, and was ready to say so, with confidence. It is roughly done, but it carries a conviction that some of his more polished statements lack.

Louis had always been in the habit of preparing for death, which may explain a little his often disarming frankness about himself, his motives, his attitudes. He wanted the record to be straight. There were those who felt that such honesty was embarrassing, or in bad taste: Louis's genial narration of how he came to write *Treasure Island*, for instance, irritated a number of his readers, who felt he should keep such mysteries to himself. But he was concerned to destroy any impression of the writer's mystique. When he wrote, in his 'Chapter on Dreams' about the workings of the imaginative process, about the 'Brownies', as he called them, who supplied his mind in his sleep, this was not a pleasing little conceit about the little people writing his books, as it has sometimes been taken, but an explanation of how the creative process was a combination of inspiration and workmanship. Only for the latter could he claim responsibility. Writing was a job. He steadfastly refused to put in any special pleading for the writer, or to veil the process by which words

were written down on the page. He pointed out that the writer
was selling a skill that brought him pleasure. 'We are whores,' he
had once written to Gosse, 'some of us pretty whores, some of us
not: whores of the mind, selling to the public the amusements of
our fireside as the whore sells the pleasures of her bed.'[4] The
analogy doesn't quite work, as Louis was to admit later. The
point was that he had no wish to elevate the writer's role, and
although he had also written to Gosse that 'the public should
know nothing from behind the scenes'[5] this was through an
anxiety to refrain from capitalising out of his private life, rather
than a desire to hide the truth.

It must have seemed a long way in time and space from the
breezes of Upolu to the 'belching winter wind' of Edinburgh; in
sending the poem to Baxter Louis was in effect sending him a
message, which told him that however distant Louis was he was
still bound fast to the old world, and not only through nostalgia.
It was an important message to convey, and Baxter probably
understood it best. In the same letter, almost casually, Louis
mentions having bought the Vailima acres as 'something to fall
back on for shelter and food', and discusses finance. For Baxter,
further apology or explanation seemed unnecessary.

The Vailima acres were, mostly, a wilderness. It is doubtful
whether Louis and Fanny realised the full extent of what they had
taken on until the purchase was already completed. Most of it
was uncultivable, at least with the resources that were available.
The stock that had been theoretically included in the sale proved
on inspection elusive. Fifty head of cattle appeared to have faded
into the landscape. By the time Louis and Fanny returned from
Sydney some progress had been made. The house was up and a
start had been made with the clearing of the bush. But one of
their first visitors, Henry Adams, who was travelling in the
Pacific with John La Farge, was scathing. The house in which
Robert Louis Stevenson lived was, he wrote in a letter home, 'a
two-storey Irish shanty'. 'A pervasive atmosphere of dirt seemed
to hang around it, and the squalour was like a railroad navvy's
board hut.' The inhabitants of this shanty with its galvanised
iron roof matched their abode.

Imagine a man so thin and emaciated that he looked like a
bundle of sticks in a bag, with a head and eyes morbidly

Vailima, Samoa

intelligent and restless. He was costumed in a dirty striped cotton pyjamas, the baggy legs tucked into coarse knit woollen stockings, one of which was bright brown in colour, the other a purplish dark tone. With him was a woman . . . she wore the usual missionary nightgown which was no cleaner than her husband's shirt and drawers, but she omitted the stockings. Her complexion and eyes were dark and strong, like a half-breed Mexican.[6]

Adams was appalled at finding a noted author unselfconsciously slumming it in a Pacific jungle, unashamed of the dirt and making no pretence to be civilised. 'Their mode of existence

here is far less human than that of the natives,' he wrote
superciliously. Yet in spite of himself he comments with
something like awe on Louis's fragility and his endurance,
although the awe rapidly turned acid. 'Stevenson gloats over
discomforts and thinks that every traveller should sail for
months in small cutters rancid with cocoa-nut oil and mouldy
with constant rain, and should live on coral atolls with nothing
but cocoa-nuts and poisonous fish to eat.'[7]

The work before them was frightening. Louis hacked away at
the threatening jungle as much as his strength would allow – 'I
wish you could see me at work in the garden. First I fall down,
then do my planting until I wish to move on, when Henry lifts
me up, and I go through the same process again.'[8] He derived
satisfaction from this outdoor existence, but time spent trying to
tame the vegetation was time spent away from his writing. 'The
rest of my life is a prospect of much rain, much weeding and
making of paths, and little letters and devilish little to eat.'[9]
Henry Adams had been somewhat peeved at what seemed to
him a lack of hospitality, for there was not much food
forthcoming. Louis and Fanny were by this time used to
improvising odd meals: 'my wife and I have dined on one
avocado pear; I have several times dined on hard bread and
onions'.[10] Speculating on the problem of how to entertain
guests in such circumstances, Louis wondered if the only answer
might be to eat him. Henry Adams may have been luckier than
he knew.

Although they had hoped for better progress before their
return to Apia, Louis and Fanny were not disappointed with
what had been achieved. Fanny's assessment of their quarters
was rather different from Adams'. 'A very neat and expensive
building, very like a bandstand in a German beer garden', was
how she described it.[11] They had brought pigs and chickens on
the *Lübeck* and a priority was the construction of suitable abodes
for the stock. Until the hens were confined there was the
unrewarding task of hunting for eggs in the bush. Getting the
seeds into the ground was another urgent task, and that was
mainly Fanny's province. She planned and instructed and did
much of the planting herself. Melons, tomatoes and lima beans
were amongst the first seeds to go in. Once the ground was more
extensively cleared and an assault made on the weeds she would

grow more ambitious. She was to be found most often
dishevelled and dirty, barefooted in the soil, her skirt hooked
up, stooping over her seedlings.

   She and Louis moved into the three rooms in the upper part
of the house, while below them lived the man and wife, and
three others, who were working for them. They were dependent
on their workers; Vailima could not even have been thought of
without them. The servant population expanded to nineteen,
including married couples. Lloyd had returned to England to
settle Skerryvore affairs and have furniture and possessions
packed up and sent out. There were in the early days only the
two of them, the far from robust Louis, weakened by two bouts
of critical illness in Sydney, and the fifty-year-old Fanny. Their
relationships with those who worked for them over the years
were a crux in their lives. Key figures in the establishment were
Lafaele and Henry Simele, there from the beginning – key
figures because they were able to liaise between Louis and Fanny
and the other workers. Of Henry Simele, who also helped Louis
to learn Samoan, Louis said, 'He does good work for us; goes
among the labourers, bossing and watching; helps Fanny; is
civil, kindly, thoughtful.'[12] The 'bossing and watching' were
indispensable. Louis believed that the instilling of the Protestant
work ethic into a people who in European terms were likely to
be considered fundamentally idle, was a duty. He succeeded
remarkably well, with the help of Henry, and was to pride
himself on the good labour relations – he did not consider them
labour relations, for his attitude was classically paternalistic, and
his workers a part of the 'family' – that reigned at Vailima. There
was other assistance, although this at times proved of a dubious
nature, in the shape of Paul, a German drifter they had
encountered on the *Lübeck* and to whom a job was offered as
general helper and handyman. He was useful, but difficult.

   Fanny presided watchfully over her seeds. Tomatoes,
artichokes and eggplants were sown in seedboxes, and whenever a pineapple was eaten the top was planted. Peas, onions,
lettuces and radishes went into the ground. They stumbled on
what had once been a banana plantation, and Mr Carruthers, a
lawyer in Apia, got for them trees and plants to put in, including
two mango trees. The lean time they went through initially must

only have encouraged their efforts. 'I am a mere farmer,' Louis
wrote:

> . . . my talk, which would scarce interest you on Broadway, is
> all of fuafua and tuitui, and black boys, and planting and
> weeding, and axes and cutlasses; my hands are covered with
> blisters and full of thorns; letters are, doubtless, fine things,
> so are beer and skittles, but give me farmering in the tropics
> for real interest. Life goes in enchantment; I come home to
> find I am late for dinner; and when I go to bed at night, I
> could cry for the weariness of my loins and thighs. Do not
> speak to me of vexation, the life brims with it, but with living
> interest fairly.[13]

He was apologising to Burlingame for having come to a halt on
The Wrecker. Other things were demanding his attention. To be
actively engaged in constructive physical work was good
medicine, all the stronger for the fact that for so much of his life
Louis had been quite unable for the kind of strenuous activity he
was now engaged in.

There were problems, setbacks, disasters one after another.
Fanny tried to bake bread in the cookhouse several yards distant
from the main house, but as it was pouring with rain, the
firewood was wet, and keeping the rain off the dough in its
journey from house to kitchen almost impossible even with an
umbrella held over it, it was an unrewarding enterprise. The
stock escaped frequently. Paul, the German, got drunk. The
misunderstandings of their numerous workers were incessant.
The cock kept eating the eggs. The seedlings were destroyed.

Slowly life became less precarious. Aunt Maggie joined them
once more, having sold 17 Heriot Row and made the trip out via
Sydney. Some of the Heriot Row furniture followed her. In a few
months Fanny's vegetables were well established, although the
job of clearing was endless and mishaps continued to beset the
garden. The Vailima horses regularly trod the path to Apia, two
large, strong pack horses to bring up supplies and building
materials, sometimes in the charge of Austin, who led a blissful
existence at Vailima until he was packed off to school in
California, and saddle horses, an ex-circus pony (who couldn't
quite shake off the memory of circus days) for Aunt Maggie, and

Louis's Jack, to whom he became very attached. It was on Jack that Louis would ride down to Apia to talk with Harry Moors, or with Clarke, or with James Chalmers, another missionary, whom he admired greatly, or with US Consul Henry Ide to whose daughter Louis presented the gift of his own birthday to be held in perpetuity, because her own was on Christmas Day, or with Bazett Haggard, British Land Commissioner and brother of Rider. In his white clothes and yachting cap, laced-up riding boots, on the not very prepossessing Jack, Louis was a familiar figure making his way between the town and Vailima. When a British warship called he was a welcome visitor on board, and enjoyed entertaining the officers at Vailima. On the whole the naval men were more congenial companions than the administrators.

Their diet improved, too. 'Dinner: stewed beef and potatoes, baked bananas, new loaf-bread hot from the oven, pineapple in claret,' Louis recorded, all of which sounds very appetising.[14] But although there was a marked improvement in the quantity and quality of food available there was not much change in the style of dress at Vailima. Bare feet were the rule, casual, cool and comfortable clothes. Later, when the move into the new house was complete, things were done with rather more style. Louis wore white shirt and trousers, with a red sash around his waist. They dressed for dinner, and sometimes entertained, for Samoa, quite grandly. By this time most of the cooking and domestic work, as well as the plantation work, was done by servants.

As progress was made on the new house it became clear that neither Fanny nor Louis was going to hold back on the achievement of something worthy of their own ideas of style and comfort. Louis was pushing himself hard at his writing. Worry about money runs as a strong current through these years, but initially at least he had no urge to stint the house. California redwood was imported for panelling. The Skerryvore furniture came, as well as some pieces from Heriot Row. Slowly there emerged a striking combination of European bourgeois comfort and individualistic Pacific decoration, with an American flavour detectable in places. The estate hummed around them, planting, harvesting, stock raising. Supervision of the work was demanding, and often Fanny's charge. She was probably not as tactful or patient as the supervision of a large number of only partly comprehending islanders – for Upolu had never seen such an establishment before – required. Louis was not unaware of the implications of this lifestyle; he referred, with apparent cheerfulness at first, to his 'Subpriorsford'.[15] The echoing of Walter Scott's Abbotsford was ominous. Scott killed himself in his attempt to keep his household going on the scale he found irresistible. Louis could never have been a landed gentleman in late nineteenth-century Scotland, at least not on that kind of scale, yet here he was, thousands of miles away, presiding over a scene that ten years earlier would have seemed laughably unreal. He took his responsibilities with great seriousness, and because of that probably underestimated the time and the energy such an operation demanded, not only in writing to keep the cash flowing in, but in maintaining his position, as employer, as chief of his clan, as a man of reputation, 'Tusitala' (story teller), and finally as a moral and political centre in the island's life. All this time, as he describes and celebrates Vailima in his letters, as he rejoices in his health and his capacity for work, as he takes pride in the position he has found for himself in a community's life and in virtually the world's imagination, there are ominous and disturbing ripples. It was perhaps inevitable, with a man like Louis, that the very conditions that seemed to nourish him were combining to kill him. Throughout his life the war in the members would not let him go.

With pride Fanny described in her diary the home that by the middle of 1891 Vailima had become. The big house was now finished.

The dining room we have hung with a yellowish tapa [barkcloth], the window casings and door being a strong peacock blue, and the ceiling a sort of cream colour. With the chairs and pictures, the colours make a most delightful harmony. At the double window I have put a curtain of Indian gauze, cream-white and silver, lined with soft orange-coloured silk and edged with lace. My own room is beginning to have the softly jewelled look that I am so fond of. . . . The ceilings and walls are natural California redwood, varnished. . . . The edges of the floor are stained with a native

dye and waxed. The furniture is old mahogany, with a little
brass. I had a rather raw Turkey carpet, very deep in the pile
and delicious to the bare feet. Now that is spread on the floor
with a border of native mats . . . it looks quite subdued, and
harmonizes very well. The window and door casings are a
dark peacock green.[16]

In planning this kind of thing Fanny was in her element. Henry
Adams would have noticed a change. There were now leather-
covered chairs and Chippendale in the dining-room. Fanny's
own room in the early months had been a repository for a
multitude of stray objects, bridles, tools, ropes, buckets,
cartridges and numerous island artefacts. Now Fanny and Louis
occupied a house with a hall large enough to hold a ball
in – which they would do – pervaded with a flavour of unconventional distinction.

In May 1891 the Strongs joined the Vailima community, and
lived in the cottage, the first Vailima house, joining the company
in the 'big house' in the evenings. Routines were established.
Louis got up early to write, about 5.30 in the morning, and
usually worked until midday. After lunch he would often play
his flageolet for an hour or two, then work again before an early
dinner. The evenings tended to be social occasions, almost
inevitable when a good half-dozen usually assembled. Louis
might read to the company what he had written that day. A game
of charades might develop, or cards, or music. Once a week the
entire household would gather for family prayers, a ritual Louis
may ostensibly have established to please his mother, but it
became something he felt deeply about and enjoyed, although
he would have resisted the idea that he was going through
gestures of conventional piety and he continued to resist
institutionalised religion. He was then usually in bed by eight
o'clock, returning to his own room (he and Fanny had separate
rooms) where he could sleep and rise early the next day to begin
his work without disturbing the household.

    Life was strongly coloured by the patterns of human
relationships at Vailima. Fanny and Louis were at the centre of a
complex web of involvements in which every difficulty and
disagreement washed back on them. It wasn't just the attitude to
work and the private lives of the Vailima islanders, although

there was always an at least incipient confrontation between island ways, American enterprise and Scots sense of responsibility. The immediate family generated a tangle of problems. During these years Fanny's health deteriorated. Her throat had been completely cured, but towards the end of 1893 Bright's disease, a disease of the kidneys, was diagnosed, and this can only have intensified the nervous disorders to which she had always been liable and which became at Vailima serious to the point of alarm. Joe Strong was not only in bad physical shape, his behaviour became an embarrassment, even to Louis, who had always liked him and been ready to find excuses for him. Belle, as his wife, was in a difficult position. Lloyd was causing problems too, which culminated in the discovery of his affair with a Samoan girl, a natural if not an inevitable result of his prolonged stay on the island. Beset by the overactive sensitivities and exposed feelings of the domestic scene Louis tried to maintain an equilibrium, to give everyone a share of his time and attention, to stay good humoured and hard-working. But at worst it was a situation in which whenever he seemed to be doing right by one, he was offending another. There were times when he could not disguise the fact that it was barely tolerable.

It was impossible for Louis to be a calm centre in all this. He had always himself been volatile and excitable. Middle age did not necessarily tone this down. H. J. Moors described him as prone to over-react, especially in trivial matters. Injustice and unscrupulous behaviour of any kind made him indignant; he was surrounded not only by family problems that affected him personally but also by a volcanic political situation which did indeed erupt around him, though he often remained cool in emergencies while small things could ignite him. Moors described him. He was, he said, highly strung, nervous. An impression is given of a man of exposed nerve ends, tautly stretched, acutely sensitive.

When in a rage he was a study. Once excite him, and you had another Stevenson. I have seen him in all moods. I have seen him sitting on my table, dangling his bony legs in the air, chatting away in the calmest manner possible; and I have seen him, becoming suddenly agitated, jump from that table and stalk to and fro across the floor like some wild forest

animal. . . . His face would glow and his eyes would flash,
darkening, lighting, scintillating, hypnotizing you with their
brilliance. . . . They carried in them a strange mixture of
what seemed to be at once the sorrow and joy of life, and there
appeared to be haunting sadness in their very brightness.[17]

Moors, in his account of Louis at Vailima, was anxious to
emphasise the extent to which the household and Louis
especially were dependent on him. He lent Louis substantial
sums of money, advised him and continually assisted him in
disentangling practical difficulties. At the same time he was
systematically overcharging him for goods, of which Louis
bought large quantities from his store, a fact which his
reminiscences do not include. Moors was astute enough to
recognise that Louis was a kind of innocent. His reliance on
others could be careless. Moors could not resist taking
advantage. Louis discovered the fraud, and furiously broke off
relations to do business with his rivals, the Germans, the
*Deutsche Handels und Plantagen Gesellschaft für Süd-See Inseln zu
Hamburg*, known shortly as 'the longhandled firm'.

Clearly, Louis's low ignition point created its waves of effect.
He was aware of the fact that he was becoming increasingly
irritable, as he built up around him the outward signs of
stability, more rather than less likely to flare up. To what extent
Louis himself may have contributed to the problems of the
Vailima household is impossible to establish. One can only
guess, and it is perhaps not very helpful guesswork. The
numbers of people in the house meant that Louis had to spread
his favours, and he had always been a man whom individuals
had tended to want to have as their own. The comradely
relationship with Fanny, so vital for so long, was inevitably
eroded although there are moments when it comes vividly back
into focus. They did not share a bedroom. Fanny, in her early
fifties and probably by now post-menopause, was perhaps
touchy on sexual matters, though not long before they had had
a pregnancy scare. Louis had just adjusted to the prospect of a
child when the alarm passed. He had always before that been
sure that it would not be right for him to father a child, and the
thought of having a child to lose one was appalling to him.
Although it has been suggested that illness may have drastically

interfered with Louis's sexual urges, it was likely that, having gained so much in physical well-being, he was full of sexual energy. Fanny was often jealous of attentions he paid to other women, even jealous of Belle who acted as his amanuensis when he suffered from writer's cramp and could not wield a pen. But it can be said without any doubt that Louis remained totally committed and faithful to Fanny from the moment he was aware he loved her. It can also be said that, acutely sensitive though he so often was towards the feelings of others, he was not always tactful or thoughtful in his behaviour. It is difficult to reconcile tactfulness with a tendency towards spontaneity and precipitate action. Sometimes the very qualities that seemed so attractive, the spontaneous generosity, the unhesitating enthusiasm for a worthwhile cause, the unconventional responses to people and situations, were just those characteristics that could breed trouble. As Louis and Fanny grew older, and as they could no longer move away from the troubles that gathered around them, these internal contradictions increased. It cannot always have been easy to live with the master, the teller of tales, straining his mind and

Louis and Belle in the library at Vailima

his imagination and his right hand to produce the words on which Vailima's future depended.

It was in the very early days at Vailima that Fanny recorded in her diary a remark of Louis's that she took to heart. Whether it was intended as a joke, or was the source of a real quarrel between them, is difficult to tell, but it was clearly important to her and was significantly, very much later, suppressed in the manuscript of the diary.

> Louis says I have the soul of a peasant, not so much that I love working in the earth and with the earth, but because I like to know that it is my own earth that I am delving in. Had I the soul of an artist, the stupidity of possessions would have no power over me. He may be right. I would as soon think of renting a child to love as a piece of land. When I plant a seed or a root, I plant a bit of my heart with it and do not feel that I have finished when I have had my exercise and amusement. But I do feel not so far removed from God when the tender leaves put forth and I know that in a manner I am a creator. My heart melts over a bed of young peas, and a blossom on my rose tree is like a poem written by my son. After I had made a perfect garden and it had been sold and bought several times I beheld it ploughed up, the vines torn down, my trees cut for firewood, the flowers uprooted – planted in potatoes. I could not have felt worse had I seen my favourite riding horse, hock-kneed and ruined, dragging the plough. After all, I believe we present our home the best of it: we possess something deep and strong and never the evanescent sport of the artist. I love the earth not only when she is beautiful but when she is called ugly. I cannot play with her and love her. My things, my house have favoured me, and I cannot loosen the strings that bind us without something breaking.[18]

Fanny is here trying hard to make something positive and creative out of her love of the earth, but it was painful for her to be told that she had the soul of a peasant rather than of an artist, especially as Louis was now on dubious ground when criticising her need for possessions. It is a revealing passage in several ways. It shows that Louis was quite capable of being, presumably unthinkingly, hurtful. And we see the bristly personality of

Fanny reacting to this, almost making a religion of her garden, and showing that she wanted to see her role as emotionally and spiritually important as well as physically productive.

Later, Fanny would react hysterically to suspected criticism. It makes it easier to understand this if we remember that Louis was at times critical and that she had always been extremely sensitive and extremely uncertain about her role. Having others in the house who might be seen to be supplanting her in some of her functions did not ease the situation. Lloyd returned, Skerryvore having been sold for £1500, and the Strongs were there. All three should have been useful additions to the household, when there was so much to be done, but it is clear that Lloyd, trying to write and inevitably under the shadow of his stepfather, was not keen on a role as either farmer or works supervisor, and Joe was a supernumerary in the household of a famous man, which again cannot have helped him to overcome his failings. The latter were only too manifest, drink summing up many of them. By the end of 1892 Vailima couldn't take him any more. Fanny noted the crisis in her diary.

> . . . we found Joe Strong out in various misdeeds: robbing the cellar and store-room at night with false keys. In revenge, when he found that he was discovered, he went round to all our friends in Apia and spread slanders about Belle. We turned him away and applied for a divorce for Belle, which was got with no difficulty, as he had been living with a native woman of Apia as his wife ever since he came here. . . .[19]

This happened when Fanny was going through one of her bad times, prone to hysteria, jealous, hypersensitive. The two things may not have been unconnected. With Joe gone, Louis's paternalist role in relation to Belle and Austin became that much more direct. He became guardian of Austin, who was sent to school in California under the care of Fanny's younger sister Nellie, who now had herself a son called Louis for whom Louis Stevenson had written that haunting little poem about the beach at Monterey.

Fanny's bad spell was intensified, perhaps brought on, by the visitation at this time of Lady Jersey, wife of the Governor of New South Wales, and members of her family, who monopolised much of Louis's time and attention. Louis

enjoyed their visit, and took the opportunity to encourage
people who could be of influence to become acquainted with the
political situation in Samoa. This involved a somewhat risky
expedition to pay a call on the chief Mataafa, the rival to the
German-supported Talietoa and the man whom Louis himself
approved. The whole business was conducted in a melo-
dramatic, cloak-and-dagger fashion, meeting at dawn on
horseback, and Louis loved it. Fanny was annoyed. Her verdict
on Lady Jersey was touched with venom, 'Very selfish and
greedy of admiration, a touch of vulgarity, courageous as a
man, and reckless as a woman.'[20] Fanny resented the fact that
her own husband gave Lady Jersey some of the admiration of
which she was greedy. Curiously, it is a judgment that might
have been passed with some justification and with little criticism
implied on Fanny herself.

Fanny had been described as suffering at this time a condition
that was close to psychotic. It is difficult to be clear as to what was
happening to her. Louis was very reticent about her condition,
although there is enough in his letters to indicate that he was
profoundly disturbed by what was happening, and a Sydney
doctor identified mental imbalance. Her hypersensitivity and
tendency towards paranoia brought her to hysteria. She at times
hallucinated, and had to be held down raving to her bed. It is
possible that these manifestations were aggravated by drugs she
was taking for other symptoms. There was certainly a degree of
imbalance in her make-up, as there was in Louis's. The strains of
Vailima life may well have caused quite trivial difficulties and
irritations to appear vastly enlarged. The borderline between
'over-reaction' and psychosis is hard to define.

There are a number of currents involved in Fanny's illnesses.
By the first part of 1893 it is clear that she is often 'ill',
but illnesses of various kinds had been frequent visitants
throughout her life with Louis, and it is not clear whether, when
Louis describes her in his letters as 'ill' he is referring to a
physiological condition, the Bright's disease, for instance,
which was diagnosed in November of that year, or whether he is
referring to a condition even more disturbing. 'Well, there is no
disguise possible; Fanny is not well, and we are miserably
anxious,' he is saying cryptically on 5 April.[21] She had had heart
trouble and stomach trouble. If at this time she was coping with

the menopause as well, and trying to run Vailima, and trying to accommodate the complicated lives of numerous other people, and to maintain a private and personal relationship with her husband, it would not have been surprising had she exhibited some signs of strain and discontent. But her symptoms were clearly more than that. All her failings are suddenly writ large. Her temper does not just fray, it shatters. She felt that she could not control what was going on at Vailima – this can be guessed from her jealousies. She was no longer able to give Louis the support and judicious encouragement he still badly needed. In that same April, Louis was writing, just two days later,

> I am thankful to say that the new medicine relieved her at once. A crape has been removed from the day for all of us. To make things better, the morning is ah! such a morning as you have never seen; heaven upon earth for sweetness, freshness, depth upon depth of unimaginable colour, and a huge silence broken at this moment only by the far-away murmur of the Pacific and the rich piping of a single bird. You can't conceive what a relief this is; it seems a new world. She has such extraordinary recuperative power that I do hope for the best. I am tired as a man can be. This is a great trial to a family, and I thank God that it seems as if ours was going to bear it well. And oh! if it only lets up, it will be but a pleasant memory. We are all seedy, bar Lloyd, Fanny, as per above; self nearly extinct; Belle utterly overworked and bad toothache; Cook, down with a bad foot; Butler, prostrate with a bad leg. Eh, what a faim'ly![22]

This is quoted at length because it seems to express so much of Louis's life at Vailima at this time. The intense worry, and the relief over Fanny, is patent, as is the strain of so many responsibilities. Louis was the man who had to try to hold it all together. What a family, indeed, and much disapproved of by Colvin, the recipient of this. Yet Louis's senses remained attuned to the qualities of his environment, the sound of the sea, birdsong. He was full of ideas for future work, though there were periods of depressing inaction, and his sense of humour is unimpaired – or his ability to make the effort to pull himself out of the doldrums by seeking out a vein of humour. It had always

been one of his talents, and it was rare, even at this stage, for him
to forget that he could do it.

During this time, the last two years of his life, Louis's letters to
Baxter are full of his concern with money, publishers and
writing projects. Vailima was an immense and continuing
financial drain. The house itself was a thorough extravagance,
full as it was of imported materials. H. J. Moors commented
acidly on the stone fireplace that was constructed at great
expense and which was almost never used. The plan had been to
be at least self-sufficient, if not to make a profit from the
produce, but working the land was arduous as well as accident-
prone, and although some of their agricultural enterprises were
a success the estate was never going to make money for them.
And then there were people. Lloyd was to say after Louis's death
that Louis had begged him to stay in Vailima as he could not do
without his help. It is difficult to see what concrete contribution
Lloyd was making, although collaboration offered Louis the
opportunity of maintaining a dialogue about his work,
something which was of great use to him. Once Joe had been
expelled from the premises Belle and Austin became Louis's
responsibility legally as they had been in practice before. Belle
worked for him, but added to the emotional tangles at Vailima.
She and her mother had always had a relationship full of
potential conflict. Fanny was often very critical of her daughter,
and Belle was in a situation that could not have been easy for
her, although she was to write blandly enough about it many
years later. She was beholden to the man who had ousted her
father; her son was being supported, his education paid for, by
that man. Her security and her comfort and her livelihood
depended on him. It could well have been better for both Lloyd
and Belle had they been forced into some kind of independence.
Louis considered them his family, and was proud to do so.
Without children of his own, they provided an important
dimension in his life. But they added heavily to the punishing
strain on all his resources – financial, physical, emotional.

Half way through 1892 there was an addition to the
household in the shape of Louis's cousin Graham Balfour, who
arrived for a lengthy stay before going on to explore other
Pacific regions. Graham at once fell into the casual ways of
Vailima, and was an energetic participant in events during his

stay. He was in an excellent position to witness and to understand what was going on there, the difficulties with Fanny, the strain on Louis. His biography, undertaken with conscientious affection, published while Fanny was still very much alive, is cautiously veiled. The job was not any easy one, as he was much more personally involved than the book's tone suggests. His affection and loyalty towards Louis, his respect for Fanny, and the fact that Belle had grown fond of him while he was at Vailima, must have made it very difficult for him to decide what should be left out.

The household at Vailima, 31 July 1892. L. to r.: Joe Strong, Margaret Stevenson, Lloyd, RLS and Fanny

Around the emotional turmoil within, the sickness and conflict, the flaring up of jealousies, hysterical exchanges between Belle and Fanny, Louis losing his temper and flogging himself to write, the germ of a love affair between Belle and Graham Balfour, swirled battles of a different kind. In fact the outbreak of open hostilities in Samoa may have helped Fanny to focus her mind on something beyond herself, and by July 1893,

when war erupted, she is commenting in her diary fully and
succinctly on the political scene. She is active again, out on the
roads, and angrily partisan.

Louis's involvement in Samoan politics had really begun long
before he had set foot on Upolu, in so far as Samoa had been
Kalakaua's first target in his grandiose Pacific schemes. The
situation was that Britain and America were uneasily inactive as
Germany energetically consolidated political and economic
power. The presence of the German 'longhandled firm' in Apia
reflected attempts to monopolise South Pacific trade. Upolu was
patterned with German plantations. The Berlin Treaty had
theoretically established the need for a native kingship
responsible to this trio of powers, but inevitably there was
considerable disagreement as to who the king should be. Each
of the Powers had a vested interest in engineering a king who
favoured them, but this kind of manipulation did not fuse well
with the sophisticated hierarchical structure of Polynesian
society. Polynesian chiefs traced their ancestry back to the
origins of their race; aristocracy, its proof and its symbols were
of the highest value, and Polynesians were unlikely to have
much regard for one whose status was not properly established
in the traditional way. Characteristically none of the three
Powers were well versed in the factors that could contribute to
Polynesian prestige.

Germany favoured Malietoa, and had installed him in Apia,
and there was little attempt to disguise his puppet status. There
were two possible rivals, but only one was a serious threat,
Mataafa, who received some support from the British and
Americans, and fiercely that of Louis and Fanny, who saw the
German manipulation of Malietoa as an insult to the Samoans.
The third claimant, Tamesese, was never a serious contender.
But it wasn't a straightforward contest between Germany and
Malietoa, and Mataafa, with the United States and Britain
behind him, for Mataafa was a Catholic, and thus looked on
with disfavour by the British Protestant missionary presence. All
this, and further complications, Louis was primed to take an
interest in when he arrived in Samoa. The book that materialised from his concern and his researches was *A Footnote to
History*, a piece of work that made his own commitment quite
explicit and caused some problems for him, including the threat

of a libel suit, thereby. Of course, that he should be turning his attention at all to such things worried Colvin and others at home, and the letters to *The Times*, so public a means of broadcasting his political concerns, were considered by many to be an embarrassment. It was not good for the image of the author of romantic tales to be exposing his partisanship in what must have seemed at that distance to be parochial tribal quarrellings rather than a power struggle that would profoundly affect the future of Polynesia and the reputations of the imperialist countries concerned.

Louis visited Mataafa, whose village was within riding distance, several times. He had no intention of sticking to the imperialist rules and did not hesitate to make his feelings open, although he certainly knew he was being provocative. He seems to have maintained a reasonably amicable relationship with the British Consul, Cusack-Smith, although the Consul found Louis's activities extremely irritating, and complained about him giving advice to Mataafa. Apparently, no more than irritating, although Louis wrote him regular letters of complaint and criticism: he did not accuse Louis of being dangerously interfering. The little episode with Lady Jersey was difficult to countenance, as her position as wife of the Governor of New South Wales (although she was masquerading as Louis's cousin) made the situation tricky. But for Louis it was part of the preliminaries of war, which by this time was anticipated. Vailima prepared for the hostilities, not sure whether they might not be a major target for the forces of Malietoa. They had weapons. When war did break out their servants mysteriously disappeared, either to participate in the fighting or to keep out of the way.

Mataafa, who never really had a chance, was defeated. Louis and Fanny were convinced that the fighting was stirred up by the whites. Louis saw the Samoans, who prepared for war by blackening their faces, as sacrificial victims. The incongruity between the invisible confrontation between the three Powers and the exhibition of primitive traditions of warfare which Louis witnessed – 'The boats have been coming from the windward, some of them 50 strong, with a drum and a bugle on board . . . and a sort of jester leaping and capering on the sparred nose of the boat, and the whole crew uttering from time to time a kind of menacing ululation'[23] – has a strong note of tragedy. There were some dead and many wounded. The wounded were brought to the Apia mission house. Louis, Lloyd and Fanny rode down at night with lanterns to offer their assistance, but there wasn't much that they could do. Fanny related that 'eleven heads had been presented to the government and were hanging in baskets on a tree near the king's hut'.[24] The trophies included the heads of three girls, which was shocking to Polynesian and white alike.

Mataafa and his chiefs were rounded up and detained at Apia. Shortly after the fighting Louis had departed for Honolulu, needing a change and a rest, but became so ill that Fanny had to follow after and bring him back. On their return they made an ostentatious visit to the prisoners bringing with them the makings of a feast, by which action Louis once again successfully fluttered the European dovecot. Mataafa himself was finally deported, a desperate fate for a Polynesian, but Louis, if he had not done so already, won many Polynesian hearts by his behaviour after the war. The chiefs were released. As a token of their gratitude they undertook a task without precedent in their lives and traditions. They built for Louis and Fanny, whose fierce partisanship equalled if not surpassed Louis's, a road linking the track that crossed the island with Vailima. With their own hands they cleared the brush and dug the road, using Vailima tools but otherwise asking for nothing. By October 1894 the road was finished. To celebrate, Louis gave a feast, for the builders, for Vailima, and for Apia, although Apia, on the whole, declined to come. Louis made a speech praising hard work and co-operation, which he hoped might be a solution to Samoa's difficulties. It was an occasion and a speech that symbolically cemented his own commitment to Samoa.

A sign was erected which, with some dignity, stated the road's meaning. 'We bear in mind the surpassing kindness of Mr R. L. Stevenson and his loving care during our tribulations while in prison. We have therefore prepared a type of gift that will endure without decay forever – the road we have constructed.'[25] Twenty-two names followed. The road became known as the Road of the Loving Heart. Six weeks after the occasion on which it was opened, when Louis spelt out his place in Samoa, his feeling and his sense of purpose, the man for whom it was named was dead.

A year earlier, the war and it seemed the worst of Fanny's ill-health behind them, Louis was writing to George Meredith telling him about life at Vailima.

. . . I am now living patriarchically in this place six hundred feet above the sea on the shoulder of a mountain of 1500. Behind me the unbroken bush slopes up to the backbone of the island . . . without a house, with no inhabitants save a few runaway black boys, wild pigs and cattle, and wild doves and flying foxes, and many particoloured birds, and many black, and many white; a very eerie, dim, strange place and hard to travel. I am the head of a household of five whites, and of twelve Samoans, to all of whom I am the chief and father: my cook comes to me and asks leave to marry – and his mother, a fine old chief woman, who has never lived here, does the same. You may be sure I grant the petition. It is a life of great interest, complicated by the Tower of Babel, that old enemy. And I have all the time on my hands for literary work. My house is a great place; we have a hall fifty feet long with a great red-wood stair ascending from it, where we dine in state – myself usually dressed in a singlet and a pair of trousers – and attended on by servants in a single garment, a kind of kilt – also flowers and leaves – and their hair often powdered with lime. The European who came upon it suddenly would think it was a dream. We have prayers on Sunday night – I am a perfect pariah in the island not to have them oftener, but the spirit is unwilling and the flesh proud, and I cannot go it more. It is strange to see the long line of the brown folk crouched along the wall with lanterns at intervals before them in the big shadowy hall, with an oak cabinet at one end of it and a group of Rodin's . . . presiding over all from the top – and to hear the long rambling Samoan hymn rolling up. . . .[26]

In this picture, which leaves out a great deal yet contains so much of what deeply appealed to Louis Stevenson in the life he had made for himself at Vailima, the incongruities are summoned together into a settled whole. Whatever the difficulties, domestic and practical, of arranging existence on a Polynesian island to suit the needs of this distinctly untypical household, whatever the demands that Louis's commitment to local affairs entailed, whatever the struggle that writing had to be sometimes, and whatever the intensity and pain of Fanny's disintegration and the complication of other personal relationships, Louis stamped on the island of Upolu a life that was real, complete and individual. He was known by now as 'Tusitala', the teller of tales. It is worth remembering that for the Polynesians, with no written language, the oral tradition meant not just stories but history, not escape into the world of the imagination but continuity, a way of maintaining contact with the events, the personalities and the rituals of the past. And it is worth remembering that Louis was a great talker. Whatever he was doing, shut up in his room for hours with his pen on the move, it was through the spoken word (although he wrote 'The Bottle Imp' for a Samoan audience), that he made himself known to the Samoans. Louis may have seen himself as a patriarch, but was probably seen by the Samoans as something closer to a shaman, a figure of significant function and symbolic status, a man who had the power to preserve and to cure.

Chapter 14

NO REST BUT THE GRAVE

No rest but the grave for Sir Walter! O, how the words ring in a man's head.

Letter to Charles Baxter

Towards the end of 1893 Louis's friend Edmund Gosse wrote to him commenting on the fact that he had become something of a living legend. The idea of the frail Scots writer exiled in the tropics awakened the public's imagination. 'Since Byron was in Greece, nothing has appealed to the ordinary literary man as so picturesque as that you should be in the South Seas.'[1] A year that had been full of stress and difficulty was coming to an end. There is a curious discrepancy between the legend growing in Gosse's London and the realities of Vailima. In July of that year Louis was summoning the courage to write to Baxter, 'We'll come through it yet, and cock our bonnets.'[2] It was hard to write; months passed and little work was done. The extent of his emotional wounding, over Fanny and the problems of her family, he never fully revealed. The man who had stripped himself bare to friends and lovers, who had happily shared so much of himself with so many, who had throughout his life spontaneously expressed his feelings, laughed and wept without repression, was keeping a close guard on his emotions. It was perhaps a final lesson in his progress to maturity, and it contained a truth that he had all along suspected, from the time when as a young man in Edinburgh he had been intensely, often painfully, aware of his isolation. The lesson told him that ultimately growing up meant coming to terms with the singleness of his identity. However much he loved and wanted to give and to share, to whatever extent he wrote for a large and sympathetic public, however much he wished to enact the lives of adventurers and soar above routine tedium, he could only be himself, and ultimately it was himself he had to face.

He was drawn in two directions. Vividly and inescapably he

was living in the present, and now writing of it, but ineluctably he was being pulled back, back to Scotland, with an urgency that was much more than nostalgia. 'Eh, man, it was a queer time,' he wrote to Baxter, thinking of their Edinburgh days, 'and awful miserable, but there's no sense in denying it was awful fun, and life – yes, sir, it was deadly living.'[3] Deadly living, too, at Vailima, and much more complicated. It wasn't just that he was thinking of the past, or that he had begun to write with a kind of nervous eagerness on Scottish themes. It wasn't just that he wrote poems in these last years that catch the essence of his exiled relationship to his country. As soon as one looks at the language he puts into the mouths of his characters of this time, into Weir, into the elder Kirstie, into the briefly glimpsed characters of the fragment *Heathercat*, Louis at last turning to the Covenanters for what would have been a novel, into the splendid woman who dominates all that was done of *The Young Chevalier*, one sees that humanity and Scottish humanity in particular were coming to life in a way it had not done before.

Out of the uneasy narrative of *Weir of Hermiston*, unfinished and perhaps because of that too readily taken for the great novel Louis so hoped it would be, leaps the bold, rich language of Kirstie.

> Man, do ye no' comprehend that it's God's wull we should be blendit and glamoured, and have nae command over our ain members at a time like that? My bairn . . . think o' the puir lass! have pity upon her, Erchie! and O, be wise for twa! Think o' the risk she rins! I have seen ye, and what's to prevent ithers? I saw ye once in the Hags, in my ain howf, and I was wae to see ye there – in pairt for the omen, for I think there's a weird on the place – and in pairt for puir nakit envy and bitterness o' hairt. It's strange ye should forgather there tae! God, but yon puir, thrawn, auld Covenanter's seen a heap o' human natur since he lookit his last on the musket-barrels, if he never saw nane afore. . . .[4]

As a little boy it had been the sound of language, above all, that had spellbound him and enriched his life. Listening to Cummy, her Scots tongue flavouring Bible stories and tales of martyrdom, it must have been apparent even then how natural was the marriage of Scots and the language of the Old

Testament, and of the violence of Scotland's past and that of the Bible. Louis remembered Cummy 'reading the works of others as a poet would scarce dare to read his own; gloating on the rhythm, dwelling with delight on assonances and alliterations'.[5] The hearing of words was the first and perhaps the strongest influence on his imagination. Now he was writing to make his readers hear.

Over the years Louis had discovered that situations that might at one time have appeared to belong only to the past, to legend or to romance, were in fact a substantial part of reality. Human personality was a great deal more complicated and various than romance would allow, although at one time it had seemed to him that only through romance was he able to explore the more extreme in the range of human behaviour. But inside *Treasure Island*, boys' adventure story, psychological realism is struggling to get out, and inside *Jekyll and Hyde*, 'crawler' and fable, fully grown, contemporary character is in embryo. Stevenson had to find a language for realism before he could fulfil the potential of his talent and do justice to his acute and humanist sensibility. At times he found it in *Weir of Hermiston*. He had found it, admirably suited to the book's special circumstances and constraint, in *Kidnapped* and wavered again in *Catriona*, the sequel written at Vailima. *The Master of Ballantrae* revealed Stevenson's ability to produce a language of real depth and authority, but it was not consistent enough to carry the book over faltering moments.

It is probable that so long as Stevenson had stayed with Scottish subjects he would have had a problem, because Scottish subjects were rooted in Scottish history. He could hear the Scots voices in his ears, the voices out of the past, of Covenanter and Jacobite, of John Knox and Robert Fergusson, the voices of his childhood and youth, Cummy, the Swanston shepherd, Lewis Balfour at the pulpit, the irreverent language of Baxter and Simpson rollicking home after a bibulous evening, the prostitute, the tavern-keeper, the voices of argument and dissension, his father. And when those voices spoke in his novels directly, or indirectly as in the case of the first person narratives of *Kidnapped* and *The Master*, the result was vibrant and authentic – it was 'real', whatever the story offered as escapist adventure or historical drama. But Stevenson never mastered the language of narrative, because he never quite knew what to do with his own personality, so insistent, so intrusive, so inevitably rooted in anything he had to say about Scotland. And he never mastered historical perspective, possibly because it was too intimately a part of the present, just the reason *for*, or the motive for, Scott's mastery of it. As a young man Louis had exercised himself time and again in the attempt to decorate the surface of his personality in such a way as would make it literarily pleasing. That is what is amiss with his early essays and such early books as *An Inland Voyage* and *Travels with a Donkey*. It was an exercise that arose out of his own self-consciousness, his sense of isolation, the uneasiness of the period itself as to what literature should be, an uneasiness reinforced by growing up in Calvinist Edinburgh at a time when London was the country's literary centre. Although it had set him on the road to success, or appeared to do so, it might be argued that it had pointed him in a sterile direction. There is little doubt that he changed direction, and that France and her writers, and America and the Pacific, had everything to do with the change.

The change of direction did not, as far as can be judged with so many Scottish subjects begun and unfinished at his death, radically solve the problem of his handling of Scotland. *Weir of Hermiston* is perhaps a red herring, best left out of the final assessment, certainly if it is only to be used to indicate what Stevenson *might* have done. The vigour of the living language his characters speak is not enough to tell a good story well, without putting the story directly into their mouths. Louis was compulsively a Scottish novelist yet, if we are looking for clues as to what he might have done, the evidence suggests that he might have become most memorably a novelist of the contemporary Pacific scene, an explorer of alienation and isolation, an analyst of values, akin to Joseph Conrad.

For confirmation that Stevenson *had* found a language of reality, and could use it with control and consistency, it is more rewarding to look at what he was writing about the world he was living in in those last years. *The Wrecker*, over which Louis professed himself pleased to be collaborating with Lloyd, is an uneven book, ambivalent, transitional. Neither narrative nor characters are happily handled. The novel did not entirely satisfy Burlingame, who complained about its apparent anti-

Americanism, and it did not sell well in America, something which greatly displeased Louis. But turning to Stevenson's subsequent attempts to write about the Pacific, *The Ebb-Tide* and *The Beach of Falesá*, one realises that *The Wrecker* is full of clues about what was likely to happen next in Stevenson's writing. It is when the amoral ambience of the Pacific itself takes over that the novel becomes commanding, when Stevenson shows us people and situations stripped of the decent clothing conventional society usually affords. As the mystery of the *Flying Scud* unfolds we realise that there is nothing to protect anyone. Normal moral values do not operate. It points straight to *The Ebb-Tide*, which began also as a collaboration with Lloyd, but was taken up later by Louis alone, and reworked.

It is interesting that Louis began apologising about *The Ebb-Tide* as he was writing it. For some time before its completion he was discussing it with his distant friends and commenting on the unsavoury nature of his material: 'A brutal, brutal story about three first-class dead beats.'[6] He tried to prepare Colvin for it. Colvin, predictably, did not like it, and did not like *The Beach of Falesá* either. He did not want Louis to expend his energies writing about South Sea derelicts. He did not recognise, or did not want to recognise, that this was precisely the area of Louis's fascination. He was writing again about morally ambiguous situations and personalities. He was writing about men adrift, not literally adrift on the sea, for they are able, just, to put together the seamanship necessary to sail the schooner they have hijacked, but morally adrift. What Louis found in the South Pacific was an area of the world where conventional moral restraints and control just did not, or could not, operate. He had seen at close quarters moral and political corruption. He had witnessed exploitation and degradation. It was an ambience in which a man did not need to change his personality or his form, Dr Jekyll did not need to transform himself into Mr Hyde, in order to manifest the capacity for evil within human nature. In the South Seas that capacity might be said to emerge naturally and readily, with a minimum of external prompting.

But Louis saw something else as well that was equally important to him. He saw all kinds of unlikely characters coming into their own, and heroism in unlikely places. He saw that in the Pacific situation it was not always evil that emerged. It

was not always greed and weakness or corrupt power that
triumphed. In *The Ebb-Tide* his central character Herrick just
manages to hang on to a sense of his moral self although at every
stage in the story it would have been so much easier for him just
to give up. He resists the alternatives that appear to engage him,
the attractions of enslavement to corrupt power or of total evil.
He is not a good man, but he is not ultimately a bad man. It was
now important for Stevenson to be able to say that to be a not
totally bad man was positive. He was also by implication
rejecting his earlier, and simplistic, view of the synonymity of
evil with possession by the Devil. Huish in *The Ebb-Tide* is at the
same time the most vicious and the most human of Stevenson's
portraits of evil.

The message emerges with restrained clarity in *The Beach of
Falesá*, another product of the Vailima years, which was first
published under the title *Uma*. It is a short story, surely amongst
the best things that Stevenson ever wrote, the tone sustained, the
substance and pace controlled, and it is precisely about how, in a
situation where men are free from the conventional rules of
behaviour, in fact are positively encouraged to behave 'badly',
fundamental humanity can prevail. It is probably significant
that it is another of Stevenson's narratives in the first person, like
most of his best writing. His central character, Wiltshire, finds
himself in a situation where out of self-interest, which he had
always assumed ruled his life, emerge qualities of courage,
genuine love, and decency. When he insists on marrying the
island girl who has been his mistress, when he commits himself
to living out his life with her and their children, in spite of his
dreams of going back home and running a pub, when he does
these things without shedding the limitations of his personality,
he amounts to a character in a sense as profound and positive as
anything Stevenson created. Wiltshire is not magically reformed
or transformed. He is the same man at the end of the story as he
is at the beginning, and it is in just that that the story's exceptional quality lies. The last sentences catch the ambiguity that
Stevenson wanted to convey.

> My public-house? Not a bit of it, nor ever likely. I'm stuck
> here, I fancy. I don't like to leave the kids, you see: and –
> there's no use talking – they're better here than what they

would be in a white man's country, though Ben took the
eldest up to Auckland, where he's being schooled with the
best. But what bothers me is the girls. They're only half-castes
of course; I know that as well as you do, and there's nobody
thinks less of half-castes than I do; but they're mine, and
about all I've got. I can't reconcile my mind to their taking up
with Kanakas, and I'd like to know where I'm to find the
whites?[7]

This is the language of reality, ungrammatical, yet slightly self-
consciously educated – 'reconcile my mind'; ambivalent, honest
but limited, and true to Louis's experience of the Pacific.

It was this kind of truth that he really cared about. He was
determined not to be seduced by the exotic, he was not going to
allow coral reefs and palm trees, the shimmering loveliness of,
for instance, the almost dream-like island in *The Ebb-Tide*
(Stevenson's last word on islands, interestingly, suggesting their
illusory and dangerous nature, for *The Ebb-Tide*'s island houses
destruction) to tempt him away from the overwhelming reality
of the moral erosion of Europe in the Pacific. It was this that he
emphasised when he wrote to Colvin about the story. It was, he
said, 'the first realistic South Sea story'. 'Now I have got the
smell, and the look of things a good deal,' he went on. 'You will
know more about the South Seas after you have read my little
tale than if you had read a library.'[8] He had wanted to get it
right.

And of course, he wanted to get the Scottish experience right.
He was thinking of Fergusson, again, 'so clever a boy, so wild, of
such a mixed strain, so unfortunate, born in the same town with
me, and, as I always felt rather by express intimation than from
evidence, so like myself'.[9] That Louis was now thinking of
himself as having slid into Scottish cultural folklore is clear. He
considered himself to be Fergusson's inheritor. He wished to
pay tribute to the ghost that had haunted him in his youth, but
all he could do at this distance was to raise the matter of
improving the monument to Fergusson in the Canongate
kirkyard. He suggested to Baxter that something might be
added: 'This stone, originally erected by Robert Burns, has been
repaired at the charges of Robert Louis Stevenson and is by him
re-dedicated to the Memory of Robert Fergusson as the gift of

one Edinburgh lad to another.'[10] The sense of kinship had not
diminished; that Louis could even have thought of adding a
third Robert to those already on the stone suggests his sense of
responsibility as well as of achievement.

It reads almost as a foreknowledge of death that Louis should
have wanted his name carved in stone in his native city. When
the news of Robert Louis Stevenson's death reached London,
early in December 1894, it was received with shattered disbelief.
With communications so unreliable there was for a few days
room for doubt. It was soon dispelled. When Louis died Charles
Baxter, stricken by the death of his wife, was on his way to Samoa
to see his old friend for the first time in seven years. The news
reached him in San Francisco. The anguished cry of Henry
James is perhaps most eloquent of the widely-felt reaction: 'Of
what can one think or utter or dream, save of this ghastly
extinction of the beloved RLS.'[11] Louis Stevenson had become
a part of the literary dream of the time. To his friends and to his
public his death was indeed the extinction of a bright light. With
the personality there died a quality that was rare and dazzling, a
quality of generous and vivid humanity that seemed to lift late
Victorian Britain out of the doldrums of middle-class religious
and moral conviction.

In 1901 Graham Balfour published the authorised biography
of Stevenson, and one of those to review it was W. E. Henley in
the *Pall Mall Magazine*. It was the breaking of a long silence.
Louis had in his last years received and praised some of Henley's
work, and had anonymously provided financial assistance when
he was in trouble, but since the quarrel Louis had not heard
directly from him. The *Pall Mall* article has achieved some
notoriety. In attacking Balfour's version of Stevenson, Henley
was in effect attacking Stevenson himself.

I take a view of Stevenson which is my own, and which
declines to be concerned with this Seraph in Chocolate, this
barley-sugar effigy of a real man; that the best and the most
interesting part of Stevenson's life will never get written – even
by me; and that the Shorter Catechist of Vailima, however
brilliant and distinguished as a writer of stories, however
authorised and acceptable as an artist in morals, is not my
old, riotous, intrepid, scornful Stevenson at all. . . .[12]

The 'real' Stevenson was the man Henley had known in Edinburgh, 'the unmarried and irresponsible Lewis' (the 'unmarried' and the spelling are equally significant), the irreverent, rebellious iconoclast. Henley had failed to recognise that the 'Shorter Catechist' had always been there – or perhaps he had just forgotten, for his earlier and most affectionate poem on Louis acknowledges that presence.

The article is full of insights that are twisted into half-truths. For instance, 'To him there was nothing obvious in time and eternity, and the smallest of his discoveries, his most trivial apprehensions, were all by way of being revelations, and as revelations must be thrust upon the world; he was never so much in earnest, never so well pleased . . . never so irresistible, as when he wrote about himself.' Henley's own awkward personality intrudes here, and his motives are conflicting. We can detect his jealousy. But we can also detect his profound distaste for what happened to Louis's reputation. The man was being idolised by just those people who represented all that Louis had tried to cast off and oppose. The real Louis had been tamed, and remained so for many years. The irony was genuinely painful for Henley. He allowed that, and the old difficulties, to cloud his judgment.

It was another fifty years before the life of Louis Stevenson was rescued from the whims of a public who could not or would not see the whole man, and almost as long before his works began to receive the treatment they deserve. We are perhaps still waiting for Stevenson's writing to be done full justice in the context of both his Scottishness and his period. But in spite of the vagaries of attitude, and the extreme pendulum swings that have occurred in the process of redressing the balance, the essential Louis has survived. To get to know the man is an exciting and moving experience.

Louis would never have wanted to adjust to the world so successfully that he accepted what he found. If life had ceased to be a challenge, to be full of questions, if, in other words, life had become unrebelliously circumscribed by the walls of a comfortable home and the values that such walls normally contain, then he might have become what Henley was suggesting. But that did not happen. The world was still a wonder to him, and a mystery, and full of tangled difficulties, on the day he died. In his last year he was writing to Bob, old and intimate companion.

> I cannot get used to this world, to procreation, to heredity, to sight, to hearing; the commonest things are a burthen; THE SIGHT OF BELLE AND HER 12 YEAR OLD BOYÇ ALREADY RATHER TALLER THAN HERSELF, IS ENOUGH TO TURN MY HAIR GREY; AS FOR FANNY AND HER BROOD, IT IS INSANE TO THINK OF. The prim obliterated polite face of life, and the broad, bawdy, and orgiastic – or maenadic – foundation, form a spectacle to which no habit reconciles me.[13]

Sex and death, sex as the mainspring of human impulse, death as the inevitable result, the seeming contradictoriness of it all, and its tantalising nature, and lurking beneath this, almost certainly, a regret sometimes that there was no child of his own, filled his mind. We know that at one time Fanny thought she was pregnant, and it turned out to be a false alarm. Of course, at Fanny's age childbirth was not to be regarded lightly. By this time we can assume that Fanny was past the age of conception. The realisation that she would never have a child by Louis, although this had been a positive decision on the part of both of them, may well have contributed to her psychological problems during the Vailima years. Louis had, at a very early age, made up his mind that to father a child would be irresponsible, because of the likelihood of that child inheriting his own physical disability. He had been too near death too often to view the prospect of nursing an ailing child with equanimity. The death of Fanny's Hervey, of Fanny Sitwell's Bertie of tuberculosis at Davos, and of Henley's only and adored daughter were all agonising reminders. Hearing of this last he wrote, 'I never envied anyone more than I did him when he had that child, and it proved – or seemed to prove – healthy. Alas! I might have spared my envy. After all, the doom is common to us: we shall leave none to come after us, and I have been spared the pain – and the pleasure. But I still sometimes wish I had been more bold.'[14]

He was acutely aware of inheritance and continuity. He was writing of the Stevenson family, *A Family of Engineers*, digging into the past, tracing the process of his own making, firing queries back to Scotland about origins. He needed to root himself in Scotland's past, he needed to know that he belonged to a continuum. There was no child for him, and no grandchild for his father, to tend his thoughts towards the future rather than the past. In the last months of his life he was almost prophetically aware of his own maturing, and in a number of ways, in his letters, his poetry, his preoccupations, appeared to be reviewing his life. In that same letter to Bob, he was writing,

If I had to begin again – I know not – si jeunesse savait, vieillesse pouvait – I know not at all – I believe I should DO AS I HAVE DONE – EXCEPT THAT I believe I should try TO BE MORE CHASTE IN EARLY YOUTH, and honour Sex more religiously. THE DAMNED THING of our education is that Christianity does not recognise and hallow Sex. It looks askance at it, over its shoulder, oppressed as it is by reminiscences of hermits and Asiatic self-torturers.[15]

Such a line of thought may have been partly prompted by Lloyd's indiscretions with the Samoan girl, but it was also an important part of the review. There were areas of life that had had to be a secret exploration, and which he had not felt himself able to write about. It was one of his difficulties in *Catriona*. He brought a young man and a girl together, conveyed an awareness of the situation, but could not successfully express sexuality. It was a young girl's sexuality that baffled him. When he came to create the elder Kirstie in *Weir* and the matron of the tavern in *The Young Chevalier* he conveys splendidly a mature, substantial sexuality. As far as we know he had never had a fully realised love-affair with a woman who was not older than himself. If the prostitutes he had visited had been young, they were his elders in experience of both life and sex. Virginity was the stumbling block. Even in *Weir* it is the elder Kirstie, with her resonant awareness of the force of physical needs, that lends a sexual dimension to the love of Archie and young Kirstie.

The letter to Bob suggests that he would certainly have tried to 'honour Sex' in subsequent fiction; in fact, he had already begun. It underlines the change of direction in his writing. Like *The Wrecker*, *Catriona* can be seen as a transitional novel, not only a sequel to *Kidnapped*, but a necessary step, like *The Wrecker* unevenly done but with striking moments, between the completeness of *Kidnapped* and the bolder, more exploratory writing of the fragments he left behind him. It was a step *away* from a convincing Scottish narrative mode. It is possible that a large theme and diverse material would have defeated him, whatever the place or time he wrote about. He was at his best with a short tale or a limited and confined number of characters. My own choice of his best fiction would put *Kidnapped* and *The Beach of Falesá* at the top of the list.

His thinking about life and his thinking about fiction had by this time become inseparable. But other immediate worries dominated his mind, one of them being money. His letters to Baxter are full of agonising over finance, and only Baxter really knew what the situation was. The delays in communications were such that at the time Louis was drawing on the funds he hoped existed in Edinburgh he could never be sure they were there. The extensions at Vailima worried him; they had been undertaken against his better judgment. 'Now I seem to be let in for an addition to my house,' he grumbled. 'It is no choice of mine.'[16] He wrote *Catriona*, or *David Balfour* as it was at first called, with dollars and pounds sterling dancing in his vision.

The ghost of Sir Walter was dancing too. In September 1892, he was writing with hopeful confidence to his 'Doer', as he called Baxter, but there is a barely disguised sinister undertone.

> I must be well-to-do, I fancy: which is the magnum bonum – maximum, in my strategically false position here, with Abbotsford going the way Abbotsfords have to go. But don't blame me. The tale is this: Lloyd has no room; I wished to build him a cottage ad interim; and my mother, who saw it would postpone, perhaps prevent, the rest of the house, objected.[17]

This letter baldly hints at some of the difficulties. His family were not scrupulous in the making of financial demands and did not suppress conflicting interests. Whatever Lloyd may have contributed to the general good at Vailima – and it does not seem to have been much – he clearly took out a great deal more. Aunt Maggie had made a financial contribution, but had strong ideas about how the money should be spent. Each member of the clan, whatever contribution they could make, and did make, drew on the lifeblood of the provider. They probably did not know what they were doing.

In the last years Louis relied heavily on Baxter to handle his financial relations with publishers, for which, having assisted him for nothing since his first trip to America in 1879, Louis paid $2\frac{1}{2}$ per cent and expenses. American publishers as well as British had to deal with Baxter, which did not please them. The Vailima years were crowded with publication. The summer of 1891 saw the serialisation of *The Wrecker*, with book publication the following year. Louis had insisted on a 15 per cent royalty, but was so disappointed in the book's sales that he rather bad-temperedly decided to revert in the future to a lump-sum payment, so that his income from a book would not depend on its sales. *Across the Plains*, with other pieces, at last saw the light in 1892, and *A Footnote to History* in the same year. In 1893 there was *Catriona* and *The Ebb-Tide*, and a collection of stories called *Island Night's Entertainments*, which included *The Beach of Falesá*. The latter had been first published in the *Illustrated London News* the year before, after some difficulty. The editor had wanted the wording of the bogus marriage certificate which united Wiltshire with Uma, the island girl, changed from stating that Uma was 'illegally married to *Mr John Wiltshire* for "one night" to "one week"'. Louis replied indulgently to the request, but was furious when the story appeared to find that the document had been entirely suppressed.[18] It did not encourage him to believe that he could write frankly about sexual matters and get away with it.

Each article and story and book required negotiations on several fronts, first for magazine publication on both sides of the Atlantic, then for book publication. In America McClure and Burlingame both considered themselves to have a special claim on anything Stevenson produced. They did not like having to deal with Baxter, who was a tough negotiator. In dealing with both Baxter and McClure, Louis had two middlemen between him and eventual publication. As Colvin saw what he wrote before publication, in a sense he had three. It did not always make for happy relations, and his correspondence often shows this. Difficulties and misunderstandings with publishers were an added irritant to life at Vailima, especially as Louis felt he simply had to strike hard bargains whenever he could and hold out for as much cash as seemed realistically possible. He did not like having to do this.

The financial drains built up. Apart from paying for the building of a house there was the maintenance of a large household. Fanny, for her health, needed a time away, and went to Fiji. Lloyd wanted a holiday. Early in 1893 Fanny and Louis were both in Sydney and consulted a London doctor, another major expense. The doctor's verdict on the pair of them was not encouraging. The suggestion was that Fanny's mental condition was shaky, and the unequivocal diagnosis of Louis's state of health was that he was badly overstrained and overworked. He had been well, with haemorrhaging making an unlooked-for reappearance. That Louis wrote frankly to Colvin we can intimate from a letter Colvin sent to Baxter, worried, as ever, by the state of things at Vailima, which just seemed to prove what he had known all along, that the South Pacific was not the place for Louis.

> Louis's weak lung is doing it's best to recover, & would almost certainly do so, if he gave it any chance: by freedom, that is, from exposure, malaria, worry, & overwork; all of which things, he says, are doing him harm, so as to make the issue doubtful: but under good conditions he might get well and live as long as any of us.[19]

Fanny was not now in a position to protect Louis from the disturbances that could make him worse. Ironically, if it was her loss of function that was partly responsible for her mental condition, she was now incapable in a situation that called for her talents.

At Vailima the writing progressed in fits and starts. There were long periods of depression and inaction. Louis suffered badly from writer's cramp, and Belle was still acting as amanuensis, a situation that did not please Fanny. Quarrels between Fanny and Belle were now a common feature of life. 1893 saw the war. Belle, too, was sometimes unwell, but when she was active her assistance does seem to have been invaluable. Louis dictated fluently, when things were going well, sometimes from notes he had made previously, but often composing spontaneously as he went. The writing of *Weir* came with particularly insistent fluency.

Moors was sure that Louis was being ground down by the women at Vailima. Fanny, he felt, had too much influence over him, and Belle too. They were altogether too powerful and abrasive a combination. But it is really impossible to single out any one feature of the last two years at Vailima which contributed more than another to the erosion of Louis's life, and it would be a mistake to suggest that life at this time had no pleasant aspects. There was the excitement of mail days, when the heap of letters and packets was ceremonially divided, and no one was allowed to open one until everything was distributed. There was the afternoon bathing in the river pool, music-making, tennis, welcome guests, conversation. Louis may have been impatient with Fanny, tactless sometimes, there may have been quarrels, but he loved and valued her too deeply for this to affect his attitude towards her. His dedication of *Weir* to his wife is a tribute not only in what Louis says about Fanny, but in the way he links her firmly with his Scottish background, as if to suggest that the partnership worked on a level deeper than surfaces suggest.

> I saw rain falling and the rainbow drawn
> On Lammermuir. Hearkening I heard again
> In my precipitous city beaten bells
> Winnow the keen sea wind. And here afar
> Intent on my own race and place I wrote.
>
> Take thou the writing: thine it is. For who
> Burnished the sword, blew on the drowsy coal,
> Held the target higher, chary of praise
> And prodigal of censure – who but thou?
> So now, in the end, if this the least be good,
> If any deed be done, if any fire
> Burn in the imperfect page, the praise be thine.[20]

The poem contains more conviction and more feeling than the earlier and more often quoted 'Trusty, dusky, vivid, true'.[21]

It was, perhaps, his refusal to retreat that killed Louis, as much as the thoughtlessness of others, or the magnitude of Vailima's demands. Whatever the pressures and however strong the feeling that he *had* to write, he was eager to write. He had, at last, so much clearer an idea of what it was he wanted to say. He had found subjects, too many subjects now perhaps, all demanding attention, all clamouring for treatment and expression, and he could not give his entire attention to any single one of them. He could not retreat from the demands of his mind and imagination just as he could not retreat from the realities of his daily existence. And he could not retreat from the giving of himself in countless directions at the same time.

He cared intensely about what he was writing. Success did not make him complacent. 'I fear with every book that it may have no merit,' he wrote to the aspiring Scottish writer S. R. Crockett, who was sending him admiring letters.[22] He worried about having to please the public who would buy his books. He kept his ear tuned to new literary voices, to Kipling for instance, about whom his friends wrote him and whose books they sent him. If there was any guarantee of the promise of the future it lies perhaps in Louis's undiminished caring about what he wrote. If circumstances were eroding his vitality, they were not eroding his literary commitment. Perhaps, even, they were augmenting what he produced. It was part of that coming together of life and literature.

Late in 1893 Colvin and Baxter, anxious to establish a source of income for Louis that would not involve him in more work, had a proposal. It was that there should be published a complete and uniform edition of his works. It became the Edinburgh Edition. Baxter had with him the first volumes when he set off on the journey to Samoa which would take him only to his old friend's grave. Louis could only advise, plan and approve. The hard work was done by Baxter and Colvin, Baxter as business agent, Colvin as editor. Louis's distance from the centre of activities of course made it virtually impossible for him to be more involved than he was, but he was also very willing to leave editorial problems to Colvin – in spite of the fact that he did not trust Colvin's judgment on some issues. It was in the end very much Colvin's edition, although Louis had had time to make it clear what he wanted to go in it. Colvin's anxiety that Louis should not queer his own pitch was as strong as ever. In February 1894 he was worrying at Baxter over a piece Louis had written about how he came to write *Treasure Island*. Louis was being embarrassingly frank again – 'Please join with me in begging that there should be no such public dissections,' Colvin pleaded.[23] But however heavy his hand on the Edinburgh edition, and however cavalier, or preoccupied, Louis's own attitude – and as the months went on he found it increasingly irritating to be called upon to make up his mind on editorial details – it was on Colvin's part a labour of love. There would not be, quite, a uniform edition within the author's lifetime. That plans were as far forward as they were, the first volumes complete and ready though Louis never saw them, was as solid a proof as could be wished of the reputation of Robert Louis Stevenson.

In October 1894 the Road of the Loving Heart was finished by the grateful and defeated Samoan chieftains. Louis feasted them at Vailima, sitting cross-legged and garlanded with his household and his guests, with food delectably arranged on the ground before them. The following month was Louis's forty-fourth birthday, and there was another celebration. The road, symbol of Louis's place in Samoa, was completed, another year of his life begun. He had been working on *St Ives*, intended as a money-spinner, another adventure story, but had set it aside to give his attention to *Weir of Hermiston*. On the morning of 3 December he dictated some pages of *Weir* to Belle. It was going well and he had great hopes of the novel. Belle was to remember how cheerful he was. In the early evening he left the little room off the library in which he worked and went down to help Fanny with the supper. He chose a bottle of burgundy from the cellar, and mixed a dressing for the salad. Fanny had been worried over the last few days, for she had got it into her head that some catastrophe was about to hit someone near to them. She could not get rid of the thought. Louis had been trying to reassure her. The two of them were alone at the end of the working day, before the family gathered to spend the evening together.

Louis had once written that it was necessary to half close one's eyes against the dazzle of reality. They were together out on the veranda. Louis was bright with talk, the adrenalin still flowing after a good day's writing, and anxious to shake Fanny out of her gloom. His hand went suddenly to his head. His fluency came to a halt with a question – 'Do I look strange?' Did he know he was looking at the starkest reality of all? Fanny with the help of the devoted Sosimo got him inside and on to a chair. She shouted for Belle and Lloyd and Aunt Maggie. Lloyd galloped to Apia for the doctor, whom he thrust on his own horse and sent belting back to Vailima, following himself on a horse

*One of the last photographs
of RLS*

snatched from a hitching rail. The extended family gathered, shocked and hushed. The doctor could do nothing but wait for the ineluctable progress of brain haemorrhage. Fanny stood rigid at the foot of the stairs. Shortly after eight o'clock that evening Louis died.

He was buried on the summit of Vaea mountain. With love and grief his Samoan workers cut a path through the dense undergrowth and bore the Union-Jack draped coffin up the steep slopes. From the top they could see the ocean. Louis had once written an epitaph for himself, not a surprising thing to do for a man who lived so close to death, which has become the only lines of his poetry many people know. I will not quote them, for I prefer another. To Colvin he had once said, 'If I could only be buried in the hills, under the heather and a table tombstone like the Martyrs, where the whaups and plovers are crying.'[24] The year before his death he had written a poem for S. R. Crockett, moved by Crockett's dedication of a book to him. The poem goes,

> Blows the wind today, and the sun and the wind are flying,
> Blows the wind on the moor today and now,
> Where about the graves of the martyrs the whaups are crying,
> My heart remembers how!
>
> Grey recumbent tombs of the dead in desert places,
> Standing-stones on the vacant wine-red moor,
> Hills of sheep, and the howes of the silent vanished races,
> And winds, austere and pure:
>
> Be it granted to me to behold you again in dying,
> Hills of home! and to hear again the call;
> Hear about the graves of the martyrs the peewees crying,
> And hear no more at all [25]

I would like to think that in that last dazzle of reality he saw the bleak tombstone of a Covenanting martyr, saw a curlew rising above the scarred Pentland slopes.

A list of works by Robert Louis Stevenson, including all titles in book form, arranged chronologically

An Inland Voyage, 1878
Edinburgh. Picturesque Notes, 1879
Travels with a Donkey, 1879
Deacon Brodie, with W. E. Henley, 1880, revised edition 1888
Virginibus Puerisque, 1881
Familiar Studies of Men and Books, 1882
New Arabian Nights, 1882
The Silverado Squatters, 1883
Treasure Island, 1883
Admiral Guinea, with W. E. Henley, 1884
Beau Austin, with W. E. Henley, 1884
Prince Otto, 1885
A Child's Garden of Verses, 1885
More New Arabian Nights, The Dynamiter, with Fanny Van de Grift Stevenson, 1885
Macaire, with W. E. Henley, 1885
The Strange Case of Dr Jekyll and Mr Hyde, 1886
Kidnapped, 1886
The Merry Men, and Other Tales and Fables, 1887
Memories and Portraits, 1887
Underwoods, 1887
Memoir of Fleeming Jenkin, 1887
The Black Arrow, 1888
The Misadventures of John Nicholson, 1888
The Wrong Box, with Lloyd Osbourne, 1889
In the South Seas, 1890
Ballads, 1890
Across the Plains, 1892
The Wrecker, 1892
A Footnote to History, 1892
Island Nights' Entertainments, 1893
Catriona, 1893
The Ebb-Tide, 1894
Vailima Letters, 1895
Weir of Hermiston, 1896
St Ives, 1897
Letters to His Family and Friends, edited by Sidney Colvin, 1899

SELECT BIBLIOGRAPHY

The following list includes all works directly referred to in the text, plus a selection of other works consulted.

Adams, Henry: *Letters 1858–1891*, Boston, 1938
Archer, Charles: *William Archer: Life, Work and Friendships*, London, 1931
Archer, William: 'R.L.S. at Skerryvore', cf. Hammerton, J. A.: *Stevensoniana*
Baildon, H. B.: *Robert Louis Stevenson*. A Life Study in Criticism, London, 1901
Balfour, Graham: *The Life of Robert Louis Stevenson*, London, 1901
Balfour, Michael: 'How the Biography of Stevenson Came to be Written', *Times Literary Supplement*, 13 January 1960
Barrie, J. M.: *An Edinburgh Eleven*, London, 1913
—— *Letters*, ed. Viola Meynell, London, 1942
Bay, J. C.: *The Unpublished Manuscripts of Robert Louis Stevenson's Record of a Family of Engineers*, London, 1929
Boodle, Adelaide: *R.L.S. and His Sine Qua Non*, London, 1926
Brown, George: *Pioneer Missionary and Explorer*, London, 1908
Brown, George E.: *A Book of R.L.S.*, London, 1920
Brown, Horatio: *see* Symonds, J. A.
Buckley, J. H.: *William Ernest Henley*. A Study in the 'Counter-Decadence' of the 'Nineties, Princeton, N.J., 1945
Burlingame, Roger: *Of Making Many Books*, New York, 1946
Caldwell, Elsie Noble: *Last Witness for Robert Louis Stevenson*, Norman, Oklahoma, 1960
Chalmers, Stephen: *The Penny Piper of Saranac*, Boston, 1916
Charteris, Evan: *The Life and Letters of Sir Edmund Gosse*, London, 1931
Chesterton, G. K.: *Robert Louis Stevenson*, London, 1927
Clarke, Rev. W. E.: *Reminiscences of Robert Louis Stevenson*, n.d.
Colvin, Sidney: *see* Robert Louis Stevenson, *Letters*.
—— *Memories and Notes of People and Places*, London, 1921
—— *Robert Louis Stevenson. His Work and His Personality*, London, 1924
Conan Doyle, A.: *Through the Magic Door*, London, 1907
Connell, John: *W. E. Henley*, London, n.d.
Cooper, Lettice: *Robert Louis Stevenson*, London, 1947
Cornford, L. Cope: *Robert Louis Stevenson*, Edinburgh and London, 1899
Cunningham, Alison: *Cummy's Diary*, edited by Robert T. Skinner, London, 1926
Daiches, David: *Robert Louis Stevenson*, Glasgow, 1947
—— *Robert Louis Stevenson and His World*, London, 1973
Dalglish, Doris N.: *Presbyterian Pirate*, London, 1937
Daplyn, A. J.: 'Robert Louis Stevenson at Barbizon', *Chambers' Journal*, 7th series, July 1917

Dark, Sidney: *R.L.S.*, London, 1932

Eaton, Charlotte: *Stevenson at Manasquan*, Chicago, 1921

Edel, Leon: *Henry James: The Middle Years*, London, 1963

Elwin, Malcolm: *The Strange Case of Robert Louis Stevenson*, London, 1950

Ferguson, DeLancey and Marshall Waingrow, *R.L.S., Stevenson's Letters to Charles Baxter*, London, 1956

Fiedler, Leslie: *No! in Thunder*, London, 1963

Fisher, Anne B.: *No More a Stranger*, Stanford, California, n.d.

Furnas, J. C.: *Anatomy of Paradise*, New York, 1937

—— *Voyage to Windward*, London, 1952

Gosse, Edmund: *Critical Kit-Kats*, London, 1913

—— *Questions at Issue*, London, 1893

—— *Some Diversions of a Man of Letters*, London, 1919

Gross, John: *The Rise and Fall of the Man of Letters*, London, 1969

Grosskurth, Phyllis: *John Addington Symonds*, London, 1964

Guthrie, Charles: *Robert Louis Stevenson. Some Personal Recollections*, Edinburgh, 1920

Hamerton, P. G.: *Philip Gilbert Hamerton. An Autobiography, and Memoir* by his wife, London, 1897

Hamilton, Clayton: *On the Trail of Stevenson*, London, 1916

Hammerton, J. A.: *In the Track of Stevenson*, London, 1907

—— *Stevensoniana*: an Anecdotal Life and Appreciation of Robert Louis Stevenson, Edinburgh, 1910

Hart, James, ed.: *From Scotland to Silverado*, comprising *The Amateur Emigrant, The Silverado Squatters*, and Four Essays on California, Cambridge, Mass., 1966

—— *Private Press Ventures of Samuel Lloyd Osbourne and Robert Louis Stevenson*, California, 1966

Hellman, George: 'The Stevenson Myth', *Century Magazine*, December 1922

—— *The True Stevenson. A Study in Clarification*, Boston, 1925

Henley, W. E.: *Essays*, London, 1921

'R.A.M.S.', *Pall Mall Magazine*, July 1900

—— 'R.L.S.', *Pall Mall Magazine*, December 1901

Hennessy, James Pope: *Robert Louis Stevenson*, London, 1974

Hinkley, Laura: *The Stevensons: Louis and Fanny*, New York, 1950

Issler, Anne Roller: *Happier for His Presence*, Stanford, California, n.d.

James, Henry: *see* Janet Adam Smith, *Henry James and Robert Louis Stevenson*

Japp, Alexander: *Robert Louis Stevenson: A Record, an Estimate and a Memorial*, London, 1905

Kiely, Robert: *Robert Louis Stevenson and the Fiction of Adventure*, Cambridge, Massachusetts, 1965

Kinghorn, Alexander Manson, ed.: *Poems* by Allan Ramsey and Robert Fergusson, Edinburgh, 1974

Lang, Andrew: *Adventures Among Books*, London, 1905

—— *Essays in Little*, London, 1891

—— 'Modern Men: Mr R. L. Stevenson', *Scots Observer*, 26 January 1889

Le Galliene, Richard: *The Romantic '90s*, London, 1925

Low, Will: *A Chronicle of Friendships*, London, 1908

Lucas, E. V.: *The Colvins and their Friends*, London, 1928

McClure, Samuel S.: *My Autobiography*, London, 1914

MacCulloch, J. A.: *Stevenson and the Bridge of Allan*, Glasgow, 1927

McGaw, Sister Martha Mary: *Stevenson in Hawaii*, Honolulu, 1950

Mackay, Margaret: *The Violent Friend*, London, 1968

McLaren, Moray: *Stevenson and Edinburgh*, London, 1950

Maitland, Frederic William: *The Life and Letters of Leslie Stephen*, London, 1906

Masson, David: *Memories of Two Cities*, Edinburgh and London, 1911

Masson, Rosaline: *A Life of Robert Louis Stevenson*, Edinburgh and London, 1923

—— ed.: *I Can Remember Robert Louis Stevenson*, Edinburgh, 1922

Mattheison, D. E. and Millgate, M.: *Transatlantic Dialogue*, Austin, Texas, 1965

Moors, Harry J.: *With Stevenson in Samoa*, London, 1910

Muir, Edwin: *Scott and Scotland. The Predicament of the Scottish Writer*, London, 1936

Neider, Charles, ed.: *Our Samoan Adventure* by Fanny and Robert Louis Stevenson, London, 1956

Osbourne, Katherine Durham: *Robert Louis Stevenson in California*, Chicago, 1911

Osbourne, Lloyd: *An Intimate Portrait of R.L.S.*, New York, 1924

Paul, C. Kegan: *Memories*, London, 1899

Prideaux, W. F.: *A Bibliography of the Work of Robert Louis Stevenson*, London, 1918

Quiller-Couch, Arthur: *Adventures in Criticism*, London, 1896

Raleigh, Walter: *Robert Louis Stevenson*, London, 1919

Ralston, Caroline: 'The Beach Communities', *Pacific Island Portraits*, ed. J. W. Davidson and Deryck Scarr

Rickett, Arthur: *The Vagabond in Literature*, London, 1906

Ruskin, John: *Lectures on Architecture and Painting*, London, 1907

Saintsbury, George: *A History of 19th Century Literature*, London, 1896

Sanchez, Nellie Van de Grift: *The Life of Mrs R. L. Stevenson*, London, 1920

Simpson, Eve Blantyre: *Robert Louis Stevenson's Edinburgh Days*, London, 1898

—— *The Stevenson Originals,* Edinburgh and London, 1912

Smith, Janet Adam: *Henry James and Robert Louis Stevenson*, London, 1948

—— ed.: *Collected Poems* by Robert Louis Stevenson, London, 1971

—— *Robert Louis Stevenson*, London, 1937

Stephen, Leslie: *Robert Louis Stevenson*, London, 1903

—— *Studies of a Biographer*, London, 1902

Steuart, J. A.: *Robert Louis Stevenson: Man and Writer*, London, 1924

Steuart, Marie: *Old Edinburgh Taverns*, London, 1952

Stevenson, Fanny: *The Cruise of the Janet Nichol*, London, 1915; see also Charles Neider, ed., *Our Samoan Adventure*

Stevenson, Lionel: *The Ordeal of George Meredith,* New York, 1953

Stevenson, Margaret Isabella: *From Saranac to the Marquesas and Beyond*, London, 1903

Strong, Austin: 'The Most Unforgettable Character I've Met', *Reader's Digest,* May 1944

Strong, Isobel: *Robert Louis Stevenson*, Saranac Lake, N.Y., 1920

Strong, Isobel: *This Life I've Loved*, London, 1937
Strong, Isobel, and Lloyd Osbourne: *Memories of Vailima*, London, 1903
Swinnerton, Frank: *R. L. Stevenson* A Critical Study, London, 1924
Symonds, John Addington: *Letters and Papers*, ed. Horatio F. Brown, London,
   1895
Thompson, Francis: *The Real Robert Louis Stevenson* and Other Critical Essays,
   New York, 1959
Trudeau, Edward: *An Autobiography*, New York, 1916
Twain, Mark (Samuel Clemens): *Mark Twain's Autobiography*, New York, 1924
Watt, Francis: *Edinburgh and the Lothians*, London, 1912
—— *R.L.S.,* London, 1918
Yeats, W. B: *Autobiographies*, London, 1955

NOTES

In the case of Stevenson's works, unless otherwise stated the date is the date of first volume publication, the volume and page reference to the Skerryvore Edition. The 'Beinecke Collection' is the collection of Stevenson material in the Beinecke Library, Yale University.

Chapter 1

1. James Dick, who worked in the Stevenson firm, wrote to Mrs Thomas Stevenson on the death of RLS, 'I often said to his father, it is no use pressing Louis to study Engineering, his heart is not in it, and he is too fragile for such work, with the risks of exposure to all kinds of weather.' Beinecke Collection.
2. Mrs Stevenson's diary, 8 April 1871 Beinecke Collection.
3. *Edinburgh, Picturesque Notes*, 1878, XXVI, pp. 6–7.
4. Ibid., p 6
5. Ibid., p. 4.
6. *Memories and Portraits*, 1887, XXV, p. 35.
7. 'Auld Reekie, a Poem', *Poems* by Allan Ramsay and Robert Fergusson, edited by Alexander Manson Kinghorn and Alexander Law, Scottish Academic Press, 1974, p. 147.
8. 'The Bonnets of Bonny Dundee', in Scott's *The Doom of Devorgoil, Collected Poems*, XII, p. 196.
9. John Ruskin, *Lectures on Architecture and Painting*, 1854, pp. 61–2.
10. *Edinburgh, Picturesque Notes*, XXVI, p. 9.
11. J. M. Barrie, *Letters*, Peter Davies, 1942, p. 252.
12. *Edinburgh Sketches and Miscellanies*, 1884, pp. 35–6.
13. J. A. Steuart, *Robert Louis Stevenson*, Sampson, Low, Marston and Co., 1927, p. 75. Although Steuart is not an entirely reliable biographer, and the contemporaries he quotes remain anonymous, this description could be authentic.
14. Walter Simpson to RLS, Beinecke Collection.
15. J. C. Furnas, *Voyage to Windward*, Faber and Faber, 1952, p. 53.
16. *Edinburgh, Picturesque Notes*, XXVI, p. 40.
17. RLS to Charles Baxter, *R.L.S., Stevenson's Letters to Charles Baxter*, edited by DeLancey Ferguson and Marshall Waingrow, Geoffrey Cumberlege, Oxford University Press, 1956, p. 48.
18. *Memoir of Fleeming Jenkin*, 1887, XVII, p. 140.
19. Ibid., p. 153.
20. RLS to Mrs Sitwell, National Library of Scotland.
21. Diary, quoted in Graham Balfour, *The Life of R.L.S.*, Methuen, 1901, p. 108.

22. 'A College Magazine', 1887, XXV, p. 39.
23. Ibid., pp. 42–3.
24. Ibid., p. 35.
25. RLS to Maud Babington, *Letters*, edited by Sidney Colvin, Chatto and Windus, 1911, I, p. 30.

Chapter 2

1. *Records of a Family of Engineers,* in *The Unpublished Manuscripts of Robert Louis Stevenson's Records of a Family of Engineers*, edited by J. C. Bay, 1929, p. 40.
2. *Records of a Family of Engineers*, 1896, XVIII, p. 211.
3. J. C. Bay, op. cit., p. 52.
4. Graham Balfour, op. cit., p. 31.
5. 'Travel', *Collected Poems*, edited by Janet Adam Smith, Rupert Hart-Davis, 1971, p. 366.
6. 'The Land of Nod', ibid., p. 371.
7. Ibid.
8. 'North-west Passage', ibid., p. 387.
9. Francis Watt, *R.L.S.,* Methuen, 1918, p. 13.
10. Mrs Stevenson's diary, Beinecke Collection.
11. Graham Balfour, op. cit., p. 37.
12. Mrs Stevenson's diary, Beinecke Collection.
13. Ibid.
14. 'Stormy Nights', *Collected Poems*, p. 363.
15. 'To Alison Cunningham', ibid., p. 361.
16. RLS to Alison Cunningham, *Letters*, Vol. I, p. 32.
17. 'Memoirs of Himself', XXV, p. 225.
18. Ibid., pp. 220–1.
19. 'Young Night Thought', *Collected Poems*, p. 363.
20. 'A Penny Plain and Twopence Coloured', 1887, XXV, p. 128.
21. Ibid., pp. 128–9.
22. 'The Manse', 1887, ibid., pp. 62–3.
23. 'To Minnie', *Collected Poems,* p. 409.
24. 'To Auntie', ibid., p. 408.
25. 'The Lantern-Bearers', 1892, XXVI, p. 112.
26. Ibid., p. 115.
27. Rosaline Masson, *I Remember Robert Louis Stevenson*, Chambers, 1922, p. 21.
28. Ibid., p. 29.
29. Ibid., p. 24.
30. 'Memoirs of Himself', XXV, p. 227.
31. Rosaline Masson, *The Life of R.L.S.,* Chambers, 1923, p. 39.
32. Mrs Stevenson's diary, Beinecke Collection.
33. *Cummy's Diary*, Chatto and Windus, 1926, p. 28.
34. Graham Balfour, op. cit., p. 60.
35. RLS to Mrs Sitwell, National Library of Scotland.
36. *Edinburgh, Picturesque Notes*, XXVI, p. 45.
37. Masson, *I Can Remember . . .*, pp. 4–5.
38. 'The Coast of Fife', 1892, XXVI, p. 89.
39. Ibid., pp. 93–4.

40. 'Thomas Stevenson', 1887, XXV, p. 82.
41. Vailima Prayers, XIX, p. 7.
42. Quoted in Balfour, op. cit., pp. 62–3.
43. RLS to Thomas Stevenson, *Letters*, I, p. 12.
44. Ibid., p. 13.

Chapter 3

1. RLS to Mrs Thomas Stevenson, *Letters*, I, p. 44.
2. 'Hail! Childish slaves of social rules', *New Poems*, 1916, p. 34. This volume, edited by George Hellman, is the publication of poems Hellman alleged had been suppressed by Fanny Stevenson. More likely, they were rejected for publication by Stevenson himself. Significantly, Janet Adam Smith does not include the poem in her *Collected Poems*.
3. Masson, *I Can Remember . . .*, p. 127.
4. Autobiographical fragment, Beinecke Collection.
5. RLS to Sidney Colvin, *Letters*, II, p. 283.
6. RLS to Trevor Haddon, Beinecke Collection.
7. 'Let Love go, if go she will', *Collected Poems*, p. 76.
8. 'My brain swims empty and light', ibid., p. 82.
9. Writer to the Signet, in Scots law, a solicitor.
10. RLS to Charles Baxter, Ferguson and Waingrow, op. cit., p. 23.
11. RLS to Baxter, ibid., pp. 23–4.
12. 'The Edifying Letters of the Rutherford Family', Beinecke Collection.
13. Ibid.
14. E. V. Lucas, *The Colvins and Their Friends*, Methuen, 1928, p 64
15. Sidney Colvin, *Memories and Notes of Persons and Places*, Edward Arnold, 1921, p. 100.
16. Ibid., p. 101.
17. RLS to Mrs Sitwell, National Library of Scotland.
18. Ibid.
19. RLS to Mrs Sitwell, N.L.S.
20. RLS to Mrs Sitwell, N.L.S.
21. RLS to Mrs Sitwell, N.L.S.
22. RLS to Mrs Sitwell, N.L.S.
23. RLS to Mrs Sitwell, N.L.S.
24. RLS to Mrs Sitwell, N.L.S.
25. RLS to Mrs Sitwell, N.L.S.
26. RLS to Mrs Sitwell, N.L.S.
27. RLS to Mrs Sitwell, N.L.S.
28. RLS to Mrs Sitwell, N.L.S.
29. RLS to Mrs Sitwell, N.L.S.
30. RLS to Mrs Sitwell, N.L.S.
31. RLS to Mrs Sitwell, N.L.S.

Chapter 4

1. *Edinburgh, Picturesque Notes*, XXVI, p. 58.
2. RLS to Baxter, Ferguson and Waingrow, op. cit., p. 31.
3. There has been some speculation that as well as everything else Stevenson

was suffering from venereal disease. It has been suggested that a sentence in a letter to Baxter suggests this: 'That walk down from Queen Street has made a fine sore of my burning, and here I am' (Ferguson and Waingrow, p. 27). The evidence seems rather slender, and there is absolutely nothing in subsequent correspondence between the friends, or anywhere else, to suggest that v.d. was part of Louis's problems. Probably if it had been he would have reflected at length and moralistically on the subject, and harked back to it in later life.

4. RLS to Baxter, Ferguson and Waingrow, op. cit., p. 31.
5. RLS to Baxter, ibid., p. 35.
6. RLS to Mrs Sitwell, *Letters*, I, p. 91.
7. RLS to Mrs Sitwell, ibid., p. 95.
8. RLS to Mrs Stevenson, ibid., p. 103.
9. RLS to Mrs Sitwell, N.L.S.
10. Ibid.
11. RLS to Mrs Sitwell, N.L.S.
12. RLS to Mrs Stevenson, Beinecke Collection.
13. RLS to Sidney Colvin, Beinecke Collection.
14. 'Preface, by Way of Criticism', *Familiar Studies of Men and Books*, 1882, XXIII, p. viii.
15. 'Victor Hugo's Romances', ibid., p. 27.
16. Leslie Stephen to RLS, Beinecke Collection.
17. 'Virginibus Puerisque', *Virginibus Puerisque*, 1881, XXII, pp. 18–19.
18. Ibid., p. 23.
19. RLS to Mrs Sitwell, N.L.S.
20. Henley to RLS, J. H. Buckley, *W. E. Henley*, Princeton University Press, 1945, p. 69.
21. W. B. Yeats, *Autobiographies*, Macmillan, 1955, p. 124.
22. Ibid., p. 127.
23. 'Invictus', *New Oxford Book of English Verse*, 1972, p. 792.
24. RLS to Mrs Sitwell, *Letters*, I, p. 132.
25. Will Low, *A Chronicle of Friendships*, Hodder and Stoughton, 1908, p. 53.
26. Ibid., p. 153.
27. Ibid., p. 33.
28. 'Fontainebleau', *Memories of Fontainebleau*, 1892, XXVI, p. 199.
29. Low, op. cit., p. 60.
30. RLS to Mrs Stevenson, quoted in Low, op. cit., p. 138.
31. 'Fontainebleau', XXVI, p. 202.
32. Low, op. cit., p. 143.

Chapter 5

1. Margaret Mackay, *The Violent Friend*, Dent and Sons, 1968, p. 12.
2. RLS to Charles Scribner, Beinecke Collection.
3. Lloyd Osbourne, Introduction, *New Arabian Nights*, 1882, I, p. vii.
4. Bob Stevenson to RLS, Beinecke Collection.
5. Bob Stevenson to RLS, Beinecke Collection.
6. Lloyd Osbourne, op. cit., I, p. ix.
7. Margaret Mackay, op. cit., p. 41.

8. Ibid., p. 143.
9. Will Low, op. cit., p. 185.
10. Nellie Sanchez, *Life of Mrs R. L. Stevenson*, Chatto and Windus, 1920, p. 40.
11. Fanny Stevenson to Timothy Reardon, Beinecke Collection.
12. Fanny Stevenson to Timothy Reardon, Beinecke Collection.
13. Fanny Stevenson to Reardon, Beinecke Collection.
14. Cf. Isobel Strong, *This Life I've Loved*, Michael Joseph, 1937.
15. Bob Stevenson to RLS, Beinecke Collection.
16. Bob Stevenson to RLS, Beinecke Collection.
17. Bob Stevenson to RLS, Beinecke Collection.
18. RLS to Henley, N.L.S.
19. RLS to Bob Stevenson, Beinecke Collection.
20. John Gross, *The Rise and Fall of the Man of Letters*, Weidenfeld and Nicolson, 1969, p. 133.
21. 'To Andrew Lang', *Collected Poems*, p. 124.
22. Andrew Lang to RLS, Beinecke Collection.
23. Edmund Gosse, *Critical Kit-Kats*, Heinemann, 1913, p. 278.
24. Ibid., p. 281.
25. RLS to Colvin, Beinecke Collection.
26. *Travels with a Donkey*, XV, p. 236.
27. Ibid., p. 143.

Chapter 6

1. RLS to Henley, Beinecke Collection.
2. 'Virginibus Puerisque', XXII, p. 24.
3. 'On Falling in Love', ibid., p. 27.
4. RLS to Colvin, Beinecke Collection.
5. RLS to Edmund Gosse, Beinecke Collection.
6. RLS to Colvin, Beinecke Collection.
7. *The Amateur Emigrant, From Scotland to Silverado*, edited by James Hart, Harvard University Press, 1966, pp. 4–5.
8. Ibid., p. 11.
9. Ibid., p. 12.
10. Ibid., p. 91.
11. Ibid., p. 99.
12. Ibid., p. 101–2.
13. Ibid., p. 120.
14. RLS to Colvin, Beinecke Collection.
15. Op. cit., pp. 128–9.
16. Ibid., p. 124.
17. Ibid., p. 141.
18. Lloyd Osbourne, *An Intimate Portrait of R.L.S.*, Scribner's, 1924, p. 17.
19. RLS to Baxter, Ferguson and Waingrow, p. 68.
20. Ibid.
21. Ibid., pp. 68–9.
22. 'Monterey', *From Scotland to Silverado*, p. 167.
23. Colvin to Baxter, Beinecke Collection.
24. Ibid.

25. Ibid.
26. Thomas Stevenson to Colvin, Beinecke Collection.
27. Thomas Stevenson to Colvin, Beinecke Collection.
28. RLS to Colvin, Beinecke Collection.
29. 'To My Name Child', *Collected Poems*, p. 411.
30. 'Simoneau's at Monterey', *From Scotland to Silverado*, p. 177.
31. RLS to Colvin, Beinecke Collection.
32. RLS to Henley, N.L.S.
33. RLS to Baxter, Ferguson and Waingrow, p. 76.
34. Ibid.
35. Henley to Colvin, Beinecke Collection.
36. Henley to Colvin, Beinecke Collection.
37. RLS to Gosse, Beinecke Collection.
38. Gosse to R.L.S., Evan Charteris, *The Life and Letters of Edmund Gosse*, Heinemann, 1931, p. 126.
39. RLS to Colvin, Beinecke Collection.
40. 'San Francisco', *From Scotland to Silverado*, p. 185.
41. RLS to P. G. Hamerton, *Letters*, II, p. 37.
42. *The Silverado Squatters, From Scotland to Silverado*, p. 207.
43. Ibid., p. 224.
44. Ibid., p. 276.
45. RLS to Colvin, Beinecke Collection.
46. Fanny Stevenson to Mrs Stevenson, Nellie Sanchez, op. cit., p. 79.
47. RLS to Jacob Van de Grift, Beinecke Collection.
48. Colvin to Henley, E. V. Lucas, op. cit., p. 28.

Chapter 7

1. Mrs Stevenson's diary, Beinecke Collection.
2. 'To My Wife', *Collected Poems*, p. 326.
3. Fanny to Dora Williams, Beinecke Collection.
4. Fanny to Dora Williams, Beinecke Collection.
5. Fanny and RLS to Dora Williams, Beinecke Collection.
6. 'On Some Ghastly Companions at a Spa', *Collected Poems*, p. 337.
7. Mackay, op. cit., p. 92.
8. Fanny to Mrs Stevenson, ibid.
9. RLS to Baxter, Ferguson and Waingrow, p. 81.
10. RLS to Thomas and Margaret Stevenson, Beinecke Collection.
11. *Stevensoniana*, edited by J. A. Hammerton, John Grant, 1910, p. 64.
12. Ibid., p. 65.
13. 'Robin and Ben: or the Pirate and the Apothecary', *Collected Poems*, p. 436.
14. RLS to Bob Stevenson, Beinecke Collection.
15. *Collected Poems*, p. 561.
16. Lloyd Osbourne, op. cit., p. 37.
17. Phyllis Grosskurth, *John Addington Symonds*, Longmans, 1964, p. 4.
18. John Addington Symonds, *Letters and Papers*, edited by Horatio F. Brown, John Murray, 1923, p. 111.
19. Mackay, op. cit., p. 99.
20. RLS to Colvin, *Letters*, II, p. 24.

21. RLS to Colvin, Beinecke Collection.
22. Introduction, *Treasure Island*, II, p. xxx.
23. Preface, ibid., p. xxxiii.
24. Introduction, ibid., p. xxxii.
25. Fanny's Preface, ibid., p. xxii.
26. Introduction, ibid., p. xxxii.
27. Alexander Japp, in *Stevensoniana*, p. 57.
28. Edmund Gosse, op. cit., p. 291.
29. RLS to Henley, N.L.S.
30. Mackay, op. cit., p. 108.
31. RLS to Baxter, Ferguson and Waingrow, p. 86.
32. RLS to Baxter, *Letters*, II, 61.

Chapter 8

1. RLS to Fanny, Beinecke Collection.
2. RLS to Fanny, Beinecke Collection.
3. RLS to Fanny, Beinecke Collection.
4. RLS to Baxter, Ferguson and Waingrow, p. 106.
5. RLS to Mrs Stevenson, *Letters*, II, p. 93.
6. RLS to Mrs Stevenson, ibid., p. 105
7. RLS to Mrs Sitwell, ibid., p. 109.
8. RLS to Thomas and Margaret Stevenson, Beinecke Collection.
9. Fanny to Henley, Beinecke Collection.
10. Fanny to Henley, Beinecke Collection.
11. RLS to Henley, *Letters*, II, pp. 119–14
12. RLS to Coggie Ferrier, Beinecke Collection.
13. Mrs Ferrier to RLS, Beinecke Collection.
14. RLS to Henley, National Library.
15. RLS to Will Low, *Letters*, II, p. 145.
16. *Kidnapped*, V, p. 75.
17. RLS to Colvin, *Letters*, II, p. 191.
18. Ibid.
19. Lloyd Osbourne, op. cit., p. 59.
20. William Archer, in *Stevensoniana*, p. 77.

Chapter 9

1. RLS to Gosse, *Letters*, II, p. 230.
2. Adelaide Boodle, *R.L.S. and His Sine Qua Non*, John Murray, 1926, p. 8.
3. Ibid., p. 76.
4. Leon Edel, *Henry James: The Middle Years*, Rupert Hart-Davis, 1963, pp. 61–2.
5. Ibid., p. 41.
6. Ibid., p. 39.
7. Janet Adam Smith, *Henry James and Robert Louis Stevenson*, Rupert Hart-Davis, 1948, pp. 65–6.
8. Ibid., p. 62.
9. Ibid., p. 67.
10. Ibid.

11. Ibid., p. 79.
12. Introduction, ibid., p. 9.
13. Ibid., p. 91.
14. Ibid., pp. 91–2.
15. Henry James to RLS, ibid., p. 101.
16. Fleeming Jenkin to RLS, Beinecke Collection.
17. RLS to William Archer, *Letters*, II, p. 253.
18. RLS to William Archer, ibid., p. 248.
19. RLS to Archer, ibid., p. 256.
20. Ibid., p. 257.
21. RLS to Archer, ibid., p. 254.
22. RLS to Archer, ibid., p. 255.
23. Ibid.
24. Fanny to Colvin, Beinecke Collection.
25. Fanny to Dora Williams, Beinecke Collection.
26. Fanny to Dora Williams, Beinecke Collection.
27. Fanny Stevenson's Preface, *Dr Jekyll and Mr Hyde*, IV, p. xix.
28. RLS to Will Low, Beinecke Collection.
29. RLS to J. A. Symonds, *Letters*, II, p. 274.
30. *The Strange Case of Dr Jekyll and Mr Hyde*, IV, p. 71.
31. J. A. Symonds to RLS, op. cit., p. 405.
32. RLS to Thomas and Margaret Stevenson, *Letters*, II, p. 292.
33. Mrs Stevenson's diary, Beinecke Collection.

Chapter 10

1. RLS to Bob Stevenson, *Letters*, IV, p. 303.
2. Rosaline Masson, op. cit., p. 135.
3. RLS to Colvin, Beinecke Collection.
4. Charteris, op. cit., p. 217.
5. Mrs Stevenson's diary, Beinecke Collection.
6. RLS to Henry James, *Letters*, III, p. 6.
7. Mrs Stevenson's diary, Beinecke Collection.
8. Lloyd Osbourne, op. cit., p. 70.
9. RLS to Archer, *Letters*, III, p. 16.
10. 'Pulvis et Umbra', XXII, p. 225.
11. RLS to E. L. Burlingame, *Letters*, III, p. 39.
12. Henley to RLS, John Connell, *W. E. Henley*, Constable and Co., n.d., pp. 116–17.
13. Ibid.
14. RLS to Henley, Ferguson and Waingrow, pp. 191–2.
15. RLS to Baxter, ibid., p. 196.
16. RLS to Baxter, ibid., p. 205.
17. RLS to Baxter, ibid., p. 208.
18. RLS to James, *Letters*, III, p. 59.

Chapter 11

1. W. E. Clark, *Reminiscences of Robert Louis Stevenson*, n.d., no page numbers.
2. RLS to Colvin, *Letters*, III, p. 66.

3. RLS to Adelaide Boodle, ibid., p. 114.
4. RLS to Colvin, ibid., p. 64.
5. Margaret Stevenson, *From Saranac to the Marquesas and Beyond*, Methuen, 1903, p. 63.
6. *In the South Seas*, 1896, XVIII, p. 5.
7. Ibid., p. 11.
8. Ibid., p. 42.
9. Margaret Stevenson, op. cit., p. 86.
10. RLS to Baxter, Ferguson and Waingrow, p. 236.
11. RLS to Colvin, *Letters*, III, p. 66.
12. RLS to Baxter, Ferguson and Waingrow, pp. 235–6.
13. J. C. Furnas, op. cit., p. 278.
14. Margaret Stevenson, op. cit., p. 152.
15. *In the South Seas*, XVIII, p. 178.
16. RLS to Baxter, Ferguson and Waingrow, p. 237.
17. RLS to Colvin, *Letters*, III, pp. 70–1.
18. Fanny to Colvin, E. V. Lucas, op. cit., p. 213.
19. Margaret Stevenson, op. cit., p. 170.
20. RLS to Baxter, Ferguson and Waingrow, p. 239.
21. RLS to Baxter, ibid., p. 238.
22. Margaret Stevenson, op. cit., p. 192.
23. Ibid., p. 193.

Chapter 12

1. RLS to Baxter, Ferguson and Waingrow, p. 240.
2. RLS to Colvin, *Letters*, III, p. 90.
3. RLS to Bob Stevenson, ibid., p. 99.
4. *Collected Poems*, pp. 497–8.
5. Ibid., p. 493.
6. RLS to Baxter, Ferguson and Waingrow, p. 243.
7. Ibid., p. 242.
8. RLS to Colvin, *Letters*, III, p. 110.
9. RLS to James, ibid., p. 108.
10. RLS to Colvin, ibid., pp. 111–12.
11. RLS to Adelaide Boodle, ibid., p. 115.
12. RLS to E. L. Burlingame, ibid., p. 39.
13. RLS to E. L. Burlingame, Beinecke Collection.
14. RLS to Fanny, *Letters*, III, pp. 124–5.
15. Ibid.
16. RLS to James Payne, ibid., p. 131.
17. RLS to Colvin, ibid., p. 129.
18. An Open Letter to the Reverend Dr Hyde of Honolulu, XXI, p. 30.
19. RLS to Andrew Chatto, Ferguson and Waingrow, p. 271.
20. Fanny to Colvin, Beinecke Collection.
21. Ibid.
22. *In the South Seas*, XVIII, p. 290.
23. Ibid., p. 231.
24. Ibid., p. 250.

25. RLS to E. L. Burlingame, Beinecke Collection.
26. *In the South Seas*, XVIII, p. 298.
27. Cf. Arthur Grimble, *A Pattern of Islands*, John Murray, 1952, p. 178.
28. Ibid., p. 230.
29. RLS to Colvin, *Letters*, III, p. 135.
30. Ibid., p. 136.
31. RLS to Colvin, ibid., p. 138.
32. Caroline Ralston, 'The Beach Communities', *Pacific Island Portraits*, edited by J. W. Davidson and Deryck Scarr, Reed, 1970, p. 83.
33. Menu, Beinecke Collection.
34. RLS to Adelaide Boodle, *Letters*, III, p. 115.

Chapter 13
   1. RLS to Baxter, Ferguson and Waingrow, p. 255.
   2. Ibid.
   3. *Collected Poems*, p. 268.
   4. RLS to Gosse, Beinecke Collection.
   5. RLS to Gosse, Beinecke Collection.
   6. Henry Adams to Elizabeth Cameron, *Letters of Henry Adams 1858–1891*, Houghton Mifflin, 1938, p. 90.
   7. Ibid., p. 94.
   8. RLS to Lloyd Osbourne, Beinecke Collection.
   9. RLS to E.L.B., Beinecke Collection.
  10. RLS to James, *Letters*, III, p. 229.
  11. *Our Samoan Adventure*, edited by Charles Neider, Weidenfeld and Nicolson, 1956, p. 25.
  12. RLS to Colvin, Beinecke Collection.
  13. RLS to E. L. Burlingame, *Letters*, III, pp. 217–18.
  14. *Our Samoan Adventure*, p. 59.
  15. RLS to Colvin, *Letters*, IV, p. 29.
  16. *Our Samoan Adventure*, p. 115.
  17. H. J. Moors, *With Stevenson in Samoa*, Small, Maynard and Co., 1910, p. 29.
  18. *Our Samoan Adventure*, p. 54.
  19. Ibid., p. 208.
  20. Ibid.
  21. Ibid., p. 210.
  22. Ibid., p. 211.
  23. Ibid., p. 226.
  24. Margaret Mackay, op. cit., p. 287.
  25. J. C. Furnas, op. cit., p. 348.
  26. *Our Samoan Adventure*, p. 307.

Chapter 14
   1. Edmund Gosse to RLS, Charteris, op. cit., p. 233.
   2. RLS to Baxter, Ferguson and Waingrow, p. 336.
   3. RLS to Baxter, Ferguson and Waingrow, p. 300.
   4. *Weir of Hermiston*, XIV, p. 129.

5. 'Rosa Quo Locorum', XXVI, p. 84.
6. 'A Chat with Robert Louis Stevenson', *Today*, 2.12.93.
7. 'The Beach of Falesá', XII, p. 86.
8. RLS to Colvin, *Letters*, III, p. 292.
9. RLS to Baxter, Ferguson and Waingrow, p. 354.
10. Ibid, p. 355.
11. James to Gosse, Janet Adam Smith, op. cit., p. 11.
12. Henley, 'R.L.S.', *Pall Mall Magazine*, December, 1901.
13. RLS to Bob Stevenson, *Letters*, IV, p. 303.
14. RLS to Baxter, Ferguson and Waingrow, p. 350.
15. RLS to Bob Stevenson, *Letters*, IV, pp. 306–7.
16. RLS to Baxter, Ferguson and Waingrow, p. 303.
17. RLS to.Baxter, Ferguson and Waingrow, p. 305.
18. Cf. 'The Beach of Falesá', XII, p. 13. The document was reinstated in book publication, but the change from 'one day' to 'one week' remained.
19. Colvin to Baxter, Beinecke Collection.
20. 'To My Wife', *Collected Poems*, p. 236.
21. 'My Wife', ibid., p. 262.
22. RLS to S. R. Crockett, Beinecke Collection.
23. Colvin to Baxter, Beinecke Collection.
24. RLS to Colvin, *Letters*, IV, p. 212.
25. 'To S. R. Crockett', *Collected Poems*, pp. 283–4.

Index

Academy magazine, 213
Across the Plains (Stevenson), 325
Adam Smith, Janet, 209
Adams, Henry, on the Stevensons at
  Vailima, 291–3, 298
Adirondack Mountains, 230, 235,
  272
Admiral Guinea, play by RLS and
  Henley, 202
Ah Fu, Chinese cook, 253, 274
All Sorts and Conditions of Men (Besant),
  207
Amateur Emigrant, The (Stevenson),
  127, 128, 133, 137, 149, 236
Amazing Marriage, The (Meredith), 172
American Civil War, 102, 103
Anstruther, Fife, 51
Antwerp, 83, 99, 104, 105
Apemama, Gilbert Islands, 278, 280,
  290
Apia, Samoa, 245, 264, 281–4, 293–6,
  303, 308, 310, 329; conditions in
  the town, 283
Appin murder, 188
Archer, William: stays at Skerryvore,
  197, 216; his description of it,
  197–8, 216; and of RLS, 198; and
  A Child's Garden of Verses, 213;
  article on RLS, 213; letters from
  RLS, 213–15, 233; friendship with
  him, 216; Archer's son, 216
'Art of Fiction, The', essay by James,
  207–9
Arthur's Seat, Edinburgh, 4, 28

Babington, Rev. Churchill, 63, 64
Babington, Maud (*née* Balfour),
  cousin of RLS, 63, 64
Baker family, of Saranac Lake, 231,
  232

Balfour family of Pilrig, 27
Balfour, Dr George, uncle of RLS,
  225, 230
Balfour, Graham, cousin of RLS: at
  Vailima, 306–7; and Belle Strong,
  307; authorised biography of RLS,
  320
Balfour, Jane, aunt of RLS, 38
Balfour, John, uncle of RLS, 27
Balfour, Rev. Lewis, grandfather of
  RLS, 27, 29, 38, 39, 315
Balfour, Margaret Isabella, *see*
  Stevenson, Margaret Isabella
Balzac, Honoré de, 166, 189
Bannockburn, battle of, 41
Barbizon, 96–8, 107; Barbizon
  School, 96; Hôtel Siron, 96–8
Barrie, J. M., 16, 159; meeting with
  RLS, 14
Bass Rock, 40, 170
Baxter, Charles, 53, 78, 79, 90, 116,
  152, 175, 177, 225, 226, 233, 315,
  319, 326; friendship with RLS, 7, 8,
  12, 13, 23, 58, 82; lends him
  money, 117; and RLS's journey to
  California, 123; RLS's letters from
  America, 131–4, 148; continues to
  help RLS, 139; *Kidnapped*
  dedicated to him, 186; and RLS's
  quarrel with Henley, 240–2, 290;
  correspondence with RLS, 242–3,
  252, 254, 258, 264, 289, 290, 306,
  313; RLS's closeness to him,
  290–1; RLS's message in poem for
  him, 290–1; and RLS's finances,
  324; handles his financial relations
  with publishers, 325; and the
  Edinburgh Edition of RLS's
  works, 328; death of his wife, 320;
  leaves for Samoa to see RLS, 320;

Baxter, Charles—*cont.*
    learns in San Francisco of his
    death, 320, 328
Baxter, Gracie, 225, 320
Beach of Falesá, The (Stevenson), 255,
    276, 279, 317, 318, 324, 325
Beachcombers, The, projected work by
    RLS, 279
Beau Austin, play by RLS and Henley,
    203
Beecher, Henry Ward, 101
Bell Rock lighthouse, 48; Turner's
    engraving, 197
Besant, Sir Walter, 207–10
Black Arrow, The (Stevenson), 41, 180,
    186–8
'Body Snatchers, The', 165, 221
Boodle, Adelaide, 204–5, 232, 247,
    271
Boston, Massachusetts, 231
Bothwell Brig, battle of, 27
Bough, Sam, 52
Bournemouth, 194–7, 200–1, 204,
    211, 214; Alum Chine, 196; *see also*
    Skerryvore
Braemar, 164, 166–70, 203
Bridge of Allan, 41, 58
Brodie, Deacon, 4, 125, 202
Burke and Hare, 4
Burlingame, E. L., 232–6, 295, 325;
    influence over RLS, 233; and *The
    Master of Ballantrae*, 271; and *The
    Wrecker*, 316
Burns, Robert, 86, 319
Butaritari, Gilbert Islands, 276, 277,
    281
Butler, Samuel, 35
Byron, Lord, 313

Calistoga, California, 142, 146
Calvinism, 32, 84, 190, 214, 215, 221,
    222, 316
Camisards, the, 120–1
Canonmills, Edinburgh, 28, 46;
    RLS's first school, 42
Carruthers, Apia lawyer, 294
Casco, yacht, 244; voyage to the
    Pacific, 247–51, 254, 257, 258, 266,

    268; crippled, 262–4; paid off, 265
Cassell's Family Paper, 35
Catriona (Stevenson), 188, 315, 323–5
Cévennes, the, 115, 120
Chalmers, James, missionary, 296
'Chapter on Dreams', 290
Charles Edward, Prince, 4, 50, 118
Child's Garden of Verses, A (Stevenson),
    26, 30, 36, 182, 213, 216
Clark, Dr Andrew, 76–7
Clarke, Rev. W. E., missionary,
    245–6, 296
Cockfield Rectory, Suffolk, 63–6, 174
Colinton, 26, 27, 33, 236; RLS at,
    37–9, 159
Colvin, (Sir) Sidney, 79, 80, 83, 84,
    86, 92, 101, 114, 120, 135, 137,
    141, 144, 153, 156, 163, 166, 183,
    196, 198, 212, 216, 233, 241, 246,
    266, 275, 305, 309, 317, 319, 326,
    331; and Mrs Sitwell, 65–7, 73;
    meets RLS, 65; description of him,
    65–6; friendship with him, 66–8,
    73, 76–7, 122, 155; in Menton,
    81–3; and Fanny Osbourne, 114,
    122, 228; *Travels with a Donkey*
    dedicated to him, 122; and RLS's
    journey to California, 123–5,
    133–4; tries to persuade him back,
    139–40; on RLS's marriage and
    return, 148–9, 153; and *Treasure
    Island*, 168; farewells to RLS, 228;
    correspondence with him, 236,
    242, 246, 252–4, 263, 264, 269–70,
    281, 305, 326; and the purchase
    of Vailima, 284–5; sees RLS's
    works before publication, 325;
    and the Edinburgh Edition
    of RLS's works, 328–9; photo-
    graph, 67
Conan Doyle, Sir Arthur, 221
Conrad, Joseph, 316
Cook, Captain James, 250, 256–7
Cornhill magazine, 88, 93, 116
Covenanters, the, 5, 21–2, 27, 32, 37,
    66, 86, 120, 188, 315, 331;
    fascination for RLS, 50
Cramond, 1, 13

Crockett, S. R., and RLS, 328; RLS's poem for him, 331
Culloden, battle of, 188
Cunningham, Alison ('Cummy'), RLS's nurse, 32–6, 46, 48, 50, 182, 314–15; her Calvinism, 32; influence on RLS, 32–6; his love and gratitude for her, 34; and the nature of sin, 34; photograph, 35
Cusack-Smith, British Consul in Samoa, 309
Custer, General George A., 130

Dalyell, General Tam, 22
Damien, Father, and Molokai leper colony, 272–4; the Damien letter, 273–4
Dangerous Archipelago, 253, 255
Daniel Deronda (Eliot), 87
Darwin, Charles, 12, 93
David Balfour, original title of *Catriona*, 324
Davos, 156–64, 172–4, 322; Hotel Belvedere, 156, 157, 160; Chalet am Stein, 173
Deacon Brodie, play written with Henley, 125, 202; unsuccessful in USA, 237
De Mattos, Katharine (née Stevenson), cousin of RLS, 218, 237–40
Democratic Vistas (Whitman), 83
Deutsche Handels und Plantagen Gesellschaft für Süd – See Inseln zu Hamburg, 300, 308
Devonia, RLS's voyage in, 123, 125–7, 137
Dhu Hearteach lighthouse, 52, 195
Dickens, Charles, 35, 87
Disruption, the (1843), 32
Drummond, Kate, 54
Drummond Street, Edinburgh, 12, 253
Dumas, Alexandre, 50
Dunblane, 41, 58
'Dynamiter, The', 194, 216

Ebb-Tide, The (Stevenson), 256, 279, 282, 317–19, 325

'Edifying Letters of the Rutherford Family, The', 61–2
Edinburgh: Georgian heyday, 6–7; in RLS's youth, 7–8; inspires his imagination, 8–10; its expansion, 13; *Picturesque Notes*, 121–2, 245
Edinburgh Academy, The, 36, 42–5
Edinburgh Edition of RLS's works, 328–9
Edinburgh Infirmary, 92–3
Edinburgh University, 3–4, 15–18, 24, 50, 216; Speculative Society, 18, 19, 24, 70; RLS fails to obtain History Chair, 120–1
Eleven Thousand Virgins of Cologne, barge, 100
Eliot, George, 35, 87
Encyclopaedia Britannica, 86
Equator schooner, 246, 270; and the Stevensons' voyage to the Pacific, 274–9, 281, 283
Erraid, Isle of, 52, 165

Fairchild family, 230, 231
Fakarava, 252–4, 260
Family of Engineers, A (Stevenson), 322
Father and Son (Gosse), 89
'Feast of Famine, The', ballad by RLS, 266, 267
Fergusson, Robert, 183, 184, 315; and Edinburgh, 9–10; RLS and Fergusson's monument, 319–20
Ferrier, Coggie, 185; friendship with the Stevensons, 194
Ferrier, Walter, 12, 18, 24, 58, 184–5, 192; death, 184, 185, 194; his mother's accusations against RLS, 185
'Fiction as one of the Fine Arts', lecture by Besant, 207
Fife, 47–8, 51
Fontainebleau artists' colony, 89, 98–101, 105, 114; RLS's essay on Fontainebleau, 98
Footnote to History, A (Stevenson), 308, 325
France: RLS's early visits, 43; his love for, 113–14, 176

Furnas, J. C., 19, 254

Garschine, Mme, 81–2
Germany, RLS visits, 43, 53
Gilbert Islands, 270, 275, 287
Gissing, George, 87, 162
Glencorse chapel, 22
Gosse, (Sir) Edmund, 65, 84, 86, 90,
    123, 126, 155, 224; meeting with
    RLS, 52; *Father and Son*, 89;
    friendship with RLS, 118–19;
    correspondence with him, 140–1,
    291, 313; seeks to persuade him
    back from America, 141; on RLS's
    a-materialism, 145–6, 193;
    comments on Fanny, 153; and
    Treasure Island, 168, 170; farewell
    to RLS, 228; on RLS as a living
    legend, 313; photograph, 90
'Gossip on Romance, A', 215
Great Malvern, 58, 212
Grez-sur-Loing, 98–100, 113, 114,
    124, 131, 147; Chevillon's Hotel,
    101, 105, 107, 109; the Osbourne
    family at Grez, 101, 105–11
Gross, John, 117

Hackston of Rathillet, 47–9, 121
Haggard, Bazett, 296
Haggard, Sir H. Rider, 118, 221, 296
Hanson, Rufe, 143–4
Hardy, Thomas, 162, 204; visit from
    the Stevensons, 218–19
Hawaii, 261, 263, 284; the
    Stevensons in, 264–74; political
    situation, 267–8
Hawthorne, Nathaniel, 50, 117, 166
Heart of Midlothian, The (Scott), 10
Heathercat, fragment by RLS, 314
Henderson, proprietor of *Young
    Folks' Magazine*, 169
Henderson's school, India Street,
    Edinburgh, 42
Henley, Teddy, 237
Henley, W. E., 84–6, 90, 92–5, 115,
    116, 123–5, 133, 137, 139–40, 149,
    150, 153, 171, 180, 183, 184, 198,
    216, 246, 259, 322; friendship with

RLS, 93–6; in Edinburgh
    Infirmary, 92–3; encouraged by
    Stephen, 92, 93; physical
    disability, 93; group of admirers,
    95; edits *London* magazine, 115; on
    RLS's marriage, 149, 154;
    deteriorating health, 185; writes
    plays with RLS, 201–3, 237;
    quarrel with RLS, 237–42, 290;
    review of RLS's official biography,
    242, 320–1
Heriot Row, Edinburgh, 13, 42, 226;
    No. 17, RLS's family home, 6, 11,
    12, 14, 18, 20, 55, 58, 61–4, 68, 69,
    76, 87, 89, 93, 95, 136, 150–2, 154,
    203, 223–5, 246, 253, 260, 261,
    277, 295, 296
Hiva-Oa, Marquesas Islands, 252
Honolulu, 262, 264–5, 270, 274, 285
Hope, Anthony, 221
Howard Place, Edinburgh, RLS's
    birthplace, 28, 29
Howells, William Dean, 207
Hugo, Victor, 165, 166, 189; RLS's
    essay on, 86
'Humble Remonstrance, A', 209–11
Hume, David, 6
Hyde, Rev. Dr, and Father Damien,
    273–4, 286
Hyères, 136, 186, 195, 242, 265; La
    Solitude, 179–80, 187, 192–4, 224;
    cholera outbreak, 194

Ide, Henry, US Consul in Apia, 296
Illustrated London News, 325
Indianapolis, 101, 102, 232
Inland Voyage, An (Stevenson), 88, 99,
    116, 120, 207, 316
Inverleith Terrace, Edinburgh, 28
Island Night's Entertainment
    (Stevenson), 325

Jacobites, the, 4, 5, 171, 188, 315
James, Henry, 186, 204, 216, 241,
    242, 269; correspondence with
    RLS, 200, 211, 229, 244, 269;
    friendship with him, 201, 206–12;
    early opinion of RLS, 206–7; 'The

James, Henry—*cont.*
Art of Fiction', 207–9; on the
French naturalist writers, 207–8;
James and RLS on the novel,
209–11; visits to RLS, 211–12; and
the purchase of Vailima, 285; and
RLS's death, 320; photograph, 208
Janet Nichol, S.S., 287
Japp, Alexander, 169, 170
Jenkin, Ann, 19–21, 41, 64, 88, 97,
213
Jenkin, Professor Fleeming, 19–21,
41, 73, 88, 97, 198; RLS's tribute to
him, 20, 213; employs RLS as
secretary at Paris Exhibition, 114,
180; death, 212
Jersey, Lady, 303–4, 309
'John Knox and His Relations to
Women', essay by RLS, 86

Kalakaua, King of Hawaii, 267–9,
275, 308; photograph, 268
Kidnapped (Stevenson), 3, 52, 118,
186–91, 201, 216, 223, 233, 234,
236, 315, 323–4; characters of
David Balfour and Alan Breck,
189–91
King Solomon's Mines (Haggard), 221
Kingsley, Charles, 35
Kipling, Rudyard, 328
Knox, John, 86, 315

La Farge, John, 291
Lang, Andrew, 84, 117–19, 206;
friendship with RLS, 118
'Lantern Bearers, The', 236
Leaves of Grass (Whitman), 83
Leith Walk, Edinburgh, 6, 26, 36, 46,
175
Le Monastier, 115, 120
Lister, Joseph (Lord Lister), and
W. E. Henley, 92–4
L.J.R. Club, 58, 59
Lloyd, John, 103, 104
Loing, river, 99
London magazine, 115, 180
London Missionary Society, 245
Longman's Magazine, 207, 209

Lothian Road, Edinburgh, 6, 8, 175,
225, 226, 253
Low, Will, 96–9, 109, 185, 221, 243;
visit from the Stevensons, 223
Lübeck S.S., 286, 288, 293, 294
Ludgate Hill, cargo boat, the
Stevensons' voyage in, 227–9, 232

Macaire, play by RLS and Henley, 202
McClure, Sam, 232–3, 325
Mackenzie, Henry, 13
Macmillan's Magazine, 80
Magus Moor, 47–8
Malietoa, Samoan chief, 304, 308
Man of Feeling, The (Mackenzie), 13
Manasquan, New Jersey, 243
'Manse, The', 236
'Markheim', 166, 221, 222
Marquesas Islands, 248–54, 256,
266
Marriage, RLS's attitude to, 90–2
Marshall, George, 102
Marshall Islands, 271, 287
Marshall, Josephine (*née* Vandegrift),
102
Masson, Professor David, 42, 55
Masson, Flora, 55, 226–7
Masson, Rosaline, 42
Master of Ballantrae, The (Stevenson),
50, 225, 227, 234–6, 251, 258, 262,
266, 268, 271–2, 315; character of
Ephraim Mackellar, 235, 272
Mataafa, Samoan chief, 304, 308–10
Melville, Herman, 247–8, 257
Memoir of Fleeming Jenkin, A
(Stevenson), 213, 224
Memories and Portraits (Stevenson), 224
Menton, RLS's visits to, 43, 44, 49,
77–83
Meredith, George, 87, 160, 162, 175,
186, 204; and RLS, 172, 175; on
Beau Austin, 203; letter from RLS,
311
Merritt, Dr, owner of the *Casco*, 247
Merry Men, The (Stevenson), 52, 165,
180, 224
'Misadventures of John Nicholson,
The', 4

Modestine, the donkey, 115, 120–1, 149
Moe, Princess, 258, 262, 263, 266, 267
Molokai leper colony, 272–4
Montaigne, 83
Monterey, 131, 134, 136–8, 303
Monterey Californian, 137
Montpellier, 177, 182
Moors, Harry J., 284, 286, 289, 309, 326; description of RLS, 299, 300; acts fraudulently, 300
More New Arabian Nights (Stevenson), 194, 212
Morning Star, US mission ship, 270
Mound, The, Edinburgh, 6, 93
Mount St Helena, California, 142
'Movements of Young Children', 159
Murdoch, George, 278

Napa Valley, California, 142–6
New Arabian Nights (Stevenson), 180
New Caledonia, 287
New Town, Edinburgh, 1–7, 13, 14, 21, 28, 46
New York, 128–9, 229–30, 232, 243
Newport, Rhode Island, 230, 232
Nice, 43, 44, 179, 182
'Nixie, The', story by Fanny Stevenson, 237–9
North Berwick, 39–40, 47, 170, 236
North, Christopher (John Wilson), 185
Noumea, New Caledonia, 287
Nukahiva, Marquesas Islands, 249, 251, 253

Oakland, California, 137, 139
Old Town, Edinburgh, 3–7, 10, 13, 15, 222; the High Street closes, 4; the lands, 4; abandoned by well-to-do, 4, 5
O'Meara, Frank, 109, 111
Open Letter to the Reverend Dr Hyde of Honolulu (Stevenson), 274
'Ordered South', 79, 80
Ori a Ori, of Tahiti, 258–60, 262, 263, 267

Osbourne, Fanny Vandegrift, 64, 70, 88, 90, 92, 94, 114, 121–4, 134, 137; at Grez, 101, 105–10; and her husband Sam, 101–5, 108, 112, 115, 124, 133–5, 137; in San Francisco, 103–4; studies art, 104; journey to Europe, 104–5; death of younger son, 105, 106, 108; impact on RLS, 108–10; he visits her in Paris, 110; his commitment to her, 112–13; leaves for California, 115, 119, 120
cables to RLS, 123; and his arrival, 131, 132, 134; in Monterey, 131, 133, 136–8; divorce, 133, 138, 139; RLS moves to her house, 139; marriage, 142
For later references *see* Stevenson, Fanny
Osbourne, Hervey, 104; death, 105, 106, 108, 322
Osbourne, Isobel (Belle), 102–4, 111, 112, 115, 137–9, 141, 142, 217, 218, 252, 270, 275, 283, 286, 299, 301, 305, 327, 329; at Grez, 107–10; and Bob Stevenson, 111; and Frank O'Meara, 111; marriage to Joe Strong, 135, 138; in Hawaii, 265–6, 268; RLS's financial support, 275; lives in cottage at Vailima, 298; divorce, 303; relations with her mother, 307, 326; and Graham Balfour, 307; photograph, 307
Osbourne, Lloyd, 103, 105, 107, 108, 110, 115, 131, 135, 136, 138, 139, 144, 147, 153, 181, 216–18, 224, 227, 230, 236, 244–7, 281, 283, 289, 294, 310, 317, 324, 329; at Davos, 157–60, 175; companionship with RLS, 157, 160; and the writing of *Treasure Island*, 167–8; at school in Bournemouth, 194, 216; on the Stevensons at Skerryvore, 196–7; at Edinburgh University, 216–17; and *The Wrecker*, 236, 279, 316–17; in the Pacific, 248, 252, 263, 268; and

Osbourne, Lloyd—*cont.*
  The Wrong Box, 278–9; affair with
  Samoan girl, 299, 323; at Vailima,
  303, 305–7; photographs, 135,
  232, 268, 307
Osbourne, Sam, 101–6, 108, 112,
  115, 124, 133–5, 137, 150, 266,
  280; silver- and gold-prospecting,
  102–3; Fanny leaves him but
  returns, 103–4; divorce, 133, 138,
  139; interest in his children, 217;
  disappearance, 218
Otis, Captain, master of the *Casco*,
  247, 249, 252, 253, 258, 262, 263,
  265
Ouida, 67

Pall Mall Magazine, 221, 242, 320
Papeete, Tahiti, 256, 257, 262, 263,
  282
Paris, 83, 89, 105, 110–14, 132, 223,
  279
'Pavilion on the Links, The', 137, 180
Peebles, 39, 47
'Penny Plain and Twopence
  Coloured, A', 36
Penny Whistles, original title for *A
  Child's Garden of Verses*, 180
Pentland Firth, 51
Pentland Hills, 4, 10, 21, 22, 53, 280,
  331
Pentland Rising, the, 49
Picturesque Notes (Stevenson), 121
Pirate, The (Scott), 51
Pitlochry, 164–5, 203, 221, 231
Poe, Edgar Allan, 166, 220
Polynesian society, 254, 257, 260,
  265, 267, 308, 312
Portfolio, The, 76
Prestonpans, 179
Prince Otto (Stevenson), 175, 180, 186,
  216
Princes Street, Edinburgh, 5, 14, 19,
  226
'Pulvis et Umbra', 234, 236

Queen Street, Edinburgh, 18;
  Gardens, 12, 13, 170

'Rajah's Diamonds, The', 180
Reardon, Timothy, 104, 105, 110
Reid, Captain, master of the *Equator*,
  275, 277–9
Rick, trading agent, 277, 281
RLS and His Sine Qua Non (Boodle),
  204
'Roads', essay by RLS, 76
Roch, Valentine (the Stevensons'
  servant), 192, 204, 227, 231, 236,
  237, 244, 247, 252, 263; her
  services dispensed with, 270
Royal High School, Edinburgh, 42
Ruedi, Dr, physician at Davos, 156,
  163
Rullion Green, battle of, 21–2, 49
Ruskin, John, on Edinburgh, 12–13
Rutherford's howff, 12, 14, 253

St Gaudens, Augustus, 243–4;
  medallion of RLS, 243–4
St Ives, unfinished work by RLS, 329
St Marcel, near Marseilles, 176;
  Campagne Defli, 178–80
Samoa, 304; the Stevensons' arrival,
  245–6; and political manipula-
  tions, 267–9, 282; German activity,
  269, 308; RLS's commitment, 284,
  287; his impressions of it, 289;
  outbreak of open hostilities, 307;
  RLS's involvement, 308–10; chiefs
  build road to Vailima, 310, 329
San Francisco, 138, 141, 142, 147,
  244, 247
Sanchez, Adolpho, 135–6
Sanchez, Louis, 303
Sanchez, Nellie (*née* Vandegrift),
  sister of Fanny, 135, 136, 141, 303
Saranac Lake, 230–2, 235, 243, 244,
  265, 271, 280
Sargent, John Singer, portrait of
  RLS, 198, 230
Saturday Review, 76
Savile Club, 88–9, 118, 153
Scott, Sir Walter, 6, 7, 36, 84–5, 87,
  117, 187–9, 191, 297, 324; and
  'Bonny Dundee', 10; and Robert
  Stevenson, 51

Scribner, Charles, 103
Scribner's, publishers, 230, 232, 233
Scribner's Magazine, 233, 234, 236,
    237; RLS's articles about the
    Pacific, 252
Sea Cook, The, original title for
    Treasure Island, 168, 170, 172
Sharp, Archbishop James, murder
    of, 27, 47–8
Shelley, Sir Percy and Lady, 206
Sheriffmuir, battle of, 41
Silverado, 143–6
Silverado Squatters, The (Stevenson),
    144, 145, 149, 180, 186, 236
Simele, Lafaele and Henry, 294
Simoneau, Jules, 136–7
Simpson, Eve, 55–6
Simpson, James Young, 12, 19
Simpson, Walter, 12, 18–19, 53, 55,
    58, 88, 100, 153, 315; canoe trip
    with RLS, 99; at Grez, 109, 110
Sitwell, Bertie, 63; death in
    Switzerland, 174, 322
Sitwell, Frances, 76–7, 80, 82, 86, 89,
    92, 109, 112, 280, 322; meeting
    with RLS, 63, 109; relationship
    with him, 63–73; unhappy
    marriage, 63, 70; and Sidney
    Colvin, 65–7, 73; correspondence
    with RLS, 55, 66, 68–76, 78, 79, 81,
    181; visits from him in London,
    72, 73; mother and son role, 73–5;
    and Fanny Osbourne, 114; in
    Switzerland with her dying son,
    174
Six Saints of the Covenant (Walker),
    32
Skelt, model theatre, 36–7, 41, 203
Skene, Edwards and Bilton, Writers
    to the Signet, 58
Skerryvore, the Stevensons' house in
    Bournemouth, 196–8, 203–4, 206,
    214, 216, 219, 221, 224, 226, 228,
    229, 233, 237, 265, 271, 286, 294,
    296; Thomas Stevenson buys it for
    Fanny, 195, 200, 212; visits of
    friends, 201; let, 227; its sale, 303
Smith, Adam, 6

'Song of Rahero, The,' ballad by
    RLS, 266, 267
Spencer, Herbert, 12, 93
Spring Grove School, Isleworth, 44,
    49
Stephen, (Sir) Leslie, 83, 86, 137, 160,
    165, 172; encourages RLS, 87–8,
    117; and Henley, 92–3; publishes
    Will o' the Mill, 116
Steuart, J. A., 54
Stevenson, Alan, uncle of RLS, 23,
    195
Stevenson, Bob (R. A. M.), cousin of
    RLS, 15, 22–3, 36, 37, 69, 82, 90,
    97, 104, 107, 110–12, 176, 177,
    180, 183, 218, 224, 265, 322, 323;
    influence on RLS, 23; and the
    L.J.R. Club, 58; allegations against
    him, 61, 63, 68; with RLS in
    Paris, 83, 89; serious illness,
    89; at Fontainebleau, 98, 100,
    101; at Grez, 107–10; and Belle
    Osbourne, 111
Stevenson, David, uncle of RLS, 226
Stevenson family and engineering, 2,
    26, 322
Stevenson, Fanny (for earlier
    references see Osbourne, Fanny
    Vandegrift), 147, 167, 174, 177,
    185, 186, 191, 216, 218–20, 223,
    224, 230, 232, 243, 244, 246, 265,
    266, 268, 270, 281, 283, 307, 322;
    married life in Napa Valley and
    Silverado, 142–6; and RLS's
    parents, 146–8; in Heriot Row,
    150–2; her influence on RLS,
    153–4; and his friends, 153–5; at
    Davos, 156–7, 160–3, 173, 175–6;
    in South of France, 176, 178–83,
    192–4; nurses RLS, 182; her own
    ill-health, 174, 182; letters to
    Colvin and Henley, 183; as
    housewife and gardener, 192–3;
    her writing, 193–4; at Skerryvore,
    195–6, 200, 202, 204–6; and Henry
    James, 211–12; problems with her
    son, 216–18
        voyage to New York, 227–30; at

Stevenson, Fanny—*cont.*
Saranac Lake, 231–2, 236, 237;
and 'The Nixie', 237–9; and
RLS's quarrel with Henley, 240,
241; voyage to the Pacific, 247,
248; in the Marquesas, 251, 252,
254–6; in Tahiti, 256, 257, 260–3;
and Valentine Roch, 265; and Joe
Strong, 275; in the *Equator*, 275;
and Vailima, 284–5, 288; life there,
293–7; deterioration of health,
299; emotional problems, 300–1,
304; and RLS's criticisms, 302–3;
and Lady Jersey, 303–4; illness,
302–3; and her daughter, 306,
326; involvement in Samoan
politics, 308–10; consults doctor in
Sydney, 326; mental condition,
326; *Weir of Hermiston* dedicated to
her, 327; and RLS's death, 329–30;
photographs, 106, 232, 259, 268,
307
Stevenson, Katharine, *see* De Mattos,
Katharine
Stevenson, Margaret Isabella (*nee*
Balfour), mother of RLS, 3, 20, 28,
39, 44, 49, 51, 58, 61, 68, 113, 117,
123, 155, 168, 176, 178, 191, 195,
200, 206, 212, 244, 252, 307, 324,
329, upbringing, 27; marriage, 26,
28; ill-health, 29, 31, 34, 41, 43,
45; devotion to her husband, 45;
her son's feelings for her, 75; and
RLS's illness, 76–7, 82; and his
journey to America, 133; and
Fanny, 146–8, 150–1; and Lloyd
Osbourne, 216; her husband's
death, 223–5; voyage to New York,
227–30; voyage to the Pacific,
247–8; in the Pacific, 252, 254, 256,
260–1, 263, 268; goes back to
Edinburgh, 251, 270; sells 17
Heriot Row, 295; returns to the
Pacific, 295; photographs, 39, 268,
307
Stevenson, Robert, grandfather of
RLS, 26–8, 48; and Scott, 51
Stevenson, Robert Louis: birth, 28;

his childhood and his verses for
children, 30–1; illnesses in youth,
3, 8, 29, 42; and Cummy, 32–6;
preoccupation with sin, 32–4;
make-believe, 36–8; and Skelt,
36–7, 41; growing up in
Edinburgh, 5–8, 46; at Colinton,
37–9; holidays, 39–41; early
schools, 42; at the Edinburgh
Academy, 42–5; trips abroad,
43–4, 49; other schools, 45
at Edinburgh University, 3–4,
15–18, 24, 50; urge to write, 8, 11,
12, 25; discarded attempts at
novels, 49; wide reading, 50;
abandons thoughts of
engineering, 1, 11, 24; law studies,
2, 12; bohemianism, 15–17;
friendships, 18, 19; amateur
dramatics, 20, 41, 73–4, 88, 95;
and his parents, 21, 24, 44, 45, 49;
and Swanston Cottage, 21–2, 58,
88, 89, 95; and his cousin Bob,
22–3, 61; university magazine, 24
possible love affairs, 54; and
prostitutes, 55, 56; appeal to
women, 54–6; romanticism, 56–7;
in law office, 58; Bar examinations,
58, 85; and L.J.R. Club, 58, 59;
trouble with his parents, 58–61,
68–9; confesses his agnosticism,
59–60, visit to Cockfield, 63–6; and
Mrs Sitwell, 63–82, 89, 92, 109,
112; and Sidney Colvin, 65–8, 73,
81–3, 122, 126, 144, 155; first paid
literary contribution, 76; ordered
South for health, 76–7
life in Menton, 78–83; financial
dependence on his father, 80, 86,
171, 223; in Paris, 83, 89;
concentrates on writing, 84–6; and
Leslie Stephen, 87–8; and the
Savile Club, 88–9, 118; attitude to
love and marriage, 90–2; *Virginibus
Puerisque*, 90, 157, 171; and W. E.
Henley, 92–5, 115; at Fontainebleau and Grez, 89, 96–100;
barge trip with Simpson, 99–100

Stevenson, Robert Louis—*cont.*
  meets the Osbournes, 101;
  impact of Fanny Osbourne,
  108–10; commitment to her,
  112–13, 117; tells his parents
  about her, 113, 117; nursed by
  Fanny in London, 114; walking
  tour in the Cévennes, 115, 120–1;
  An Inland Voyage, 116; *Will o' the
  Mill,* 116–17; and Andrew Lang,
  118; and Gosse, 118–19
    journey to California to join
  Fanny, 113, 123–4; the voyage,
  126–8; encounters with emigrants,
  126–8; *The Amateur Emigrant,* 127,
  128; in New York, 128–9; by train
  across America, 129–31; stricken
  in health, 129–31; arrival at
  Monterey, 131, 134; seeks health in
  the mountains, 131–3; illnesses,
  132, 138–9; in Monterey, 136–8; in
  San Francisco, 138, 141; moves to
  Fanny's house, 139; supports her
  household, 139; offered money by
  his father, 141; his wedding, 142;
  married life in Napa Valley and
  Silverado, 142–6; *The Silverado
  Squatters,* 144, 145, 149, 182, 186;
  return to Britain, 148
    in Edinburgh and London,
  150–6; Fanny's influence on him,
  153–4; at Davos under doctor's
  orders, 156–64; and J. A.
  Symonds, 160–3; summer in
  Scotland, 164–72; renewed illness,
  164, 166; his tales of witchcraft and
  the supernatural, 164–6; the
  writing of *Treasure Island,* 166–73;
  fails to obtain History Chair,
  170–1; and George Meredith, 172,
  175
    return to Davos, 172–4;
  seriously ill again, 173–4; Mrs
  Sitwell and her dying son, 174;
  Prince Otto, 175, 180, 186, 216;
  moves to South of France, 176; St
  Marcel, 178–80; Hyères, 178–80,
  186, 187, 192–5, 242; *A Child's*

  Garden of Verses, 180, 213, 216;
  The Black Arrow, 180, 186–8; *New
  Arabian Nights,* 180; worse attacks
  of illness, 181–3; the death of
  Walter Ferrier, 184–5; *Kidnapped,*
  186–91, 201, 216
    at Skerryvore, Bournemouth,
  195–8, 200–1, 203–4, 206, 214,
  216, 219, 221, 224, 228; and Henry
  James, 201, 206–12, 241, 242;
  writing plays with Henley, 201–3;
  'A Humble Remonstrance',
  209–11; *Memoir of Fleeming Jenkin,*
  213, 224; and William Archer,
  213–16; *More New Arabian Nights,*
  216; renewed ill-health, 216, 219,
  225; visits Thomas Hardy, 218–19;
  political enthusiasms, 219–20;
  Jekyll and Hyde, 220–3, 229–30;
  visit to the Lows in Paris, 223;
  death of his father, 224, 225, 227,
  234
    The Master of Ballantrae, 225, 227,
  234–6, 251, 258, 262, 271–2;
  bequest from his father, 226;
  departure from Edinburgh,
  226–7; voyage to New York,
  227–30; in New York, 229–30; at
  Saranac Lake, 230–2, 235, 237,
  243, 244; articles, for *Scribner's
  Magazine,* 233, 234, 236; quarrel
  with Henley, 237–42
    voyage to the Pacific, 247–9; in
  the Marquesas, 248–54, 256; at
  Fakarava, 252–4; voyage to Tahiti,
  254–5; in Tahiti, 256–63, 265; *The
  Ebb-Tide,* 256, 279, 282, 317–19,
  325; more ill-health, 257, 258; in
  Hawaii, 264–74; at Waikiki beach,
  266, 271, 272, 275, 283; and King
  Kalakaua, 267–9; *The Wrong Box,*
  268, 278; concern in Polynesian
  affairs, 269, 274; letters to *The
  Times,* 269, 274, 309; and Molokai
  leper colony, 267, 272–4; and
  Father Damien, 272–4; voyage in
  the *Equator,* 274–8; in the Gilbert
  Islands, 276–8; *The Wrecker,* 279,

Stevenson, Robert Louis —*cont.*
295, 316–17, 323, 325
    arrival in Apia, 245, 246, 281–3;
    purchase of Vailima, 283–5, 291;
    commitment to Samoa, 284, 287;
    in Sydney, 286–8; in residence at
    Vailima, 288; impressions of
    Samoa, 289; condition of Vailima,
    291; life there, 293–7; diet and
    clothes, 296; 'Tusitala', 297, 312;
    family problems, 298–303;
    responsibilities and worries,
    305–6; involvement in Samoan
    politics, 308–10
    Weir of Hermiston, 314–16, 323,
    327, 329; *Catriona*, 315, 323–5; and
    Scottish subjects, 315–16; and
    Fergusson's monument, 319–20;
    on sex and death, 322–3; *Across the
    Plains*, 325; *A Footnote to History*,
    325; *Island Night's Entertainment*,
    325; medical opinion in Sydney,
    326; overstrain and overwork,
    326; and S. R. Crockett, 328, 331;
    and the Edinburgh Edition,
    328–9; *St Ives*, 329; brain
    haemorrhage and death, 329–30;
    buried on summit of Vaea
    mountain, 330; news of his death,
    330; portraits and photographs,
    iv, 39, 45, 59, 174, 232, 243,
    268, 276, 301, 307, 330
Stevenson, Thomas, father of RLS, 1,
    6–8, 10, 18, 20, 21, 23, 28, 29, 32,
    41, 42, 44, 45, 47–9, 55, 69, 82, 113,
    123, 168, 170, 171, 176, 185, 195,
    202, 212, 216, 220, 224, 227, 260;
    lighthouse and harbour engineer,
    1, 2, 26, 27, 48, 51, 52; early life,
    26; and his father, 26; courtship
    and marriage, 26, 28; and the
    Disruption, 32; illnesses, 29, 43,
    45; Commissioner for Northern
    Lights, 51; rift with his son, 58–61,
    68–9, 89; allegations against Bob
    Stevenson, 61, 63, 68; and RLS's
    illness, 76–7
    RLS financially dependent on

    him, 80, 86, 141, 150, 171, 223,
    and RLS's literary career, 86–7;
    tries to persuade RLS back from
    America, 133–4; and Fanny,
    146–8, 150–1; and *Treasure Island*,
    167; failing health, 191–2;
    business difficulties, 191; buys
    Skerryvore for Fanny, 195, 200,
    212; visits to Skerryvore, 212;
    death, 6, 223–5, 227, 234; funeral,
    225; complications of his estate,
    225–6; bequest to RLS, 226;
    photograph, 45
Stoddard, Charles Warren, 247, 262,
    263
*Strange Case of Dr Jekyll and Mr Hyde,
    The* (Stevenson), 220–3, 229–30,
    233, 236, 315
Strong, Austin, 265, 270, 271, 286,
    295, 303, 306
Strong, Belle, *see* Osbourne, Isobel
Strong, Joe, 139, 144, 145, 217, 252,
    269, 270, 281, 283, 299, 307;
    marriage to Belle Osbourne, 135,
    138; in Hawaii, 265–6; and King
    Kalakaua, 268; confrontation with
    RLS, 274–5; RLS's financial
    support, 275; lives in cottage at
    Vailima, 298; his misdeeds, 303;
    sent away from Vailima, 303, 306;
    divorced by Belle, 303;
    photograph, 307
'Suicide Club, The', 180
Swanston Cottage, 21–2, 58, 88, 89,
    95, 280, 315
Sydney, 286–7, 290, 291, 294, 326
Symonds, John Addington, 221; at
    Davos, 160–3, 173; acquaintance-
    ship with RLS, 160–3; suffers
    from tuberculosis, 160; homo-
    sexuality, 161; comments on RLS,
    161, 163; and *Jekyll and Hyde*, 222;
    photograph, 162

Tahiti and the Tahitians, 254–63, 289
Tamesese, Samoan chief, 308
Tantallon Castle, 40
Taravao, Tahiti, 257

Tautira, Tahiti, 258–62, 266
Taylor, Sir Henry and Lady, 205–6
Telford, Thomas, 13
Tembinoka, local tyrant in Gilbert
    Islands, 278
Thompson's school, Edinburgh,
    44–5
Thoreau, H. D., 50; RLS's essay on
    him, 137, 169
'Thrawn Janet', 164, 165, 198, 221
Times, The, RLS's letters on
    Polynesian affairs, 269, 274
'To My Name-Child', poem by RLS,
    136
Tolstoy, Count Leo, 220
Torquay, 49, 224
Travels with a Donkey (Stevenson),
    120–2, 316
Treasure Island (Stevenson), 3, 40, 118,
    166–73, 181, 186, 203, 204, 209,
    221, 233, 236, 315; character of
    Long John Silver, 173, 220, 221
'Treasure of Franchard, The', 178
Trudeau, Dr E. L., 231
'Tusitala' (story-teller), Samoans'
    name for RLS, 297, 312
Twain, Mark, 243
Twelfth Night, Fleeming Jenkins's
    production, 73–4, 97
Typee (Melville), 248

Uma, original title of The Beach of
    Falesá, 318
Under Two Flags (Ouida), 67
Underwoods, poems by RLS, 224
Upolu, Samoa, 246, 247, 283, 291,
    297, 308, 312

Vaea mountain, Samoa, 283; RLS's
    burial on summit, 330
Vailima, Samoa, 146, 242, 262; its
    purchase, 283–5, 291; the
    Stevensons take up residence, 288;
    condition of the estate, 291;
    building of the house, 291, 298;

furnishing, 297–8; financial drain,
    306; chiefs build road to it, 310,
    329
Vandegrift, Jacob, 101
Vendetta in the West, A, unfinished
    story by RLS, 137, 169
Virginia City, 102, 103
Virginibus Puerisque (Stevenson), 90,
    157, 171

Waikiki beach, Hawaii, 266, 271,
    272, 275, 283
Walker, Patrick, 32
Water of Leith, Edinburgh, 1, 13, 26,
    28, 46
Waverley station, Edinburgh, 7, 10,
    226
Weir of Hermiston (Stevenson), 50, 227,
    314–16, 323, 329; character of the
    elder Kirstie, 314, 323; dedication
    to Fanny, 327
Weybridge, George Meredith's
    house at, 172
Whitman, Walt, 50; RLS's essay on
    him, 83, 86
Will o' the Mill (Stevenson), 116, 117
Williams, Dora, 141, 142, 151, 217,
    247
Williams, Virgil, 104, 141, 142, 247
World magazine, 233
Wrecker, The (Stevenson and Lloyd
    Osbourne), 236, 279, 287, 295,
    316–17, 323, 325
Wrong Box, The (Stevenson and Lloyd
    Osbourne), 268, 278

Yeats, W. B., on Henley, 95
Young Chevalier, The, unfinished work
    by RLS, 314, 323
Young Folks' Magazine, serialization of
    Treasure Island, 168, 169, 171; of
    The Black Arrow, 180; of Kidnapped,
    223

Zola, Emile, 207, 208, 211